TRAVELS IN THE REGIONS OF THE UPPER AND LOWER AMOOR AND THE RUSSIAN ACQUISITIONS ON THE CONFINES OF INDIA AND CHINA

TRAVELS IN THE REGIONS OF THE UPPER AND LOWER AMOOR AND THE RUSSIAN ACQUISITIONS ON THE CONFINES OF INDIA AND CHINA

WITH ADVENTURES AMONG THE MOUNTAIN KRGHIS;
AND THE MANJOURS, MANYARGS, TOUNGOUZ,
TOUZEMTZ, GOLDI, AND GELYAKS:
THE HUNTING AND PASTORAL TRIBES.

BY
THOMAS WITLAM ATKINSON, F.R.G.S., F.G.S.

AUTHOR OF
"ORIENTAL AND WESTERN SIBERIA,"

WITH A MAP AND NUMEROUS ILLUSTRATIONS

GYAN

Published by

Gyan Publishing House
5, Ansari Road
Daryaganj, New Delhi-110002
Phone: 011-47034999, 9811692060
E-mail: books@gyanbooks.com

Distribution Network
gyanbooks.com
India, USA, Canada, UK, Australia, France

ISBN : 978-81-212-4157-1 (PB)
First Published, 1860

2nd Impression 2020

Printed at: Gyan Press, Delhi.

Travels in the Regions of The Upper and Lower Amoor
and
The Russian Acquisitions on The Confines of India and China
Author: Thomas Witlam Atkinson

TRAVELS

IN THE REGIONS OF

THE UPPER AND LOWER AMOOR

AND

THE RUSSIAN ACQUISITIONS

ON THE CONFINES OF

INDIA AND CHINA.

WITH ADVENTURES AMONG THE MOUNTAIN KIRGHIS;
AND THE MANJOURS, MANYARGS, TOUNGOUZ, TOUZEMTZ, GOLDI, AND GELYAKS:
THE HUNTING AND PASTORAL TRIBES.

BY

THOMAS WITLAM ATKINSON, F.R.G.S., F.G.S.

AUTHOR OF

"ORIENTAL AND WESTERN SIBERIA."

WITH A MAP AND NUMEROUS ILLUSTRATIONS.

LONDON:
HURST AND BLACKETT, PUBLISHERS,
SUCCESSORS TO HENRY COLBURN,
13 GREAT MARLBOROUGH STREET.
1860.

TO

HER MOST GRACIOUS MAJESTY

VICTORIA, QUEEN OF GREAT BRITAIN AND IRELAND

SOVEREIGN OF THE VAST INDIAN EMPIRE

ETC. ETC. ETC.

This Volume

BY SPECIAL PERMISSION

Is Dedicated

WITH FEELINGS OF DEVOTION AND GRATITUDE

BY

HER MAJESTY'S MOST HUMBLE AND OBEDIENT SERVANT

THE AUTHOR

PREFACE.

My former work was published for the purpose of introducing to the English reader scenes in a remote part of the globe, of which no other descriptions were available, and I attempted nothing beyond a narrative of incidents and observations as they were noted down from day to day, such as I considered would suffice to explain and illustrate my pictorial representations. In the present work the higher interest of the subject has induced me to attempt to produce information of a more elevated character, intended to satisfy, in some respects at least, the wishes of the Geologist, Botanist, Ethnologist, and other scientific scholars, who invariably expect to find in an account of a new country materials likely to extend the circle of their favourite study, or strengthen the truths on which it is founded.

There were other demands to satisfy, to which, it will be found, I have tried to pay the same deference. Our commerce, prodigious as are its operations, is, it is well known, capable of infinite expansion, and I have laid open a field of almost incalculable extent, where enterprise, skill, and industry are sure to find a profitable investment. Having suggested the establishment of a Fair on the Indian frontier, I may be permitted to say that this was not made without a knowledge of what is passing in another part of Asia. The "Yermak" at Irbit, on the frontier of Siberia, has within the past ten years risen from one of comparative insignificance to great importance. Its commercial transactions in February last amounted to more than 12,000,000*l.*

For those of my compatriots who have been alarmed by the approaches of Russia to our Indian Empire, I have faithfully stated every step that has recently been made in this direction, and afforded them an opportunity of learning her present position on the north of the Himalaya. Her existing relations with China, now that we are engaged in a war with its Government, will doubtless give increased interest to the facts I have been enabled to collect respecting the several advances she has skilfully made into Chinese territory, and the consequent extraordinary development of her own.

I am indebted to several of the Russian officers who were employed in the great expedition into Manjouria for facilities in acquiring information during my travels, and I beg them, and numerous Asiatic friends, to whom I am under similar obligations, to accept my grateful thanks.

With regard to the Illustrations, it is here necessary to state that to the numerous landscape series, engraved from my own drawings, I have added a few characteristic portraits, copied from a work recently published by the Russian Government.

I have only to express an earnest hope that the efforts I have made to render this second production more valuable than the first, will be accepted as a proof that I am not insensible of the indulgence I have received from my critics.

Brompton, July, 1860.

CONTENTS.

PAGE

APPENDIX.

LIST OF ILLUSTRATIONS.

THE UPPER AND LOWER AMOOR.

CHAPTER I.

FLIGHT OF CIRCASSIAN PRISONERS.

INTELLIGENCE has reached England from time to time, for the last ten or a dozen years, of Russian acquisitions in central Asia, stretching out far towards the Himalaya; and in 1857 of that vast tract of country, the valley of the Amoor, said to have been ceded by the Emperor of China to the Emperor of Russia. Letters and paragraphs on the subject have frequently appeared in the public prints, some of them having an apparent air of truth from the details set forth: but they had evidently been written without a proper knowledge of the country, and had no foundation in fact. Up to the latest advices no modern geographer has published any reliable description of these regions; and no recent traveller, it was believed, had penetrated its alleged interminable steppes and Cyclopean mountain chains. In short it was regarded as a *terra incognita* quite as much by the scientific as by less learned readers.

As I had passed several years exploring this remote portion of the globe, and was the only European who had been permitted to enter the new Russian territory, it suggested itself to me, that a detail of my wanderings in these enormous tracts of mountain, valley, and plain, which Russia has added to her empire and colonised with a warlike race, might be considered of some interest to my countrymen. It must be understood, in the first place, that this additional Russian territory extends over more than two-thirds of her southern Siberian frontier, which is about 6500 miles in length, commencing on the Caspian in 44° lat. N. and 51° long. E., and ending in 53° lat. N. and 142° long. E. Its most southern point is in 42° lat. N. and 80° long E. The breadth of these acquisitions varies very much at different points, and will be best understood by a reference to the map.

The importance of such an increase of power to a state, previously one of the most considerable of the European monarchies, cannot be understood without knowing the sources of material prosperity which exist within these new provinces. Mineral wealth of incalculable amount and agricultural produce in prodigious abundance, form but two items in their resources. The various tribes that inhabit distinct portions will also be found to claim attentive consideration.

I am far from being an alarmist, and, with the opportunities I have enjoyed of knowing the state of feeling in Russian society, I ought to be the last person to suggest apprehension of evil from the accumulation of the elements of a predominating influence in the hands of an absolute sovereign: but the English statesman will not, I am sure, shut his eyes to the fact, that Russian territory has now very nearly approached the possessions of Great Britain in India, and whatever my opinions may be, he may not unreasonably expect that a government which advances in the East at this rate of progress, may desire sooner or later, to expand her territorial limits to the southward. To him the contingency may seem inevitable, of a further stride across the Himalayas to Calcutta: but even if such intentions were entertained, of which there is no proof, ample employment for many years to come will be found for the present enlightened ruler of this colossal empire, in the development of the resources of Russia on the vast steppes of central Asia, in the region of the Amoor, and on the island of Karapta or Saghalien with its commodious harbours and extensive coalfields, and in the establishment throughout these regions of that civil and military system which will bring it in perfect harmony with Russia on the Dwina, Don, Oural, and the Volga.

Unwilling to detain the reader by merely prefatory matter, I commence my explorations from the Siberian frontier.

Semipalàtinsk, or Seven Palaces, stands on the frontier between Siberia and the Kirghis Steppe, in lat. 50° 30′ N. and long. 80° E., and at above 775 feet above the level of the sea. It is so named from seven mounds lying near the town, traditionally the remains of royal residences; but if this be the case they were erected when the art of building

Ruins near Semipalàtinsk.

palaces was in its infancy. Unless a great change has taken place in this district, it is difficult to account for such edifices being raised here, for the country around is a barren plain, with several stagnant lakes, occasional patches of grass, and numerous hillocks formed by the wind whirling the sandy soil into heaps.

The town, consisting principally of wooden buildings, stands on the eastern bank of the Irtisch. It is a long line of houses set back about 150 yards from the river, facing the south-west, with a view over the Kirghis Steppe, which stretches out in that direction for more than a thousand miles. A wide road separates the houses from gardens that extend along the river bank. Here melons and water melons are grown of a large size, and of a most delicious flavour, without the aid of glass. They are sold at a very cheap rate—five or six for tenpence.

The buildings are scattered over a considerable space forming several streets; each house, great and small, has its court-yard enclosed by a wooden fence ten to twelve feet high, with large gates in the centre. The government offices, and other edifices connected with the military department, are at the northern end of the town. These, and the custom-house, are mostly built of brick, and have an imposing appearance when seen at a distance. A numerous body of Cossacks is always stationed here with a strong force of artillery; so that this is really a military town of great importance in connection with the government of the Kirghis.

There is one mansion in the town,—the residence of a Siberian merchant from Tomsk; this had been furnished without regard to cost. The hot-houses and green-houses attached to the dwelling were on an extensive scale, and contained a choice collection of tropical and other plants, brought from Europe at great expense. The arrangement of the whole establishment proved that a most luxurious style of living had reached this distant spot, on the verge of nomade, almost of savage life. The proprietor possessed lead and silver mines in the Kirghis Steppe at about 200 miles distant, which were at one time a source of considerable wealth. Afterwards, through mismanagement and peculation, the working entailed a serious loss—persons employed by him in offices of trust becoming rich at his cost.

Among other refinements of civilisation imported from Europe into this region, is litigation, in which some of the Siberians are fond of indulging. This gentleman became involved in a lawsuit, respecting a claim of 475,000*l.* It lasted several years, and then he not only lost it but also enormous sums expended in law proceedings and bribes. This so affected his circumstances that the mansion was suffered to fall into decay; and the shattered windows now admit the swallow and the bat, which have taken up their abode and rear their young in its magnificent apartments. The vines and the pines have ceased to bear their luscious fruit, and the flowering plants no longer put forth their splendid blossoms. The lead and silver mines have passed into the hands of the Crown, and are now being extensively worked.

Many Tatar merchants in Semipalàtinsk are engaged in trade with the Chinese towns of Tchoubachack and Kuldja; also with Bokhara, Khokan, and Tashkend, between which and Semipalàtinsk caravans are frequently passing. They take out printed Russian goods, copper, iron, and hardware, returning with tea, silks, and dried fruits, which are forwarded to the fair at Irbit and are then dispersed,—the greater portion being sent into Siberia, the rest into Europe. The dwellings of the merchants engaged in this trade are commodious and clean, and the rooms contain a great deal of valuable property,—in some rich carpets from Persia and Bokhara are hanging on the walls as well as spread on the floors,—in others they are piled up in bales. In another room are magnificent silks, shawls, and Kalats (or dressing gowns), beautifully embroidered with gold and coloured silks. Ornaments and large vases in porcelain from China, tea services, plates, dishes, and similar works of singular taste and beauty; diamonds, rubies, emeralds, and a few other precious stones, form parts of their stock in trade. At my visits, shortly after entering the house, tea and dried fruits were handed. Low divans are placed round the rooms, but most generally the inmates are found seated on carpets spread on the floor drinking tea and sewing. Forged Russian notes are frequently found among these Tatars, twice they passed them upon me; although I knew from whom I received them, my friends advised me to burn the notes, as the loss would be far better than the trouble and annoyance if the affair was placed in the hands of the police.

Beside these merchants there are others who carry on a great trade with the Kirghis, supplying them with silk dresses, tea, raisins, and wooden bowls from China, kalats of printed calico from Khokan, Russian hardware, iron, copper and leather; for which they receive in exchange black and grey fox skins, black lamb skins, horses, oxen and sheep. The horses and oxen are driven into eastern Siberia to the different gold mines. One of these Tatar traders told me that he imported 50,000 horned cattle into Siberia annually, and these are chiefly consumed at the gold mines. I have met the Kirghis with herds of from 3,000 to 4,000 oxen 1,500 miles from their homes and 500 from their destination.

When the cattle are delivered at the mines, the men remain a few days and then start on their return,— a very long ride. Their journey homeward is by the post as far as Semipalàtinsk, and then to their hovels in the Steppe on horseback. The sheep are driven across the Steppe to Petropavlosk on the frontier of Siberia, and thence to Ekaterinburg, where they are killed and their fat melted down into tallow. More than one million sheep are brought from the Kirghis Steppe yearly which are disposed of in this manner. The whole of the tallow was (till within the last five years) forwarded to Europe; now the bulk is converted into sterine at a large works near Ekaterineburg. This establishment supplies all Siberia with candles, besides sending a great quantity into Russia.

Before taking leave of Semipalàtinsk, I will mention an event which might have terminated my explorations; with the chance of a ride to the mines of Eastern Siberia, at his Imperial Majesty's cost. One Saturday evening, in October, 1850, I arrived at Semipalàtinsk from Chinese Tartary, when

The Ferry across the Irtisch at Semipalàtinsk.

the director of the customs informed me that Prince Gortchikoff was in the town. After my few articles had passed the scrutiny of the officers and a lodging was procured, I prepared to pay the Prince a visit. During a two years' travel my wardrobe had become exceedingly scanty and tattered; nor was it possible to obtain any apparel on my journey, unless the Tatar costume was adopted.

It was just dusk in the evening when I presented myself at the gate of the house occupied by His Excellency. While passing through the court-yard a group of Cossacks eyed me with scrutinizing glances, evidently meditating the operation of kicking me out. Returning their stare with a determined look, I proceeded on, and entered the house. An officer was in attendance in the hall, from whom I inquired if the Prince was within. A very haughty reply in the affirmative was vouchsafed me, accompanied by a surly demand as to who I was and what I wanted. This was answered by handing my card and desiring it should be given to His Excellency. My person and appearance were carefully inspected; the card critically examined; after which the officer declined delivering it. Finally he ordered me out in a tone intended to enforce instant obedience, and turned away clanking his sabre as he strode to the window.

I now quietly repeated my demand and insisted on the card being instantly delivered, or that his conduct should be reported. This astonished him and raised his ire; striding towards me he asked in a most imperious tone how I dared to remain after his orders, — ending his sentence with a German expression in nowise flattering to me. Again he demanded who I was, and what business I could have with His Excellency. Finding that he spoke German, I looked coolly at him, saying in that language that my card answered his first question, — his duty was to inform his commander I was there by delivering it, and my business should be stated to the Prince only. He then told me that the Prince attended to no beggars, and advised my speedy departure without an escort of Cossacks, with which he would soon accommodate me if I lingered.

Our conversation had brought out another officer who stood scanning me with a look of supreme contempt. The two took several turns to and fro, probably contemplating some amusement at my expense. At last the gentlemen called a Cossack to remain in the hall, — a quiet hint that they did not deem the coats safe. After this they left me and entered the rooms beyond; in a few minutes my first acquaintance returned, and in a most affable manner invited me to follow. He conducted me through several rooms into a small cabinet in which I found the Prince, who instantly rose from his seat and shook me cordially by the hand. The bullying adjutant was greatly amazed and somewhat crest-fallen, not knowing who I was, and fearing that a complaint might be made against him.

After learning from me how long I had arrived, he assured me that I had been the cause of his having made a rapid journey to this place, and to my extreme surprise acquainted me with the particulars I shall now lay before the reader.

About the latter end of the month of September, 1850, an event occurred in the Altai which caused great sensation throughout Western Siberia. In one of my journeys in the autumn of 1848, I had visited the towns of Kouznetsk, Bisk, and all the Cossack posts on my way to the Altin-Kool; remaining two days with the officer in command at Sandypskoï, the last Cossack fort on the river Bëa. There is a body of 500 men at this fort, which stands in a delightful situation on the east bank of the river. The Cossacks and their families are well off, having all the comforts of life and many luxuries. Nearly all the mining officers in the Altai knew me, and I had frequently visited the military commanders in their different districts, and thus all the authorities had a full knowledge of my identity.

Thirteen months had elapsed since I had shaken the Siberian sand from my feet, and left Oustkamenogersk. It was late on a Sunday night when a ball was given in honour of a lady's names-day, that I said good-bye to my friends and started eastward towards Mongolia. A great storm was raging in the mountains at the time, causing me to watch the forked lightning as it played round the summits of the Altai, and illuminated the whole country with a crimson glare, dimming the flickering lights in the festal mansion, while the crashing thunder silenced the music. During the early part of this period, I had forwarded letters through the Cossack piquets to Prince Gortchikoff, the Governor-general of Western Siberia, and his replies reached me through the same channel. From this circumstance the Prince knew that I was far from Siberia, and pushing my way south into regions over which Russia had no control.

One night in the month before mentioned, when all my friends in Barnaoul had quietly retired to rest, little thinking that danger was fast approaching their abodes, they were awakened from their slumbers a little after midnight by a party of Cossacks galloping up the quiet street, to the house of the chief of the mines. A loud thundering at the door roused the inmates, when a dispatch was delivered informing the Colonel that Siberia was being invaded by 3,000 Asiatics, who were descending the valley of the Bëa, and the officer in command of the Cossacks at Sandypskoï required troops to be sent to Bisk forthwith: upon which town he intended to retreat, not having a sufficient force to check the invaders.

In a few minutes Cossacks were sent to rouse up the officers, and desire them to repair to the house of their chief without delay. On their assembling, the dispatch was read; causing great consternation among those who dreaded the advancing savages. Similar dispatches had been sent to the Governor of Tomsk, to Prince Gortchikoff in Omsk, and to the Emperor in Petersburg. The director of the mines ordered the colonel in command of the military, to have his men (about 800), ready to march at daybreak. After this he turned his attention to the safety of the town, and what it contained. Nearly all the gold obtained from the mines of Siberia had been delivered in Barnaoul, to be smelted into bars, ready to send by the first winter roads to Petersburg. It was supposed that the Asiatics knew this, and that their object was plunder. There were about 43,200 lbs. weight of gold, and 28,800 lbs. of silver in the cellars at the smelting works: a prize worth having. Besides the precious metals, there were the stores belonging to the crown, and other property of considerable value,—even the dwellings of the officers would have afforded a rich booty. The shops and warehouses contained supplies of every thing needed by the inhabitants, and an immense stock of wodky was stored in the government cellars.

The chief assigned to each officer the duty he had to perform, some to provide for the security of the precious metals, and others to make arrangements for defending the town. Having placed the whole under the command of Colonel Kavanka, the Director prepared to lead the troops to the scene of action on the Bëa.

The approaching dangers were now made known to the ladies. The idea of being captured and carried away by the savage tribes, filled their minds with horror; as many traditions remäined in Siberia of the barbarities inflicted by the Asiatic hordes in former invasions. When their husbands announced the orders they had received, the excitement increased; the news spread into every dwelling, as usual much exaggerated on the transit. Many believed that the invaders were close at hand, and fear caused some to fancy that they heard their savage cries. The Cossacks galloping to and fro with orders, strengthened this idea; and the panic filled every female heart when the shrill notes of the bugles and the roll of the drums echoed in the night.

Just as the grey dawn began to break in the eastern sky

two Cossacks dashed through the gate into Barnaoul, and galloped on to the house of the Director. One of them leaped from his horse and delivered a second dispatch from the officer at Sandypskoï, with the information that the invaders were rapidly descending the valley of the Bëa. Also that they had commenced burning the *aouls* of the Kalmucks, and were murdering every man, woman, and child they could lay hands on. Instead of 3,000, they were now announced to be 7,000 strong, great numbers of whom were armed with rifles. Further, this army of savages was led on by the Englishman Atkinson,—a fact affirmed to be beyond all doubt, as the writer of the dispatch stated that he had seen him. This account caused general alarm. Some thought that the wild hordes of Asia were bursting forth, as in the time of Genghiz Khan, to spread desolation over the country on their march towards Europe. All felt that the affair had become serious, and the Cossacks declared that the people at all the villages on their route were packing up their goods and preparing for flight.

The Director and the officers in Barnaoul did not doubt the fact of my being with the invaders, but not as their leader. It was thought that I had been taken prisoner in the regions to the south of the Altai, and being so well acquainted with the passes in the mountains, it was supposed that the commanders of the hordes had compelled me to act as their guide. When this was made known, some of the ladies betrayed a gleam of hope, assured that I should try to save my friends. The officers were most anxious about my safety, and many plans of rescue were suggested. The chances of success were however considered doubtful, and all feared for my fate. This last communication hastened the preparations, and at six o'clock the troops were on their march. The chief intended joining them at a point about fifty miles distant, to which he could travel by more difficult but a much shorter route. The Colonel who remained in command of the town, began placing the Zavod in a state of defence, and then barricaded his own dwelling. Some of the

Troops crossing the Obi at Goubena.

ladies proposed that the Governor's mansion, a large brick building, should be made the citadel; and that in the lower story all the precious metals belonging to His Imperial Majesty, as well as their own valuables, should be deposited; while they and their children should occupy the upper rooms; satisfied that fear of the Emperor would insure such a defence of the position as might lead to their preservation. At ten o'clock in the forenoon a third dispatch arrived, informing the Director that the Cossacks had retreated from Sandypskoï; the number of the enemy had now advanced to 10,000, and it was stated that the inhabitants of the towns of Bisk, and Kouznetsk, were leaving their homes and carrying what little property they could along with them. In fact wheresoever the news had reached, the people were fleeing from their dwellings with the utmost precipitation.

Three similar dispatches had been forwarded by couriers to General Anossoff, the governor of Tomsk, to Prince Gortchikoff at Omsk, and to the Emperor. The distance from Barnaoul to Sandypskoï was more than 250 miles, and the troops were pushed on at their greatest speed. Immediately the intelligence reached Prince Gortchikoff he left Omsk and travelled to Semipalàtinsk, a distance of more than 600 miles, in forty hours. From this place he sent a regiment of Cossacks with six guns to secure some of the passes in the Altai; while another with six guns was ordered from Oustkamenogorsk to cut off any bodies of men making their way westward.

General Anossoff called out a body of soldiers in Tomsk with one field gun. At the same time he ordered the general commanding the forces in the government of Tomsk to march with a strong force and four guns. Shortly these two divisions were on their march by different routes; the commanders of each believing that they would find me a prisoner in the hands of the enemy. At the end of their third day's march they observed the villagers deserting their homes; and on the fourth day they met the people in great numbers fleeing away in the utmost dread. News had reached them of the massacre of the Kalmucks, accompanied by such ferocious acts of cruelty that no persuasion could induce them to remain,—in short, the whole population was panic struck and had lost all courage.

On the fifth day the troops from Barnaoul reached Bisk, and found the town deserted by all the inhabitants, except a few civil officers and a small body of Cossacks; the latter in guard of the warehouses in which were stored the valuable furs belonging to the Crown. During the night news reached the commander which cast a doubt on the accuracy of the dispatches. Gradually reports were received reducing the number of the invaders, and containing reliable information that they were not continuing their march down the valley of the Bëa. This delayed the further advance of the soldiers; and Cossacks were sent to stop the march of the troops under the command of the two generals from Tomsk. In the course of two days it was ascertained that this alarming invasion had its source in a party of forty Circassian prisoners who had escaped from the gold mines on the Birioussa. When this discovery was made the troops returned to their respective stations, and the local officers were left to deal with the affair.

These fugitive Circassians had no intention of invading the Russian dominions, their object being to escape from the great Siberian prison to their far distant homes. They were prisoners of war, and had been sent to work in the mines of Siberia, which was considered an act of great cruelty. Surely soldiers who had bravely defended their homes deserved a better fate than to be mixed with Russian convicts, many of whom were criminals of the worst class. These brave fellows had been employed at the gold washings on the Birioussa, a river which forms the boundary between the governments of Irkoutsk and Yenissey. From this place they determined to escape, and, after many difficulties, made the attempt.

By the aid of small quantities of gold, which they managed to secrete during their labours, they procured a rifle and ammunition for each man from the Tatars, who concealed them in a cavern in the mountains about seven miles from the mines. The most essential requisites for their future success had now been obtained, but at a cost of ten times their value. There was no fear of the Tatars betraying them, as their own safety depended on their secrecy, and a terrible punishment awaited them if detected with gold in their possession.

On a Saturday afternoon in the latter end of July, 1850, when the labours of the day were ended, the Circassians quietly left the mines in small parties, going in different directions. This was done without exciting any suspicion, and they met in the evening at a rendezvous, a ravine in the mountain, about six miles from the mines, in a southerly direction. A stud of spare horses were kept at pastures in the forest several miles from their place of meeting, and at about seven from the mines. A large party of Circassians proceeded towards this place, and arrived near it just at dusk, and three were sent on in advance carrying their rifles, as if returning from the hunt. The horse-keepers were driving the animals into the inclosure to secure them for the night. When this was accomplished, they discovered three rifles pointed at them, and were told that they would be shot if they attempted to escape. A shrill whistle called up the other exiles, who instantly secured the three men ; the best horses were at once selected out of a stud of between three and four hundred, and as two of their attendants were great hunters, and well acquainted with the mountain regions around, the Circassians carried them all away to act as guides to the Chinese frontier, and to prevent the discovery of their means of flight till they had got a good start : moreover, they turned the remainder of the stud out of the inclosed ground, and drove them into the forest, to make it appear that they had broken loose, and that the absent men were searching for them. They departed, carrying off fifty-five horses. No time was lost in reaching their friends in the glen, who received them with shouts of joy. An hour before midnight, when the moon rose to light them on their way, they commenced their flight.

The hunters led them southward, through rugged passes and over several ridges, without once stopping till they reached, a little before sunrise, a high summit, whence they could look down upon the gold mine, and distinguish the smoke curling up from the fires that are constantly kept burning to drive away those pests, the musquitos.

Having taken a last look at the place of their exile, they hastened onward into a grassy valley, where they fed their

Exiles departing.

horses and breakfasted. After a rest they pushed on again. They presently came upon a mountain torrent, over which they crossed with great difficulty. Their march was continued till near nightfall, when they encamped in perfect security, still keeping strict guard over their guides. On the evening of the fourth day they ascended the last summit of the Saian, crossed the crest of the chain, and descended into a narrow valley, where they encamped for the night.

They had now passed the Chinese frontier, and the guides knew nothing of the region beyond this point; they were therefore set free, and their rifles handed to them. A goodly supply of venison had been obtained on the march, and this evening was passed in feasting and enjoyment. At day-break they separated—the Siberians to return to their homes; the Circassians were left to their own resources in a wild region abounding in deep and rapid torrents, that forced them to seek a route near the head waters of many large streams which fall into the Yenissey.

This led them in a south-westerly direction, and after a ride of four days they reached that river, in its basin between the Saian and Tangnou Mountains. Here it is broad, deep, and rapid, rendering it dangerous to swim; while to follow the stream up towards its source would take them too far to the eastward, and might place them in a dangerous position if pursued.

A little below them the rapids commence, and extend several miles to the head of a gorge rent in the mountain, in which are the great falls. At this place a body of water, 250 yards in breadth, rolls over a succession of cascades 2,800 feet in height. These are contained in the space of about a mile, and the thundering of the water is echoed far over the mountains. Under these circumstances, the fugitives were obliged to swim the river without delay, which was not accomplished without danger, as they were carried far down the stream.

They now entered into a most rugged region, with no guide but the setting sun, and they watched it descend daily over the land of their birth; towards which they constantly directed their course. This was their first error — their route ought to have gone southerly to the Tangnou chain. After many days of severe toil they reached the river Annü, which rolls over its rocky bed in an immense torrent. This they could not cross, and they were compelled to turn towards its source, which brought them where nature wears her most savage aspect, into a group of mountains, extending over a vast space, that reaches up to the shores of the Altin-Kool, to the Tchoulishman,—and to the high plateau of the Tchouia,—the most elevated steppe in the Altai.

I had found this region a chaos of rocks, high precipices, deep ravines, and roaring torrents; often forming impassable barriers.

More than three weeks were passed by the exiles in these labyrinths of rock, wood, and water; while many vain efforts were made to cross the Abakan. The numerous ravines through which the mountain torrents find their way into this river, and the high precipices rising along its course, eventually forced the wanderers to the south-west. In a few days they reached the region of eternal snow, and succeeded in crossing the Abakan far up towards its source. Another difficulty now beset them—winter had already commenced in the higher regions to the south; which, with the rugged nature of the country, turned them to the northward—a most dangerous course.

Had the unfortunate warriors known but a little of the geography of these regions, they would have continued their route to the south, and crossed the Tangnou Mountains; but their immense snowy peaks no doubt alarmed them, while the lower ranges to the west seemed to invite them towards Circassia. After passing the Tangnou, and reaching the country of the Kalkas, all danger from Siberia would have been at an end, and a ride of twenty-five days to the westward would have brought them to the Kirghis tribes, among whom they would have found a language they understood and a religion like their own, and have met with friends to aid them in their long ride over the vast Asiatic plains, in the direction of their homes. Instead of this they entered into a region, the physical nature of which gradually forced them to the north-west, and at length they struck upon the eastern shores of the Altin-Kool. Here their last chance of success presented itself—a malignant fate, however, seems to have pursued them. This large lake, with its rock-bound shores, stopped their progress westward; still, a route was open for them toward the Tchouia, whence a ride of fifteen days would have taken them across the Kourtchume, and into a place of security. But here, again, a singular fatality turned them towards the north.

They came upon that part of the lake which extends in a north-easterly direction for about fifteen miles, to where the river Kamga falls into it. After considerable difficulties they succeeded in reaching the river, and rode along its bank for many miles before finding a ford. Leaving the Kamga, they crossed a high ridge, and struck upon a Kalmuck trail, which they followed. This led them along the mountains which skirt the northern shores of the lake, till they reached the Bëa, the only outlet of the Altin-Kool. Immediately on issuing from the lake the river enters a rocky gorge, in which it runs for about thirty miles. Throughout this distance it is a succession of rapids and falls, over which neither man nor animal can pass.

More than two months had now elapsed since the poor fellows left the Beroussa, and they were still in their Siberian prison; during this period they had suffered both from hunger and fatigue. Although game was abundant in many of the regions through which they passed—when hunting is the only source of a man's subsistence, the supply often proves precarious, as all will find who try. Following the mountains along the eastern bank of the Bëa, they reached a part of the country thinly inhabited by Kalmucks, living under Russian sway. At length they arrived at a Kalmuck aoul, and got into difficulties with the people, but whether the Kalmucks attempted to stop them, or threatened to call in the aid of the Cossacks to take them prisoners, it is impossible to say. The dispute unfortunately ended in a battle, when several Kalmucks were killed, and their aoul burned. Those who escaped conveyed the terrible news to other tribes, and all became alarmed. Some retreated into the forests with their families and cattle, while others carried the alarm to the Cossack fort at Sandyp. The officer in command was drunk when the news arrived; hence those exaggerated dispatches which followed each other in rapid succession.

The Circassians committed a fatal error by engaging in this conflict with the people, as the alarm rapidly spread in every direction, and left no chance for their escape. Continuing their course to the northward, they passed beyond the rapids, and succeeded in swimming their horses over the Bëa. From this point they turned to the south, which led them into the mountains between the Bëa and Katounia. This river in the mountains is one succession of rapids, so that there are but few places where it can be crossed even in canoes; it is impossible to swim the torrent.

The higher mountains to the south being deep in snow, placed the fugitives in a trap. When their real number was discovered, the illusion respecting their force was destroyed; and the Kalmucks prepared with a savage determination to avenge the blood that had been shed. A body of men were soon collected; they were stanch as bloodhounds, and had been seldom foiled in running down their prey.

Scouts, sent forward to follow the trail, were followed by Siberian hunters who knew every mountain pass and torrent. Mounted on good fresh horses, they rapidly closed upon the fugitives; and on the evening of the third day of their pursuit encamped within three miles of them.

The Circassians were on their march with the first gleam of dawn, towards the upper end of the narrow valley, which led them into a pass. They observed that their enemies were proceeding in two divisions,—one riding up the

A view on the Bëa.

ridge a little to the westward, and the other following on their track. This caused them to hurry onward, fearing to be caught in the pass. As they were on a good track their horses were not spared, and in little more than an hour they reached another valley, which extended for several miles to the east and west. The object of that division of their pursuers who were crossing the ridge was now visible—it was to prevent their escape to the westward.

The prisoners continued their ride to the eastward, and found, after going a few miles, that they were in a succession of small valleys, that led them up between the mountains toward the snowy region. Before turning a jutting point, they ascertained that both parties of the Kalmucks were now following on their track, at about three miles distant, without apparently making any attempt to approach nearer. It was not till long past mid-day that they were observed to be rapidly gaining upon them. Pushing on their tired steeds availed nothing, as each few minutes brought their enemies in closer proximity. Presently a spent ball struck one of their horses, which showed that the hunters were trying the range of their rifles, and that they intended mischief.

At length the hungry and way-worn warriors were driven into a mountain pass, and rifle balls began to drop fast around them. Having reached a narrow part of the gorge, where it was strewn with fallen rocks, they made a stand and returned the fire with effect—for several saddles became vacant. In a few minutes they received a heavy volley, when some of the exiles were wounded, notwithstanding their shelter, and several horses were killed. They now stood at bay, determined never to yield. Their pursuers outnumbered them five to one, and knew every crag and turning in the ravines, which enabled them to take shelter where no bullet could touch them, whence they could pick off their opponents, and force the survivors to retire from every position they sought. Each new post was held with undaunted courage, till diminished numbers compelled the Circassians again to retreat; every call to surrender being answered with a shout of defiance.

While the work of slaughter was going on, night shrouded the combatants, and under cover of the darkness fifteen of these brave men escaped on foot, ascending further into the mountains, and leaving their horses to their merciless enemies. Though their position had become desperate, they scrambled on, hoping to find shelter from the cutting blast. At length they reached some deep recesses in the rocks, where they decided to pass the night; they however dared not light a fire, as that would guide the Kalmucks to their retreat. The night passed without their being disturbed.

With the first grey dawn of morn they commenced their weary march and scaled the rocky heights before them, whence they had a view of the vast snow-clad peaks above, which stopped all farther progress in that direction. Dark clouds were gathering around these rugged crests, betokening an approaching storm, an evil omen for the exiles. After carefully scanning the country in search of their pursuers, not one of whom was visible, they turned to the west, skirting along the base of one of the giants of the chain towards a forest of cedars which covered a low rocky ridge.

The hunters had not been idle; long before daylight appeared two parties had been sent forward to form ambushes where it was expected the Circassians would be obliged to pass, while the main body remained behind to clear the ravine. Being convinced that the forest would afford them the only means for their escape, the fugitives pushed on in that direction. They had reached within about two hundred yards of the wood when a puff of white smoke appeared in a thicket, sending a leaden messenger which proved fatal to one of their comrades. They now made an attempt to reach the shelter of some rocks, but before they had proceeded twenty paces five others had fallen. A savage shout to surrender greeted their ears from a large party in their rear that were fast closing in upon them. Their last few shots were spent on the advancing body, and not without effect;

then they made a rush to reach the forest; but only four were destined to gain its cover, and some of these were wounded. The thick underwood screened the poor fellows from the volley which whistled after them, and stopped the firing, as they were soon lost in the dense and tangled branches.

The clouds, which had become blacker, began pouring down rain and sleet, accompanied by a fierce gale, which brought their enemies to a stand and caused them to prepare an encampment under the cedars. Two small parties were sent on in pursuit, but these were shortly compelled to return without having discovered the retreat of the remnant of the gallant band. The storm had now become a hurricane, driving the snow into the balagans and whirling it into eddies, which made it difficult to see objects at a few yards' distance. This continued for three days without intermission, and then the mountains were covered deep in snow, which deterred the hunters from making any further attempt to find the fugitives. The winter had also set in with a piercing frost, and this no doubt soon accomplished that which the rifles of the Kalmucks had spared. The four Circassians were never seen again, nor any trace of them found.

Having heard from the Prince these details of an adventure in which I, unwittingly, had been implicated, he endeavoured to dissuade me from pursuing my course to Barnaoul, fearing that the villagers on my route might treat me as a conspirator; but after remaining a few days at Semipalatinsk, I started for that town, and reached it without the slightest molestation. There during the winter I gathered from the chief of the mines numerous particulars respecting this tragic story, which I have added to the account I received from Prince Gortchikoff.

CHAP. II.

RUSSIAN POSTS AMONG THE KIRGHIS.

I CROSSED the Irtisch, which is about a quarter of a mile in width, by a ferry boat to the Tatar village on the Kirghis side of the river. Here exists a curious population of Russian Cossacks, Tatars, Kalmucks, and Kirghis, and a singular mixture of races is springing up, which will greatly puzzle the future ethnologist. There are many Tatar merchants in this village, which at times presents a very busy and singular scene. Numerous caravans start from here, and several had just arrived. There were groups of Bokharians, Khivans, Khokanians, and men from Tashkent; each in their gay and picturesque costume. The caravan drivers are generally Kirghis, and their tattered garments showed that they had made a long journey.

Numerous camels, with their long shaggy necks and huge loads, were waiting to be unburthened,—others were patiently lying down while the bales were being removed from their saddles. Many Cossacks were watching these operations, to prevent smuggling ; but, notwithstanding their vigilance, the people succeed in conveying into Siberia considerable quantities of tea and silks which have never passed his Imperial Majesty's customs.

The Cossack post for carrying government dispatches starts from this place to Ayagus, a Cossack fortress about two hundred miles distant,—the piquets are built about fifteen miles apart, serving as stations, and forming a line of posts guarding the Kirghis. After leaving the village a vast plain is entered upon, in parts slightly undulating and covered with rough grass, now dried up by the sun. The driver seated himself firmly on his box as the steeds swept along the steppe, and the other two Cossacks rode on each side as a guard—this route not being particularly safe. For

Caravans on the Irtisch.

the three first stations we met nothing on this desert except the piquets,—it was a solitude unbroken by any sound, save the tramp of our horses and the rattling of our wheels. Not a bird was seen in the air, nor was there a cloud to break the monotony of the clear blue sky. Nothing seemed in motion but our little party. One might have fancied that all nature slept, and that everything possessed of life had sought repose in some subterranean abode. At last a small chain of misty purple peaks was seen rising out of the steppe to the south-west — a relief to the apparently interminable plain which surrounded us.

A fourth station had been passed, still without any sign of either man or beast—the Kirghis having left this region for other pastures among the mountains far to the south-east. At each piquet our Cossacks and horses had been changed; the former were wild-looking fellows, and the latter strong and fiery. We were now approaching the rocky ridge which had been so long our landmark, when, at some seven or eight miles before us, we observed a black object in motion. We rapidly gained upon it, and at length came up to a large van drawn by four horses abreast; passing this, we shortly reached the piquet.

The small chain, which had appeared gradually rising out of the steppe as we approached, was within four or five miles of the station, and its singular and picturesque forms were distinctly visible, some of the crags being exceedingly curious; the Cossacks had named them after animals, to which, as they fancied, they bore a strong resemblance. Having informed the officer of my desire to visit the mountain, he immediately ordered horses to be got ready and two Cossacks to accompany me. While these preparations were being made, the carriage we had passed arrived, and then I found the owner was a travelling wine merchant from Semipalatinsk, on his way to Ayagus. His van was stowed full of various wines, including claret and champagne which had never seen France: these spurious beverages he expected to sell to the Cossack officers, the former at 10*s.* a bottle and the latter at 15*s.*

When the merchant heard that I was going to visit the crags, he asked to be my companion, to which I consented. The Cossack officer told me to take my rifle, as the Argali (wild sheep) were numerous in the mountain; besides which, he added, there were some roving bands of Kirghis about, whom it would not be prudent to meet unarmed. On hearing this the merchant ordered his servant to bring in his gun, and its case, after some delay, was dragged out from beneath hampers of wine. More time was lost in searching for the key. At length the case was unlocked and the weapon produced. The officer advised him to keep his gun in readiness for use, or the Kirghis would carry off both his carriage and himself.

On approaching the mountain I observed that a precipice, about 400 feet high, rose abruptly from the steppe, extending for several miles to the south-west. As we rode along, the Cossacks pointed out the different objects standing on the precipice. One huge mass, about 250 feet long and 100 feet high, was called the Tiger, another the Camel, another the Cock. At some distance from these a singular mass rose out of the plain, crowned by a number of pillars, one far overtopping the rest,—these they called Shaitan and his legions guarding his domain. Beyond these, rugged crests rose to about 2,000 feet above the plain. The whole of the higher masses appeared to be of granite, without a blade of grass growing upon them. Beneath were several small valleys covered with rich grass, on which the wild sheep feed; but the Kirghis, apparently from a superstitious influence, never ascend to them.

Several hours were spent in sketching these curious scenes, while my companion was firing at a piece of paper pinned against a rock. He had not as yet planted a ball within two feet of it, at only fifty yards' distance; indeed, it became evident, from the way in which he handled his weapon, that danger from it would be greater to himself than to any Kirghis who might stop him. Night was drawing on fast when we returned to the piquet. At the wine-merchant's request I permitted him to travel with me, provided he could proceed at my pace; but shortly after we started I observed that he was losing ground; and as the Cossacks had no idea of wasting time, their horses were urged forward, and we soon left him behind. When we reached the next piquet

Shaitan and his Legions.

it was dusk; still we could see his van some miles distant on the plain. Having delayed my departure till his arrival, he now informed me that he had determined to sleep at the station, apparently not desiring to bring his van in contact with a Kirghis battle-axe. In a few minutes we left him, and I saw him no more.

We had not gone far when the night set in, and the gloom presently increased to total darkness. Our escort had been doubled by the officer at the last station, and one led the way at a gallop. The sparks from his horse's hoofs guided my driver, and, as before, the others rode on each side the carriage. On one side of the road pyramids of earth are thrown up ten feet high, at about one hundred yards apart, each looking blacker than the gloom beyond; these guided us on our way to the piquet.

While here drinking tea, the officer told me that I had a dangerous district to pass through, in which there were some most daring bands of Kirghis. Our escort was therefore again doubled, with orders to carry muskets in addition to their swords and pistols, and their firearms were loaded in my presence. After preparing my own arms for immediate use, I got into the carriage, wished the officer good night, and we were once more plunged into darkness.

Not without considerable excitement, arising from a sense of danger, four piquets were passed during the dark hours, and we reached a fifth just as the day began to dawn, crossing several low hills on our way. This post was in a narrow valley formed by some abrupt and rocky hills of no great elevation; in the centre a small river was winding its course, and the place looked dismal and dreary. On our way we were twice challenged by sentinels, and at our arrival found the guard had been increased to twenty-five men.

A few months previous, a most tragic event had occurred here. The piquet had been attacked in the night by a large body of Kirghis, and its defenders, eight in number, murdered. This was not done without a terrible struggle; no firearms had been used by the Kirghis, only their battle axes, as the mutilated bodies of the guard clearly proved. The fight was a desperate one, and many of the assailants fell before the Cossacks were killed; but the Kirghis carried off all their dead, fearing they might lead to the detection of the tribe engaged. Plunder was not the object of the attack, for the arms were not taken away; and the muskets were broken, but whether in defence or by the enemy no one could tell. The cause of this massacre is unknown,—perhaps it was an act of vengeance for some injury or insult to their chief.

Hurrying from the still bloodstained walls without taking any refreshment, my way for a few miles was along the bank of a small stream. We then crossed a low ridge, from the summit of which the plain extended in a south and westerly direction far beyond the reach of my vision, while to the south-east were seen the blue and misty crests of the Tarbagatai. Far away in the steppe to the northward, a salt lake appeared with its border of various-coloured salsola, but no Aoul or even a Yourt could be observed in any direction. Shortly the sun rose, but his beams fell on a dreary waste, browned by his scorching rays. The Cossacks gave me little time for contemplating the scene; their horses were put into a gallop, scattering dust and pebbles from their hoofs as they bounded towards the plain. In about an hour the next piquet appeared like a black dot, but no puff of smoke showed that it was inhabited. At length we were near enough to distinguish horses feeding on the steppe, and presently dashed up to the station, where we found the Cossacks had just turned out, preparing to proceed with us.

After our morning meal we again started. The country was still slightly undulating, but not rich in pastures; rough grass and patches of sand seemed scattered over the vast waste.

We were fast approaching the remotest Cossack settlement in these regions: Russia, however, is not likely to stop here, as in a few years her boundary will be far to the south. After riding about eight miles, we came to the river Ayagus, which at this time was a small stream running in a rocky bed. In the spring, when the snow is melting on the steppe and on the Tarbagatai, a great body of water finds its way through this channel to the lake Tenghis or Balkash. Soon after crossing the river we entered the town of Ayagus, and continued our way down a broad street, formed by the small wooden dwellings of the Cossacks, which led to the government buildings on the south side of the town. Nine hundred Cossacks are stationed here, most of whom have families; there is also a battery of Cossack artillery, and a small body of infantry. The officers consist of the commander of the Cossacks, with several subordinates, the artillery officer, three military officers, and the surgeon. At the head of the civil department is the Sessedatal or chief magistrate, who has a secretary and several assistants. These constitute the governing power over the Kirghis in this region. The men sent to fill these departments look upon their position as a species of banishment; and it has always been a principle among the employés to abstract the greatest amount of profit from the nomades, who are ground by every man, from the chief to the common soldier. This makes the Kirghis give Ayagus a wide berth; nevertheless, means are devised to bring many of the tribes within the grasp of the greedy officials.

The travelling wine merchant always finds his journey to this place a profitable one. Besides his vinous supply, wodky is sent here by the brandy contractors, who pay a premium to the officials on the quantity consumed. This, and the love they individually have for the spirit, induces them to set a bad example to the men. The commander at the time of my visit was equal to any man in Europe as a toper. His regular quantity of wodky every evening was three bottles, "taken pure;" for, as he said, "no good Russian ever watered his brandy". Many of the officers tried to emulate his drinking powers; thus an example was set which the men eagerly followed, and an enormous quantity of this degrading spirit was consumed in Ayagus.

The sessedatal was a tall, burly, and hard-drinking man from the south of Russia, and in no way scrupulous how profit was obtained from the inhabitants of the steppe. His duties are wholly with the Kirghis; and he has officers residing among the different tribes wherever Russia has obtained any influence, who lose no opportunity of extending her power. The chief is courted, paid, and some mark of distinction given him; perhaps a medal, a sabre, or a gold-laced coat and cocked hat,—with the privilege of attending a council at Ayagus once a year; when laws are made to govern the tribes, that rivet still faster the fetters with which he and his people are being bound. From this meeting he returns to his aoul, "dressed in a little brief authority." A young Russian who understands his language is appointed to reside with him, to translate all official papers sent to him, and write his answers; to which he attaches his seal, without understanding a word they contain. The youth is also a spy upon him and those who visit his aoul, reporting regularly to the chief at Ayagus. Thus the power of the empire is quietly and gradually creeping on into the plains of Central Asia; and when it is sufficiently secured, the nomades will have to pay both in men and money.

Three Cossacks were now appointed to be my escort, and a party of eight Kirghis, with twelve horses and two camels, sent for from a distant aoul. They arrived early in the forenoon, when the baggage was packed into leather bags and loaded on the camels. Shortly after mid-day, having made our adieu to the different officers assembled to see us depart, we rode away in a southerly direction.

The river Ayagus for a short distance led us among low hills, in some of which slate rocks cropped out; others, being almost destitute of herbage, bore a sterile aspect. In this direction Ayagus seemed to stand on the verge of a desert that could not afford a mouthful of food to man or beast. Having ridden more than three hours over these barren hills, we reached a plain covered with good pastures, on which great herds of cattle were feeding. In the distance a number of Kirghis yourts were seen on the shore of a small lake. We found that they belonged to a Tatar merchant; his wife and family occupied one, the others were inhabited by his people. The wife and daughter came out of the yourt and invited us to drink tea in their dwelling; but their hospitable offer was declined, as we had still a long ride to the aoul where we intended stopping for the night. The merchant was returning with the produce of his summer trading among the Kirghis. He informed me that he had above 3,000 horses, about 7,000 horned cattle, and more than 20,000 sheep, which he was now driving to the frontier of Siberia. These were worth about 15,000*l.*, and the whole had been obtained by barter: it is generally admitted that these Tatars make more than cent. per cent. by their dealings.

We continued our ride over the plain, through great herds of cattle, and in little more than two hours reached our destination. This was the aoul of Syrdak, a wealthy chief, who received us with marked kindness. A yourt was quickly placed on a clean piece of grass near the bank of a stream, and the ground inside the dwelling covered with Bokharian carpets. Tea was brought in, with dried apricots and raisins —no bad substitute for bread. While I was having this refreshment, a sheep was killed and cooked; in due time portions of the boiled mutton were served up on a wooden tray, with boiled rice.

The chief was a man about fifty years old, rather good-looking, with great shrewdness expressed in his countenance. He was dressed in a Chinese silk kalat of varied colours, having a fine shawl round his waist, and on his head a brown conical cap, turned up at the sides like a cocked hat. A pair of green leather boots, with over-shoes or slippers, completed his attire. Vast numbers of horses, camels, cattle, and sheep were assembling round the dwelling, guarded by men and dogs, to secure them against wolves and robbers. Not far from the aoul dark purple slate rocks rose up from the steppe to the height of about sixty feet, extending to the south for about a mile, and then terminating abruptly on the plain; when these rocks were seen from a distance, they had the appearance of a great fort.

The following morning a sharp frost had crisped the grass, which, when the sun rose, sparkled like diamonds. Having obtained horses, camels, and men, from my host, he offered to accompany me some distance. After riding about an hour we reached the summit of a hill, whence the vast Asiatic plain lay stretched out around me, extending more than 2,000 miles in length, from the Caspian on the west, to the Barluck Mountains on the east. Its breadth is about 1,200 miles; and over this enormous space the nomade tribes wander with their flocks and herds. It was a scene never to be forgotten, causing me to stop my horse and look around in wonder at the desolate landscape to the southward. Herbage there was none, all appeared scorched up by the sun. At some ten miles' distance there was a broad tract of country covered with a substance of dazzling whiteness,—beyond, was a lake some twenty-five or thirty miles in length and about fifteen miles in breadth; the shores quite flat, with a belt of reeds about two miles in width extending round it. To the east, and at a great distance, the purple peaks of the Tarbagatai were visible; but on the whole space within the range of my vision not a single abode for man could be seen.

As we rode along, I perceived Syrdak in earnest conversation with Petrouka, one of my Cossacks, and presently both came to my side, when the latter related to me what had passed between them. Syrdak was dissatisfied with his lot in life, although surrounded by everything which makes a nomade wealthy He had recently discovered that a chief of much less rank than himself, had been decorated with a gold medal, sent by the Emperor. This was the iron which had pierced his soul, and rendered his life miserable.

He had desired the Cossack to tell me that he regarded my visit to his aoul a great boon, inasmuch as he thought it would afford a channel through which a communication from him on this interesting subject might reach the ear of "the Great White Khan." I desired Petrouka to tell Syrdak that I was not a Russian, only a traveller visiting the country by the Emperor's permission. My host did not appear satisfied, and proceeded to tell me of his importance among the tribes, adding that the Great Khan ought to be informed of his power, and that his friendship was ten times more valuable than that of the man who had been honoured.

I suggested that any claims he might have for distinction should be made through the officials in Ayagus to Prince Gortchikoff, who, I was sure, would give them attention.

To this Syrdak objected, saying that the people in Ayagus would devour half his herds and leave him the hoofs; but that, if I would speak of him to the Great Khan, he was sure the medal would be sent.

Again I urged that I was a stranger whom the Emperor had permitted to visit his country, to see the Kirghis and their steppes, and that I was entirely without power.

"But the Cossacks serve you," he exclaimed.

"Yes," I said, "by order of the Emperor."

"Did the Great Khan tell you to take them?" he demanded.

Showing my passport, I replied, "This orders them to serve me; without it they would refuse." He examined the paper minutely, turning it in every direction—the large red seal producing a great effect on his mind.

"How many horses did you give to the Khan for it?" he at last asked, earnestly.

"None," said I.

"In Ayagus," he added with increased gravity, "they took from me five camels and fifty horses, for only looking at a paper much less than that. How many can you take with it?"

"Not one."

"Will the Great Khan come here?"

"I think not."

"Has he many aouls, men, camels, horses, and cattle?"

"Yes, more aouls than you have horses—some so large they would cover this valley; and more men than there are animals on the Kirghis steppes."

"He is a great Khan, and will surely send me the medal if you speak to him."

"I cannot help you in the matter; the Emperor only gives the medals to good men for their services."

"Then tell him he has given one to a great rogue who plunders the caravans."

This ended our conference.

From this spot Syrdak led us towards the south-east, saying it was most likely that we should meet with a tribe in that direction; and a ride of three hours carried us across the broad valley, and to the eastern end of another ridge. Here are several ancient tombs, which are held in great veneration by the Kirghis. They say that one of these edifices contains the graves of two mighty Genii, who ruled over the whole region between Nor-Zaisan and the Balkash,—to whom all the Sultans of the steppe did homage. They also tell of the terrible battles which were fought between these great spirits, and others who inhabited a part of the Gobi. Some of the fearful ravines in the mountains to the south, are attributed to strokes from their swords, when a path was required to bring up their legions. Extravagant as are such legends, it would not be safe to venture to express to the Kirghis any doubt respecting their authenticity.

Two of these tombs are alike both in form and dimensions. They are circular on the plan, and conical, or more properly an elongated dome, with an aperture on the top. From the ground to the apex of the dome the height is about fifty-five feet; on the south side, and about eight feet from the ground, there is an opening four feet square, and higher up in the dome there is another about two feet square. I succeeded in entering the tomb through the lower aperture, and found the

Tombs of the Genii.

interior diameter twenty-one feet. The walls are four feet thick, and built of stone obtained from rocks near at hand. In the centre of the tomb there are two graves, nine feet long and three feet six inches wide, and on each side of these are three other graves six feet long. The Kirghis say the two large ones contain the Genii, and the smaller ones are the sepulchres of six inferior spirits, their attendants, who were sacrificed when the former were overpowered by the Genii of the Gobi. Around this spot there are several smaller tombs and numerous mounds of earth.

We sat down at the foot of these ancient monuments and partook of some refreshment, while our horses fed on the rough grass at no great distance. The frugal meal being ended, I said, "Amanbul" to my host, who urged us to make a rapid ride, as it was far to the aoul we were seeking. Almost immediately after leaving the tombs we got into a morass, which was probably the bed of a shallow lake from which the water had been evaporated, leaving incrustations of salt on the grass and mud. Not far from this place we reached a part of the steppe covered with efflorescent salt, which is beautiful to look upon, but exceedingly bitter to the taste. Although we proceeded at a rapid pace, we were more than two hours in crossing this crystallised spot. We then entered on a sterile steppe, covered with sand and pebbles, on which only a few stunted thorny bushes were growing, bearing yellow and purple flowers, that greatly resembled the wild rose in form.

We were now on a level plain, but no pastures could be seen in any direction, and the Kirghis urged us on at greater speed. Hour after hour passed with the same monotony around us, while the sinking sun was watched with anxiety, as his slanting rays were cast along the steppe. At last a wreath of smoke was descried in the distance, to the infinite delight of all. We stood for a few minutes while I scanned the horizon with my glass. To our great disappointment no aoul was visible, nor could the yourt be seen from whence the smoke curled up. We had been nine hours on horseback, still it was necessary to push the poor animals on. Having gone a few miles the horses scented the pastures, pricked up their ears, and bounded forward with fresh vigour.

As we approached nearer, a belt of green became visible; though neither cattle nor yourts could be seen, smoke there was to a certainty, and no doubt a Kirghis aoul. In somewhat more than an hour we perceived that the green was a belt of reeds, extending for many miles,—still no water could be seen; and on reaching the reeds the smoke seemed to be about a mile from us. We tried to cross the swamp, but found this impossible, as the plants were ten feet high, and so thick that the horses could not force a passage, while at a few paces from the bank the water became deep. Turning to the south, we rode along the edge of this vegetable barrier in the hope of finding a track. We had ridden several miles and left the smoke behind us; still no place was found by which we could cross towards it. Darkness was fast approaching, and there appeared no hope of our finding a path. Our horses were again urged forward to reach the southern end of the reedy border, when, to our great satisfaction, we perceived a Kirghis. Two of my men rode up to him, explained our position, and desired him to guide us to the aoul.

He good-naturedly complied, leading us to the eastward for more than two miles, and then turned into the reeds along a well-trodden track. In about half an hour we were greeted by the barking of dogs as we rode up to the aoul; night had, however, set in, and nothing could be seen but a few yourts around us. These were located in the pastures of a numerous tribe occupying a region to the west of the Ala-Kool, and the people told me that the aoul of the chief, "Hade-Yol," was at the distance of a five hours' ride to the eastward.

Being aroused at daybreak the following morning by the noise of the cattle, I left the yourt, and saw that we were surrounded by a countless multitude, and that three other aouls were at a short distance. A busy scene in pastoral life was presented to me. The women and children were milking the cows, sheep, and goats. Not far from the yourts three large iron cauldrons were placed over holes dug in the ground; into these the milk from the different animals was poured from the leathern pails, while three boys were keeping up a constant blaze beneath the cauldrons, by adding small bushes to the fire. At each of these seething pans stood a woman, stirring and skimming the bubbling mass. The tattered garments, pointed caps, and haggard looks of these poor creatures, as they flitted to and fro in the steam of their cauldrons, forcibly suggested the witch scene in Macbeth. The preparation they were engaged upon was "Hyran." After boiling about two hours the fluid becomes thick, when it is cut into squares and subsequently dried in the sun. This forms a considerable portion of the winter food of these people.

In another place the young women were at work making "Voilocks"— felt coverings for the yourts ; these are made in pieces twenty-five feet long and seven feet broad, by a simple process. Their workshop was a space forty yards long and fifteen wide, within a reed fence seven feet high. At one end a number of old women and girls were beating the wool and camel's hair with rods. When this is rendered sufficiently soft and is properly mixed, it is handed to the young women at the other end, who are the felt makers. The first article required is a reed mat, which is made as follows :—reeds are obtained seven feet long and three-eighths of an inch in diameter, being carefully selected to this size. Six inches from each end of the reed a small hole is bored, and five others at equal distances between them. Through these holes strings like catgut are passed—the reeds are thus placed close together; when formed to a sufficient length, the ends are secured, and the mat is complete.

It is next spread on the ground, when the young women bring the wool and camel's hair which have undergone the beating process, and begin laying it evenly on the reeds. This is a work of time and labour, but when finished it forms a perfectly even mass about nine inches thick. Four of the workwomen kneel down at one end and begin carefully rolling up the mat, and the woolly substance is pressed together. When this has continued for some time the article is unrolled, sprinkled with water, and again rolled up. The process is continually repeated, till the material becomes almost solid and about half an inch thick, — then the manufacture is complete. These voilocks are waterproof; they are exceedingly warm coverings for their yourts, and wear for years.

While I had been watching the manufacturing operations, the Cossacks had made preparations for our departure. My horse was brought; then, thanking the Kirghis for their hospitality and shelter, we departed with fresh horses, camels, and men. After going a short distance from the yourts, it became evident that a plain extended to the horizon on every side. Over this vast space a number of aouls were scattered, with large herds of camels, as well as thousands of horses and oxen, all moving towards their pastures. As we rode along we passed through flocks of sheep spread over miles of country; they appeared numberless, and the whole steppe seemed teeming with life.

The tribes had only returned to these pastures a few days before. In some parts there was most luxuriant grass, on which the sheep were browsing, in other places we rode through steppe grass reaching to our saddle flaps. Having travelled southward for about four hours, and constantly through multitudes of cattle, we met a Tatar merchant following his trade among these people. I accepted his invitation to stop and drink tea with him, which was speedily produced, and was excellent in quality. Bread he had none, but dried apricots supplied its place. He told me that five tribes were assembled on this part of the steppe, and all within a two days' ride. They were returning from the mountains, visiting their pastures on the way, towards their winter quarters on the Balkash. He assured me that these Kirghis had about 2,500 camels, 60,000 horses, more than 100,000 horned cattle, and sheep beyond calculation. One chief had more than 9,000 horses. No doubt this was a fair estimate, as my informant was well aware of the numbers each Sultan and tribe possessed.

On leaving the hospitable Tatar we changed our route, by his direction, more to the south-east; still over pastures on which thousands of cattle were feeding. Soon after mid-day we reached the aoul of "Nour-Ali," who rode out to meet me, having been informed of my visit. He was between seventy and eighty years old, but hale, and sat his horse like a man of half his years. We stopped and dined with the old chief, who, surrounded by his family, presented quite a patriarchal tableau. From him we learned that another tribe would be found at a six or eight hours' ride to the southward, and that beyond was a sandy desert; but I could get no further information. I obtained a fresh supply of men and cattle, and immediately after dinner continued my journey.

We were 16 in number, and two of the Kirghis had some knowledge of the place where it was expected we should find the next tribe. After riding about an hour we left the pastures and entered on a sandy plain, on which tufts of steppe grass were growing. Gradually these were left behind, till at length we were on a dreary waste, on which nothing was visible to guide us or break the dull uniformity. The guides suggested that a party of us should go on at a good speed, leaving those with the camels to follow in our track. I ordered one Cossack and five Kirghis to remain and bring on the tired beasts as fast as they could. It was also arranged that a fire should be lighted as a beacon when we reached the aoul, when men should be sent to guide them to us.

All were well mounted on steeds caught fresh from the herd, and by command of "Nour-Ali" one of his best horses had been saddled for me. This animal, by the fire in his eye, showed that he had a touch of Shaitan in his temper.

While we stood for a few minutes telling off the men, he displayed a disposition to return to his pastures, and that too without his rider. He pawed the ground in his rage, sending the sand and gravel far behind him, and then plunged forward with a bound like a deer. One of the guides was also mounted on a fiery animal equally impatient

Starting to cross the Desert.

of control. All being settled we started, but our horses could not be kept in; the clanking of sabres was new to their ears, and put them into a perfect fury. The sand was smooth and hard, our speed soon became a gallop, and the sound of hoofs could be heard far over the plain.

There is no mode of travelling that creates so profound a

sensation of independence as riding over these steppes, uncertain whether the next tribe will be friendly or turn out a band of plunderers. After proceeding about two hours, our friends were seen far behind, diminished to the size of specks on the vast plain. The Kirghis pointed to the descending orb, and urged my going on at speed, as no time was to be lost; assuring me that if night caught us before reaching the pastures, we should probably have a sandy couch, without either grass or water for our horses.

Several hours had passed, yet nothing was seen to indicate that we were drawing near a grassy region, and our companions were left so far in the distance that they were lost in the grey vapour. The sun was just setting when we turned our horses, and went on at a brisk pace. In a little time we observed a change on the horizon; small mounds now appeared in the distance, but whether they were yourts, camels, or bushes, no one could tell. In about half an hour we came upon small tufts of grass, and shortly afterwards the pastures were before us. After riding about a couple of miles we approached the edge of a slight depression on the plain, and then beheld herds of cattle proceeding to an aoul about a mile distant; while several others were scattered over this little valley.

Presently there was a great commotion, and men were seen galloping from one aoul to another. The people had observed our approach, and doubts were entertained about our intentions. A party of six horsemen came to meet us, when two Kirghis went forward to explain who we were; they met, and a few minutes sufficed to convince them that we were honest travellers. A man was sent back to give this assurance to the tribe, and the others rode up to welcome and conduct me to their chief. My Kirghis having explained that a party were left behind with the camels, two of the men started on our track, to meet and conduct them to the aoul.

I was led to their lord, who I found standing at the door of his yourt; on riding up, he laid hold of my bridle, offering me his hand to dismount; he then gave me the usual salutation, and ushered me into his dwelling. A fire was burning in the middle of the yourt; a large cauldron, on its tripod, standing over it, and two females were stirring the contents with wooden ladles. Soon a large bowl of-brick tea was handed to me. As this is a beverage not generally known to the ladies of England, it may be useful to tell them how it is concocted. Brick tea is a solid mass about eleven inches long, six inches wide, and one and a-half inches thick, and is made from the last gatherings and the refuse of the tea crop. Instead of the leaves and stalks being dried, they are made wet, mixed with bullock's blood, and pressed into a mould, when the mass becomes more solid than a brick. When it is used, a man takes an axe and chops off some small pieces ; these are bruised between two stones, rubbed in the hands, and then thrown into the cauldron. A bowl of "Smitanka," sour clotted cream, is added, with a little salt and a handful of millet meal; these ingredients are boiled for half an hour, and then served up hot. Before handing it to the guests, small portions are taken out of the cauldron with a spoon, and thrown to the four winds as an offering to the gods. I cannot say that the beverage is either bad or particularly clean, still hunger has often caused me to make a very good meal of it ; but I think it is rather *tea soup* than tea.

My host's name was "Joul-bar," the chief of a powerful tribe. Several of his friends came in from the different aouls around, anxious to know the cause of the visit of so many armed men ; it was soon explained, and then all seemed satisfied. The alarm caused by our appearance was accounted for,—a numerous band of Kirghis had made a descent on an aoul only three days before, carrying off men, women, and children, with a great number of horses and cattle. It was also known that these freebooters were still hovering about at no great distance. Looking at the chief and those around him, I thought they were not the men to be plundered with impunity; and all the aouls of the tribe were concentrated on these pastures as a security.

Joul-bar was a determined and fine-looking man, about forty-five years old ; and many of his associates were nearly the same age. There were several older men in the tribe, but all contentedly acknowledged him their chief. His father had died three years previously, and he had been elected unanimously by the whole body. On two occasions, during his father's life, he had saved them from pillage by his prudence and bravery. He had also conducted several successful "Barantas" (plundering expeditions) against Kirghis who had been engaged in robberies on his tribe: this had obtained for him the full confidence of his people. The chief was rich, having nearly 10,000 horses; others of his tribe had from 5,000 to 7,000 ; they had also a great number of camels and vast herds of horned cattle, and they estimated their sheep at more than 250,000. It was a splendid sight watching these enormous herds and flocks spread over the steppe,—nor is it uncommon to see a herd of 8,000 to 10,000 horses, more than 1,000 camels, 20,000 horned cattle, and 50,000 sheep. But great as these numbers are, the animals appear to occupy a comparatively small space on these vast plains.

My host told me that in the direction I proposed going, after quitting his pastures, I should find a sandy desert, destitute both of food and water for the horses. The ride, with horses alone, would occupy from eighteen to twenty hours, and if attempted with camels it would take more than two days. He therefore advised that we should cross the desert with horses only, saying that we could defend ourselves better should we meet any of the roving bands. I then arranged with him to supply me with men and horses for the journey.

CHAP. III.

HOW TO CROSS THE DESERTS OF ASIA.

Early in the morning I found Joul-bar directing the arrangements for our long ride. Calling his people together, he pointed out twelve Kirghis who were to be my attendants, saying that they were men on whom I could depend, and some of them had a knowledge of the country. Thirty-six horses were provided, two for each man, and four for the baggage, which would enable us to ride across the desert in the shortest possible time. Joul-bar and his people were greatly interested with the various articles of my baggage, particularly my arms and costume. The stockings, shirts, and under garments were minutely examined, these being articles entirely dispensed with by the Kirghis. My rough cloth coat, with its pockets, afforded matter for much speculation, and the quality of the material was exceedingly admired, but its sombre colour did not please. A strong hunting knife was found in a pocket; this the chief turned about in all directions, but could not succeed in opening. As he held it in his hand, I pressed the spring and the blade flew open, causing him and those around to gaze at the instrument with amazement. My pen-knife with two blades was also a great curiosity, and this he named "Barant-chuck," (a baby). These articles were handed round, and as they passed from one person to another, each exclaimed, "Yak-she," (good).

Having closed the hunting knife, I showed him how to open it by touching the spring; with this he was delighted, and would have continued playing with it for a day had time permitted me to stop. He inquired if I had more, when I answered "Jock" (no): he was greatly disappointed, and wished to keep the one in his hand, desiring to know how many sheep he must give in exchange. I told him I could not part with it, having no other, and my country being so far off, I could not procure one. He now asked how many days it would take to go to England and return, with a caravan of camels. My reply was, twelve moons. "That is a long time," he said, and asked if many such knives were made for barter. When I told him that he could load a caravan of a thousand camels in a few days, with knives of all sorts, some much larger than the one he admired, others smaller even than the barantchuck, with a few that contained a hundred blades, he held up his hands in wonder.

Desiring to leave as speedily as possible, and on good terms with my host, I took out of my baggage a pair of woollen gloves, which proved a great curiosity. Having drawn one on, I gave the other to Joul-bar: when he had succeeded in getting his fingers into their proper places, he looked at his gloved hand with intense satisfaction. I then presented the other. Had they been scarlet instead of grey, their value would have been much enhanced. Thus I got out of the difficulty. I took my morning meal, within a few feet of the carpet on which the ladies were sleeping; after which, with the usual ceremonies, I was suffered to depart.

In a little more than an hour the sun rose, as if from the sea, casting his slanting rays into the desert, and lighting up the whole plain. This enabled me to examine my party. They were wild-looking fellows, dressed in varied costumes. Several had horse-skin coats, with flowing manes down the centre of their backs; the skirts tucked into their tchimbar of yellow leather. On their heads they had horse-skin caps, with part of the mane on the top falling back like a helmet, which gave them a most ferocious aspect. Others had sheep-skin coats, leather tchimbar, and fox-skin caps, with lappets hanging over their ears. Each man had his battle-axe, and three of them carried long lances, with tufts of black horse-hair hanging beneath the spear. Thus armed and costumed, we formed an imposing cavalcade. Among the horses were animals of great beauty. Joul-bar had ordered for me a pair of dark iron-greys, of a race celebrated for speed and endurance. The spare ones were divided among nine Kirghis; leaving the Cossacks, three Kirghis, and myself, free for defence, if necessary. Although the chief and the tribe thought it probable that we might meet with some of the roving gentlemen of the steppe, neither the Cossacks nor myself entertained any apprehension. We were well mounted, and our rifles could give a good account of our assailants, should we be attacked. For the first hour we rode slowly over rich pastures, that were soon to be cropped bare by the vast herds feeding upon them. After this our horses were put into a quicker pace, and we shortly began to leave the grassy steppe behind.

There was a belt along the edge of the desert, about two miles in width, on which tufts of rough grass were growing, and broad patches of plants having succulent leaves and deep crimson flowers. These were quickly passed, and we entered upon a sandy waste, which, to the south, the east, and the west, appeared a sea of sand. Stopping my horse, I glanced back at the aoul and the herds we had left: a few camels and horses only could be seen, now diminished almost to specks; but the yourts and the people were no longer visible. I desired the Kirghis to point out the direction of our route, which was nearly south-west, and then we started onwards.

For many miles the sand was hard like a floor, over which we pushed on at a rapid pace. After this we found it soft in places, and raised into thousands of little mounds by the wind. Our horses were now changed, and in an hour these mounds were passed, when we were again on a good surface, still riding hard.

Hour after hour went by, and our steeds had been changed a second time; those we started with seeming as fresh as when they left the aoul. In our route there was no change visible,—it was still the same plain; there was not so much as a cloud floating in the air, that, by casting a shadow over the steppe, could give a slight variation to the scene. At noon I called a halt, to look round with my glass; but nothing appeared on the sandy waste. When mid-day had passed, my attendants desired to stop. The horses were piqueted in three groups, but we could procure them neither grass nor water. The Kirghis produced smoked horse flesh and their Koumis bottles, and they and the Cossacks dined. A piece of boiled mutton having been secured from last night's feast, on this I made my repast.

While the men were taking their meal, I walked along about half a mile. The whole horizon was swept with my glass, but neither man, animal, nor bird could be seen. One of the Kirghis galloped up to me, bringing my horse, and urged me to be gone. Having resumed my saddle, we rode on for several hours, but there was no change of scene. One spot was so like another, that we seemed to make no progress; and though we had gone over a considerable distance, nothing could be observed to indicate that we were drawing near a grassy region. No landmark was visible, no rock protruded through the sterile soil; neither thorny shrub, nor flowering plant, appeared, to indicate the approach to a habitable region. All around was "Kizil-koom," (red sand).

What a solemn stillness reigns on these vast arid plains, deserted alike by man, beast, and bird! Men speak of the solitude of dense forests: I have ridden through their dark shades for days together; but there was the sighing of the breeze, the rustling of the leaves, the creaking of the branches; sometimes the crash of one of these giants of the forest, which, in falling, woke up many an echo, causing the wild animals to growl, and the frightened birds to utter shrieks of alarm. This was not solitude: the leaves and trees found tongues, and sent forth voices; but on these dreary deserts no sound was heard to break the death-like silence which hangs perpetually over the blighted region.

On the Desert.

Fourteen hours had passed, and still a desert was before us. The sun was just sinking below the horizon. The Kirghis assured me that two hours more would take us to the pastures and to water; but they doubted our finding an aoul in the dark. Our horses began to feel the distance we had travelled, and now we changed them every hour. We still kept on at a good speed; and though two more hours had elapsed, there were no signs of herbage. It had become quite dark, and the stars were shining brilliantly in the deep blue vault. My guides altered their course, going more to the south. On inquiring why they made this change, one of them pointed to a star, intimating that by that they must direct their course.

We travelled onward, sometimes glancing at the planets above, and then anxiously scanning the gloom around, in the hope of discerning the fire of some dwelling that would furnish food and water for our animals. Having ridden on in this manner for many miles, one of the men stopped suddenly, sprang from his horse, and discovered that we had reached vegetation. The horses became more lively, and increased their speed, by which the Kirghis knew that water was not far off. In less than half an hour they plunged with us into a stream, and eagerly began to quench their terrible thirst, after their long and toilsome journey.

While they were drinking, several of the men alighted, and with their hands examined the ground to trace the footprints of animals; but this proved fruitless. It was then decided that two parties, of three men each, should follow the stream upwards and downwards, and examine the banks. They had proceeded but a few hundred yards when those to the east called loudly for us to follow; fortunately, they had found a well-trodden track. By feeling the footprints, the men knew that horses and cattle had recently passed. After fording the stream, we rode on, in the hope of finding the yourts; and when we had gone about a couple of miles, we were suddenly brought to a stand by what appeared to be the distant barking of a dog. We stood still, but the sound was not repeated. We proceeded onward, listening with intense anxiety for a repetition; and having gone a few hundred yards, distinctly heard several dogs raise a chorus of canine alarm—to us, most welcome music. As we advanced, the barking became furious; we could also hear the clattering of hoofs, made, apparently, by the guards riding at full speed over the turf to call out the tribe. Presently there was a great commotion; men were shouting to each other, while others galloped from the aoul to support the sentinels. We stood still, and two of our Kirghis advanced slowly, calling out that we were friends, and not robbers. They rode up to the watchmen, who, when satisfied, came and conducted us to their chief. With him we found an armed assemblage ready for the fray; women and children were huddled together, and all looked anxious, if not apprehensive. In a few minutes I was seated, taking my customary refreshment, in the chief's yourt. On looking at my watch, I found that we had been riding eighteen hours.

When I awoke the next morning, the chief, with several men and women, were sitting in the yourt. I threw off my covering, sprang to my feet, and my toilet was finished. The traveller who visits these Asiatics will be disappointed should he expect better accommodation. His lavatory must be the nearest piece of water, and the broad steppe, with its blue canopy, his dressing-room. Nor will he lack spectators of either sex; all will be interested in (to them) the novel and extraordinary scene. Cleanliness is not a Kirghis virtue; they are economical in soap, and the washing of either person or clothing apparently forms no part of their domestic duties.

The summer costume of both men and women consists of two, sometimes of three, silk or cotton Kalats (long dressing gowns). These are made double, so that when one side is dirty, the garment is turned, and a new side appears. In time this also becomes more foul than its precursor, and then in it goes and forth comes the other: so alternate changes take place, till the garment falls off, a compound of rags and filth, when a new one goes through the same process. The summer costume of the children, up to eight years of age, is still more economical. The juveniles take a roll on the bank of a muddy pool; the scorching sun quickly bakes the coating they thus obtain, and their dress is complete. When this is worn off or looks shabby, either by sleeping in their furs or by their gambols on the grass, they add a new one of the same material. In winter, men, women, and children of all ages, wear fur coats, making it exceedingly difficult to distinguish the sexes.

The Kirghis who had accompanied me intended remaining here another night, and would start on their return before dawn on the following morning: they expected to reach their aoul in 18 or 20 hours. Their horses will then have gone over not less than 240 to 250 miles. Our average rate of travelling had been 6 to 7 miles per hour. On inquiring from my host, he informed me that the country onward was rich in pastures, and that tribes and numerous aouls would be found on my route.

Before two o'clock we were all in our saddles. At a little distance from the aoul we found great flocks of sheep, and then came upon the camels, cows, and oxen. Further on we passed through herds of horses; these were feeding six or seven miles away, attended by mounted herdsmen. The people were rich in flocks and cattle, and my guide told me that their pastures extended a two hours' ride beyond where the horses were feeding. We were now riding over a rich carpet of grass, intermingled with flowers. What a change from the arid and desolate scene of yesterday! Herds of antelopes were feeding, to which the dogs gave chase: we had several splendid runs, but their fleetness soon placed them out of danger. They stood in groups, gazing at us with their large black eyes, within rifle range, but I would not shoot at them or permit the Cossacks to do so. They were very small and beautifully shaped, with exceedingly slender legs, and bounded over the steppe, apparently scarcely touching the grass.

Sometimes they were seen in herds of more than a hundred. The country was undulating, and several small lakes could be discerned in the distance. Far away to the west, a belt of dark green was observed, which the men said was Kamisch (reeds) on the shores of a large lake; but the water could not be seen from our position.

About an hour before sunset, we perceived dark objects on the steppe; they were the camels and horses belonging to the Kirghis on whom we were going to intrude for a night's lodging. Our horses were put into a gallop, hoping to reach the aoul before dusk; and just as the sun went down, we came upon the herdsmen. They were in great alarm, and driving in their horses; for our appearance, and the direction we came from, caused them to watch our approach with suspicion. News of our advance had been sent to the aoul; but when the people were assured that we were travellers, the herds were left to feed, and one of the herdsmen sent to guide us to the chief, an hour's ride distant. We had not ridden far, when a number of horsemen approached us at full speed, uttering shouts of defiance, and brandishing their battle-axes; but when within 200 yards, the herdsmen dashed forward, and explained who we were. The chief met us at the head of his retainers, gave me a welcome, and conducted me to his aoul. Our arrival had again caused great consternation, and all the men were prepared to do battle for their wives, children, and cattle. When it was known that we had crossed the desert, many inquiries were made about the roving bands that were hovering, it was supposed, on the skirts of the arid region, and plundering every tribe they could attack.

The people we had fallen in with belonged to the tribe of the celebrated Sultan Batyr; and a man was sent to his aoul, at a two hours' ride to the eastward, to announce my approach. The chief, whose acquaintance I had just made, gave me fresh horses, and accompanied us. Having good ones, our ride over the pastures was rapid. As we came near the aoul, three Kirghis met us, to guide me to the Sultan, whose yourt was easily distinguished from the others, by a spear standing at the entrance, with a long black tuft of horse-hair floating in the breeze.

As we rode up, he came forward, took the reins of my bridle, giving me his hand to alight, saluted me, and then led the way into his dwelling. A Bokharian carpet and some tiger-skins were spread, on which a seat was offered me, and the Sultan sat down opposite. Tea and dried fruits were immediately placed before us, of which my host urged me to partake, setting me a good example. He was a hale old man, was said to be more than eighty years of age, possessed good and pleasing features, a ruddy complexion, and had but little hair, which was very white. He was still above the average height of the Kirghis, and must have been a fine-looking man when in his prime. Several of his aged followers had taken their seats near him, while the younger ones stood around.

The yourt was a spacious one, nearly forty feet in diameter, and thirteen feet high; a boy was feeding a blazing fire in the centre, and a great number of boxes and bales were close behind me, containing the old man's treasure. On some packages to my left were the Sultan's saddle and richly-decorated horse trappings, ornamented with iron inlaid with silver. Near these was the chair of state, which is carried on a camel before Batyr when on the march; at the four corners it is decorated with peacock feathers, signifying his descent from "Timour Khan," (Tamerlane). A fine hawk was perched on one side of the yourt; on the opposite, a large "Bearcoot" (black eagle), was chained to a stump, shackled but not hooded. Both these birds are used in hunting by the Kirghis; the hawk for pheasants and other feathered game, and the bearcoot for foxes, deer, and wolves.

Later in the evening an aged woman and three young ones, with four children, came in; they were the Sultan's family, and had been at their evening occupation; the Sultana and the young ladies milking the cows, sheep, and goats; the younger children assisting. Night and morning this is the customary duty of the wives and daughters of these princes of the steppe; who are as proud of their descent from the great conqueror, as any English noble of his Norman origin. The maiden feels no degradation in milking her kine nor in saddling her horse, and when mounted, with hawk on wrist, manages her steed like an Amazon.

Several years before my visit, the fine old man had witnessed on this very spot one of the most heartrending scenes that can afflict a father. Some time before the event occurred which I am going to relate, his eldest son had attained his manhood, when the Sultan decided that he should begin life on his own account. To enable him to do this in a manner befitting his station, the father gave him 1,000 horses from his stud, a proportionate number of camels, about 2,000 horned cattle, and 5,000 sheep; appointing several young men of the tribe to be his attendants and herdsmen. The animals, however, fell far short of the number the son considered he was entitled to. He demanded half his father's live stock, but this was refused.

Already the youth had been engaged in several of their "barrantas," or great plundering expeditions; and, unknown to his parent, was forming a band of the most desperate characters in the region. He now tried to induce the young men of the tribe to join this band of marauders, and, unfortunately, was successful. This accomplished, he left his father's pastures, driving his horses, sheep, and cattle about 300 miles to the south-east, into a wild district. When his band had become sufficiently numerous, he commenced plundering on a great scale. Many aouls were swept away, the pastures rendered desolate, and the people sold into slavery by these robbers. Their depredations were carried on far and wide, no one daring to pasture cattle in the vicinity of their retreat.

Accounts of his atrocities frequently reached his parent and the tribe, but no one thought him base enough to make a descent on his own kindred. One night, when the guards were on their usual duty, the dogs appeared to scent a distant danger by whining and growling frequently; which made the men imagine that tigers were prowling about near the herds. Shortly they became more restless, giving forth growls and savage barks in a most unusual manner. This alarmed the watchmen, who sent to warn the Sultan, and rouse his people. In consequence, the horses were saddled and the men mounted, with their battle-axes in hand, ready for any attack. It was discovered that, whatever the danger might be, it was approaching both on the north and south, and from the fury of the dogs it must be drawing near. No tramp of horses had yet been heard, even by placing the ears to the ground. The tribe, however, were not kept long in suspense, the well-known sound of distant hoofs being at last audible, gradually advancing. Nothing could be seen through the gloom; presently the dogs rushed forward with fury, and in a few minutes battle-axes were clashing, and the work of death commenced.

While the battle raged on one side of the aoul, and the men were driven towards the yourts by the furious assailants, another party of them was attempting, in another direction, to drive off the herds. When they got among the cattle, thousands of horses began rushing to and fro, and the scene became fearful,—women and children shrieked in the yourts, while the fires cast a glare on the savage combatants around them. In the course of the conflict, one of the robbers was cut down, and fell close to the door of one of the dwellings; he was quickly recognised by the Sultana, as one of her sons; she uttered a fearful shriek, and proclaimed the discovery.

When the appalling intelligence reached the Sultan, he and those around him seemed panic-struck, and their hands ceased to wield their axes. Taking advantage of this, the robbers swept off more than 3,000 horses, and several women. Many of the tribe were wounded, and some fell in the fight.

Marauders at the Aoul.

In the morning it was discovered that the plunderers had lost several of their band, two of whom belonged to the aoul. The leader had escaped, but the people look upon him as a demon in league with Shaitan.

Having mentioned that the nomades of Central Asia are proud of their genealogy, it may also be added that each

Sultan boasts of a long line of ancestors, whom his poet traces up either to Genghiz Khan or Timour, and some even take a flight among the Genii ; besides which, they still retain all the love for barbaric grandeur as it existed in the days of these conquerors. Those feelings will be best illustrated by an account of a funeral ceremony which took place during my journey among these people.

If, when they enter their final resting-place, it is not, like the monarchs of Europe, amidst thundering of cannon, and the deep and solemn tones of the funeral march, (such as I have heard in a northern capital, where 60,000 troops lined the streets through which the pageant passed,) their obsequies are attended by ceremonies equally imposing, which, according to their ideas, prove the race and rank of the deceased.

A celebrated Sultan, "Darma Syrym," died at his pastures near Nor-Zaisan, within the Chinese frontier. He was an aged man, greatly esteemed by his people, and feared by other tribes. In early life his power had been recognised far into the country of the Kalkas, and into the region of the Gobi. The owl's feather which he wore was not the only badge that marked him a descendant of Genghiz. He was a warrior too, and had made his influence felt on the banks of the Jaxartes.

His illness was not of long duration, but his mulla had perceived in its early stage that it would be fatal. This was announced to his people, and caused a deep and painful sensation. As he drew towards his end, many came from afar to witness the last moments of the great man.

The moment he had ceased to breathe, Kirghis were despatched to the nearest aouls to announce the event. Swift horses were used, and they were ridden to the utmost of their speed. When the messenger reached his destination and delivered his sad tidings, another man was despatched to convey the intelligence to others. Thus, within the space of a few hours, the news of the Sultan's death was spread over an area of near 200 miles in diameter.

The Sultans, chiefs, or elders of each tribe, immediately repaired to Darma Syrym's aoul, to assist at the funeral rites, and before evening a vast number came pouring in. A spear with a black flag was mounted at the door of the yourt, and the deceased was laid out, dressed in his best attire. The chair of state, the emblem of his greatness, was placed at his head. His saddle, horse trappings, arms, and clothing, were arranged in piles on each side, and Chinese silk curtains were suspended from the ribs of his yourt; while his wives, daughters, and other females of his tribe, knelt with their faces towards him, chanting the funeral dirge. The effect of this music, as they sang, swaying their bodies to and fro, was solemn and pathetic. Groups of men entered, and instantly kneeling, joined in the funeral chorus, swelling the mournful harmony with their deep-toned voices. There were no shrieks, tearing of hair, or funeral wails used by these people. Theirs was really a musical service.

While this was being performed, another part of the ceremony was preparing. In the rear of the Sultan's yourt men were engaged slaughtering ten horses and one hundred sheep for the funeral feast. Near these, numerous iron cauldrons were boiling over fires in the ground, attended by men stripped naked to the waist, who, with wooden ladles in their hands, were employed skimming the boiling contents.

Groups of men with crimsoned arms and hands were engaged in the slaughter, while others dragged up the victims for sacrifice, and near were the swarthy forms of those occupied about the cauldrons. At times the whole group might be seen, some with uplifted arms pursuing the work of death,—then a shriek and a plunge, and a horse fell, having received the fatal thrust. In another moment all was obscured, then suddenly the figures were dimly visible; appearing, as the steam was wafted past, like demons engaged in some unholy rite. It was a savage scene, and, when coupled with the mournful sounds issuing from the dwelling, produced a saddening and a sickening effect.

When a sufficient portion of the animals was cooked, the guests assembled, and seated themselves in a circle on the

Funeral Sacrifice.

ground, in front of the yourt—the Sultans and elders in the centre, those of less degree around them; beyond these were the women. As this dinner differed in no way (save the number of guests) from the banquets I have described in my work on Oriental and Western Siberia, I shall not repeat it.

The festival continued for seven days, during which other Sultans and Kirghis were constantly arriving. It was supposed that near 2,000 people assembled to assist at this funeral. On the eighth day the Sultan was interred. His body was taken from the yourt in the clothing in which it had lain—another cloth was wrapped around it, and then it was placed on a camel, by which he was carried to the tomb. The chair of state was borne before him on another camel, and two of the Sultan's favourite horses formed part of the procession, being led immediately after the body. After these came his wives, daughters, and the women of his tribe, chanting the funeral hymn, in which the mullas and a vast number of the men joined—swelling the mournful strain into a mighty chorus, which was heard far over the plain.

On reaching the tomb the body was placed in the grave, when the mullas recited prayers, and told of the great deeds of the departed. While this was performing, the two horses were killed, and interred on each side of their late master. After which the graves were filled up, and the procession returned to the aoul, to partake of another grand funeral banquet. One hundred horses and 1,000 sheep were slain to do honour to the deceased Sultan.

When the women returned, they entered the yourt, and chanted their mournful dirge for an hour before the pile of arms, horse trappings, and apparel which had belonged to the departed. After which, all the family assembled before the dwelling, and were joined by the Sultans and chiefs who had attended to do honour to the memory of Darma Syrym. This great festival was continued for several days after the funeral, until the people gradually left for their homes. By the tribe it was kept up a long time, and the chanting was repeated at sunrise and sunset during a whole year.

Leaving the tomb and tribe of Darma Syrym, I shall take my readers to Tchingiz-tau, a region on the north-west of the Balkash, or Lake Tengiz,—and give them in the following chapter an account of an acquisition which has become of vast importance to Russia.

CHAP. IV.

SILVER MINES IN THE STEPPE.

In the year 1848, the Emperor Nicholas decided that the whole of the people on the Trans Baikal should become Cossacks,—a necessary measure for carrying out his plans in the regions of the Amoor. Hitherto a large body of the population had been employed in mining operations, which will be alluded to hereafter. This sudden change closed the silver mines of Nertchinsk, and stopped the supply of lead, of which about 250 tons had been sent annually to the silver smelting works in Western Siberia. When this lead could no longer be obtained, the quantity had to be made good by importing the metal from England, involving a carriage by land of more than 2,000 miles, beside a sea and river voyage of a greater distance. This supply was stopped altogether at the commencement of the Crimean war.

Thus it became a most serious difficulty, and every exertion was made to discover lead mines either in Siberia or the surrounding regions. With this view, three young mining engineers, and a party of 180 men, were sent to explore a vast country in the Kirghis Steppe, lying between the Tarbagatai and the Irtisch. They were to search for lead and silver ores, but signs of other mineral wealth were not to be neglected. The party returned, however, in the autumn, unsuccessful in so far as their principal object was concerned, although they had explored an immense tract of country. Gold, copper, topaz, and tourmaline had been found, but no silver ore exists in the region on the north of the

Tarbagatai, extending up to Nor-Zaisan on the south-east, and as far as the Irtisch on the north.

In the summer of 1852, another expedition from the Altai, consisting of three officers and 180 men, was sent into the region to the north of Ayagus, under the command of a clever and intelligent officer, Captain Tartarinoff. They were accompanied by a strong body of Cossacks, to protect them from the Kirghis, who, it was feared, might oppose their examining the country. This time their efforts were crowned with success. They having explored the steppe to the west of the Arkat Mountains, and as far as Tchingiz-tau, found some rich silver and lead mines near the latter chain, which would, if worked, prove of immense value to Russia. Vast quantities of lead could be obtained, ten times more than is required for all the smelting operations; besides a large amount of silver for the mint.

As this region was far beyond the Russian frontier, it required extreme caution in arranging with the Kirghis. To take forcible possession would have been a great risk; all the tribes would have resisted, and some of them were too powerful to be trifled with. During the winter, negotiations were entered upon through the authorities in Ayagus; when it was arranged that a meeting should take place at an aoul near the silver mines, between the Sultan, the chiefs of the tribes to whom the region belonged, and the director of the mines in the Altai. It was expected that much diplomacy would be required by the Russian officer to accomplish his object.

Some weeks before the time appointed for the meeting, (the first week in May,) the chiefs, with many people of the different tribes, had been carefully examining the excavations made by the Russian miners; but no rich veins of the precious metal were visible. The stones the miners had broken up, appeared to these uneducated men like the ordinary rocks of the steppe, without any metallic appearance indicating that they were rich in silver—a metal much prized by the Kirghis. Had they discovered any metallic veins, it is doubtful if any remuneration would have induced them to dispose of their land.

At length the important time drew near, and the Sultan, with his chiefs and tribes, were waiting with anxious expectation the arrival of the officer from "the great White Khan." Grand preparations had been made for his entertainment, consisting chiefly of horse-racing and wrestling, and a sumptuous banquet "à la Kirghis."

My friend, the director of the mines in the Altai, was pursuing his way across the lower spurs of the chain towards Semipalatinsk, which having reached, he crossed the Irtisch to a Tatar village where Cossacks were ready to receive him. Four horses were instantly harnessed to his carriage, and a pair of leaders added: a Cossack mounted the box, another one of the leaders, and two rode on each side the carriage as a guard. A crowd soon gathered around his equipage; and on its deep green colour, silver mountings, and glass windows, the Tatars, Kirghis, and Bokharians gazed with wonder. When the Cossacks put their steeds into a gallop and dashed on through the village, these nomades watched the horses bound along, expecting that every shake would demolish the glass.

Sir Robert Peel has praised the Russian yemtchicks for their excellent driving, and seems to have been delighted with the speed at which they carried him along the road from Moscow to Novgorod. If he really delights in being whirled over the country at the speed of a fox-chase, I should recommend him to go and try a gallop with the Cossacks on the plains of Central Asia. He may then sit behind animals as full of spirit as race horses, wild as deer, driven with a light snaffle bit by men who never use the lash; a word being always sufficient to put the team into a gallop or bring them up, at the pleasure of the driver. In this manner I have often crossed the country, and no horses were left *dead* on the plains. It was at such a speed that the director was travelling from one Cossack station to another. Having reached a station about 150 miles from the Irtisch, he left the Cossack post road, and turned on to the steppe. From this point his route was in a north-westerly direction, leaving the great and little Arkat Mountains far behind him.

Here he found the Kirghis sent by the Sultan to receive and conduct him to the aoul, about 100 miles distant. Some fine steeds were also in waiting for him. Kirghis horses are excellent for riding; even when caught fresh from the herd, it is seldom they cannot be managed. Putting them in harness is quite another matter; for the animals are impatient of restraint, and the rattling of a carriage at their heels makes them frantic. The director, wishing to travel onward in his carriage, the horses were brought up, and with the assistance of a number of Cossacks, were at last harnessed. A Cossack seated himself on the box, and Kirghis rode the leaders. But when an attempt was made to put the vehicle in motion, some of the team began to plunge, and others to kick so furiously, that my friend gave up the idea of taking his carriage forward, fearing that it would soon have been a wreck on the plain.

The author, with an artillery officer, in a light tarantas, had once been driven with Cossack horses to an aoul about sixty versts from the piquet, where our attendants left us to return home with their horses the following morning. Having spent some days in pheasant shooting, we prepared to leave our hospitable host, to visit another chief, who lived at a five hours' ride distant. Our friend provided us with horses and an escort of his Kirghis, who, with the help of our two Cossacks, succeeded in fastening six to our tarantas. One of our men mounted the box, and took the reins of the wheelers, and four Kirghis rode the others.

But all their efforts could not make them move the carriage a single yard.

The old chief was exceedingly angry, and ordered six more to be attached, with broad straps of hide across their chests, and ropes forming traces—rather slender tackle for

Kirghis Horses harnessed to a Tarantas.

rampant and plunging animals. The lines of horses and men made a formidable contrast with our small vehicle at their heels; but the chief felt that the honour of his cattle was at stake. When the word was given to proceed, some of the team reared and plunged on one side, as they felt the traces tighten against their ribs; others bounded in the opposite direction, seemingly intent upon tearing the carriage in half. During the confusion which followed, the leaders made a double, and rushed up to the carriage, appearing more inclined to ride than draw. After many efforts they were once more got into line, with mounted Kirghis on both sides of each pair. This succeeded, and away they went at a gallop, while the Kirghis shouted with joy as they rushed onward over the plain.

This was a scene I shall never forget. The men were enraptured, caring nothing for the bounds of the carriage, which rendered it no easy matter to keep our seats. Even the horses entered into the spirit of the race, for this it more resembled than travelling. After about an hour's gallop the steeds became more reconciled to their work; still, some refractory animal occasionally showed a desire to be free and range over the vast plain around him. Night was closing in fast when we dashed up to the aoul of the chief, the team white with foam, greatly to the surprise of the people. I have mentioned this incident to show what the Kirghis will do with horses that have never been in harness; but the danger is too great to be pleasant, and my fellow traveller, as well as myself, thought one such risk sufficient.

The chief of the mines commenced his journey on horseback, attended by a party of thirty Cossacks, and a considerable retinue of Kirghis, sent by the Sultan to escort him to the aoul. His baggage and other valuables were loaded on camels, and placed under a special guard of Cossacks. It was near noon when they left the piquet, having to ride about twenty-five miles to a group of yourts, at which they were to sleep. A Kirghis feast, of the usual character, awaited him here; mutton killed a few hours before, and now placed smoking hot before the guests; horse flesh, both cooked and smoked, and large heaps of boiled rice, formed the principal viands.

The following day the party travelled fifty miles, dining

and sleeping at some yourts sent by the Sultan, and on the third day they reached their destination. A detachment of Cossacks and Kirghis had been forwarded to announce the director's approach to the Sultan: and when he was within about a mile of the aoul, several chiefs came up to guide him to their lord.

The aoul was a large one, as all the Sultan's tribes had assembled, each being interested in disposing of a portion of their pastures. Two large yourts were seen standing on a rising ground, at about 200 yards from those in the aoul, and about 100 yards apart. At the door of one of these a spear was standing, decorated as usual with its long black horse-hair streamer. A number of saddled horses were piqueted near, and a group of men were standing round the spear: these were the Sultan and his elders, waiting for their guest.

When the director rode up, the Sultan advanced a few paces to aid him in dismounting, then saluted in the usual manner, by placing first one hand and then the other on his breast. The ceremony being ended, the director and his officers were ushered into the yourt, and regaled with tea and dried fruits. While this was proceeding, the Sultan inquired after his guest's horses, cattle, and his sons, and then about his journey. All these questions having been answered by the young Russian interpreter, the director paid the same compliment to his host. When the tea had been disposed of, the Sultan attended his guest to the yourt prepared for him, in which the Cossacks had arranged his baggage. Chairs or tables there were none, but they had covered the floor with Bokharian carpets, which gave the place a comfortable, even an elegant appearance. The director and his friends were now left alone, while other yourts were being prepared for the officers of his staff. The Cossacks secured yourts for themselves, and had them placed about fifty paces from that of their chiefs; thus forming an independent settlement. In about an hour the Sultan sent two of his followers to announce that he was preparing to visit his guest, and hoped the director could receive him. An answer was returned, expressing the pleasure the visit would afford. The Russian's turn was now to be host, and to entertain the Sultan and his followers; tea again forming the principal refreshment, but this time it was made in a more civilised manner.

Presently an officer and a few Cossacks mounted their horses, and crossed the small space between the two yourts to escort the Sultan, who, as soon as he had got into his saddle, with his mulla by his side, proceeded to the director's yourt surrounded by his chiefs. The Cossacks had formed a table by placing several boxes together; on these a cloth was spread, a China tea service displayed, and a number of dishes placed, containing bread, sweet cakes, dried fruit, and sweetmeats; these the Kirghis looked upon with great astonishment, they being seen for the first time. The splendid uniforms of the director, his officers, and the guard of Cossacks, also produced a striking effect.

During the repast there was little conversation, and that little not edifying; but the hissing somervar, the porcelain cups, and glass tumblers were examined minutely. The silver spoons and forks, however, and the table knives, were the greatest attraction. Then the Sultan and chiefs looked at the spoons placed in their cups with amazement. The loaf-sugar was also regarded with curiosity, and enjoyed like children: while the table, covered with valuables and luxuries, formed a spectacle beyond their comprehension, but they were under the conviction that all had been sent by the emperor. The entertainment having come to an end, the Sultan and his followers departed, escorted back as they came. Not a word had been breathed on the subject of the director's visit, and shortly after dusk every one save the watchmen was sound asleep.

In the morning the Kirghis brought fresh horses for the Russian officers, who were going to ride about the country, and inspect the mines. From the number of horses piqueted, it was evident that all the tribes were greatly interested in these proceedings.

When breakfast was ended, the Sultan and his chiefs came to conduct the director to the district which had been selected by the mining engineers. The specimens carried to Barnaoul proved the value of this little spot, and a map laid down by the engineers showed whence each had

Silver Mines near Tchingiz-tau.

been procured. These rich minerals were distributed over a space near twenty miles in length and eight in breadth ; but the chief of the mines saw at a glance the absolute necessity of securing a district considerably broader, including a small river,—otherwise it would be impossible to carry on the necessary mining operations.

Here was a difficulty. Although the Sultan and the chiefs were willing to sell the arid land, with its rocks and metals, the value of which they could not perceive—the water flowing through the country and fertilising their pastures they could appreciate; besides which, it quenched the thirst of vast herds of cattle belonging to tribes far beyond their region.

Few men have had such an escort as that which accompanied the director; it comprised all classes, from the prince to the herdsman. A great addition to its picturesque effect was caused by the Sultan having ordered the aoul to be removed to a point about fifteen miles distant, it being a more favourable resting-place for his guest while surveying the mines. The scene was striking and novel even to a Siberian, and the Russian officers were much astonished at the rapidity with which the aoul was dismantled. In less than two hours the yourts, the household goods, and other matters, were loaded on camels, and the whole tribe on their march. A vast herd of camels led the van, followed by a multitude of horses, oxen, and sheep; while the Kirghis, decked out in their holiday attire, gave colour and variety to the scene. Great numbers of the people followed this prince of the steppe and his guests, evidently expecting that prodigious quantities of silver would be discovered; and intense was their disappointment when they saw the director throw down the specimens which were broken off the rocks for his inspection.

On his arrival at the aoul, the director regaled the Sultan and his companions with tea, and in about two hours the Sultan led his guests to the banquet in nature's spacious and lofty hall, carpeted with fresh green turf. Some large Bokharian carpets were spread for the guests, near which the Sultan took his seat; and the chiefs arranged themselves in semicircles, leaving a good space in front of their lord. This was a large dinner party, as, including the Russian director, it consisted of more than 300 people.

The flesh of the horse forms (served up boiled, broiled and smoked) to Tatar, Kirghis, or Kalmuck gourmands, the most delicate dishes that could be placed before them. Mutton is also produced at every dinner, but beef is rarely eaten by the

Kirghis; hunger only could induce them to partake of it. The flesh of the camel is sometimes used, but only on great festal occasions, or when the animal has been killed by accident.

When all were placed, a number of Kirghis passed round, pouring warm water from iron jugs upon the hands of each person, to enable him to make his ablutions. These being ended, the cooks entered the circle, bearing long wooden trays piled up into heaps, and containing the various meats. When the trays were placed on the ground, they nearly filled the whole space between the Sultan and his chiefs. It was indeed a prodigious quantity, and all eyes were turned upon it. The Sultan tucked up the sleeves of his kalat, and thrust his hand into the reeking mass: this was the signal to begin, and his example was instantly followed by all who could reach the trays. But the first and second circle took care to appease their appetites before passing anything to those behind them.

The Cossacks had prepared a dinner apart for the director and his friends, which they placed on the table in a somewhat more civilised manner. Their host sent them several large bowls of rice, boiled with "Ouroukus" (dried apricots); this is a great dainty, and seldom produced at a Kirghis banquet. Vegetables they have none; in fact, the people of Central Asia disdain such trifles, nor are there any grown by the nomades. This festival was kept up with noisy revelry till darkness threw a veil over the scene.

When day broke the following morning, the people were busily engaged with their preparations for the races, as these were to commence directly the bargain was completed. The Sultan, his mulla, and several of the chiefs, were invited to breakfast with the director, after which they were to proceed to business. The other members of the tribes having no control over the property to be negotiated, were not admitted to the council. In due time a good substantial repast was placed on the board (or rather boxes). The bread, biscuits, cakes, and sweetmeats were luxuries they could not obtain in the steppe; and being served with tea in cups and glasses by men in uniform, produced a great impression on their minds, making them think that the wealth and power of the great White Khan were unbounded.

Their appetites having been fully satisfied, the director deemed it a favourable moment to commence proceedings. He therefore desired his interpreter to ask the price at which the Sultan valued the stony tract, and the pastures on its western side, with the stream of water which bounded it in that direction. In reply, the Sultan stated that he and the chiefs were willing to sell the land with the minerals on the following terms, viz: That two hundred and fifty pieces of silver (meaning silver roubles) should be paid to him, and a gold medal added, like the one presented by the Emperor Alexander I. to Sultan Boulania. Also, that another sum of one hundred silver roubles should be paid to the mulla and the chiefs, to be equally divided among them. But he said that the river they could not dispose of, as that was necessary for their pastures, and for watering their cattle.

The director now told them that he must absolutely insist on the river being included, as he could not purchase the mines without it. Nor would it, he said, be injurious to the tribes, as their cattle could drink at the stream before it entered the mining district, where it passed for many miles through their pastures. He, however, promised to add something more to the amount named by the Sultan, if this point was ceded to him. Having stated this, he ordered the 250 new and shining roubles to be placed on the table; the large gold medal, with its broad red ribbon, was taken out of its case and placed near the money; and 100 roubles more counted down for the mulla and the chiefs. A gold-laced scarlet coat and a sabre were now added to the heap intended for the Sultan; a kalat or long robe, of vivid colours, and a gold imperial, were put on the table for each of the chiefs and the mulla. The interpreter was instructed to tell the Sultan that all these things would be given if the river were included in the purchase; if not, the negotiation would be at an end, as no further offer would be made. They were not prepared for this mode of settling the matter: it seemed far too abrupt, as their transactions usually occupy days; indeed, sometimes weeks are consumed in settling their bargains, time being no object with them. They looked at each other with astonishment, and then at the valuables spread out before them, anxious to secure them, but still desiring to get more.

Having spoken together for some minutes, the Sultan said that it would take time for them to consider the matter; adding, that they would consult all the tribes about it, and give an answer in a few days. The director fully understood what was meant by this, and that they intended delaying their decision until something more was offered; and knowing that this would be continued for an indefinite period if once permitted, he told the Sultan that, as the matter had been under the consideration of himself, the mulla, chiefs, and tribes, for several months, they could not require any further time. Besides, he had taken a long journey to meet them, and now he could not, under any circumstances, admit of delay. It therefore became necessary that they should definitely decide, before the council broke up, whether they accepted his offer or not; finally he assured them that, if they once left his yourt without concluding the bargain, he should start on his return within an hour.

Without further remark the Sultan began examining the sabre and the coat, desiring that the latter should be tried on. He was quickly invested with it, and viewed the extraordinary change that appeared in his person with perfect satisfaction. The gold medal was hung on his breast, producing a great effect; but when a Cossack buckled the sabre on his waist, this settled the point. He would have given half the rivers in the steppe sooner than be stripped of his weapon and finery.

In a few minutes the mulla and chiefs were bedecked in their new clothing, evidently on the best terms with themselves, and vastly admiring each other. The money was handed to the Sultan, which he rolled up in his shawl and secured round his waist, as this was too precious in his eyes to be trusted to any other hands. The mulla and chiefs followed his example. Shortly afterwards the Sultan stamped his seal on a document transferring to the great White Khan the whole district shown on a map prepared beforehand, with all the gold, silver, and other minerals it might contain, its pastures, and the river. Thus, for a sum of about one hundred and fifty pounds, his Imperial Majesty acquired mines and a freehold property in the Kirghis Steppe, which will, I have no doubt, expand rapidly towards all the points of the compass. These mines are of immense value, and are now sending their contributions to the Imperial Mint.

The council broke up, and all parties were satisfied. When the Sultan left the yourt and appeared before his tribe in all his splendour, nothing could exceed their astonishment; they evidently thought no earthly monarch could surpass him in grandeur. The mulla and the chiefs also appeared in their gaily-coloured robes, producing a striking effect, as they stood on each side of their prince.

Carpets were now spread in front of the yourt for the director and his staff; and as the whole party seated themselves, the Sultan ordered the wrestlers to come forth. Several men threw off their fur coats, when they appeared *au naturel*, except a small piece of calico tied round their loins. They stepped forward on to a clear space in front of their prince, who seemed to eye their brawny forms and muscular limbs with great satisfaction. Having exhibited themselves, they retired, and the Sultan gave the signal to begin. A couple were presently engaged grappling each other's naked and greasy limbs: both competitors displayed skill and dexterity. This was a severe trial, and continued a long time before one of them was thrown. Immediately this occurred, other wrestlers entered the arena, and some terrible falls were given.

Kirghis Cemetery, and the Tomb of Tursun in Tchingiz-tau.

These contests, when between different tribes, are conducted in a most savage manner. The men engage in them with a full determination to conquer or die on the turf. Usually the Sultan stops the conflict between men of his own tribe, when he sees them become angry, before the last terrible throw, which almost invariably proves fatal. I regret to say that these Asiatics are somewhat like the ancient Romans in the arena, generally expressing their disapprobation if the last savage act is not fully accomplished. The inhuman customs of a barbaric age are found among the people of these regions, and he who can count the greatest number of opponents sacrificed to his prowess, receives the highest honour during his life; after his death tradition makes him a hero.

The athletic sports being ended, the races began; but these are not like either the Derby or St. Leger. At Doncaster and Epsom the courses are short—rarely long enough to test the endurance of a horse; great speed for a short distance being the grand object in England. Among the Kirghis it is quite different; the horse that possesses the most enduring physical power is most valued. The course they were going to run over would try their mettle to the utmost, as it was fifty versts, or about thirty-three miles, in length. This distance was chosen to show the director the value of the different studs owned by the Sultan and the chiefs. Forty horses were brought up to the starting point, all mounted by young Kirghis, and each rider feeling confident in the quality of his steed. It might have been called a steeple-chase, as the course was over the country to a place twenty-five versts distant; then each rider had to pass round a yourt marked by a flag, and return to the Sultan's aoul. Members of the tribe were stationed at different points, carrying spears and small flags to mark the route.

After some little trouble the horses were marshalled nearly in line, when the signal was given and away they went, with a great number of horsemen following in their rear. For the first ten versts the speed was not fast, and they kept well together. After this jockeying was resorted to, each trying to keep the lead without distressing his horse, as the return would try his metal sufficiently. Before they reached the turning point it became evident that the race would be well contested, and it was expected that it would be run in considerably less than two hours. When the horses reached within about a mile of the yourt a terrible struggle began, to obtain a place in the inner circle, — nearly all of them came up in a compact mass. But in rounding the yourt several shot ahead, getting nearly 200 yards in advance before the last had passed the spear. This was one of the favourite horses; his rider had been jockeyed out of his place, and when he saw the whole group before him he urged his steed onward at a tremendous pace, soon passing several of his opponents, and gradually drawing near the leading group.

The speed was carefully maintained when they had passed about one third of the distance homeward, yet no one of the competitors was left far behind. A number of well mounted Kirghis were waiting about ten versts from the aoul, where the real contest and excitement commenced. Several horses began to lose ground, and were rapidly being left behind. Still there were upwards of twenty close together, more than half that number galloping neck and neck. The clattering of the hoofs on the turf, and the wild shout of the men cheering on the riders; the spectators dressed in their varied and brilliant costumes, mounted on fiery steeds, rushing onward at full gallop, and heralding their favourites on to victory, presented a scene in Asiatic life which finds no parallel in Europe.

The Sultan and those around him were in a state of great excitement when they saw the advancing throng, now within a verst, and the shouts of the people came floating tumultuously on the air, becoming gradually louder as they approached. Horse and rider were distinctly visible, each straining every nerve to reach the goal. Nearer and nearer the foaming steeds rushed on, eight of them so close abreast that it was impossible to say which was in advance. Onward they fly, and when within a few strides of the spear three horses bound forward from the group and pass it at the same moment, amidst the loud hurrahs of the Kirghis. The distance had been run in one hour and forty-two minutes. Such is the horse-racing among the Kirghis:

but sometimes they make the course sixty versts, or forty miles.

This finished the festivities, and the director started on his return the following day, attended by a numerous escort. The engineer officers were left to see the boundary marked out by pillars of stone heaped up by the miners and Kirghis.

CHAP. V.

RUSSIA'S FIRST ADVANCE INTO THE GREAT HORDE.

The next point of interest to me was the region of the Kara-tau, which bounds the Kirghis Steppe to the south. Here were the pastures of the Great Horde; and in one of the valleys Russia was just commencing a fort. A ride of ten days after leaving Ayagus brought me to the river Bean, the boundary between the pastures of the Great and Middle Hordes. The country I passed over varied greatly in its aspects; arid steppes were frequently crossed, on which the grass was withered by the sun; and the only patches of green were the salsola bordering the numerous salt lakes. On approaching the mountains the country becomes more fertile, and affords good pasture for vast herds of cattle,—indeed, wherever there is moisture grass is abundant.

The ancient inhabitants of this region rendered it extremely productive. The numerous canals which still exist show their engineering skill, and the extent of the irrigation it produced. In some of the channels the water yet runs, and, where it overflows, the sterile soil is covered with a luxuriant carpet of vegetation, adorned with flowers of singular beauty. There is abundant proof that it has once been densely inhabited, and it is probably destined to be a great theatre when occupied by Russia. The vast number of tumuli scattered over the plain, the extensive earthworks, which have been either cities or strongholds, afford convincing evidence that a great people were once located here.

One of these ancient works on the Lepsou, near its outlets from the Kara-tau, is a parallelogram, about 700 yards in length and 300 in breadth. The earth walls are now about twelve feet high, and have been considerably higher; their thickness is about sixteen feet at the bottom, and nine feet at the top. This enclosure was entered by four gates, one being in the centre of each side; but the eastern end has been partly destroyed by the river, which is gradually cutting down the bank. Half a mile to the north and south are numerous mounds; and at about a mile from the western end there is a large tumulus, about 150 feet in diameter, and 50 feet high. The people who produced them were a very different race to the present occupiers of the country, and had made an extraordinary advance in agriculture and mining. In one of the small mountain ridges on my route, I found a fine specimen of malachite, and came upon the remains of ancient mines,—most probably worked at a period long before those of Siberia were discovered by the Chutes, who left many of their flint instruments in the depths of the Altai.

As we approached the Kara-tau from the north-east, the mountains were seen rising abruptly from the plain, — some to the height of near 7,000 feet. Their dark purple colour has obtained for them the name of "Black Mountains." On our ride towards this rocky barrier, I got an occasional glimpse, through the great rents in the chain, of the snowy crests beyond. These appeared so near, that I was almost deceived into the belief that an hour's ride would take me to them; and each new opening only made me the more anxious to cross into the valley. After a long day on horseback, we were glad to rest in the aoul of some herdsmen belonging to a chief, who gave us a welcome reception.

In the morning I discovered that the habitation was about ten miles from the foot of the Kara-tau, near its western end, where it descends on to the great plain, along which it runs in low hills to a considerable distance. Here I obtained horses and men to take us over the mountains into the valley lying between the Kara-tau and Ala-tau. Shortly after leaving the aoul, we got entangled in a deep morass, which compelled us to ride two hours to the westward before we were able to cross this dangerous quagmire. We then rode towards a great gap in the chain, seeking a pass

Lake and Kara-tau.

by which we could ascend. On reaching the place we found the dry bed of a small torrent, so narrow that we could only ride in single file, and the bottom covered with small pieces of sharp slate, which rendered it dangerous for our horses. The narrow ravine soon became so exceedingly steep that we had to dismount and lead our animals up its serpentine course, that more resembled a staircase than a track for travellers.

In about an hour we reached the head of a little gully, that led to a steep mountain slope, covered with short grass and moss, through which the slate rocks protruded. This was not difficult to ascend; and we presently rode up the incline and reached the summit, consisting of dark purple slate rocks without any vegetation. We descended into a stony valley, where great disruptions have taken place. Beyond, to the south, there was a very abrupt, craggy ridge, which the Kirghis said was the crest of the chain; and this we had to scale. I was advised to proceed in a south-easterly direction, towards a great depression in the mountain, where it was thought we might be able to cross. This I reached in a little more than an hour, and succeeded in ascending to the summit without difficulty, whence I obtained a view of the Ala-tau, with its snow-clad peaks, and the valley lying between the chains. The latter appeared to be about twenty miles in width, and extended to the eastward forty or fifty miles, while to the west it terminated on the great plain. I perceived that it was intersected by several deep ravines, in which small streams found their way into the Kopal, that was seen winding its course westward to the Karatal, and thence to the Balkash.

Although I was aware that the Russians were constructing a fort on the Kopal, no indication of this could be seen, nor any mark to guide us towards the presumed locality. I, however, felt convinced it was across the valley near the foot of the mountains, and more to the eastward. This induced me to hasten our march towards the south-east, where we found the descent exceedingly abrupt, causing us much trouble in picking our way among large fragments of slate. We rode over places on which it was difficult for the horses to keep their footing; while in one part the mountain slope was covered with *débris* fallen from the cliffs above, that extended about 200 yards in width, and terminated on the brink of a deep ravine. This we were compelled to cross at a short distance from the brink of the chasm, and in a little more than an hour reached the valley, that, instead of being a plain, as it appeared from the mountain top, proved undulating ground, intersected by many small gullies and deep ravines. One was about 300 feet deep, with nearly perpendicular sides, down which it would have been no easy matter to descend on foot; on horseback it was impossible. This obstruction obliged us to turn to the north-east, when, after riding about two miles, we came upon a torrent running in a deep gully. After carefully scanning the bed, we concluded that it afforded us a chance of descending into the deep ravine. Passing over its precipitous banks, we rode slowly down the stream, and ultimately reached the bottom of the gorge, which was covered with trees and thick brushwood. During our progress several pheasants had sprung up, and we saw other indications of game.

Ascending the opposite porphyritic cliffs, we continued our ride over undulating ground till we reached the top of a low hill, whence a great smoke was seen near the foot of the mountains to the south-east, but far away; towards this I directed our course, hoping to find either Cossacks or Kirghis. We were now on good turf, which enabled us to gallop on at a rapid pace; and after riding about two hours we could discern some low sheds and yourts a few miles from the foot of the Ala-tau. At length we reached a round hill near the middle of the valley, from which we had a splendid view looking to the eastward.

On the north was the Kara-tau, with its dark serrated ridge, and on the south the Ala-tau. The lower part of the chain appeared clothed with luxuriant vegetation, having three distinct zones of red, orange, and blue; hence the name, " Variegated Mountains." Many of the high crests rose far into the region of eternal snow. Looking along this chain, the snowy peaks appeared to vanish in endless perspective, till the eye rested upon a stupendous mountain mass near the sources of the Ac-sou and Sarcand. Its snow-clad summits and glaciers received a glowing golden tint from the descending sun, while the rocky crests beneath looked black and grim.

Having examined the country, I hastened forward, passing several large tumuli, while many more were seen scattered over the valley. Just at dusk we reached a group of yourts, to the great astonishment of the Cossack inhabitants; their officers, however, received me kindly, and gave me a hospitable welcome. They had been here a month, and did not appear to have done much. I sat up with them till a late hour relating tidings from Europe, which interested them greatly.

On leaving the yourt in the morning I found a small body of Cossacks occupied throwing up the earth-work for the fortress, while others were engaged preparing timber for the log buildings. I had now reached Kopal, the most southerly fort Russia has planted in Chinese Tartary. This military post is situated in about 43° lat. N., and 82° long. E., and is only three days' journey from Kulja, a large Chinese town containing about 40,000 inhabitants. The fort is in the region belonging to the Great Horde of the Kirghis, and is significant of the fate which awaits these warlike tribes.

Four years before my arrival a battery of artillery, consisting of six guns and 100 men, had been sent into the Ala-tau, and the officer in command had taken up a position in a pass about eight miles to the southward of the site of the new fort. From Ayagus to their camp was a journey of eighteen days, with hostile tribes inhabiting the plains between this little band and their friends; while to the south-west, on the opposite side of the mountains, there were legions of Chinese convicts occupying the region around Kulja. The officer had formed his camp in the mouth of a gorge; a few men stationed up in the cliffs were sufficient to defend the place against one hundred times their number; and the guns would have caused terrible slaughter had any body of men attempted to force the pass. The captain and his men arrived here in the autumn, after a most arduous march of forty-two days over a country in which there were no roads. Deep rivers often delayed their march; and extensive morasses, capable of swallowing vast armies, frequently compelled them to make a détour that occupied several days.

Route over which the Artillery marched, and Kirghis Tombs.

Notwithstanding that everything now around them wore a summer aspect, they knew that winter was fast approaching, and that no time ought to be lost in preparing for it. The numerous glens and small sheltered valleys afforded plenty of grass for their horses, where they could be left to pasture in safety; but the season was past for making hay for their winter fodder. This, however, was not of vast importance, as these Asiatic horses are accustomed to seek their food beneath the snow, like wild animals, and instinct tells them where grass is to be found. Nor do they require any shelter from the weather; stable, grooming, and corn being luxuries unknown to them.

Stone was lying in the bottom of the gorge, ready quarried by time and water; and with these rough materials the men soon erected huts for their winter dwellings. Trunks of trees and branches formed the flat roofs; over these was thrown a covering of earth, about nine inches thick: thus they were secured against both wet and cold. Glass they had none; Chinese silk, strained on to small frames, formed the windows, and rough doors were made out of bark. Logs of wood were their seats, and dried fern their beds. In this way the men were soon housed, and their dwellings furnished.

Much, however, remained to be done; wood had to be collected for their winter fuel, and this could only be obtained in the upper glens, whence it was difficult to transport it; a supply of game had also to be provided for their daily consumption. Luckily for them, the whole region abounded with animals. Deer were exceedingly numerous on all the lower ranges, while the maral (a large stag) and the argali (wild sheep) were found in all the higher regions. A large party of men were constantly employed hunting; and both venison and wild mutton were plentiful in the camp. As the season advanced, the upper regions became covered with snow, causing the animals to descend to the lower valleys. The men now began to lay in their winter store. The officer told me that he had often shot the maral and deer from the door of his hut; showing how completely unaccustomed they were to the sportsman and to his rifle.

This was no enviable position for Captain Abakamoff; the men had society among themselves, but he was shut out from companions of his own class. Fortunately, he was a good naturalist, and the country afforded him opportunities of acquiring much valuable information, as well as of adding a great number of choice specimens of birds and insects to both public and private collections; besides which he was a distinguished Nimrod. Many a day we spent together in the chase, when the pursuit of game led us into the wildest recesses of the mountains, where only the excitement of hunting the maral could have induced him to risk his life. The sublime scenery, however, was a powerful inducement to me, and the prospects I then beheld repaid me for the toil and danger I underwent in seeking them.

Some of the scenes we have passed together are so deeply impressed on my memory, that they can never be effaced. We often encamped amidst scenery of marvellous grandeur. Sometimes this has been in terrible storms, when the warring elements might have made the stoutest heart quail; at others, when the fading sunbeams were bathing the snow-clad peaks above us in ruby tints, and lighting them up with all the glories of declining day. As night crept over us, the scene changed; the blaze of our fires lit up the groups of men, while the trunks and branches of the trees under which we were encamped were coloured with a crimson glare. After our evening meal, my friend would call our party around him, and, taking his seat in the centre, would lead them in some of their soul-stirring songs, making the forest resound with wild harmony. When the music ceased, the sighing of the breeze was heard among the leaves, and sometimes the sound of a distant waterfall was wafted towards us. Then again these soothing sounds were broken by the tinkling of the bells attached to some of our horses. This reminded the men of their duty; and the animals were presently picketed near us. Then all became quiet; each man turned down on his saddle-cloth, and soon slept soundly.

Before the end of October the winter came upon this little band in the mountain gorge; their stony dwellings were covered with snow, and their usual occupations were stopped. Their horses were in a valley at some distance, access to which was impossible, in consequence of the deep new-fallen snow. They were, however, under no apprehension about them, as a thick forest of cedars skirted the foot of the mountains, and under these they would find shelter. As time passed on, it became more dreary, till the snow was sufficiently hardened; then the chase afforded the usual excitement.

In the early part of November, bourans began to blow, that lasted two and three days at a time, during which the men could not proceed twenty paces from their dwellings. This was but a foretaste of what was in store, for on the morning of the 23rd it began to blow a gale, which gradually increased to a hurricane, sweeping the snow into clouds like flour, and rendering it almost dark at midday. During the night and the following day it became worse, and Abakamoff assured me that the roaring of the wind, as it swept up the gorge, was appalling. Already their huts were covered deep with snow, and almost as soon as passages were made from one to another, they were filled up. At length each party became prisoners in their dwellings, from which they could not proceed five paces. They had now great difficulty in cooking; and those most distant from the kitchen found it a constant labour to keep up a communication with that necessary establishment. When the snow became deep enough, a gallery was formed in it, and then they passed to and fro without difficulty.

This bouran continued till the 4th of December,—eleven days without intermission,—after which came calm weather, with 20° Reau. of frost. Immediately the storm had ceased, a party was sent up to the valley to look after the horses. On reaching the spot, they were found completely sheltered in the thick forest, where but little snow was lying on the ground. It also had afforded them a good pasture. These fearful bourans were of frequent occurrence during the months of December and January. Before the middle of February their fatal effects were visible on man and animal, for thirteen of the men died, and fifty-seven horses perished in the snow.

From this it will be easily inferred that the great valley between the mountain chains was exposed to the full force of these terrible gales. Bad as it was in the sheltered gorge, it was far worse on the plains; in fact, no Kirghis tribes ever attempted to winter there. Nevertheless, here a place had been selected for the fort, in spite of the reports of men who had experienced three winters in the region. At this period a pair of large epaulettes was deemed sufficient in Russia to qualify a man for any position, and stow his head with an extraordinary quantity of brains; giving him a thorough knowledge of every subject, however foreign to his previous occupation. Though in many instances this decoration was placed on the shoulders of men of singular talent and genius, I have known examples, and not a few, where the reverse was the case; and in some the wearers combined in their own persons the talents of Falstaff and Dogberry.

A brace of generals, with a numerous staff, were sent into the steppe to determine upon the site of the new fort. Stores and creature comforts of all kinds accompanied the two heroes, among which champagne was a prominent item. A strong guard of Cossacks formed their escort; and numerous cooks and bakers were also attached to the expedition. A party of Cossacks and cooks were always sent on in advance to select the place for encampment, and to prepare a sumptuous entertainment; and strict orders were given that the day's march should not be a long one. After a journey of thirteen days, which ought to have been performed in six, they reached the valley of the most easternly branch of the Lepsou. This was a delightful spot, covered with luxuriant pastures, on which fine clumps of birch and poplar trees were dotted over a plain three miles in breadth, extending to the foot of the lower spurs of the Ala-tau. These were clothed to their summits with magnificent pines, larches, and birches; and far overtopping them were seen the rugged crests of the upper chain.

It was decided that the expedition should repose a few days in this beautiful valley, after their extraordinary toil.

Valley of the Lepsou.

Hunters were despatched to the mountains to procure game; and men were engaged netting the river for fish. Others were employed building ovens (which I stumbled upon in my wanderings), in which to bake calatchkies or rolls. Men were also sent into the upper mountains for ice to cool the champagne, and other preparations were made for the festal banquets. These were continued for several days before the gallant generals were sufficiently recovered to resume their journey.

At length, after four days' feasting, they started, and ultimately, after two more rests, reached the river Kopal, in the valley between the Ala-tau and Kara-tau. Here and beyond, the country appeared so desolate, that they determined to proceed no further, and at once decided that here should be the site of the fort. Having come to this wise decision, they hastened back to a more genial region, and there took the repose they fancied they so much needed. Unfortunately, it is too often thus that the Emperor's plans are carried out.

The fort was placed on a rising ground about 400 yards to the east of the river Kopal, and about eight miles north from the mouth of the gorge in which Abakamoff had his battery. A vast number of tumuli are scattered over the plain, and some are of large dimensions; proving that the region has once been densely populated, or else it has been a vast cemetery, in which apparently a nation has been interred. The spot had a most desolate aspect; not a single tree was visible, and scarcely a bush could be found, except on the banks of the river, and even there they were few.

The plain around was covered with coarse gravel and sand, among which there was little vegetation. In early spring, or from the middle of February to April, a little grass grows, and numerous flowers bloom; subsequently all is burnt up, and then it becomes an arid waste. So furious are the storms in this valley, that I have seen the coarse gravel torn up and swept along by the wind, forming a shower of sand and stones. Such was the enviable spot where 500 Cossacks, with their families, were sent to form a permanent settlement, and 200 others to remain three years to aid in carrying on the works.

One short month before my arrival, or on the 20th of August, these poor people had reached the place, having been told that they were going to a warm and rich country, where all kinds of produce grew in abundance. Their horror and dismay on reaching their destination may be better imagined than described. The journey hither had been one of great hardship; and they had been sent from comfortable homes, and from a region of plenty, to inhabit a dreary waste on which nothing would grow.

A very clever engineer officer had been sent from Russia to direct the works and carry out the plans prepared in Petersburg. He arrived a few days after the Cossacks, and was even more astonished than they had been when he beheld the place, knowing what had to be done before the winter, which the resources at his command afforded little hope of accomplishing. A report had been placed in his hands stating that timber could be procured in an unlimited quantity within a distance of eight versts. One glance at the country proved this to be a falsehood. To obtain a supply quickly was now a matter of vast moment, and Abakamoff, with a party of men, led the engineer to the nearest accessible place from which it could be procured. They rode along the plain for about twenty miles, to a gorge leading up into the mountains, and then ascended the bed of a torrent for about three miles before reaching the forest.

Here they found plenty of large pine trees, but they had to be cut down and transported to the plain, and the ravine formed a serious obstacle. In a few days 150 men were engaged felling the trees; and a great number of bullocks were obtained from the Kirghis to drag the timber to the fort. The official buildings, storehouses, and hospital, were to be erected forthwith; and each Cossack had to provide his own dwelling. He had to cut the timber, transport it to Kopal, and then to erect a house in which to shelter his miserable wife and children. All that he could expect to accomplish before the winter set in, was one room. A great number were built only twelve feet square, in which two families, consisting of ten persons, were glad to take shelter, and thought themselves comfortable; while many had to be content with excavations in the earth, without a hope of being housed during the winter. So long as the fine weather continued, the subterranean abodes sufficed, but it was obvious that the time was rapidly approaching when there would be no sufficient security from the cold.

Having obtained valuable information from my friends, I determined to cross the Ala-tau and visit the upper valleys of the Ac-tau. Captain Abakamoff advised me to lose no time, as the winter commenced early in these regions. The engineer intended to accompany me for three or four days, in the hope of finding a forest whence he could obtain a further supply of timber and firewood. My company now numbered seventeen,—all well-tried men.

Leaving our friends at the fort, we rode to the gorge where the artillery had encamped; but as they had removed to the Kopal, near the works, the place looked desolate. Our way was up the ravine for nearly two miles, and then we ascended to the mountain slope, on which we found thick turf, forming good pastures. This had been a famous hunting-ground to Abakamoff's people, where a vast number of animals had been shot. As we rode along several herds of deer were seen in the distance, but they were soon lost in the numerous valleys. In about two hours we reached a deep, rocky, and well-wooded glen, running nearly east and west, that we had to cross. The cliffs were of limestone, in some parts very abrupt; in others there were steep slopes, down which we led our horses, and passed over the glen without difficulty. On emerging from the ravine we came upon a black fox, playing with her two nearly full-grown cubs. They were beautiful animals, and stood looking at us for two or three minutes before they scampered off into their home in the rocks.

From this point our course was directly south, and up towards the ridge. As we proceeded, vegetation gradually diminished, till we left it behind us, and entered a rocky region with snow lying in patches around. An hour's ride brought us to the summit, whence we looked down into a small valley, with another ridge beyond rising far above us. To the east the crest rose still higher, being deeply covered with snow, with dark rocks protruding, while beyond were seen the white summits of the Ac-tau. We lost no time in crossing towards some lofty crags, near the base of which a great gap was formed in the ridge. On reaching this we passed round the base of the peaks, and saw the deep, narrow valley of the Kora lying beneath.

As we stood looking into the depth, probably 5,000 feet below us, the river appeared like a band of frosted silver; we could also hear the roaring of the water as it rushed over its rocky bed. Near this place we found a track formed by the maral, argali, and wild goat, but it seemed doubtful if we should be able to descend by it. Men were sent to the east and west for a few hundred yards, along the ridge, searching for a better path, but they were unsuccessful. This side of the valley was exceedingly abrupt; indeed, in many parts the precipices were perpendicular; in other places the declivity was so steep that neither man nor horse could maintain a footing, nor were there either trees or bushes growing on any part.

The opposite side, facing the north, was well wooded, the trees extending from the bank of the river upwards, till they diminished to dwarfs at the snow line; and a few were struggling to live even in the icy region. The bottom of the valley appeared clothed in rich verdure, while the trees there were covered with luxuriant foliage, coloured with the deep and glowing tints of autumn. As there was no time to spare for scanning the region with my glass, I ordered one of my Cossacks, an old hunter, to lead the way downward. I followed close behind, and the rest came after in single file. We had not proceeded far when we were obliged to dismount and lead our horses over a most dangerous place, — on a ridge of rocks extending more

Argali.

than 100 yards, where a false step would have sent us rolling down a rocky declivity for more than 2,000 feet.

Having passed this fearful spot we remounted, and succeeded, after encountering several other difficulties, in reaching the bottom, but far to the east of the point whence we began to descend. At one place the ground was covered with fallen rocks, and among them were many large masses of beautiful ribbon jasper, of yellow, red, and green; but I fear these must ever remain as nature has left them, for there is no possibility of transporting such blocks up the side of this deep and rugged valley. Taking my last look at them, with some reluctance I turned from the spot, and led the way down to the bank of the Kora, seeking a place on which to encamp. We soon found that the torrent must be crossed, as there was no wood on our side of the river.

It was at once obvious to all that fording this stream would be a difficult and dangerous task; indeed, at the point where we had struck the river, it was utterly impossible. My old hunter advised our going up the bank to the eastward, as below us to the west the torrent was more than a rapid, — it was a continuous succession of falls, and the noise was positively deafening. Having gone near three miles, as directed, we came to a part where the stream was broader, and here we determined to cross. The engineer, myself, three Cossacks, and four Kirghis, decided to make the attempt; the others were to remain on the bank, and follow if we succeeded.

Our first difficulty was finding a place on which we could form in line and ride into the water side by side, as we were quite certain that three or four horses could not stem the torrent. Having accomplished this, we rode into the stream. When we had proceeded two or three paces we were caught by the full force of the water, that seemed strong enough to sweep us down the torrent, — it drove us at once into a compact body. Still we went steadily on: each man knew his fate if our line was once broken; he knew also that to turn back was now impossible. Step after step brought us near the middle of the stream, where the rushing water was fearful; several times it dashed over our saddles, and splashed above our heads. At last we reached the bank, and turning to look back upon the danger we had passed, I believe every man thought it had been accomplished at too great a risk. The other men were sent farther up the stream; and we had the satisfaction of seeing them cross without much danger.

Our encampment was chosen under some magnificent pine trees, standing near the river, where a level space extended about 100 yards in breadth to the foot of some rocks, and about 500 yards in length. Here was an excellent pasture for our horses in front of our camp. While the balaghans were preparing, Sergae, the hunter, and three others, started in search of game. They had not been gone more than half an hour when we heard the echoes of their rifles. A little after dusk they rode into our camp, with a young maral and two fine fat bucks; another maral had been wounded and traced up to the snow, where the crimson dye had marked his track. As night was at hand they were obliged to return and leave him till morning, when they were certain to find him either alive or dead.

Shortly after their arrival our camp presented a busy scene. The Cossacks were engaged grilling venison for the engineer and myself, and preparing their own soup. The Kirghis were also occupied cooking their suppers in front of their balaghan, from portions of the game just brought in. Huge piles of wood had been heaped on the fires, which were now blazing splendidly, and soon aided in qualifying the cold baths we had taken in crossing the river. As it was known that tigers, bears, and wolves inhabited this region, our horses were allowed to feed, and then they were picketed near our camp fires. A Cossack and two Kirghis were appointed sentinels, to be changed every two hours; and the first watch began at ten o'clock. The engineer and myself sat till our guards were changed, discussing the prospect of Russia in these regions, and her object in building so many forts.

The next morning a clear sky and the rosy tints of the rising sun betokened a fine day, causing great activity in our camp. These men love to contemplate nature. A magnificent sunrise, or storms which envelop the snow-white peaks with black portentous clouds, whence the red lightning hurls its fearful shafts, or a glorious sunset, when plain and mountain are bathed in glowing light, and the fleecy clouds are constantly changing from a golden yellow to a deep crimson, and then gradually fading into twilight, — are watched with intense interest, having great charms for their uncivilized minds.

I stood watching for the moment when the sun's first rays should light up the crags and snow-decked peaks, some of them 8,000 feet above me, then others were seen so far distant that they seemed like scarlet vapour assuming mountain forms, floating in the air. In strong contrast with these stood the jasper cliffs to the south, rising to an enormous height, with trees growing on every ledge, and bushes hanging from the fissures. In two places near the summit, water was seen dashing over the brink and forming numerous cascades, which appeared like streams of foam leaping among the dark rocks. At times they were lost in thick foliage, then they burst forth from under the trees, and bounded from rock to rock, throwing off spray and vapour at each leap, till they became almost shadows before entering the dense forest beneath.

I had promised that I would, before commencing my own labours, accompany my friend in search of a forest whence he could obtain a supply of timber, as well as aid in seeking a track by which men could drag it to the summit of the mountain. The Cossacks had discovered a place about a mile above our camp, where the river could be forded easily; this induced me to decide on returning each evening to our present lodging, as the place afforded plenty of grass for our horses. Sergac and three other men were ordered on a hunting expedition, and to look after the wounded maral.

Our morning meal of broiled venison and tea being ended, we prepared to explore this savage and picturesque valley. Proceeding down the bank of the Kora, we shortly reached a dense forest of magnificent pines. Here was timber enough to satisfy my friend, could it be conveyed over the river; unfortunately, at this part the rapids and falls formed an insurmountable obstacle. Having forced our way through thick underwood for about three miles, we rode out into an open glade, and disturbed a bear and her two cubs while enjoying a game at romps. The moment we appeared they scampered off into the forest, among rocks where it was impossible to follow.

Continuing our ride onward, we came to a beautiful park-like spot, where splendid clumps of cedars, pines, and birches were dotted over this side of the valley, with a fine grassy turf beneath. This extended along the bank of the Kora for several miles, varying from 300 to 500 yards in width, and rising rather steeply to the base of the high cliffs. At a short distance on our left the two waterfalls were pouring down; I turned out of our route and rode towards them, when I found that both streams fell into one channel, forming a considerable torrent, that rushed down its rocky bed and leaped into the Kora. The *débris* brought down by the water stopped my riding, nor was it easy to climb a confused mass rising abruptly 700 or 800 feet. On reaching the top I perceived that each fall fell into a small basin, after which the two streams united and were lost under the rocks for about 200 yards. The cliffs are a yellowish limestone, like that at Roche Abbey, and are worn into picturesque forms by the falling water. About

500 feet above the bottom of the fall I observed a great cavity, probably leading into a cavern, up to which it was impossible to ascend. At a point 300 feet below the basins, the stream bursts forth from its rocky prison in a column containing ten times the quantity that falls into the basins above. The force with which it is ejected proves there is an enormous pressure on this body of water; probably it proceeds from a subterranean channel, communicating with a lake on the mountains.

After leaving this place we gained a part of the valley where a spur of the mountain formed a magnificent crescent, terminating on the river in a precipice 800 or 900 feet high, with its summit broken into battlements. At some distance beyond this a ridge from the north side runs far out into the valley, appearing to close it in. On the crest of this spur the rocks are piled up in singular forms; some are in heaps like vast ruins, others are hanging on the brink of a precipice, appearing ready to slide over with the least touch. In one part three huge blocks have fallen together and formed a vast portal. My people doubted their being so placed by accident, and all wondered how they retained their position. The river forms a rapid at the foot of the precipice, over which nothing can cross. This obliged us to seek a ford higher up the stream, where, after two attempts, we succeeded in gaining the opposite bank.

Having followed the river downward about a mile, a splendid scene burst upon us. The valley narrowed to about 500 yards in width, with rugged cliffs, forming a frame through which was seen a well-wooded country, bedecked in all the glories of rich summer foliage. The Kora was winding its way through this beautiful valley, sometimes hidden among clumps of trees, then it emerged into an open glade, greatly increased in breadth. Thence it continued meandering along, shining like a mirror among the deep green grass and varied-coloured flowers that adorned its banks. Beyond this rose mountain over mountain, the lower range covered with a thick forest, where the tints of autumn were spreading fast. Then another chain coloured in deep purple-gray, through which were seen large patches of red and yellow; these were flowers covering the slopes, but no trees were visible. In the distance a rocky ridge rose several thousand feet above those nearer to me; its rugged forms standing out distinctly against the hazy summits still far above. This was again overtopped by a great snowy chain in which the Ili has its source; some of the peaks appeared glittering with ice, and beneath were vast glaciers.

Proceeding along at a short distance from the river, I found large masses of green and cream-coloured jasper cropping out; and near these a ridge of granite extended across the valley, in which the Kora has formed a great rapid. Passing round the end of the high cliffs on the north, we entered a lovely spot about two miles broad, with another narrow valley extending into the mountains to the south; and down this came a roaring torrent, adding its waters to the Kora. Looking down this river I perceived the valley gradually became narrower, and ended in a great gorge a few miles below, where it turns more to the south.

My friend found on this spot all that he required in timber and firewood. The supply was inexhaustible, and the river presented few obstacles, as it could be forded in almost every part of the valley. So far, one part of his object was attained, and now our attention was turned to the other. After riding about two miles we came to a narrow valley, running up into the mountains to the north. This we determined to explore, and ascertain if the timber could be dragged out by oxen in that direction. A short ride brought us to the bed of a torrent fifty or sixty yards wide, but now almost dry. It was exceedingly stony, large blocks having been rolled down by the stream. The lines on the rocky banks show that the water sometimes rises twenty-seven feet. This occurs either from the sudden melting of the snow in the upper regions, or during great storms. A few trees were growing close to the river, but on the slopes higher up there were none. The valley being exposed to the full blaze of the sun, accounts for their non-appearance.

We had not gone more than three miles when we reached a point where the valley turned to the north-west, becoming a mere ravine, and its sloping sides changed to high precipices, at once destroying all hope of finding a route for the oxen by this valley.—A tragic event happened at a short distance beyond this spot during the following summer, when a party of men were trying to find a path through the gorge. As they ascended, one of the horses became restive while climbing some rocks, and plunged with his rider into the torrent. They were instantly carried down to some large blocks of stone, that were just under water, where the horse gained his footing for a few minutes, and the man tried to breast the flood. His comrades threw a long rein towards him, but as that passed over his head the horse staggered and was swept down by the torrent. Notwithstanding the efforts of his companions, both man and horse perished.—Leaving our horses, six of us ascended the eastern ridge, thinking it probable we might find a way along the crest up to the higher summits. After an hour's walk we were convinced that this was impracticable, as we reached the base of some granite cliffs 500 or 600 feet in height, which it was impossible to ascend on foot. We now returned towards our companions, and as we descended the ridge the declining sun hinted the necessity of a quick ride to our encampment.

We were greatly surprised on arriving at the Kora to find the stream considerably swollen: in fording, the water reached to our saddle-flaps; a few inches more it would have given us a swim. The warm day had melted the snow on the mountains, and the river was rising fast. This in-

A Torrent into which a Horse leaped with his Rider.

duced us to push on, as we had the torrent from the water-falls between us and home. The engineer and I led the way at a gallop; nor was it long before we heard the loud roaring of the stream, — a bad omen for us. On reaching the bank it was obvious not a moment was to be lost. We instantly rode into the flood five abreast; and both parties crossed safely, but not without a thorough wetting: ten minutes later would have stopped our fording. We must then have gone dinnerless and supperless to our grassy couches on the bank of the torrent, and listened to its deafening music.

Again we hurried onward, but darkness caught us before we reached the forest, through which we had much trouble in finding our way. After a two hours' ride among the thick and tangled bushes, and often in total darkness, it was with no small delight that we looked upon the cheerful fires at our encampment. Sergae and his hunters had long arrived, bringing back the maral wounded yesterday, that had led them a good chase in the snowy region before he received the fatal bullet. They had also shot two wild goats, and added them to our stock.

The maral or large stag is found in all the higher regions of the Ala-tau, Ac-tau, and Mus-tau; he affords noble sport for the hunters, and his horns are highly valued by the Chinese. But it demands a fearless hunter to follow him into his haunts among the precipices, glaciers, and snowy peaks of this region. In winter and spring he is found in the valleys, but as the weather becomes warmer he ascends, to escape the flies and other insects. They are seldom found in herds, though groups of ten or twelve are sometimes seen standing on the brink of a precipice 1,500 to 2,000 feet in height, quite inaccessible to man.

At other times I have beheld them climbing the lofty crags, and cropping the velvety moss which grew on the ledges. On one occasion I saw a group of seven standing on the top of a mass of rock, rising up like a gigantic tower to the height of 700 or 800 feet; three of its sides being nearly perpendicular, and the fourth was formed by a narrow ridge of rocks running up from the top of a great precipice at an angle of 60°. In some parts this line was broken by great perpendicular steps, that appeared to render it impossible to ascend. Still, along that rugged ridge they had climbed to the summit.

A great chasm, at least 1,000 feet deep and 600 yards in width, separated us from them, much to the regret of our little party; and no place could be found by which to descend into the gorge, and scale the opposite precipices. Could we have succeeded in this, some of the maral must have fallen to our rifles. It was a tantalising sight to hungry men, one that often prompts the hunter to feats of daring; but in this instance we could only look with admiration on the splendid animals, and hope for a nearer acquaintance another time.

I have followed my game, commencing the chase without a breakfast, having had no dinner or supper the preceding day. After stalking a stag for five or six hours, his branching horns are seen above the copse in which he is lying, some 400 or 500 yards distant; another half hour of cautious creeping places me within range, whence the shining black eye can be marked as the target. Stretched at full length on the ground, yet scarcely daring to raise my head to obtain a sight along the tube, the bead of the rifle covers the speck of black, giving a certainty of an approaching banquet. At last the finger touches the trigger, but instead of the whistling bullet performing its function, the hammer falls on a bad cap. This slight crack, however, rouses the maral, and in an instant he bounds away, carrying my dinner along with him.

The Cossacks and Kalmucks display a finer sense of honour in their hunting than many highly civilized Europeans.

Two Cossacks were out hunting the maral for two objects, food and antlers. They had followed the game far up into the Ala-tau, and had been successful; sleeping at night near their spoil. The next morning they started again in pursuit, when, after some hours, they found a magnificent animal, whose horns they saw were worth 120 roubles (17*l*.), a prize well worth securing. They hunted him from

The chasm over which the Maral leaped.

one valley to another, till at last he retreated to a high craggy region.

His pursuers were not the men to be deterred by obstacles. They scaled the rugged height, still following on his track; whichever way he turned some slight mark betrayed his path. Late in the afternoon they caught sight of his branching horns in a deep rent in the mountain, whose sides were nearly perpendicular, while the opposite end terminated on the brink of a great precipice,—thus preventing all chance of escape.

When they entered the gorge he rose from his lair, about 300 yards in advance, and started forward among fallen rocks. They followed rapidly, and gained upon him fast. Having reached within about one hundred paces of the end of the ravine, he stood hesitating, and looked back,—seeming inclined to double and make a rush to pass them. From this circumstance the Cossacks knew that some other animals were in the pass; and as tigers are often found here they did not fire, but gradually approached. The stag went slowly on, evidently in fear. Having passed some large blocks, two huge bears sprang out into the ravine close behind him.

The stag suddenly bounded into the air to a pinnacle of rock, standing detached from the precipice, and leaving a chasm thirty-three feet wide. One of the bears springing after him rushed over the cliff, falling more than four hundred feet,—and thus ended his career. The other stood on the brink of the chasm growling, and in a fearful rage at his disappointment. The hunters advanced, and when they came within twenty paces he stood up and gave a savage growl of defiance. But this was his last,—a leaden messenger sent him rolling after his companion.

The maral stood gazing at the hunters without showing any sign of fear, while they admired his beautiful form and noble horns. To the honour of the Cossacks be it told, he was left in peace, great as was the temptation to these ill-paid men. Within a few paces were the coveted horns, equal in value to the annual pay of five of their body. The fellows were, however, as good as they are brave.

After noting some peculiar marks on the animal's body, by which to recognise him again, they departed. Retracing their steps was a most difficult and dangerous task, which they had not felt during the excitement of the chase. The following day they sought the bears at the bottom of the precipice, when to their great delight they discovered that the maral had re-leaped the chasm on to a ledge below the brink, and had escaped. When the Cossacks joined their companions at the piquet the whole of the circumstances

The Maral's Leap.

were related. A correct description of the maral was given; and greatly to the credit of these men he long remained king of his native wilds.

While listening to the above incident my companion charged his pipe, and began sending out clouds of smoke, each puff adding to his happiness. Before the second pipe was consumed, timber, mountain passes, and our day's ride were forgotten. The night was calm, with a gentle breeze fanning our enormous fires into flames, and lighting up all around; nor was our sleep disturbed by tiger, bear, or wolf.

CHAP. VI.

THE KORA AND TRADITIONS.

Another splendid morning greeted us, causing the arrangements to be speedily completed for our day's ride. The hunters were again ordered forth to procure fresh supplies, although the lower branches of the trees which formed our larder, presented a goodly quantity of venison. I held a council, and heard a report from Sergae and other hunters, accustomed to reconnoitre a country well when pursuing game. As they had seen a small lake in the valley, about a three hours' ride distant, and thought the mountains appeared more accessible in that region, it was at once decided to go there and search for a path by which oxen could ascend to the summit.

Leaving our camp, we shortly reached the place where the Cossacks had discovered the ford, and passed easily, as the river had subsided during the night. The water begins to increase rapidly about four o'clock in the afternoon, and continues doing so till nine o'clock in the evening,—after which it gradually subsides. From this point the valley was exceedingly rugged, the granite cliffs on the north being nearly perpendicular, and rising nearly 1,000 feet. On the south side, a dense forest commences on the bank of the river, extending up a very steep slope for about 500 yards, to the base of some huge rocky masses. These rose in three terraces till they reached the snow line; in parts they were wooded, in others the cliffs have fallen, forming a mass of *débris* that extends from the edge of the forest to the lofty crags that stand bristling out of the snow like watch-towers and battlements.

About three miles further up the valley we came upon a spot where an avalanche had swept over these terraces, forming a great gap, by tearing up the rocks and hurling them into a vast heap. This mass spread over more than a mile in length, and the rocks were piled up 900 to 1,000 feet, appearing as if half a mountain had been thrown from above. A little beyond this place, the cliffs on the north jut out nearly to the centre of the valley, terminating in high crags, which in some parts overhang their base considerably. As I passed round these, a most savage scene presented itself to me. The forest on the south side had been torn up by a terrible storm,—naked trunks with their branches wrenched off reared their shattered forms, and thousands of trees were lying strewn about in every direction. Here was seen the effect of a hurricane that had uprooted huge trees like stubble. Far beyond this scene of devastation rose the snowy chain of the Ac-tau, its vast peaks towering into the deep blue vault in sublime grandeur.

Having travelled onward several miles, I arrived at a part of the valley where the Kora makes a bend toward the cliffs on the north, leaving a space of about 200 yards in width, between the base of the rocks and the river. As I approached this spot, I was almost induced to believe that the works of the Giants were before me, for five enormous stones were standing isolated and on end, the first sight of which gave me the idea that their disposition was not accidental, and that a master mind had superintended the erection,—the group being in perfect keeping with the scene around. One of these blocks would have made a tower large enough for a church, its height being 76 feet above the ground, and it measured 24 feet on one side and 19 feet on the other. It stood 73 paces from the base of the cliffs, and was about 8 feet out of the perpendicular, inclining towards the river. The remaining four blocks varied from 45 to 50 feet in height, one being 15 feet square and the rest somewhat less. Two of these stood upright, the others were leaning in different directions, one of them so far that it had nearly lost its equilibrium.

A sixth mass of still larger dimensions was lying half buried in the ground; on this, some young picta trees had taken root and were growing luxuriantly. About two hundred yards to the eastward, three other blocks were lying, and beneath one was a cavity many a family in Kopal would have considered a splendid dwelling. Not far from these stood a pile of stones undoubtedly the work of man, as a great quantity of quartz blocks had been used, with other materials, in its construction. It was circular, 42 feet in diameter and 28 feet high, shaped like a dome: a circle of quartz blocks had been formed on the ground, enclosing a space ten feet wide all round the tomb. Finding such a tumulus in this valley, surprised me greatly; it could not have been the grave of a chief of the present race, but was as ancient as those I had found on the steppe.

My Kirghis companions looked on this place with feelings of dread, and on the tomb with veneration. Each left a strip of his garment on the grave as an offering to the soul of the departed. Their proceeding excited my curiosity; and from one of them, "Tursun," who believes himself a descendant of Genghiz, I obtained the following tradition. The word Kora implies sealed or locked.

"The valley of the Kora was once inhabited by several powerful Genii, who had a continual feud with others of their race, in the different regions of the Tarbagatai, the Barluck, and the Gobi. They frequently ravaged the nations or tribes subject to their brethren of the north, and always retreated to the Kora in security. Many towering crags commanded the region, enabling the guards to perceive their advancing enemies afar off; and the vigilant sentinels stationed on these watch-towers rendered the position impregnable. The approaching legions were lured into the rugged mountain passes, and there either overpowered or destroyed by huge blocks hurled from the crags above. At length their audacity and cruelty became so great that a combination was formed to wreak a fearful vengeance upon them; and Shaitan was invoked to aid in their destruction.

"As usual, the advancing bodies were quickly discovered, and measures taken to destroy them in the pass. Shortly two other vast legions were seen marching towards different gorges; and now all the forces of the beleaguered Genii were brought up to annihilate these hosts. The battle was terrific; and the mountains resounded with the din of war; while the crashing of the avalanches hurled into the gorges shook the mighty peaks above. Victory seemed secure to the Genii; when, at the very moment of their success, an appalling sound was heard in the upper regions, causing the mountains to tremble. Suddenly a cloud of smoke and flame burst forth reaching to mid-heaven; red lightning darted from the vapour, and the thunder found an echo in every peak and valley. Amidst this tremendous uproar, "hell's artillery" belched forth red-hot rocks, causing fearful destruction to the legions of the Kora. In these appalling sounds the Genii recognised the power of Darkness; and, becoming panic-struck, they were driven back into the valley, whither no one had yet dared to follow. The conquering legions now poured on, with Shaitan leading the van, when, on the brink of the precipices, vast rocks were hurled down, crushing and entombing the Genii beneath." After this terrible event the Kora was sealed for ages, but the tradition was handed down from sire to son.

"At length a daring chief determined to visit the valley and take up his abode there, in spite of the remonstrance of his family and friends. Attended by a number of his followers, he crossed the mountains, descended to the Kora, and encamped on the enchanted ground. The yourts were pitched, the animals slain for the festival, and his followers seated themselves around him, exulting in the prowess of their Sultan who had ventured to lead them to this

Tombs of the Genii on the Kora.

mysterious spot. When in the height of their revels, a loud crash of thunder rolled through the valley, and echoed among the crags. Suddenly, and before the sounds had died away, a Genii appeared, terrible in his rage. His threatening aspect and flashing sword filled them with horror. Addressing the Sultan in a voice that made every heart quail, he said, 'Monster! thou hast dared to bring thy slaves hither and pollute this sacred spot, and for this thou shalt die.'

"Quick as the flash of the lightning the blade swept round his head, severing the huge rock in twain, and in a moment all were entombed beneath the ponderous mass. A few of the people saw the fearful tragedy from a distance, and fled, conveying the information to the Sultan's family and to the tribe. The women became inconsolable, and mourned for years. At last a spirit called the 'white lady' took pity upon them, and through her intercession the tribe were permitted to raise the tumulus near the fatal spot. After which the valley was again closed, and no Kirghis has ever ventured to feed his flocks there."

Leaving a place rendered classical by Kirghis traditions (which are quite as true as those of Greek origin), we continued our ride up the valley; and this we found ascended rapidly. As we proceeded upward, the trees became more stunted in their growth. In little more than an hour we reached the lake; but it scarcely deserved the name, being only about 400 yards long, and 100 yards broad. It extends, however, into the mountains to the north. A stream from it rolls over a fall about 50 feet high, and then runs on into the Kora. After surveying this place, which afforded but little hope of success to our search for a path, we left the Kora and rode up a steep ascent on the west side of the lake. This led us up to a ridge, whence we got a view into the region beyond, — and a rugged one it proved.

To the north-east, summit beyond summit appeared, till the eye rested on the snowy peaks near the source of the Ac-sou. There there was no chance of a path. After crossing the ridge, we continued our ride in a north-westerly direction, towards another high summit, crowned with lofty crags. In places our way was over a mossy turf, sprinkled with flowers; other parts we found to be a stony region, over which it would be difficult for the oxen to drag the timber, though not impossible. A ride of two hours finally brought us to the fallen masses near the foot of the crags; and these compelled us to seek a path more to the westward, where the oxen would be able to cross the summit.

The engineer, myself, and three men, dismounted and climbed the high rocks that afforded a view over the country, whence we saw that there was only a narrow valley between us and the last summit. This induced us to hasten onward, and shortly afterwards we arrived at a great gap in the crags, through which we picked our way among the fallen blocks. It was evident that a path could easily be made here, if we succeeded in finding a route forward. We descended into the narrow valley and found it rough and stony, still we made our way across, and began the last ascent: it proved to be the most difficult part of our route; but by taking an oblique direction we succeeded in reaching a dome-shaped summit, the highest point over which the route would pass. Here we all dismounted, and presently piled up a landmark that was visible for a long distance. About a mile from this point a route had been traced by the Cossacks leading northward, and thus the object of my friend was accomplished.

Two miles distant to the north-east the mountain swelled up into a mighty dome capped with snow, with dark crags protruding. At its base on the north side I observed a thickly-wooded glen falling to the eastward. It was evident that this summit would afford me a view of the country around, as well as into the deep valleys extending south from the Ac-tau, which I wished to examine. I therefore left my companion to return by the route we had come, as he intended throwing up a few landmarks to provide against the obliteration of the track before next summer.

Taking three men with me I rode towards the mountain and soon began the ascent: it was far more abrupt than any of us had imagined, and occupied us an hour in riding to the snow line. From our elevated position, that was far above all other points for many miles around, we had a magnificent view of the Ac-tau, Mus-tau, and the peaks near the source of the Ili; while to the north the dark crests of the Kara-tau were visible, and immediately beneath us were several deep valleys extending to the south-east. The foreground on which we stood was composed of masses of light green slate, but the rocks above protruding through the snow were of a deep red colour; I obtained specimens, which proved to be a beautiful jasper containing veins of pure quartz. Descending towards the south, we came upon a fine red granite extending far into the valley. In these rocks I found broad veins of rose quartz, some of them eighteen and twenty inches thick, whence blocks of a splendid colour could be obtained. After crossing the valley and riding about six miles, we came upon our friends engaged erecting a landmark.

Finding that it was two hours past noon, we began to retrace our steps at a quick pace, only stopping twice to raise two more pillars; but this so delayed us, that day was near its close when we reached the valley of the Kora. As we rode down to the Giants' Tombs the last gleams of light were fading from the high peaks of the Ac-tau, while all around us was shrouded in deep gloom. On approaching by this dim light a spot which the traditions of the people have clothed with sublime imagery, it was obvious that the Kirghis advanced with superstitious dread. When they caught sight of the mighty stones, whose bases were lost in the darkness that rapidly closed over the valley, a marked change came over them. They evidently expected either

Shaitan or the Genii would appear, and cast suspicious glances at every object that came into view.

Further on we had a real danger to encounter in fording the Kora, and fears were entertained that the water was too high to permit of it. We pushed on as quickly as the ground permitted, and on reaching the ford we saw that the water was deep; but as crossing afforded the only chance for a dinner, we decided to make the attempt. We rode down the bank, stood at the edge of the stream till formed in close line, and then plunged in. The water had risen considerably, and in a few steps my horse and others were swimming; several floundered over the stones, but we crossed in safety, though not without a wetting. After this we soon caught a glimpse of our camp fires, and in a short time we also were seated around them. The hunters had long returned, adding two maral to our larder. A rough ride and a fast of twelve hours tended to promote appetite and give a zest to our venison. My friend was delighted at the success of the expedition, and pipe after pipe was exhausted by him in the excess of his gratification.

Another splendid morn beamed upon us, but the grass was crisped with hoar-frost, and a coating of ice was on the pools,—a sudden change from the balmy breezes of yesterday. Immediately after breakfast my companion and his people were ready to return to the fort. My arrangements had also been made to ascend the Kora as far towards its source as possible. This being a good region for game, I included Sergae and the two hunters in my party, leaving three men at the camp. As we rode to the ford, the engineer urged me not to remain too long in the region, and suggested my being guided by Sergae and the Kirghis as to the time of my departure, for they knew the climate well. On the morning of the 27th we crossed the ford, shook hands, and separated, — he for Kopal, and I to go up the Kora. Hurrying rapidly on through the part we passed yesterday, I reached the lake, and then entered into a new region.

A little beyond the lake the valley became much narrower, with high precipices on each side; and the river was embedded among cedar trees, that fringed its banks. Passing round the base of the northern cliffs, we entered a large oval-shaped basin, about two miles long, and nearly a mile in width, having large blocks of granite, slate, limestone, and other rocks strewn promiscuously over it. In some of these masses I observed a metallic appearance. Dismounting, I discovered this to be lead ore, almost pure. Some of it was as soft as my rifle balls; and the rocks containing the metal had been brought to their present position by the torrent. Two broad water-courses had been ploughed through this basin, and the rocks heaped upon each side; both were now quite dry. Having crossed these, we found the Kora running in a broad channel.

The mountain to the south appears to have been scooped out, and forms a deep crescent. Its abrupt face was cut into numerous terraces, now thickly wooded with pine, birch, and cedar. Many isolated crags were rising far above the trees, and over-topping these were the snow-clad summits of the chain. While examining them with my glass, I observed a group of five maral feeding at a great elevation above us. I pointed them out to Sergae, telling him they were on the slope between two high crags; but he declared there were none. Having given him the glass, and directed it towards the spot, he quickly discovered the animals, and showed them to his hunting companions, who were equally incredulous till the glass was applied to their eyes; when the three stood in amazement, first looking at the glass and then gazing up towards the deer. Sergae instantly exclaimed that he must secure some of those; and asked to go in pursuit. I consented, and directed them to meet me on this spot at sunset.

In a few minutes Sergae and his companions forded the river, and made their horses ascend the steep; then having reached the foot of the cliffs, they secured them under some trees, and began to climb the towering rocks on foot. We stood watching them a short time, when I found the temptation great, but I knew my days were limited in this region, and that time could not be spared. Turning away reluctantly, I rode through the labyrinth and entered a part of the valley with steep mountain slopes rising on each side; between which the river rushed down in a succession of falls. This was a splendid scene, and was added to my folio. In the distance of a quarter of a mile the fall is not less than 1,500 feet.

Not far beyond this place we came upon masses of ice lying on the banks, through which the water had cut a channel; some were 30 and 40 feet thick. After passing them by riding along the mountain slope, at a considerable height above the river, we reached a part where the torrent was bridged over by ice, about 100 yards in breadth, and from 50 to 60 feet in depth. This put a stop to our further progress on horseback. Two men were left in charge of the horses, and the rest accompanied me onward.

Our way was over the ice, which was cracked and broken into hundreds of fragments, having numerous fissures extending through its whole thickness. These presented constant obstructions, and our progress was slow, till we arrived at a track made by animals along the mountain side. Having proceeded about a mile, we found the river running in an open channel formed in the ice more than 100 feet deep; the sides were much undermined, and the mass had a beautiful sea-green colour. Proceeding onward, the valley rose rapidly, and the torrent made a thundering sound as it rushed along. A little further up it was lost beneath a bed of ice of great depth; still, the roaring of the water was heard. At this part the valley was narrowed to a gorge about 150 yards wide, with cliffs rising to about 600 feet in height. Beyond were rugged slopes, with patches of snow and rocks, terminating in a lofty serrated ridge; and above this were vast snowy crests.

Proceeding upwards we presently came to a turn in the gorge, where the snowy peaks and the glacier burst upon

Glacier and Snowy Peaks of the Ac-tau.

us in all their grandeur. A sea of ice and snow extended ten or twelve miles up to the base of several vast snowy peaks, whose perpendicular and riven sides showed the dark rocks protruding through. Having crossed the ice to some rocks about half a mile distant, we ascended the cliffs about 300 feet, whence the view was magnificent. In one part the surface was broken up into thousands of fragments, that sparkled like brilliants in the rays of the sun; while to the south, and nearer the mountains, several large fissures were visible; but the torrent was buried too deep beneath the crystal mass to make its voice heard. A complete solitude reigned around; nothing having life was seen either among the crags or on the icy waste. It was desolation clothed in the purest garb, rendering its aspect inexpressibly cold and chilling. Had I reached this place a month earlier, I would have crossed the glacier to the higher chain; but the risk was too great at this late season, the storms in this region being both sudden and terrible.

Having taken my last look at these giants of the chain, I turned away with regret; and late in the afternoon reached my companions and the horses. I hastened our return, as the sun was sinking fast, and would soon set in this deep valley. Drawing near the place where the hunters started after the game, all looked around, but nowhere could we see any traces of them, though it was past the time appointed for our meeting. The sun had shed his last rays on the lofty peaks, and the valley was already shrouded in a dim twilight. The men holloaed loudly, but we received no response. Two of them rode across the river, to ascertain if the horses were still at the foot of the rocks; and returned announcing that they were gone. I ordered a volley from our rifles, which echoed among the crags, but no answer was given; we therefore concluded that they had returned to the camp.

It was long after dark when we forded the river; but every stone in our way seemed to be known to our horses, as they crossed without a stumble. On our arrival at the camp I was greatly surprised to find that the missing men were not there. We all felt great apprehension that an accident had befallen them among the precipices. More than an hour after our arrival two of them rode into the camp; but Sergae was still missing, nor could I gather any satisfactory account respecting him. It appeared that they had ascended the cliffs together, and had got nearly within rifle range of the maral when the animals scented them, and galloped away, — three going in one direction, and two in another. This circumstance divided the party: Sergae followed the two marals, and his companions the other three; they pursued them far into the region of eternal snow, where they shot one on the brink of a precipice, over which he fell; and the others escaped.

Many efforts, attended with great risk, were made to reach the deer from above, but they were unsuccessful, and, much to the hunters' disappointment, they were obliged to leave him for the wolves. It was quite dark when they got down to the place where their horses were left; and Sergae not being there, they concluded that he had returned to the camp. Our anxiety became centred upon him; but after more than two hours had elapsed, a shout was heard from the opposite side of the river, calling for assistance. In a few minutes several men were in their saddles, and, riding to the ford; they crossed in a body as the water was deep, and conducted Sergae over in safety. When I saw him ride up to the balaghan, it was a great relief to my mind.

He had followed the two maral among the precipices for several hours, after which they descended to the Kora, crossed the river, and began to feed on the shores of the lake. He returned to his horse, rode over the stream, and started again in pursuit. Just at dusk he found them and shot one— this he had brought home; besides which he had killed a wild goat, and left him hanging under a tree till the morrow. He had heard our signal as he was stealing upon his game, and could not answer it.

When I turned out on the morning of the 28th there was a clear sky, and a sharp frost quite biting to the fingers. After breakfast I commenced my sketching: first, the scene so famed in Kirghis story,—the terrible defeat of the Genii, and the Sultan's tomb. This and some others near it occupied the day. The next day, which was much colder, was devoted to another part of the valley equally grand and interesting. During my absence a party of the men hunted a large black bear that had paid them a visit at the camp,—he escaped, though not with a whole skin, as was shown by the crimson spots on the stones. He was cunning enough to beat a retreat into the thick forest, among rocks where his pursuers could not follow.

My labours were continued daily, and my rambles extended far up several of the ravines running to the south, which led me among some of nature's most stupendous works. In fact, I could have spent a month exploring this part of the chain, as each day's journey opened out places full of interest. In some the slate was heaved up into perpendicular pinnacles, in others it was lying at various angles, and some of the strata were bent into curves. I was subsequently led into a granite region, among precipices whose summits were shattered by lightning, and their faces riven into picturesque forms; while in several of the ravines, and on the mountain tops, I found jaspers and porphyry of various colours.

So time passed till the 4th of October, when I awoke just as day was breaking, and ushering in one of the most lovely mornings I had ever beheld. As the sun rose, fleecy clouds were lit up with a glowing crimson light; while the snow-clad and frozen peaks gleamed phantom-like against the sky. A little later the icy masses received the rosy tint, appearing to throw out flashes of brilliant flame, and gradually the rocky crags were coloured with the glorious hue, while all beneath was in deep shade. Even my people watched the changes with astonishment: two of the Kirghis thought this the expiring effort of summer, and a token of a sudden change.

We left the camp early, as our ride would be a long one, to proceed to a magnificent waterfall in one of the ravines.

After sketching this I crossed a high ridge, and reached the western end of the glacier at a point where it was slowly advancing through a rocky gorge into the valley. Leaving our horses, four of the men ascended the lofty crags along with me, and in about an hour we looked upon the Mus-tau, with the glaciers descending from it; while to the south-east line after line of mountain peaks extended, and beyond these rose the stupendous "Bogda Oöla," so far in the distance that it appeared like a thin, airy cloud. We descended to the glacier, and returned through the gorge, which was only accomplished after considerable difficulty, the sun being far down on his course when we reached our horses.

During our march I had observed a peculiar haze spreading over the mountains, and now it descended into the valleys; this the Kirghis said betokened bad weather. These men are keen observers and excellent judges of the different phenomena that usually appear before a change, and their opinions may be relied upon with implicit confidence. They urged that no time should be lost; and our necks were often risked in the rough ride over the country we passed. Darkness caught us long before we reached the valley of the Kora, which rendered our ride really dangerous, and it was past nine o'clock when we rode into the camp. Sergae and his companions had been successful. A smoking hot dish of stewed venison was placed before me; this, and a few glasses of delicious tea, soon satisfied both my hunger and thirst. While taking my meal, I observed that Sergae and several Kirghis were in deep consultation round one of the fires. When my supper was ended, three of them came up and told me that the appearance we had seen to-day was a certain indication of a coming storm, and a forerunner of the winter. They urged upon me the absolute necessity of leaving the valley early in the morning, deeming it dangerous to delay. I told them that if at daylight they should observe any indications of a change, we would depart without delay; if no such sight appeared, I wished to remain a few days longer. With this answer they were satisfied.

Glacier in the Gorge

Several hours had elapsed, when I was suddenly roused from my night's rest by a loud crash of thunder which bewildered me for a moment. As I listened to its echoes among the mountains, a vivid flash lit up the valley in a reddish light; at the same moment another terrific roll burst over us, causing every one to sit up. This was accompanied by a great hurricane that we could hear rushing down through the trees far above us. Flash succeeded flash in quick succession, the thunder rolled incessantly, and presently it began to snow. The men rose and heaped logs on the fire, for the ground and the balaghans were quickly covered with a wintry garb, rendering it exceedingly chilly. The thunder continued to echo through the valley for more than two hours, while the snow fell fast. The storm had visited us earlier than expected, and the Kirghis were extremely anxious to leave the valley.

When morning dawned on the 5th, what a change had come over the scene! The ground was covered more than a foot deep with snow, which continued to fall so thick that both forest and mountain were hidden from our view. This was a serious matter, as we could not move while the snow fell; and both Sergae and the Kirghis were alarmed. They feared the storm might continue several days, and then we should be shut in on the banks of the Kora, without a chance of escape. Hour after hour passed without the slightest appearance of a change, till ten o'clock, when the snow-storm ceased; but a heavy, dark canopy hung over us. Looking up to the high peaks, I perceived that the clouds were driving past at a tremendous speed, although it was a perfect calm with us. I pointed this out to my companions, who at once prognosticated a fearful storm. It soon became evident that the wind was descending, as we observed snow swept over the precipices in clouds; nor was it long before the sound was heard in the upper region of the forest. Gradually the roar came nearer, when branches were torn from the trees and carried along by the blast.

Deep as we were in the valley, it was not long before a sound more appalling than the crashing thunder was heard approaching; and shortly the hurricane swept past, covering us in a cloud of snow, which it licked from off the ground like dust. Instinct had warned the horses of what was coming; and they sought shelter in the thick forest, whither it was impossible to follow them at present. The day passed; night came, and still the tempest raged; fortunately, no snow fell, and we occasionally got a glimpse of the starry heavens. Our only hope was in the wind clearing the snow off the track by which we had descended, as we might thus be enabled to escape; but this contingency appeared doubtful. The bark was stripped from several trees; and cedar branches were collected, with which we made our balaghans more habitable. By these means and large fires we became tolerably comfortable.

Another morning dawned upon us, and the storm was raging with greater fury; large trees were snapped asunder like matches; and great branches were carried high into the air. This day was spent in anxious hope that the storm would abate at sunset; and a little before dusk it lulled for a short time, only, however, to burst forth again with more terrible effect. About midnight it subsided into a perfect calm; and immediately after a severe frost set in. Sergae awoke me in the night; when he and the Kirghis urged me to depart as early as possible, saying that storms would now be frequent, and that the loss of one hour might prevent our escape. To this reasonable request I offered no objection, as our safety depended upon crossing the mountains and reaching Kopal.

Before day broke on the 7th we were all up and stirring; and soon after daylight a party of men were in search of our horses. The animals were found in a sheltered spot, near the foot of some high precipices, which completely screened them from the tempest, while it afforded a sufficient pasture. The water in the Kora was greatly diminished, and ice was formed on the pools three inches thick, while a cutting breeze made our faces tingle. At nine o'clock we forded the river, and rode down the valley, following our former track, where we found the snow driven into heaps so deep that we could not ride through them. These obliged us to turn in another direction, that shortly brought us into greater difficulties, as the first two men vanished in a moment, and both horses and riders went floundering into deep snow, from which we had great trouble in extricating them. We retraced our steps, and divided into two parties, in the hope that one or other would find a track to some rocks about 400 paces distant, where we knew the ascent commenced.

Rolls in the deep snow did not daunt us; and after many efforts we approached to within about eighty yards of the rocks. Beyond this point it seemed impossible to advance; for whichever way we turned our attempts were baffled. It was now feared that the horses must be left, and that our only chance was to ascend on foot. I, however, objected to the idea of abandoning our animals to perish without other trials, and accompanied Sergae to a place a little more to the westward. Again we turned towards the rocks, proceeding with caution, till we reached within twenty paces, when we found a deep hollow filled with snow, forming a complete barrier. Two men tried to pass on foot, and failed; others sought a path a little more to the north, and succeeded in crossing; and here we led our horses over, to our inexpressible satisfaction. Although we were only two miles from our encampment, we had been four hours in reaching this place.

Looking upwards the prospect seemed better, as there was little snow; but we soon found it was impossible to ride our horses up the rocky steep. The animals were therefore strung together, the reins being fastened to the cruppers, and now formed a long line, by means of which they would be able to hold each other up in case of accident. When all were ready, Sergae led the way; I followed, with two men close behind; then came Kirghis leading the horses, and the other people after them. Our progress was slow; and in some parts the track was really dangerous, as the rocks were covered with ice. The axes were used to roughen the surface, which enabled us to ascend to the top without accident. Standing for a few minutes on the summit, we looked down into the valley, and saw the smoke curling up in wreaths from our fires. I believe all felt thankful for our escape from a spot that would otherwise have been our last home.

We found but little snow on the summits; the gale having carried it into the valleys and ravines. This enabled us to make a rapid ride over the mountains. Without encountering further difficulties, we arrived at the fort a little before dark, when we heard from our friends that the snow-storm had been very slight, and had soon turned into rain. I visited the works with the engineer, and found that they had progressed considerably during my absence. The Cossacks were busy building up the logs; and my friend expected to place the roof on the hospital in eight days. He had most wisely suspended the earthworks at the fort, and was using all his means to get the buildings covered in. Besides, it gave the Cossacks an opportunity of roofing in their own dwellings before the winter; and this was a most important matter.

The morning of the 8th ushered in a great change: it was like summer on these low plains; but the summits of the Ala-tau had received a new covering of snow, indicating that winter was approaching. Still, Sergae and the Kirghis thought I should have time to visit the source of the river Bean, about 30 miles to the eastward. I also hoped to explore this before the winter set in; and preparations were made to start on the following day.

The nomades stated that, about twenty years since, terrible thunderings were heard in a valley near the source of this river, that continued for many days, causing the people to leave their summer pastures and hasten down to the plain. Some of the men who were in the vicinity declared that the valley was filled with steam, from out of which lightning came forth that had destroyed many of their herds. They also told me of a vast cavern in one of the gorges whence sounds often issued, and sometimes clouds of steam. In this place they say vast treasures were deposited by the Genii, which they believe to be guarded by demons. Believing the first part of this story had its origin in some volcanic outbursts, I determined to visit the region.

Sergae, two Cossacks, and five Kirghis formed my party, and we left the fort early; our route being eastward along the plain at the foot of the Ala-tau. A ride of four hours brought us to the narrow valley of the Bean, which extends far up into the mountain to the south. A wide stream was rushing along over its bed of rocks, the banks were fringed with shrubs, and the ground was still covered with summer vegetation. Farther up, the valley was studded with clumps of picta, birch, and poplar; on ascending higher it became a dense forest, which retarded our progress.

It was near evening when we emerged into a more open part of the valley, inclosed on both sides by high cliffs of limestone. Here we found good pastures, with plenty of wood for fuel: this induced Sergae to advise our encamping under the trees, as higher up there would be no shelter. In a short time we had large fires blazing, that made our camp look cheerful, while a few branches piled up on one side formed a comfortable bed-room. When night began to shroud in the valley, the horses were piqueted near the fires, and the Kirghis made another at a short distance to frighten away the tigers, that frequently destroyed their cattle; wolves are also numerous in this region. The night, however, passed without either men or animals being disturbed.

We were on horseback early in the morning, and continued our ride upward. After going about two miles, the valley turned more to the eastward, and in three hours we reached a point where it terminated in a ravine that extended far into the mountains. One of the guides led us over a ridge to the south, and a further ride of two hours brought us into the valley we were seeking. It was a rugged place, about five miles in length and two in breadth, with a small lake near the centre. Snowy peaks formed a crescent on the south and east, and it terminated on the west at the foot of some high crags. Several groups of argali were seen browsing on the slope, but they scampered off on our approach.

We rode down the declivity, picking our way among masses of greenstone, and reached the bottom of the valley. No evidence of volcanic action was visible on the shore of the lake, which appeared to be shallow, and formed by the snow melting on the high summits around. In summer, before the water is carried off by evaporation, it is considerably larger. Having ridden more than a mile to the westward, and crossed nearly to the foot of the high mountain to the south, I found nothing that would account for the phenomena the people had described; and after a careful inspection, was convinced that no volcanic eruption had occurred in the valley.

I now desired the Kirghis to guide me to the cavern. One of them pointed to a great cleft in the lofty ridge to the south-east, and said, "It is there, but the snow is deep." Notwithstanding the difficulty he had suggested, I determined to proceed: we therefore rode towards it, and in an hour were brought to a stand by snow that had recently fallen. Leaving three men in charge of our steeds, we commenced the ascent on foot. This proved no easy task, as we frequently sunk nearly overhead; and floundering in the snow was not agreeable. Having gone about two miles, we reached a part of the mountain where the rocks were rent into numerous cavities. Some were nearly filled with snow, in other places they were bridged over, and between these wintry arches we got a peep into their enormous depths. It would have been madness attempting to cross these frail structures. Even my old hunter, who was no coward, declined to proceed.

I inquired of my guides (as they had declared they knew the route) why they had led us into this labyrinth, through which it was impossible to pass. Two of them said that they had ascended by a route a little more to the north, but at this time the snow had rendered that impracticable. None of them had ever been so far to the south before, and they had no idea of the dangers we had encountered. I ventured to express a doubt of the existence of the cavern and its wonders. This roused my companions, who swore that they had been in the gorge twice when the steam was pouring out of the great mouth, but had never approached near enough to hear the voices. One man said that his father had lost several horses and two camels, which had strayed into the gorge, and that the man who went in search of them never returned. He fully believed that they had been drawn into the cavern and devoured. Had we succeeded in reaching the gorge, none of the Kirghis would have approached the cavern; the Cossacks, however, had no fear. It was not without great regret that I felt compelled to return, and leave the exploration of the cavern to others. From midsummer to the middle of August, I believe it may be reached without difficulty.

The guides now proposed to lead me into a beautiful valley to the north-east where game was plentiful, whence we could also return to the plain by another route. We therefore retraced our steps, crossed the ridge to the Bean, riding up its bank for about a mile, and then forded the stream. A ravine opened to the north, through which we passed into a most romantic spot, apparently surrounded by limestone cliffs. After crossing this place we descended through an opening in the rocks, and saw several maral bounding over a small valley beneath, having scented our approach. On discovering them, the eyes of the hunters sparkled, and Sergae proposed that we should carry some of these noble animals back with us. I consented to remain for a couple of days, and take our chances of success in hunting, which gave great satisfaction to my companions. We were soon encamped under a clump of trees, and the evening was spent in the preparations for commencing the sport on the morrow. It was arranged that Sergae should be my companion, that the Cossacks should go in another direction, and the Kirghis remain at the camp.

We were up and ready early, and started on our respective missions before sunrise. Shortly after leaving our camp we entered a singular glen, a favourite spot with the Kirghis, where they make their Ai-ran in the summer. Leaving this curious scene, we continued our ride from one small valley to another till past noon, but without seeing a single animal. Numerous trails were discovered, some of which we followed far without success. At length we saw three argali browsing high up among the rocks at about a mile distant. Our horses were speedily secured, and we started on the chase, intending to approach them from the leeward.

Sergae led the way, and we scaled the rugged slope, keeping under cover till we thought we were near them. The old hunter reconnoitred, and discovered that they had moved much higher up, where they were feeding. This compelled us to make a considerable détour, and as we approached they ascended, giving us a long chase. At last we were near the summit, and saw the animals bound away far beyond the range of our rifles — tantalizing after a four hours' chase.

We followed the ridge to the eastward, in the hope of

falling in with other animals. At length the sun went down, and this caused us to descend rapidly. On our way a group of ibex sprung out from among the rocks: Sergae dropped one as he was springing over some large stones, behind which the others had disappeared. Darkness was already shrouding in the valley, and we were not yet half way down. Although descending was far less laborious than scaling the

Curious Rocks, and Kirghis making Ai-ran.

cliffs, it was attended with much more danger. Having reached the bottom we turned to the westward, and after a walk of more than five miles, found our horses and rode quickly to the camp; but it was long after dark when we arrived.

Our companions were already seated by the blazing fire; they had been more successful, having brought home a fine maral and a wild goat; a second maral had been wounded, but had escaped in the darkness. This was a bad day's sport; and very few animals had been seen. Sergae and the Cossacks assigned as a reason that the wolves had been hunting the maral, causing them to ascend into the higher valleys, adding an assurance that we should be visited by the ravenous beasts before morning. Large fires were made; the horses piqueted near them, and two sentinels were placed outside as a guard, — all the others, except Sergae and myself, were left sleeping. He was seated on a log, puffing clouds of smoke from his short Chinese pipe; every few minutes ceasing to smoke, to answer my questions relating to his service in other parts of the steppe.

After taking a few strong pulls at his pipe, he commenced an account of his early career among the tribes, saying, "I was among the first men who were sent to establish piquets on the Karkaralla, — a small mountain chain in the Seradne (middle) Horde, north of the Balkash. The Kirghis resisted our advance into their territory; and many severe conflicts ensued at the different positions; but we maintained our ground, although it was often difficult to send provisions. At that period the Karkaralla abounded with large game, — the maral, argali, cazeole, and wild goat. Whenever any of the Cossacks were out hunting, it required great care to avoid being captured; and many of my comrades were taken by the Kirghis and sold as slaves into Bokhara, Tashkend, and Khokan; not one of whom ever returned.

"I once had a narrow escape, having been separated from two of my companions when out hunting in the Karkaralla. Knowing the danger of an attempt to return alone, I searched for them, but without success; and at last I started for the piquet. On descending one of the ravines, and when near the outlet to the plain, I saw a body of Kirghis at about 200 yards distant. Some were sitting on the ground; and a few were standing beside their horses. My appearance roused the party into action in a moment; several sprung into their saddles, and others rushed towards their steeds. I saw in an instant that my position was a critical one, and that they intended my capture.

"It was impossible to pass them; while retreating up the glen was also dangerous, as they had good steeds, which would soon overtake me. A large maral being secured on my horse that would retard his speed, I severed with my knife the thongs that held him, and pushed him down. By this time several men were riding fast towards me, when I turned my horse and galloped up the pass. There was no time to look back; and by their shouts I could hear that they were gaining upon me. My rifle was quickly unslung; and I determined that the first man who approached should pay the penalty. As I urged on my horse, they shrieked like chorts (devils) in my rear.

"Having reached the mouth of a very narrow ravine, that entered the gorge from the right, I sprang into it, and ascended up the bed of a small stream which came trickling down. I had not proceeded more than twenty paces when the Kirghis were at its mouth, believing they had me secure. Springing from my horse, I stood with my rifle pointed; and as they could only approach in single file not one dared to face it.

"A mass of rock stood out into the ravine a little higher up. I saw if this was reached I could stand a siege against three times their number; and my horse would be secure behind it. Driving him upwards, I retreated slowly, taking care to cover with my rifle any man who attempted to follow. This kept them in check; and in a short time I was safe in a fort about thirty feet above the little stream. From this place I could pick off the men as they approached; and re-load before a rush could be made on my position. All had remained quiet for about half an hour, when I observed several men examining the face of the cliffs, apparently intending to climb. Their object was obvious; but I determined not to fire a shot unless compelled. The men passed out of the ravine; and my watch was vigilantly kept both in front and on the cliffs.

"I was soon made aware of their proceedings by several pieces of rock being dislodged and falling into the ravine, which told me they were far above. The spot was scanned as if I was watching for the eye of the sable; and presently I caught a glimpse of two men creeping along the ledges towards a point above my position. I called out, 'You had better take care; you are not going to take me like a marten in his hole, without having your fingers bitten.' The Kirghis in the pass began shouting to attract my attention, but my eye was on the cliff; and I saw a man's hand grasping a projecting point of rock. My rifle was instantly raised; in a few moments his head appeared, and his eye rested on me for an instant; it was enough. I touched the trigger; he made a leap into the ravine, and fell not far from his companions, — several of whom rushed up and carried him out. They now set up some fierce shouts, but took especial care to keep under shelter."

After relating this my companion applied most vigorously to his pipe for several minutes, and then continued his narration.

"That was a lesson they did not like; and the other man crouched close behind the ledge. Could I have sighted him for a few moments, he should have jumped after his companion. They had now found I could bite, and they left me alone; but they kept guard in the pass, and frequently looked past the corner to see what I was doing. As they were inclined to keep their distance, I began smoking, and wished for darkness, when I intended to make my escape on foot. I had smoked several pipes undisturbed, when suddenly I heard a commotion; several of the Kirghis galloped up the pass, and others quickly followed.

"They had not gone far when the report of a rifle echoed among the crags; and I heard the clatter of hoofs returning. I knew that my comrades were at hand, and determined to bring down one of the horses of our enemies as they passed my fort. In a few minutes they were near the ravine; the first man galloped by, but the second I stopped, and sent both horse and rider rolling. When my rifle cracked, my comrades gave a shout; I answered, and we soon met in the pass. They had wounded one of the Kirghis, which caused them to retreat; and now they kept far out of our reach."

Sergae having finished his narrative, we prepared for sleeping, and were lying down when a distant howling was heard. "I told you," he exclaimed, "that the brutes would find us; and here they come!" We had no fear of an attack; and the horses were so well secured that they could not break away. Several choruses were howled as the wolves advanced, till they entered a belt of bushes about 200 yards from our camp. We could hear constant growling, and sundry combats among the pack. These continued till near daylight, when they departed for their dens.

At daybreak we were in our saddles, and left the camp, the Cossacks going in search of the wounded maral, while I and Sergae rode towards one of the upper valleys, where he thought we should find plenty of game. As we passed along, the hunter bestowed a curse on all the wolf race, and hoped we might make a near acquaintance with some of them. We had ridden far amid many remarkable rocky scenes, in a limestone region, and in some parts through wooded glades, but not a single maral or argali had been seen. At length we saw several bearcoots soaring aloft, when Sergae assured me that both hunters and game were not far off.

I have mentioned in my former work that the bearcoot is trained for hunting by the Kirghis. But I have said nothing of his prowess in his wild state, when he sports on his own account, and sometimes plunders other ravagers of their prey. The following incident will illustrate his power and courage, besides showing that he would prove a formidable opponent to any unarmed man, if hunger prompted him to dispute possession of his game.

Three of these dark monarchs of the sky were seen soaring high above the crags to the south, which were too abrupt to ride over. We therefore piqueted our horses to feed, and began to ascend the mountain slope. In about an hour and a half we reached the summit, and descended into a small wooded valley, when we observed the bearcoots wheeling round towards the upper end, in which direction we hastened. Having gone at a quick walk for about three miles, we reached a rocky glen that led us into a valley of the Bean, known to be a favourite resort of the animals we were seeking. A small torrent ran foaming through its centre, and mountains rose on each side far above the snow-line. In singular contrast with the rich foliage and luxuriant herbage in the valley, the lower slopes facing the south were almost destitute of verdure, while those facing the north were clothed with a dense forest.

We had scarcely entered this sylvan spot when a singular spectacle was presented to our view. A large maral had been hunted down by three wolves, who had just seized him, and the ravenous brutes were tearing the noble animal to pieces while yet breathing. We instantly prepared to inflict punishment on two of the beasts, and crept quietly along under cover to get within range. We succeeded, and were levelling our rifles, when Sergae called my attention to two large bearcoots, poising aloft and preparing for a swoop. He whispered, "Don't fire, and we shall see some grand sport."

Presently one of the eagles shot down like an arrow, and was almost instantly followed by the other. When within about forty yards of the group, the wolves caught sight of them, and instantly stood on the defensive, showing their long yellow fangs, and uttering a savage howl. In a few seconds the first bearcoot struck his prey; one talon was fixed on his back, the other on the upper part of the neck, completely securing the head, while he tore out the wolf's liver with his beak. The other bearcoot had

Bearcoots and Wolves.

seized another wolf, and shortly both were as lifeless as the animal they had hunted.

The third brute snarled when his comrades set up their wailing howls, and started for the cover: he was soon within range, when a puff of white smoke rose from Sergae's rifle, and the wolf rolled over, dead. The report startled the bearcoots, but we remained concealed, and they commenced their repast on the stag. Their attack had been made with so much gallantry, that neither the old hunter nor myself could raise a rifle against them, or disturb their banquet. When satisfied, they soared up to some lofty crags, and Sergae took off the skins of the poachers, which he intended keeping as trophies bravely won by the eagles.

My old friend had spent thirty years in the vast forests and mountains of Asia. He was thoroughly acquainted with the habits of the animals, and the feathered race that inhabit them; and the daring attack by the bearcoots was the most interesting scene he had witnessed. The number of bears which had fallen by his rifle and spear during the thirty years of his hunter's life, was enormous. In one season he had obtained thirty-two bearskins by shooting, or killing with a spear, unaided and alone.

He sought his savage game in their wild haunts, meeting Bruin on his own domain, and treating him like a noble foe; nor did he always come out scatheless from the conflict. He bore several scars that his ursine foe had printed with his paw, and has often met his opponent with a spear and hunting knife, when no one was near to watch the terrible contest. Sergae said that some of his antagonists were excellent fencers, often testing his skill, strength, and courage to the utmost. Several times the battle has been fought with his hunting knife only, when he had been severely wounded while grappling with his prey. Here was the type of a true hunter.

After witnessing this scene with the eagles, Sergae observed that we should find no game: instinct, he said, warned the wolves that winter was at hand. They were ravenous, and had driven the animals into the higher regions, where it would be imprudent for us to follow at this season. Our attention had been so fixed on the bearcoots and wolves, that we had not noted a great change in the atmosphere to the southward. The distant snowy peaks appeared to stand out on a black ground, so intense was the contrast between them and the clouds rolling up beyond. My companion urged me to make a quick walk to our horses, as he feared we should be caught in the storm.

Having returned through the rocky glen, we had a view to the south, and saw that clouds were enveloping the high summits of the chain. Presently we heard a distant growl: Sergae exclaimed, "Grom" (thunder). Instead of following our track down the valley, we turned up the mountain, and had not ascended far when another clap echoed among the mountain peaks. We were not long in climbing to the summit; but before we had crossed the crest, several heavy peals burst over the valley. The descent before us was abrupt and dangerous; if snow fell it would be more so. No time was lost nor a word spoken, but on we went, letting ourselves down from ledge to ledge by the shrubs growing in the clefts; and in about an hour reached our horses.

The clouds were already shrouding the crags above us, causing us to spring into our saddles and gallop along the valley. As we rode on, the snow fell fast; and before we reached our temporary home, the ground was covered several inches deep with snow. On arriving at our camp we found our companions busy making a balaghan with pine branches. Frail though it was, its shelter, and the large fires, made our dwelling comfortable. The Cossacks, like us, had been unsuccessful. After our evening meal, Sergae related the encounter of the eagles, to the great delight of his auditors. Shortly after dark a stiff breeze sprung up, that I feared would become a gale before morning. While snugly seated under our leafy canopy, watching the white flakes as they were wafted past, I drew Sergae on to another subject, with all the facts of which he was perfectly familiar.

Russia has exercised great prudence in her conquests among the Asiatic tribes: she has always respected their religion and superstition; and no priests have accompanied her Cossacks. She has thus avoided many difficulties which other powers have fallen into, where the soldier and the missionary have marched together. From my knowledge of these people, I believe it is impossible to make converts among them. They are not like the Africans, who are but little more advanced in civilisation than the animals of their plains. The Asiatics are descended from a race of conquerors; and their traditions extend back into remote ages. Robbers they are; but neither pilferers nor pickpockets. Great hospitality, and a wild spirit of chivalry, still exist among them. The following incident will show the danger of meddling with the religious or superstitious feelings of the Kirghis.

In the region of the Karkarella, as in many other parts of the steppe, there are numerous tumuli; some are of great size, and probably contain the ashes of men who have been "mighty in battle." About 10 miles from one of the piquets are the remains of an ancient edifice, which is held sacred by the tribes. It is named the temple of the "White Lady;" and it is said that no animal ever entered its sacred precinct and lived. No Kirghis ever approaches this spot except barefooted; and the pollution of this ground, they believe, would be followed by instant death. This had often been a subject of conversation between the Cossacks and Kirghis; and many traditions had been related telling of the wonderful power of the white apparition.

Some of the Cossacks believed these wild stories; but one dare-devil swore he would test the prowess of the "Bielaya chortofka" (white she-devil), pollute her temple, and defy her. More than two months had elapsed without any reference to the White Lady, when one morning the Cossack started on a hunting expedition alone. Three days passed over, and nothing was heard of him. This caused some apprehension; and it was feared that he had been captured by the Kirghis. One of the men suggested that he had probably gone to visit the White Lady; and a party was instantly dispatched to the temple in search of him. As they approached the spot nothing was seen but the tumuli and the ruined walls; but on nearing these a horrible spectacle was presented to them. The hands and

Tumuli near the Karkarella.

arms of their comrade were placed on a stone, and near them his loaded rifle. On another stone, at a short distance, they found his head; and then they discovered that his mangled remains were placed in a circle around the temple.

This affair still remains a mystery; all the Kirghis declare that it was the vengeance of the White Lady.

I left the valley early in the morning; descended to the steppe, and reached my friends at the fort late in the evening.

CHAP. VII.

INCIDENTS IN KOPAL.

During the night there was a great change in the weather; it blew a gale, which nearly tore up the yourts, while the rain poured down in torrents.

When I arose in the morning the Ala-tau presented a wonderful change: yesterday the high summits only were covered with snow, now the whole chain was clothed in its wintry garb, excepting the low ridges at its base; and the higher peaks were wrapped in a canopy of black clouds. This stopped my proceedings, and the Kirghis predicted that the snow would reach the steppe in a few days. The clouds began to roll about the summits, and lowered rapidly on the mountains: in the evening they were in great commotion, and presently we had a gale, which continued, with repeated changes of rain and snow, till the 15th. Then winter came in full vigour, ushered in by a bouran.

During this time every effort was made to complete the hospital; the beams were all up and part of the planking done. When one room was covered, a bed of earth, nine inches thick, was laid over the planks, rendering the room warm and water-tight. As the warehouse for the black flour and other stores was unfinished, and the provisions were exposed to the weather, the structure was hurried on, the poor fellows working through storms of rain, wind, and snow. In about a fortnight these buildings were made water-proof; but the dwellings of the Cossacks were in a very different state.

It was truly heartrending to look upon their miserable families when the storms were raging; some were seen trying to shelter themselves under strips of voilock, and others were lying down to sleep in corners of the half-roofed rooms. Elsewhere groups of women and children, with haggard looks and shivering limbs, were huddled round fires, cooking their scanty meal; and watching for the return of their husbands and fathers,—wet and exhausted from excessive toil. These were not the scenes of one day—they were continued for weeks—and soon the fatal effects were visible. First, the children sunk under this severity, and were carried in numbers to the graves; the poor miserable mothers, worn out by anxiety, fatigue, and bad food, next fell victims to the fatal maladies which assailed them. I have often watched the mournful processions wending their way to the hill selected for the cemetery, about two miles distant from the fort, and when they have passed have turned away with gloomy forebodings for the future. The endurance of the Cossacks lasted a little longer, but their turn was approaching.

Much has been said and written about the misery of our men in the Crimea; but what was theirs in comparison with the sufferings which these poor women and children endured? They had been torn from comfortable homes, where they lived in plenty, and transported to this desolate spot. Here they were reduced to black bread, salt, and brick tea; vegetables there were none, and the Cossacks had no time to spare for hunting.

On the 20th we had a great bouran and a fall of snow, that continued seven days, covering the steppe four feet deep, and rendering it impossible for me to return to Siberia. I was now doomed to winter here, and take my chance of whatever fate might bring upon us. The prospect for all was gloomy; but not one of us seemed inclined to meet misfortune half-way by useless repining.

The society among which I was thrown was of a mixed character. At the head of the civil department was a German baron, who had won glory in the Caucasus, where he had received a wound from a Circassian sabre, that nearly proved fatal. He was the Priestoff, or political agent, whose duties were with the Kirghis. He was a good soldier, had few scruples, and was a most amusing fellow, believing himself equal to Nesselrode in diplomacy. Were fiction and invention essential in the acquirements of a minister, I would back the Baron against the Count. Captain Abakamoff and the engineer, Captain Loganoff, were clever and intelligent men, who did honour to their professions. The commander of the Cossacks, Izmaeloff, was an excellent officer and a good man, though not highly educated: his life had been spent as a Cossack officer, and in these duties he was thoroughly efficient.

Captain Tochinskoi was his second in command, a good companion, and a burly little fellow; he was not a man likely to lead his troop into danger, unless he liked fire better than water. On one occasion he was sent with a party of fifty Cossacks towards the Ili to secure a strong body of daring marauders. During the march they had to ford the Kok-sou, a most turbulent current: when he saw its boiling waters, his cheek blanched, his courage evaporated, and nothing could induce him to ride into the stream. Fortunately he was a favourite with his men, who knew the consequence of disobedience to orders, and they determined he should not be disgraced. Without further ceremony he was lashed to his saddle, two men led his horse into the torrent, and the party conducted him over in safety.

There were two young lieutenants, who had been educated in Omsk: they were the sons of Cossack officers, and this was their first service. A lieutenant in the army had just arrived with fifty soldiers, accompanied by a young surgeon, who had passed his examination at the University of

Kazan, in the spring. He was sent to cure, kill, and practise on His Imperial Majesty's subjects. A topographer was also occupied in his calling; he was from Omsk, and a very good fellow. We had also a commissionaire, or store-keeper, and five of the officers were married men. These were to be my intimate associates for the next six months; and I had learned that, to induce your companions to be agreeable to you, you must be amiable to them. I must not forget one other distinguished person, a Russian Pope, who, for some cause, was made a soldier, and had just arrived with his comrades.

After the snow storm we had bright sunny days, with the thermometer ranging from 10° to 15° Reaumur, of frost —sufficiently sharp to make our faces smart and our fingers tingle. During this weather Abakamoff, Loganoff, and myself, accompanied by three Cossacks, were frequently out in search of game, and seldom returned without something for our larder. November came in with fearful storms and greater cold; but we were now housed in one of the government offices, which, however, was far from wind-proof. During the bourans snow was driven into the rooms, and lay in wreaths on the floor, and the water in my glass was frozen. Nevertheless, this poor shelter was a vast improvement on the yourts, and one learns to measure comfort by comparison.

After some delay I obtained a rough, unfinished door, propped it up with four logs, and thus formed a table, that enabled me to use my pencil. My first work was a large water-colour painting, now in the possession of Prince Gortchikoff, and, I believe, the first water-colour picture ever painted in this part of Asia. While dabbling in my colour-box, discomfort, and even hunger, were forgotten, and the occupation enabled me to smile at the disasters of a stormy winter, and to enjoy the amusements of my companions.

On the 10th the thermometer fell to 20°—Reaumur, a most unusual degree of cold in these regions, and its effect soon became apparent. Before the surgeon came, disease was making great ravages among the people, and his arrival was hailed with delight. Unfortunately, two most important things were wanting to render his healing talent useful to the community, — viz. an hospital, and medicine; the former was without a roof, and the latter had not been sent. At length, after great exertion on the part of the engineer and the Cossacks, the surgeon was housed, a few boards were nailed together for bedsteads, and skins spread on them formed the beds and covering. The patients became numerous as soon as the winter set in.

At first, when sickness seized the men, they deemed themselves fortunate if taken into the hospital, where they found shelter, and fancied that they were safe in the hands of Andra Ivanovitch. This illusion was, however, speedily dispelled; within the first week five men out of the seven who had entered, died. The number of patients increased, and so did the deaths. Before the end of a month, twenty-eight men were taken to their last resting place on the hill. Bad food, miserable dwellings, and crowded rooms brought on typhus-fever, which carried off many women and children; the Cossacks also caught the disease, which quickly proved fatal. It was painful to see the men carry one, two, and sometimes three of their comrades from the hospital; and this happened daily.

Such a mortality created serious alarm, as no patient improved under the medical treatment, and the people came to the conclusion that if a man entered the hospital, he would not leave it alive. The consequence was, no sick person would enter it, and several died in their dwellings. This caused the officer in command to issue an order for every man to be sent to the hospital as soon as the first symptoms of fever appeared; but it produced no effect, as all tried to conceal their illness.

At length the ravages of the disease became so alarming that an officer with a guard was sent to visit every dwelling, and wherever they found a sick man he was instantly conveyed to the hospital. This measure created such intense excitement that a Cossack left his cottage as the party

Kopal before the Winter set in.

approached, walked out on to the steppe, and shot himself, to avoid being carried into the ill-fated building. Notwithstanding this tragic event, men were constantly taken to the hospital by the guard, and were speedily carried from it to the grave.

A succession of bourans continued until the end of November, often rendering it impossible to go out, as the snow was swept past in such dense clouds that nothing could be seen at three or four paces distant. We were all prisoners during the storms, although the mercury rose to 5°—Reaumur, sufficiently warm for shooting could we have seen the game. Immediately the gale ceased the mercury fell to 20°—Reaumur, and this we found unpleasantly cold in such dwellings. Bad black bread, salt and tea, were almost our only provisions, and the snow was too deep on the mountains for any attempt to obtain deer in the upper valleys. Under these circumstances Abakamoff, the engineer, and myself, decided to go to Kizil-a-gash and spend a few days with Minda-boi, a Tatar merchant, who had set up his yourts in that sheltered spot. He had informed us that this wooded valley abounded with pheasants; we therefore hoped to improve the condition of our larder.

The distance from Kopal to the valley where our friend was encamped, was forty miles, and as the snow was deep on the steppe, we deemed it prudent to start at daylight. After a ride of eight hours we reached Kizil-a-gash, and arrived at the aoul shortly after dusk; Minda-boi gave us a welcome reception, and snug berths in his own yourt. The cold ride had sharpened our appetites; his mutton and rice required no other sauce, and we quenched our thirst with tumblers of tea.

Immediately after our meal an opium pipe with its apparatus was brought in and prepared by a Tatar. After spreading a large tiger skin and placing a cushion upon it, Minda-boi stretched his limbs, and the man handed him the pipe, which he commenced smoking with evident pleasure. In about ten minutes he seemed to pass from the ills of mortal life into Elysium, or into a state that appeared to afford him the highest pleasure. My companions were engaged in puffing out clouds of tobacco smoke, and moralising on the injurious effects of the more powerful narcotic. Having refilled their pipes, they turned down in their furs, and puffs of smoke curled up over their heads. These became gradually less frequent, a Cossack quietly took away the pipes, and they slept undisturbed. Minda-boi still remained in his region of bliss, and I was left to my own musings.

Opium smoking has become prevalent among the wealthy Kirghis, more especially with the sons of the sultans and chiefs: this is deeply to be regretted. The Tatar merchants have introduced the drug, and very few of these traders are found without a supply. In a country where caravans have to make such long journeys, it is a great advantage to them, the article being of small bulk and of considerable value, as they sell it for its weight in silver. Before the caravans reach the towns of Kulja and Tchoubachack they are met by Chinese, who purchase their whole stock, paying for it in silver, and these men smuggle the opium into the towns; then the merchant enters with his caravan of wares and silver ambas unmolested.

From my observations among the Kirghis and Tatars, I believe that, when opium smoking has been indulged in for a short period, there is little chance of a man leaving it off. When frequently used, it soon leaves unmistakeable evidence of its pernicious effects, in the sunken eye and emaciated features of its victim. I have known many who have smoked the drug in small quantities for several years, without its producing any visible effect; still, even with this class, it at last becomes most enervating.

We were out early, and found that our host had fresh horses ready to take us to the shooting ground, about three miles distant. It was a bright sunny morning, though piercingly cold, and the trees were covered with hoar-frost, causing them to sparkle like brilliants. These wintry landscapes were splendid, for the upper masses of thick dark pines appeared powdered with gems; near them were other trees with their naked boughs crystallised, while the birches, with their pendent branches, appeared like strings of diamonds waving in the sun. But these are pictures which the hand of nature only can produce.

Having reached the cover, we dismounted and commenced operations; but presently found that three, four, and sometimes five feet of snow formed an impediment, and often a complete stop, to our progress. At length it became a labour attended with great risk, as we often fell into deep holes; besides which, the pheasants had sought shelter in the brush during the storm, and were now buried deep beneath the snow. After several hours of hard toil we were compelled to give up, and return without firing a shot: thus all hopes of obtaining supplies in this place were at an end for the present. We spent another night with our friend, who repeated his dose of opium, and my companions their tobacco, with similar results. When they were at rest a Cossack threw some furs over me, and I slept soundly without the aid of either opiate.

We left Minda-boi early the following morning, having been informed by a Kirghis that he had seen two large wild boars the previous evening among the kamish, a few miles further in the valley. A ride of an hour brought us to the spot, when we speedily discovered their trail, as well as a place newly rooted up in the snow; but no boars could be seen. Three Cossacks and three Kirghis accompanied us. One of the latter assured me that our game were out feeding, and that they would be found at a marshy spot lower down, where the springs are never frozen.

Having proceeded about half a mile, both animals came into view, and we found ourselves between them and their lair. As soon as they discovered us, they watched our approach for two or three minutes, then made a run for the reeds. Being well mounted we presently headed them, when they separated, and the large boar turned towards the plain in the direction of a thick cover of kamish, about two miles distant. The other rushed on towards his home: two bullets followed him, but without effect, and then all our attention was given to his comrade. He went on at a rapid pace for about half a mile, then suddenly disappeared in deep snow, where we lost him for a short time near the head of a deep gulley.

When we rode up the snow had closed over him, and several of our party were galloping round to the other side of the ravine. While all were intently watching for a sign of his whereabouts, he reappeared within fifty yards of Abakamoff and a Cossack. Both their rifles cracked, and instantly crimson spots stained the plain, but without stopping his speed. A deep hollow retarded us, while he was going far ahead. Having passed this we gained upon him fast, and presently several shots were fired, some of which took effect. These caused him to double and rush at the foremost horse, when it became evident that he was furious and bent on mischief. For a few minutes he was in the middle of the party, rendering it too dangerous to fire, and several horses had a narrow escape from his formidable tusks. He then rushed straight towards a Kirghis, which gave us a chance; a volley was fired that stopped his career, and he rolled over into the snow. He was a magnificent animal, and had received nine balls before he fell.

When we reached the aoul Minda-boi was much pleased with our success, as a boar hunt in the snow is a dangerous experiment, but when food or hunger depends on the result the risk is never thought of. After spending another night with our friend, and seeing him a third time in a state of bliss, we left him, taking one of his camels to carry our spoil. It was late in the evening when we reached the fort, and most of our friends had retired to rest.

The severe weather had stopped all operations at the fort, except the transit of timber from the mountains. Long strings of oxen were seen plodding their weary way through the deep snow drawing empty sledges; by this means a good track would soon be formed, and the timber would be more easily transported than in summer.

December came in with mild weather, and the mercury rose to 2°+Reaum.; a change of 18° in the temperature foreboded no good, although the bright sunshine made us fancy that spring was at hand. This idea was, however, dispelled in the night of the 9th by a severe gale that swept furiously over the steppe. On the 10th it increased, and in the afternoon we had a fearful bouran, driving the snow along like thick clouds of flour, while gravel was torn up from the plain and hurled against the buildings with great force. The sentinels were withdrawn from their posts, nor was it possible for any man to stand on duty until the 13th, when the storm moderated for a few hours. In the evening it returned with redoubled fury, making the little dwellings rock, and exciting doubts of their stability. The roof of one of the stores was torn off, and the heavy planks scattered far over the plain.

Fears were entertained for the Cossacks who were absent, for a hundred men were in the forest cutting timber and conveying it to a point whence the bullocks could take it away. In the latter duty forty men were engaged, and it was for them that we felt the most painful anxiety. On the 16th the storm ceased, and the mercury immediately fell to 12°−Reaum. A party of twenty Cossacks were despatched to the forest to look after their comrades. Late in the evening of the 18th they returned with the bullock drivers, from whom we learned that no accident had happened.

From their report it appeared that the sledges were all loaded on the evening before the storm, and some time before daylight on the 10th the men started, believing that they could reach the fort notwithstanding the gale. All went on well with them till near noon, when they had travelled about twelve miles. After passing the point of one of the spurs of the Ala-tau, they observed a great change in the atmosphere to the westward. Instinct warned the animals of approaching danger, for they decidedly refused to proceed farther. A few minutes' observation convinced the men that their only chance of safety was by a quick return to the forest. No time was lost in unyoking the oxen, and when free they started back to the forest at their utmost speed.

The roaring of the hurricane behind alarmed both men and animals, nor had they proceeded far when the storm enveloped them in clouds of snow. Fortunately the hard track was a good guide, and after much risk they reached the forest, where their friends were sitting under their balagans, in comparative calm. When all were assembled, it was discovered that thirteen oxen were missing; they had gone off the track, and had perished in the snow.

At times I could not help thinking upon the pleasures of the festal season my friends were enjoying in England. It was not, however, with regret for their loss, for it was impossible to look at nature in all the various phases in which I beheld her, and expect to enjoy Christmas cheer and comfortable dwellings.

My journey into these regions was not without some risks, one of which was near closing my career in Kopal, and giving me a last home among the Cossacks on the hill. The circumstance happened during the Christmas holidays, when all were trying to enjoy themselves, especially those who had a dwelling to shelter their friends in. Old Father Winter had returned with grim severity, bringing with him 20° Reaum. of frost, spreading before him a spotless carpet over mountain and plain. A sharp cutting breeze accompanied him, which rendered the frost sufficiently keen to make even these poor abodes feel comfortable.

My friend Abakamoff, the artillery officer, had invited all his comrades, and as fashion had not yet established late dinners here, we assembled at an early hour to partake of his Christmas fare. If our boar's head was not placed on the table with all the ceremony in fashion in "olden times," other parts of him made a grand display at our feast. Beside, we had the remembrance of the hard chase, and the pleasure each hunter feels at escaping from his formidable tusks. Our party broke up early in the evening, as another officer had arranged that we should adjourn to his dwelling, this being the first day it was habitable.

The evening was fine and frosty, with a beautiful moon shedding her light over the snowy waste, and rendering every object almost as distinct as day. This induced Abakamoff to propose that he and I should take a drive in his sledge; to this I willingly assented, and the vehicle was ordered. The carriage-builder had not yet found his way into these regions, and we were content with a common sledge, made like those used by the peasants of Siberia. It had two strong runners, on which a light body, made of rods woven together like basket-work, was secured. In it two persons could be accommodated, sitting down on a carpet spread over straw lying at the bottom; and a few wolf skins were thrown in for covering. In front of this basket-work a narrow board was fixed, on which the driver sat, resting his feet on the runners.

The old artillery horses had recently been changed for some splendid Kirghis, which were now being broken. Three of these wild steeds were harnessed to the sledge, and in a few minutes the vehicle was at the door. Abakamoff's dwelling stood on the open plain, which extended to the eastward for more than thirty miles, and northward for about twenty. The deep ravine of Tamchi-Boulac ran along on the north-west at about five hundred yards distant.

Several of the officers went out with us to see the horses start, the driver was on his seat, and my host desired me to step into the sledge. I had just sat down when the horses made a plunge, in a moment throwing the driver from his seat and dragging the reins out of his hands. They dashed off at full speed, going straight on towards the ravine. I understood my position in an instant — to attempt to leap from the sledge would have been certain death, and I decided to take my chance in the gorge, believing this to be the least dangerous. The horses rushed madly on, and I felt that a few minutes would decide the fate of all of us, the ravine being sixty feet deep at this part.

A dangerous Ride.

As we approached the danger I clutched fast hold of the sides, determined to keep my seat while they made the terrible leap. We were within fifty yards of the ravine, when the opposite precipice was visible, and I felt that in a few moments we must bound over into the chasm. On we went, and I grasped the rods with a firmer hold, ready for the spring. When within about fifteen yards the horses turned, but the impetus of the sledge caused it to swing, and we only just cleared the edge of the precipice.

The wild brutes sprung forward at a tremendous speed, going towards the east, and soon reached a rough track, over which timber had been drawn. Now the sledge was tossed from side to side, and several times I was nearly thrown out. Still I held on, fearing my clothes might be caught by the rods, when I should be dragged along, and nothing could save me. Instead of becoming tired, the horses seemed to increase their speed, and the sledge was nearly turned over, my right hand was wrenched loose by the shock, and coming in contact with the ground was instantly rendered powerless.

The bounding of the sledge added to the fury of the horses, and I saw no hope of their stopping unless they plunged into one of the small ravines which crosses the plain. These were filled with snow, that would cool their fiery tempers and give us a soft bed. I knew that men would be sent after us, but steeds like ours would not be easily overtaken by men on horseback. We had just passed a large tumulus, five miles from the fort, and still the brutes went on at speed. Another half-mile had been galloped over when they were suddenly checked; one horse fell and rolled over into the snow. In two or three minutes we were surrounded by a number of artillerymen, some of whom dashed up to the heads of the horses, secured them, and I leaped out of the sledge.

The cause of our sudden stoppage was quickly perceived; a quantity of timber was lying on a heap, and the long reins caught on one of the trees, they became entangled on the legs of the horse, threw him down, and he rolled over into the snow.

We were soon ready to return. A driver took his seat on the sledge; I stepped into it, the artillerymen sprung to their horses, the man shook the reins, and the steeds went back at a rattling pace, but under perfect command.

My hand was much bruised, and one finger broken above the first joint, having a chip of hard wood driven far up beneath the nail. This was drawn out with pliers, and the blood flowed freely, some short splints were speedily prepared, when I set the broken bone, and my friend Abakamoff bound it up. The faculty, no doubt, would have pronounced this a piece of rough surgery, but it succeeded.

The next day it was manifest how much I had been shaken and bruised, for I was unable to stand. My friends, however, were very attentive, they gave me a good stewing in a Russian bath (which I should always recommend under such circumstances), after this I got better, and in a few weeks the bone of my finger was united. The following day Abakamoff and the officers examined the place where the horses turned away from the ravine, and discovered that the sledge in swinging round had actually projected over the brink. This spot will be long remembered in connection with my narrow escape.

Each officer who had succeeded in rendering his dwelling habitable gave a ball during the Christmas holidays, at which it may with truth be said "that dancing was kept up with great spirit." If the number and efficiency of our orchestra did not equal that of Strauss, our performers succeeded in producing extraordinary effects when under the influence of a few drops of the Chinaman's brandy. Their deficiency in musical science and melody was compensated for by the vigour of their performances. The instruments were a violin, two balalikas (a guitar with three strings), a flute and a drum, and the latter never failed hiding any discordant tones (if such there were) of the other instruments.

My youthful days had not been much devoted to Terpsichorean amusements, and in European society I should have resisted all allurements to join in a quadrille. Here, however, the case was different; I felt it a duty to add my mite to the general enjoyment, and without hesitation joined in their dances. Every one desired to be my instructor, and my first essay in a Cossack dance was with my friend Anna Pavlovna; she was moderately tall, rather stout, and good nature beamed on her laughing features. The dance usually commences by a lady stepping out into the middle of the room with a handkerchief in her hand. She then goes through some graceful movements while approaching the gentleman she wishes to be her partner. When her hand is offered it would be an insult to refuse, and I never saw a Cossack so ungallant. Anna waved her handkerchief over the stranger, and held out her hand, I accepted her invitation amidst great applause, and then began my first drill, which she made a long one. If I had not profited by the practice, it was no fault of my instructress. I was, however, honoured by several other drills during the evening, and had the advantage of seeing the ladies and some of the officers go through the exercise in a most masterly manner.

During our holidays a caravan arrived from Yarkand, they were going to Semipalatinsk, but the bad weather and deep snow stopped them, and to these circumstances we were indebted for their visit. On their way hither they had passed through Kashgar, Kokhan, and Kulja, and traded at each place. Among other products they carried, were tea, silks, and dried fruits, for the first and last of these they found a market, and their ouroukas (dried apricots), and kishmish (sultanas), afforded us a great luxury. I learned from two of these merchants that they had been in Cabul and Cashmere in the summer, and from the latter place had obtained shawls and other merchandise. They remained with us a fortnight and then proceeded on their journey, but it was doubtful if they would be in time to reach the fair at Irbit, if not, their goods would be forwarded to Nijne Novgorod.

Christmas, with its festivities, was passed, and we were in February. The snow was melting fast on the steppe, but in the night the mercury fell to 3°—and 4°—Reaum. Before the middle of the month, we had 10°+Reaum. in the shade, and 2°—Reaum. in the night. The small streams on the steppe were flowing and free from ice. Ducks and other water fowl had arrived in great numbers, a certain harbinger of spring.

An incident occurred which caused a change in our little society. On the 14th a party of five Cossacks arrived from Ayagus, bringing a despatch from the minister of war, recalling the engineer to a good appointment in Petersburg. As the despatch had been delayed more than a month in Ayagus, he had to depart forthwith. In three days he delivered over to the proper officer all matters under his charge, and on the fourth was prepared to depart. Abakamoff gave an early dinner, that we might escort our companion some distance on his way to the first aoul, and having accompanied him to a stream about ten miles distant, we said farewell and separated. Four days after his departure we were startled by a fearful phenomenon, an earthquake, which occurred on Sunday the 18th, at seven o'clock in the morning, and created a great sensation in Kopal. I was up and dressing at the time, when I heard a singular sound, apparently at a great distance. It approached from the west at a terrific speed, and presently became most appalling; in about twenty seconds it seemed to pass at a vast depth beneath me, and rushed on into the mountains to the east. As it passed there was a great motion, or rocking, from west to east, which shook the buildings to and fro. Immediately the shock had passed I went out on to the steppe, and observed that the mountains were enveloped in a dense fog. For several days before this event there was a peculiar haze in the atmosphere, and I had remarked that it was probable we should have a storm. This appalling phenomenon ushered in the Maslinitz, or Carnival, when all labour ceased; the time was devoted to enjoyment; and one distinguished character amongst us, whom I beg to introduce, aided greatly in promoting the general enjoyments.

Among the soldiers sent to Kopal, there was one who had occupied a very different position, having been a distinguished member of the "Church Militant." During the latter years of his ecclesiastical career he had shown that the Church was not the sphere for his talents. His tastes were expensive as well as criminal, and to gratify them he used the powers of his sacred office to screw all the roubles possible out of his flock. His brethren also gave him the credit of stripping the holy pictures of their gems and replacing them with paste. Be this as it may, he was not alone in this species of fraud, for it had often been done. The result was his degradation and change of occupation, and my knowledge of the man enables me to say that he was more suited for the musket than the crosier. Nevertheless, in early life he had been studious, and had gained a high position among his fellows for his learning and ecclesiastical acquirements.

He soon began to distinguish himself among his comrades in Kopal. At Christmas he arranged a comedy, and succeeded in drilling a number of his companions so well in their parts, that the piece was performed every evening. It was "a decided success," and was several times performed before two audiences the same night. This aided in establishing his popularity, while his knowledge gave him power among his comrades, and obtained for him the title of "Proto-Pope" (Arch-Priest).

In all the revels and carouses he took the lead among the

men, some of them, however, declaring that he had made a compact with Shaitan, which enabled him to take brandy in quantities that would be fatal to them. The Maslinitz is a holiday that every good Russian deems necessary to keep, and in doing so makes himself ill by eating blinneys, preparatory to the long fast. My comrades were too orthodox in their creed to neglect the important event.

Although it was only the end of February the winter on the plains had passed, and the steppe was covered with a carpet of grass and flowers. This added much to our enjoyment, and every one entered upon the festal week determined to make the most of it.

Even of luxuries we had a few, having procured a good supply of pheasants from Kizil-a-gash, and these and rice boiled with dried apricots afforded us delicious fare. Vegetables we had none, and our rye-bread was horrible. The officers had sent a party of Cossacks to Kulja (a three days' journey) for Chinese brandy, as without that there could be no feast. This is most abominable stuff, strong, fiery, and stinking. The two first qualities were greatly in its favour, and the latter they endured, as no other intoxicating beverage could be obtained. The Cossacks and soldiers had also got a supply. Two days before the festival six camels were seen wending their way into Kopal, heavily laden with the spirits.

No pantomime ever produced on a London stage was looked for by a youthful audience with more anxiety and delight than was the piece that the Proto-Pope had prepared for these warriors. No one had been initiated into the mystery, as the author was to be (like Mathews) the sole performer. The only persons called to his assistance were carpenters, whom he directed to make a platform, with a strong pole standing up in its centre. On the top of this a piece of plank was secured, with uprights at the angles, and a rail placed round the top. The platform was secured on wooden axletrees at the front and back, and four gun-wheels were obtained by permission of the artillery officer, on which this machine was mounted, with a pole in front. The Pope had been assisted in his costume by the wives of the Cossacks.

Early on Monday morning twelve artillery horses were attached to the car, with drivers in uniform to each pair. A great number of spectators had assembled, all equally anxious to see the sport, and presently the soldier-priest mounted to his rostrum on the top of the pole. His vestments were made of voilock, decorated with coloured cloth, while in shape they were exactly like those of a priest of the Greek Church. In fact, he had managed to give himself the appearance of a Russian Pope when officiating in a solemn service.

Having attained his elevated position, he was hailed with lusty cheers, and with every demonstration of delight. When this exuberance of feeling had ceased, he began solemnly chanting from a book in a deep-toned voice. As he proceeded, all listened intently for a few minutes, and then they burst forth with thundering applause. After waiting till the interruption had ceased, he continued his discourse with the utmost gravity, receiving frequent shouts of approbation from his audience. His harangue occupied nearly an hour, and when it was finished the men made the air ring with their loud hurras.

He then ordered his car to be drawn to another place, a number of men sprung on to the platform to keep it steady, and the cavalcade moved on. Having reached the house of the chief of the Cossacks, the priest commenced anew, and so it was continued from house to house till each officer had been visited. His discourse was a burlesque on the "fast and its founders," in which he rendered both the men and the ceremony perfectly ludicrous. These performances extended over six days, and on each he produced a new subject. His second discourse was a satire on the Archbishops, Bishops, and the higher Clergy, in which he exposed the doings of these Ecclesiastics, to the great amusement of his hearers.

On the third day his subject was the working clergy and the means they adopt to screw money out of the serfs.

The Proto-Pope on his Rostrum.

The fourth day's text was "the confession and its consequences;" this was a theme he treated with great humour, and it afforded intense delight to those around him. The fifth day was devoted to the "Archimandrite, the Monks, and the Monasteries," and, lastly, "the Abbess, her Nuns, and the fools who force their daughters into nunneries." The two last subjects were his masterpieces; they were painted with a free and broad pencil dipped in vivid colour, the depth of shade beautifully contrasted with flashes of light. No one but an artist with a thorough practical knowledge of the subject in all its details, could have painted them with such force.

Some of my friends declared that his descriptions were true to nature, but that had he uttered them in Russia his fate would have been chains and the mines of Nertchinsk for life.

As the first day of the Maslinitz was preceded by an earthquake, strange to say, so was the last. Late on the Saturday night the revelling had ceased, and all in Kopal except the sentinels were at rest. When, a little after midnight on the 25th, a loud crash of subterranean thunder caused great alarm, and the upheaving of the ground announced another of these fearful events.

The marauding warfare constantly carried on between the Great and Middle Hordes, kept a large portion of the country between the Ala-tau and the Balkash in a very unsettled state, rendering it dangerous to the caravans, which were often plundered by both parties. After much negotiation, Prince Gortchikoff succeeded in inducing the Kirghis Sultans and Chiefs to meet in a congress and settle the boundary between the Great and Middle Hordes.

It was arranged that they should meet in Kopal on the 1st of March, and before that day many of the nomade Chiefs arrived accompanied by their Mullas and elders. The Sessedatle with his staff came from Ayagus; he was empowered to act as umpire between the Chiefs. Several other Russian officials came from the tribes in the Middle Horde to take a part in these important proceedings. On the appointed day, the heads and representatives of the great families and tribes were assembled, many of whom had never met except in deadly strife, when on their plundering expeditions. As each had wrongs to avenge, it was doubtful if they could be kept under control.

Captain Abakamoff had received orders to exercise the artillery, and fire a salute on the day the congress commenced its sittings. All the chiefs desired to attend and witness the spectacle; when they saw the horses gallop round with the guns, and the evolutions performed with such rapidity, they were delighted. At last the guns were brought up and placed in position, about a hundred yards from the Chiefs, and the men began loading. During this operation many of the Kirghis rushed forward to get a better view. Before they had gone half the distance the first gun belched forth its flame, smoke, and thunder, instantly checking their ardour, and causing a rapid retreat. As one gun after another echoed in the mountains, they gazed with perfect horror, and were evidently greatly relieved when the salute was ended.

This military display produced a great effect on their minds, forming a subject of conversation more interesting to them than that for which they had met; indeed they could not be induced to enter on the boundary question that day. As the number of people assembled to take a part in these proceedings exceeded one hundred, a large flock of sheep was collected from the nearest tribes, considerable quantity of mutton being required for the occasion.

There was no room in Kopal large enough to contain the assembly, nor could they be crammed into a yourt; this involved the necessity of their deliberations being conducted in the open air. A spot was selected within the fort, and the turf formed their seats. In the centre the Sessedatle and his assistants sat down, their laps forming their desks, and ink horns were suspended on their kalats. Such a display of writing materials appeared to produce great astonishment. Sultan Souk and his Mulla took their places in front of this formidable array, and the other Chiefs arranged themselves around it, forming their House of Peers—the outward circle being the House of Commons.

It was the duty of the Russian official to open the proceedings, and he began by telling his audience that his Excellency the Governor-General Prince Gortchikoff had sent a despatch (which he produced and handed to Souk), recommending the Sultans and Chiefs to form a boundary between the two Hordes, which should be satisfactory to the tribes, and thus stop all feuds and plunderings in future. The despatch authorised the Sessedatle to act as mediator in case any difficulty arose between the Chiefs. This having been explained to the assembly by Souk's Mulla, the Sessedatle addressed them and expressed a wish that their deliberations should be conducted in a friendly spirit, such being the only way by which they could arrive at a just decision on a matter so important to their future welfare. Beside, he added, he was sure that it would be highly gratifying to the Prince if his suggestions aided in bringing about so important a result.

When the Sessedatle had finished speaking, all eyes were turned upon Sultan Souk, whose ancient descent and distinguished position gave him precedence. He began by saying that he had considered the suggestions of the Prince, and was willing to adopt them, and form the required boundary; but that it must be understood that the line of demarcation must be made according to his views, which he believed would be approved of by the Great Horde. "The boundary to which I shall consent," he said, "is the Ac-sou, including the shores of the Balkash. If the Middle Horde agree to this, it is well, if not the Chiefs will maintain their right, and seize every man and animal found on the pastures."

The Sessedatle suggested to Souk that the rights of both Hordes ought to be respected, and that the great extent of pasture he now claimed belonged to the Middle Horde,—their territory extending to the Bean. He produced a map with the boundary laid down by the Russian authorities. This he explained, and told the assembly that the pastures on the north of the Bean belonged to the Middle Horde, and that he was instructed to say that the Prince would not consent to any arrangement which deprived them of that district.

Souk looked at the map placed before him for some time evidently without comprehending it, and then said: "I cannot understand this paper, nor why you have marked the Bean and call that the boundary; it may remain so on the paper, but I will have the pastures to the Ac-sou. The Prince has ordered the Lep-sou, the Ac-sou, and the Bean, to be placed where he pleased on this paper. He may have them so, but I order the boundary to be on the Ac-sou, nor shall it be changed. If the Middle Horde do not consent to this, they shall soon see some of my people on the Lep-sou." Several other Chiefs of the Great Horde spoke, who declared their approval of the Sultan's proposition, and expressed a determination to carry it out to the letter by plundering every tribe that crossed the Ac-sou. This created a great sensation; the Sessedatle remonstrated with Souk, but without effect; he was obstinate, and no argument could alter his determination.

A Chief of the Middle Horde next addressed the congress, saying that they had consented to meet the Sultans of the Great Horde to settle the boundary between their pastures. They were now told by Sultan Souk that the division must be at the Ac-sou, and not at the Bean. This latter river had bounded the pastures of the Middle Horde for many generations; he would respond in the same spirit as Souk, and he hoped that all the people would agree with him: if so, the Ac-sou would never be the boundary, and if any tribes crossed either the Bean or even the Kok-sou, they would never return. His tribe would be ready to meet Souk and his marauders whenever they dared to enter the pastures.

This speech terminated the first day's deliberations, which had only created an increased feeling of hostility. Day after day passed with similar results, and no arguments could induce either horde to make concessions. At the end of a month the Sessedatle was tired out, and broke up the congress, without having made one step in advance; and the tribes separated more embittered than before.

After the departure of these nomades, Kopal settled down into its quiet habits; the earth-works were pushed on; but no timber could be procured, the gorges being deep in snow. In April another engineer arrived from Omsk to complete the fort, and we soon discovered that the change was not for the better. He constantly mourned the loss of his beloved Omsk, where, he said, "Mirth, pleasure, and elegance reigned supreme." When in his cups, which was very frequent, he has been heard soliloquising grievous complaints of his fate, in having been banished to what he styled a barbarous spot, where the men and women possessed no knowledge of life and its refinements but what they had acquired in a Cossack piquet.

He had not arrived more than a fortnight when we met at dinner. I observed that his refined tastes did not prevent him partaking too freely of coarse beverages, and when the rest had departed he remained with our host. Subsequently, when the guard went their rounds, they were startled by a strange-looking object, lying near a gate. On examination, they found that it was the engineer, who had undressed himself entirely, with the exception of his boots. He was sleeping on the turf, his clothes beside him, in the full conviction that he was in bed.

During the winter the guns were placed in position on the west side of the fort, commanding the valley; the ammunition wagons in the rear, with some stores beside them. In one of the wagons the military chest was secured, containing 700 silver roubles in coin. A sentinel was constantly on duty, and during the cold weather in winter he was changed every hour, at other times every two hours. One morning, in the early part of April, a great sensation was created by the fact transpiring that, when the relief-guard came to the guns, the man was not on duty, nor could he be found anywhere.

A large Tumulus and Altars near Kopal.

The other sentinels had not observed any people approach, nor had any circumstance occurred to excite their suspicions. That the man had been recently carried off it was evident, for he had answered the last challenge within half an hour. Notice of the matter was instantly sent to the chief of the Cossacks, the Captain of the Artillery, and to the officer in command of the soldiers, who shortly arrived on the spot; lights were procured, the guns examined and found all right, and the wagons appeared undisturbed; the one in which the money was deposited was then opened, when it was discovered that the lock of the chest was broken and the roubles gone. As no men had been observed near the place, the sentinel was at once suspected of the robbery; and it being only an hour past midnight, and exceedingly dark, it was impossible to follow him. Nothing could be done till morning, except giving orders that several parties of Cossacks should be ready to start as soon as there was light enough to see the trail on the steppe. It was supposed that the culprit would try to find his way to the upper part of the Irtisch, a journey of fifteen days with a good horse, and thence proceed into the Altai mountains, and join some of the hunters. The moment daylight appeared, Cossacks were out searching the plain near the fort; but no trace of the sentinel or other fresh trails could be found. Shortly afterwards the several parties started on their expedition, taking different routes leading to the Irtisch.

By noon the fugitive had passed the western end of the Karatou, and came upon the caravan route leading to Kulja, Kokhan, and Tashkend. This he followed till late in the evening, when he observed a few yourts at about a mile distant. He turned toward these, and found that they belonged to some herdsmen, — by whom he was hospitably received, and remained the night. Next morning he was on his road at daylight, and made a long day's ride; sleeping at night at a Kirghis aoul.

The following day he made another long march, and in the evening he reached an aoul of a Kirghis Chief, Adi-yoll. A Tatar merchant was here following his vocation, and recognised the man to be a soldier from Kopal. He questioned him about the object of his journey in this direction, and expressed surprise at his being alone. He soon discovered that he was deserting, informed the Chief, and advised him to send the man under an escort to Kopal, which was instantly agreed to, though the soldier offered the Chief three packets of silver roubles, each containing one hundred. The merchant was now convinced that the money had been stolen from the government cash-box, as he knew there was no officer in the place who could produce ten roubles in silver. All the coin found upon the man was made into a parcel by him, and sealed up by the Chief. In the morning, it was given to one of the escort, with instructions to deliver it and the prisoner to the commander in Kopal.

On the evening of the sixth day after the robbery, a party of Kirghis rode up to the little dwelling of the chief of the Cossacks; and delivered the prisoner and the parcel containing the money, not one rouble of which was missing. The man was sent to the guard-house, and the cash deposited in a place of greater security.

The following day the officers assembled, in order that, whatever the culprit might say, should be appended to the report the commander would have to send to Prince Gortchikoff, the Governor-General of Western Siberia, from whom his sentence would emanate.

The prisoner being put upon his defence, addressed the commander, as is customary, by name, saying, "Ivan Ivanovitch, I did leave my post and take the money, but another person planned the robbery, and has long urged me to commit it." The commander replied, "This is a serious charge you are making; do not attempt to criminate any man in the hope of saving yourself, unless that person is really guilty." The prisoner said earnestly, "Ivan Ivanovitch, 'Ye Bogh'*, he is guilty." His judge demanded his name, and said that if he were in Kopal the Cossacks should bring him into the court immediately. The fellow added, with every appearance of sincerity, "He was with me when I took the money, but the Cossacks will find it difficult to

* By God.

catch him, Ivan Ivanovitch; it was 'Chort.'* I wish you had him here, I would prove to his face that he has caused all this mischief. Oh! how I should like to see him run the gauntlet through our regiment, and you commanding, Ivan Ivanovitch. But I'll tell you what he has done, and then you will see what a villain he is."

He then gave a circumstantial account of a visit he had received, when at his post, from a mysterious stranger, who among the Cossacks, as elsewhere, is "the gentleman in black." He repeated at length various arguments, that were used to tempt him to take the emperor's silver, and represented himself as long holding out against temptation; but when "Chort" showed him how he might escape with the treasure, and live like an officer in China, by keeping a horse in readiness, and waiting his opportunity to plunder the wagon; then, having broken open the chest, and placed the silver carefully in his sash, how easily he might crawl away with it to a distance, mount a steed, and place himself in a few hours beyond the reach of pursuit, he gave in; but not, according to his statement, until the tempter had repeated his visit, increased his arguments and persuasions, and helped him to commit the robbery.

Though this defence was made with much earnestness and apparent candour, accompanied by the strongest asseverations, it produced very little effect upon his judges; the fellow was sent back to the guard-house, and kept secure until Prince Gortchikoff sent an order for his removal to Omsk, where he was tried for his crime and sent to work in the mines at Nertchinsk for life.

The time for my quitting this region having arrived, I visited the cemetery on the hill, and counted 107 graves, proving how active death had been during eight months.

* The Devil.

CHAP. VIII.

DEPARTURE FROM KOPAL.

On leaving Kopal I turned my steps to the eastward. A party of Cossack officers, with their wives, accompanied me to the Arasan, our first night's encampment. From the fortress our way was towards Byan-ja-rouk, a sacred mountain with the Kirghis, over which I had watched the sun rise almost daily for the past five months, and during the preceding October and November I had seen the snow gradually descend the high chains around, securing us as effectually as in a prison.

Immediately after the snow melted on the plains, the flowers began to bloom and the birds to sing. These indications of returning spring had daily increased my desire to be gone. Travellers who have been confined in such a region can fully comprehend with what anxiety the mountain masses were scanned each returning morn, and can understand the gratification I felt in listening to the crash of the avalanche above. This was a certain indication that many of the icy barriers were breaking up, and that the lately frozen-up torrents were pouring their floods towards the plains.

Though the steppes had long been covered with a carpet of grass and flowers, indeed were now withered by the scorching sun, doubts were entertained of my being able to cross the Kara-tau, and descend to the plain beyond. My object in attempting this was to meet the tribes and join them on their march to the summer pastures in the high valleys of the Ala-tau, in Chinese Tartary.

After taking leave of all our Cossack friends according to the usual custom, which is always done at their own dwellings before commencing a journey, we mounted our horses and departed. A ride of little more than an hour's duration carried us beyond the region of tombs, and on to a part of the steppe composed of bare granite on which there was scarcely a blade of grass. In some parts huge masses were thrown up, with broad veins of rose quartz protruding, that extended in parallel lines in a south-easterly direction for ten miles. Beyond was a grassy plain running up to the foot of the north side of Byan-ja-rouk, and in the distance were several groups of ancient tombs,—the burial-place of a race of whom the Kirghis have no tradition.

Not far from one of these smoke was rising, which indicated the place for our encampment, and a sharp gallop over about eight miles of rich greensward brought us to it. A party of Cossacks and artillerymen had been sent on before with yourts, and such eatables as could be procured, each family having contributed a portion from its little store to make our parting feast.

We were now at the "Arasan," or hot mineral spring, having a temperature of 29° + Reaumur both in winter and summer. At a very distant period this has been a place of some importance,—judging from the extent of the foundations of several buildings, and the heaps of ruins around. The Kirghis have a tradition that one of these has been a Kalmuck temple; they also look upon the place as holy.

A large bath has been formed with rough stone walls, 23 feet long, 8 feet wide, and 4 feet 6 inches deep, and the spring is very strong, giving a column of water three inches in diameter. It has been resorted to for many centuries by Kalmucks, Tartars, Chinese, and Kirghis. Formerly the place swarmed with serpents of a harmless species, and the bathers considered it a good omen when any of them twined round their arms and neck; nor would they on any account have them disturbed.

The water was clear, and the steam curling up from it induced the officers and myself to bathe. While enjoying the luxury my attention was directed to a serpent that was twisting his slimy body among the stones not far from my back. He was much too near to be agreeable, and I instantly gave him a wide berth, to the great amusement of my friends. About fifty yards from the bath, a cold spring gushes forth in a circular basin,—now partly filled up with stones, whence carbonic acid gas bubbles up in great quantities. Good soda-water of natural manufacture could be obtained here in an inexhaustible supply.

The sun had descended below the Kara-tau, leaving golden and crimson clouds spread over the western sky. As we sat at our evening meal these melted away, and were succeeded by a flood of yellow light streaming up in rays to the zenith. It was a lovely night, undisturbed by even a breath of wind. Shortly after dusk the moon rose and changed the scene; her pale silvery light throwing over the rocks and ruins a kind of spectral halo. While watching the twilight fade away and the moon rise, recollections were called up of many such nights passed with my companions; and as I felt that this was a final parting, it caused a deep feeling of sadness.

At this moment a Cossack began playing on his Ballalika, (a rude guitar with three strings); the effect was magical, quickly dispelling the gloom all had felt, and in a few minutes we were dancing Cossack dances on the turf to his wild music. These are eminently characteristic, full of graceful attitudes, and as wild as the surrounding scenes. Some Chinese brandy, which had been procured from Kulja, aided in raising the spirits of my friends, and no ball given in polite society ever passed off with more true enjoyment. Some of the men had been my companions for many months; we had hunted together, shared many toils and dangers, and had rambled far within the Chinese dominions. They had often enlivened my camp after a hard day's ride by their songs, and now gave me a parting farewell in some of their wildest strains, which left an impression on my mind not soon to be erased.

Byan-ja-rouk from the North.

When I looked out in the morning the sun was throwing up his rays over Byan-ja-rouk, and tipping the snowy peaks of the Ac-tau with a deep crimson light, while all the lower chain of the Ala-tau was still clothed in cold grey. After the morning repast my friends, excepting three, returned to their homes. The officer of artillery, with two of his men, rode with me to the pass in the Kara-tau, where we dined, and then separated.

A ride of half an hour brought us into the rugged ravine, with its dark purple slaty walls rising in some places a thousand feet above us; in other parts it opened into an amphitheatre, in the shelving sides of which ten times the multitude ever assembled by Cæsar in the Colosseum could have found places. A small stream ran through the centre of this area, leaping and foaming over fallen rocks: its banks were fringed with many flowering shrubs, while luxuriant grass, with beds of sweet-scented yellow poppies, were spread over the surface.

We were three hours riding from this place to the top of the pass, whence we had a view over the steppe, that stretched out like a sea beneath us, till earth and sky seemed to be united in purple vapour. Here we expected to see the tribes on their march, but were disappointed. In one direction smoke was seen, although at a great distance. We were now about five thousand feet above the steppe, and to the east the mountains rose abruptly two thousand feet higher. On some beetling crags, far above us, was standing a group of argali (wild sheep), apparently watching our movements with intense interest. It was impossible to approach them within rifle range, and shortly they scampered off to a higher summit, whence they continued gazing until we were lost in the windings of the pass.

The descent was very tedious, and occupied us four hours. After leaving the gorge and reaching the crest of a low hill, we beheld a few miles to the east a Kirghis encampment. On reaching it, we ascertained that this was an advance party on their way to the Ala-tau, and that they had only just arrived. Their yourts, fifteen in number, were being pitched on the bank of a small stream; as usual, the women were performing this laborious work, while the chief and some of the elders of the tribe were lounging on carpets, drinking koumis. A place was made for me in the little circle, and a bowl of the beverage handed to me, which, after tasting, I passed to one of my men, who proved himself a true descendant of the race by draining it to the bottom.

Large herds of camels, horses, and oxen were seen grazing at a short distance, and immense flocks of sheep were feeding around us. I ascertained from the chief that he intended remaining on this spot for two or three days, and that we should find some of the tribes a two days' journey beyond the river Ac-sou. While two yourts were being put up for our party, I strolled through the aoul, and watched the women at their labours. Poor creatures, they were miserable indeed, notwithstanding that they were surrounded by vast flocks and herds. Their forms were emaciated, and their faces careworn; even the young seemed marked with age, and all were covered with dirt. Water never comes near their skins, except from a shower in the mountains; and their clothing bespoke extreme wretchedness.

Some had sheepskin coats, others of printed calico from Kokhan, yellowish leather tchimbar (wide trousers), madder-coloured boots, short in the foot, with high heels, which rendered their gait ungainly. Their head-dresses were of calico, formed like a hood, and hanging over their shoulders, which gave them the appearance of nuns; but there was nothing prepossessing either in their looks or costume. When the yourts were finished, the voilocks spread, and their small stock of moveables arranged, they turned to their other domestic duties, milking their cows, sheep, and goats. The lambs and kids were strung together in long lines, waiting their turn; the moment the women had finished milking, children, from four to ten years old, slipped the cords from their necks, when the young animals bounded off to their dams, butting and springing over each other's backs.

A short distance from these the men were milking the mares and camels; and one of the former was kicking and plunging, evidently determined not to submit. As a Kirghis is not to be defeated by his horse, when koumis is wanted, in a short time she was secured with thongs, and notwithstanding her efforts to bite, and her attempts to lie down, was compelled to contribute to the general stock. The foals were tied up in long lines of fifty or sixty in each, and are only allowed to suck morning and evening after the milking.

This tribe had been more than two months on their march from the shores of the Balkash,—the winter resort for all the Kirghis of this region. Theirs is a life of constant migration between the higher valleys of the Ala-tau and the steppe around the Balkash. Here, during the winter season, their flocks and herds obtain food from the tops of the rough grass which protrudes through the snow. As these people make no hay for their cattle, the want of it often subjects them to great disasters, and the past winter had been a most fatal one. Early in October, 1849, there was a fall of snow, which rendered it difficult for the cattle to find the short grass on the steppe. Before the end of the month there was a bouran and a snow-storm that continued nine days, covering the whole country four to five feet deep. This prevented some of the tribes reaching the shores of the Balkash, and vast numbers of their sheep died; the Kirghis in this region lost no less than 70,000 sheep. The camels, horses, and oxen succeeded in procuring a scanty subsistence; but before the spring, vast numbers of these died also. One chief, at whose aoul I remained, had had 700 horses, 80 camels, and a great number of oxen destroyed.

Independently of such calamities, the Kirghis are subject to great personal risk and danger on these vast Asiatic plains, where the wind blows with a fury unknown in Europe. In January, 1850, the thermometer fell to 20° Reaum. below the freezing-point, and then came terrible bourans. I have known one to continue for eleven days with such fury that the yourts were blown down, and the voilock coverings rent asunder and carried away by the storm. I have also seen the household goods strewn over the snowy waste, when all had to scramble to procure the smallest covering as a protection against the cutting blast. These disasters not unfrequently happen in the night, when, in the confusion, the fur wrappers are blown from the young children; and they, miserable little creatures, are hurled into the snow, and perish. But it is not children alone who fall victims to the fury of these storms,—if men or women wander from the aoul, they can seldom return, and thus they are often frozen to death within fifty paces of their friends. Such are the fearful calamities that visit these vast steppes.

The tribe with whom I was stopping had suffered, and were mourning the loss of some of their friends. At the door of one of the yourts, a small white flag was fluttering from a spear, indicating that a young female had been lost; and plaintive music and deep sobs were heard issuing from the yourt, as the sun was setting. In some of the narrow rocky valleys of the Ala-tau I have often heard a dozen, or even more, voices singing in chorus these funeral strains. As the sounds swelled and echoed from crag to crag, it had a pleasing, but at the same time a most melancholy effect,—it was truly funereal.

During the evening I made many inquiries of my host about the passes in the Kara-tau, and expressed a wish to ascend by the gorge of the Ac-sou. This, he said, was utterly impossible, as the river ran between perpendicular precipices, without a ledge on which man could set his foot. Nor would it, he added, be practicable to ford the river within a two hours' ride from the point where it issues from the mountain. The first ten or fifteen miles after it enters the plain it is one continued cataract, the water tumbling over large rocks, forming a succession of falls, and making a roar that is heard at a long distance: over it, he said, neither man nor horse could cross.

The chief and his friends were trying to make themselves happy; and if koumis and arrak could do it, they had abundant materials at hand. The bowls were often emptied, and they were becoming noisy and quarrelsome, — of course, under these circumstances, no further information could be obtained. Having no desire that either myself or my men should take a part in a Kirghis brawl, I deemed it prudent to retire to our yourt.

At daybreak the following morning we left the aoul, long before the chief and his boosing companions had opened their eyes. Notwithstanding what had been said as to the impossibility of ascending the gorge of the Ac-sou, I ordered our march along the foot of the mountains. After riding about two hours we came upon a great number of ancient tombs; many only small mounds of earth, varying from fifteen to twenty feet in diameter and ten feet high; these were scattered far over the plain. About a mile further, I found others of much larger dimensions; one, 120 feet in diameter and 37 feet high; with a shallow ditch, 12 feet wide and 4 feet deep, running round its base. One hundred feet from the edge of the ditch was a circle of stones, two feet high, and ten feet from this there was another of the same height. Directly facing the east was an entrance twelve feet wide, having an avenue of the same width, formed of similar stones, extending eastwards 100 yards.

Having ridden my horse to the summit of the tumulus, I saw three others to the north, of apparently similar dimensions. One of them was about a mile distant, another about two miles, and the third still further, in a north-westerly direction. To the south I observed a still larger tumulus not far away. The whole intervening space was covered with smaller tombs, extending over an area nearly four miles in length by one mile in breadth — verily a vast city of the dead.

Here was a place for reflection, and for much curious speculation as to what nation or race occupied these numberless mounds. They have passed away without leaving a single record, and it is impossible to identify them or date their cemeteries. Most probably they were raised by the earliest inhabitants of these vast regions, which we are led to believe was the cradle of the human race. I turned my horse away, deeply regretting that I had not the means of examining one of the larger tombs, as articles might probably be found therein that would go far towards explaining this historical enigma.

After leaving this necropolis a ride of nearly two hours brought us to the gorge of the Ac-sou, when I was convinced that all attempts to ascend the ravine would prove fruitless. It is a rent in the mountain, with overhanging precipices, split near their summits into fearful crags, that seem ready to topple into the roaring torrent beneath. Having climbed to a high jutting mass of light green slate, I looked down into the terrific gorge, and beheld the rushing water dashed up like flakes of snow;—this and its tremendous roar produced a most appalling effect. I ascended the mountain still higher, till I stood on some crags about 3,000 feet above the plain, but not mid-way to the summit.

From this spot I obtained a view up the gorge. It was fearfully grand. Huge buttresses projected into the ravine, crowned by lofty turrets of varied form. On some, dwarf cedars had taken root, and the branches were wreathing round their heads like civic crowns. The opposite cliffs assumed the forms of mighty castles, with broad terraces and pierced battlements; among these, small picta trees were growing, that a lively imagination might easily have pictured as soldiers guarding the pass. At one place the precipice rose up like a turreted gateway, beneath which a stream of water gushed forth, and leaped into the gorge at one bound. As it descended it was wafted about like white horse-hair streaming in the breeze, and before reaching the bottom appeared like a cloud of vapour.

It was impossible to proceed further in this direction. Nature has placed an impassable barrier here, and without some great change man can never penetrate this awful depth, nor the geologist examine the strata laid bare 4,000

Gorge of the Ac-sou.

feet beneath the summit. Turning from the ravine towards the steppe, I saw at a long distance the yourts and smoke of an aoul to the east of the Ac-sou. This induced me to hasten our descent, as there was a long ride before us, and we should have to follow the river many miles to the north before we could cross it.

While riding along its bank, looking out for a practicable ford, the hissing and foaming of the water warned us against the attempt. At length we reached a point where there seemed less risk, but on making a trial, two of the men were near being carried away over a water-fall. We were compelled to seek a safer place; and having ridden about ten miles, came to a broad part of the river, where, at the lower end of a small island, alternately fording and swimming, we succeeded after much difficulty in reaching the opposite bank.

In half an hour we came to the bed of a dry river, about half a mile in breadth, covered with large stones, that gave us much trouble in crossing. As night was coming on apace, it was impossible to trace its course up to the mountain, and ascertain if it was an ancient bed of the Ac-sou. This, however, is probable, as great changes take place in a region where earthquakes are frequent and severe. About two hours after sunset we reached a high bank overlooking the aoul we were seeking, and then lost no time in riding up to the Chief's yourt, accompanied by the usual chorus of shouting men and barking dogs.

Having appeased my hunger, I had time to examine the company around. Djani-bek, the Chief, was a man about forty years of age, with a burly figure, and a jolly, Friar-Tuck-looking face, which showed that abstemiousness formed no part of his creed. Four other Kirghis were sitting in front of us, his boon companions; beyond these there sat a number of his retainers and herdsmen scanning my face and figure with their small sparkling eyes, evidently wondering from what part of the globe I had come.

In the red glare of our flickering fire the group formed a more striking picture of banditti, than any painted by

Salvator Rosa. Two of my men were sitting near me, whom the chief questioned as to whence we had come, and where we were proceeding. When told that we were going to wander in the mountains, he looked with much astonishment, and inquired if I had camels and horses. On a negative being given, all appeared alarmed and suspicious, and examined me more closely, fully satisfied that I must be either a madman or a robber.

Djani-bek informed me that several of his men had ascended the pass in the Kara-tau the day before, and had found the snow still lying on the mountains, which would delay the march of the tribe for several days. Some were already within three days of this encampment, and we were only a three hours' ride from the mouth of the pass.

The Kirghis have not yet acquired the European habits of sitting up late, and they rise with the dawn. We were therefore out early in the morning, and I took the opportunity of examining our position. The yourts were on the edge of a broad and deep gully, cut down into the sand by a small stream. This was now a beautiful green pasture, being watered by the little rivulet, which was twisted and wound about in the bottom among rich grass, sometimes half hid, and then lost under flowering shrubs, at this time in full bloom. Great herds of camels and horses were feeding on these pastures, which extended for several miles to the northward. The sheep and goats had spread themselves over a rocky hill, stretching along far to the eastward. To the south the Kara-tau reared his jagged peaks of deep purple slate, among which the snow was still lying in patches. On the crest of the lower ranges granite is thrown up in singular and picturesque forms, while to the north and west the steppes seemed interminable. It was over these that the Kirghis hordes were now marching with their innumerable herds and flocks, though not visible within the range of my vision.

Finding that it would be necessary to wait for the arrival of the tribes, and that they would not commence their emigration for several days, I determined to extend my journey to the eastward, as Djani-bek had informed me there was a mountain pass in that direction, which some of his people had said was a twelve hours' ride distant. I could obtain no particulars from him; he only knew that some of the tribes to the eastward ascended by it to their summer pastures: this decided me, and I determined to examine it. Having arranged with the chief for five fresh horses and two men, these and two Cossacks formed my little party.

At six o'clock we were in our saddles, and crossed the deep gully to the steppe beyond. For the first mile the ground was covered with short turf; after this we came upon a plain, composed of pebbles and sand, with occasional tufts of steppe grass, extending about three miles. This led to a sandy plain entirely deprived of vegetation. Far to the north we could see some green patches of verdure surrounding a lake, but with this exception the entire country appeared an arid desert.

In about an hour and a half we reached the brink of one of the dry water-courses frequently found in these regions. This was a large one, being not less than a mile and a half in width, and 130 feet deep; the banks being nearly perpendicular, formed a complete barrier to our progress in this direction. I sent three men along the bank and took my only other companion upwards, searching for a place by which we could descend. After a long and fruitless ride, the report of a gun, and the waving of a handkerchief by the men, recalled us to a spot where they had discovered a track made by deer and other animals descending for water.

We rode over the brink, and began to descend slowly, crossing a broken part of the path with great difficulty. At length two men and myself had reached the bottom. As we stood watching the other two, the sand suddenly gave way under the feet of the last horse, and both man and animal rolled down from a height of about forty feet. Fortunately the Cossack threw himself clear of the horse; still we thought both were killed. On hastening to their aid they rose to their feet; the horse gave himself a shake, and began to kick and plunge furiously, and the man burst into a fit of laughter.

All hope of returning by this track was now at an end, and we rode on with increasing anxiety, making vain guesses as to what had become of the stream which had scooped out this formidable hollow. Sand and pebbles covered the greater part of the surface, interspersed with patches of fine grass; but near the middle we found numerous pools of fresh water, with a small stream uniting them. They were surrounded by beds of fine sand, on which were the footprints of several animals of the deer tribe.

Near one pool, other footmarks attracted the attention of my men, one of whom called out that the barse (tiger) had been there. On reaching the spot, I saw distinctly the prints of huge feline paws, though not recent. Most probably this tiger had followed the other animals into the mountains, whither they had gone in search of food. Having made this discovery, we lost no time in examining the nipples of our rifles. A little further, we found the bed of a torrent covered with large stones and coarse gravel, over which a stream of water was running rapidly, rendering it very difficult to ford; and the opposite bank proved as high and abrupt as the one we had descended.

It was now past mid-day, and the pass in the mountains appeared still far distant. On questioning the guide, I ascertained that he had never crossed this country before, and could tell me nothing reliable about the pass. Quickening our pace over the sandy steppe, at seven o'clock we turned into the great ravine we had been seeking. The first few hundred yards were between grassy slopes, with a little rivulet in the centre: at last, having passed some rocky masses, the rugged mountain jaws opened upon us in all their grandeur. This was a terrific rent: the dark purple slaty rock had been riven asunder by granite, and heaved up into craggy precipices of enormous height. In some parts the rocks were broken into sharp points; in others they were piled up like huge towers, overhanging the base of these mighty cliffs. To add to the wildness of the view, three large eagles were soaring far above our heads, and several were perched upon the crags.

The Kirghis imagined from this that some of their countrymen were encamped in the pass, and, riding forward, found unmistakeable evidence that horses and other animals had recently passed on the other side of the stream. Presently three Kirghis appeared, who, after a ride of little more than an hour, brought us to a wide part of the pass, where they had pitched their yourts on some grassy slopes, at a point from which the gorge branches off in two directions. They were taking advantage of the luxuriant grass growing on this spot, intending to remain two or three days. The aoul belonged to a rich chief, Kal-matai, and some of his children, with one of his wives, were here, with their numerous attendants and herdsmen. In four days the chief was expected to join them with his other herds, by which time this part of his tribe would have selected the pastures, and established themselves in the upper valleys of the Ala-tau. All the camels, horses, and other animals, had been assembled close around the yourts, as the space on which these had been pitched was limited. It was quite dusk when the Kirghis escorted me to a yourt, where two of the sons of the chief received me, and gave me the usual welcome.

Various were the sounds that greeted my ears on waking in the morning—the sharp cry of the camels, and the bellowing of the bulls, echoing among the rocks, increased the confusion. As day dawned I turned out, and stood at the door of the yourt, gazing in wonder at the scene before me. The spot on which I stood was a green grassy mound in the middle of the gorge, and three yourts were placed upon it. A little below, on the bank of a small torrent,

Basaltic Rocks.

there were seven other yourts, while, immediately opposite, and at about 300 yards from me, rose a mighty mass of dark basaltic rocks, to a much greater elevation than the distance from me to them. They were pillared and split into most curious forms; some of them like watch-towers guarding the pass.

These basaltic masses divided the gorge, which branched off to the south and east. Looking up the southern branch, the eye rested on the snowy crests near the source of the Ac-sou, and up the other were seen the dazzling peaks in which the Başcan has its source. Nearer, some shrubs and flowers were hanging from the clefts, showing that spring was adorning these rugged forms with all her beauty. The whole space around the base of these precipices was filled with living animals: prominent among them I discovered the curved necks and shaggy heads of the camels, above the horses and oxen. Vast flocks of sheep and goats were climbing almost inaccessible cliffs in search of pasture. It was interesting to watch the latter spring from ledge to ledge, where there appeared scarcely space on which to stand; while the sheep stood gazing at them, unable to follow their agile leaders, and partake of the rich grass on which they fed. Shortly the whole aoul went forth, and engaged in various pastoral occupations.

My hostess was a woman about forty-five, with strong Kalmuck features,—showing that she had descended from that race, and most probably had been stolen from them when young. She wore a black kanfa kalat (Chinese satin), a scarlet and green shawl round her waist, and a fox-skin cap; yellow leather tchimbar embroidered round the bottom, and the usual high-heeled boots. Had she been washed, she would have produced a great effect in any town in Europe. Notwithstanding her finery she was occupied with her domestic duties, preparing cheese from a mixture of sheep and cow's milk. It is formed into squares like our cream cheese, and then dried in the sun on a rush mat. I have eaten it, and when fresh the flavour is not bad. There is one great drawback to the enjoyment of Kirghis cookery; their culinary utensils are dirty,—even their leathern pails used for milking, and all other vessels in which the milk stands, are never washed. They are lined with a thick coating of coagulated milk; and he must be a bold man who would trust his nose a second time within their rims.

Two of the sons of my hostess were fine young men,—one twenty and the other twenty-five years old. I ascertained from them that by ascending the eastern branch of the pass I could reach the Bascan; and wishing to visit the glaciers above the source of that river, I ordered our march in that direction, and they gave me a man who knew the route. There are several points in the gorge where basaltic rocks form grand features: shortly after passing these the cliffs are less abrupt, with picta trees growing on every ledge. As we advanced the pass became wider, well wooded, and terminated in a fine valley, whence I had a magnificent view of the snowy chain.

From this place the guide led the way to the north-east, up the mountain slope. As we ascended I perceived that the country to the south presented a very wild aspect; nevertheless there are numerous valleys in this region which afford good pastures for two months. At this season thousands of horses and oxen are seen grazing, and hundreds of thousands of sheep are feeding on the hill-sides. The tribes begin to retire from the higher region about the middle of August, stopping at every pasture on their return till all the grass is eaten by the herds. On nearing the summit I observed that purple slate rocks cropped out, and in some parts they rose into lofty crags.

After some difficulty we reached the crest, whence the course of the Bascan could be traced among the mountains; then continued our ride south-east, towards another ridge that was easily crossed, and we descended into a small valley with a stream running through its centre. The guide led the way down the bank of the stream to a point where it falls in a succession of cascades for more than 1,000 feet, into a valley in which runs one of the branches of the Bascan.

It was not easy to ride our horses down the rugged descent, often close to the water, where it rolled on with a thundering noise. Having reached the bottom, we passed round some high rocks and entered a deep valley, about a mile in width, and extending far to the southward. Here a scene of desolation was presented, such as I have never witnessed since. The valley had once been thickly wooded with pines and large cedars,—now not a single tree was standing. Thousands, yea, tens of thousands, were lying prostrate, their large trunks bleached by the summer's sun and winter's frost. All had been hurled down by one tremendous blast; some uprooted, and others, of large dimensions, were snapped asunder. The hurricane which caused this fearful devastation had not passed over with a revolving motion, such as I have witnessed, where the trees were torn up and strewn about in every direction. These were all lying side by side, with their tops up the valley, proving that the blast had ascended.

The guide led the way upwards for more than three miles, till we reached a part of the valley not more than half a mile in width. At this point another narrow valley branched off to the westward; this had also been well wooded. Here the pent-up hurricane had divided, and every tree was lying parallel to its neighbour. At this part we dismounted and led our horses over the fallen timber to the river, which was easily forded. The opposite ridge was soon ascended, when the principal branch of the Bascan was before me, winding through a rich valley. Some of the tribes had already reached it on their way upwards; vast herds of horses, oxen, and sheep were feeding, and a large aoul was visible at no great distance.

The ridge on which we stood was at least 3,000 feet

above the river, and in most parts the descent was too abrupt to attempt even on foot. We rode along the crest to a place where the Kirghis have discovered a practicable path. The descent was made by many a zigzag turn, frequently along the edge of granite cliffs of great depth, and over some exceedingly ugly places. At last we reached the bottom, at a place where the river runs almost close up to the rocks. Here the Kirghis have made a frail bridge, using a mass of granite that stands in the middle of the stream as a pier. These rude engineers have succeeded in throwing trunks of trees across the torrent; on these they have placed branches and a thin covering of earth. This structure was in too fragile a state to risk a ride across; however, we led our horses over, but not without danger, as three of them broke through, and one man had a narrow escape.

A ride of half an hour brought us to the aoul, that belonged to a wealthy chief, Barak, who gave me a cordial welcome. From him I learned that it was utterly impossible to ascend to the glaciers in which the Bascan has its source, as the route was still deep in snow, and the river so much swollen that it had stopped their march. I therefore accepted his offered hospitality to remain the night. At this part the valley is beautiful; high mountains rise up on each side, and many have summits far into the region of snow. Some of the lower ridges are covered with a thick forest of dark pines, and on the lower slopes are excellent pastures, studded with clumps of birches and poplars. In many places the river is fringed with magnificent trees, and the valley covered with luxuriant grass and flowers.

Few people possess such a spot: Barak could sit at the door of his yourt, and look at his tens of thousands of animals feeding on the mountain slopes. He could also enjoy a view of his domain, in which beauty and savage grandeur were combined. Having no wish to lose time, I visited a spot about four miles higher up in the valley, where a gorge opens to the south; it is formed in some high limestone cliffs, in which were several caverns. Through this opening there was a peep into the icy region beyond, where stupendous mountain peaks rose up, clothed with eternal snow, while at their base crystal masses were glittering; and to these I determined to penetrate if possible. After scanning the gorge it presented no great obstacle, could we cross the torrent. Having succeeded in other places that appeared almost as dangerous, I asked the Cossacks if they would ford it with me. They and three of the Kirghis instantly volunteered; the other three men declined.

Both banks were examined, and a place found that appeared to afford a chance of success: we formed in line, and, at the suggestion of a Cossack, each man gave the long rein of his bridle to his neighbour. A few steps brought us into the current, and the horses stood it well; but before we reached the middle the water rushed up their sides and over our saddles. Two lost their footing, and would have been swept down, had not the Cossack's precaution enabled us to hold on and draw them out of deep water. The other men rode in to our assistance, and we got out with a ducking, but fully convinced that the passage was impracticable. The source of the Bascan and its glaciers were thus sealed to me, and I returned to the aoul disappointed. A month later, Barak said, it might be accomplished.

My host was a Bee (magistrate), and had great influence with the people. During the evening a man was brought before him, charged with having stolen five horses and two camels. The theft was observed by a couple of witnesses, and the animals were discovered among his herds.

The first part of the charge he denied with great indignation, and attempted to prove an alibi, but failed.

The Bee asked one of the witnesses if he was sure this was the man who drove the horses off, and by what marks he knew him.

"By his ugly face and his seat on horseback," replied he; "also by the pattern and colour of his kalat, which was red, yellow, and green. It is not the one he has on. I also know his horse."

In answer to this evidence the culprit replied that his face was less like that of a thief than was that of the man who had accused him. As to the kalat, he never had such a one as had been described, and there were so many horses like his own, that the resemblance was no proof of guilt.

The Bee asked, how many kalats have you?

"Three," he answered.

"Where are they?"

"I have them on."

"All?"

"Yes."

"Are any of them like the one described?"

"No."

"I should like to see them: take one off."

"I have no objection, but there is no occasion, as none of mine are so fine."

The Bee insisted.

The culprit took one off, and held it up to the witness inside and out — but that was not the garment; the second and third passed the same ordeal with a like result.

The Bee exclaimed, "There must be a mistake—the man is free." This result greatly astonished his accusers.

The prisoner resumed his clothes, and began abusing the witness, applying to him sundry epithets which will not bear translation. Presently the court, or circle, was in a state of confusion, and the prisoner retired towards his horse. The owner of the animals, and the witnesses, seeing this, rushed upon him and dragged him back to the Bee, insisting on his garments being re-examined.

He called upon the Bee for protection; but his persecutors proceeded, without further ceremony, to strip him. His kalats were again examined; but they afforded no proof of his guilt. This, however, was not satisfactory to his accusers; and I am sorry to say that, without taking heed of the presence of the ladies, his tchimbar was torn off, and the identical garment pulled from its hiding-place in triumph. This condemned him, and the Bee ordered the restitution of the stolen animals, at the same time imposing a fine of ten horses and four camels. The trial did not last more than an hour, and speedy justice was awarded. Thieving of this kind is instantly punished among the Kirghis; but a baranta, like the sacking of a town, is honourable plunder.

Early in the morning I left the hospitable Bee, accompanied by two of his people, to guide me to a lake in one of the small

A Lake near the Bascan.

valleys that branches out to the south-east of the Bascan. A ride of an hour carried me to this picturesque spot, where I found work for my pencil. The mountains around the lake are rugged, and its shores rocky, affording no pastures. The Kirghis say the ice is seldom melted before June. Looking up the lake, there is a splendid view of the higher parts of the chain; and the summits of the Ac-tau are seen in their full grandeur, overtopping the rocky heights.

Before leaving this place the men proposed to lead me to a ford on the Bascan, and thence to our old route; the bridge we had crossed yesterday being deemed unsafe. Having retraced our steps into the valley of the Bascan, a ride of about three miles brought us to the ford, which we crossed without much difficulty. An incident happened to me as we ascended from the river, that left an impression on my mind which is still as vivid and fresh as the moment it occurred; nor can I, even at this time, contemplate the scene of it without a shudder.

At a short distance from the ford, we commenced a very abrupt ascent, by which we reached a ledge on the precipice about 500 feet above the river. Shelving rocks rose up to a great height above, and in several parts the path was so narrow that the left foot hung over the brink. I proceeded along this perilous path for about 300 yards, one of the Bee's men and a Cossack leading, I following them, and the rest of the party behind. At last we reached a broader ledge about twenty-five feet long and eight feet broad; the side and farther end of this small platform descended nearly perpendicular to the stream, more than 600 feet beneath.

The rocks rose so steep on the right that there appeared no possibility of proceeding farther; but the Kirghis turned his horse and rode up the incline about fifteen feet, to an opening in the rocks: when he gained the top, the Cossack followed. I then turned towards the steep, and my horse began to climb. Having made an attempt, and found it difficult, he rose on his hind legs, tried to turn round, and leap over the brink. By a great effort I pulled his head against the rocks and sprang off his back, when two Kirghis, who were on the platform, backed their horses, fearing to be carried over with us. The Cossack, who had witnessed the circumstance from above, leaped from his horse and hastened to my assistance. In a short time the animal was quieted and led up the ascent; nor did any other man attempt the risk—all dismounted, and passed the spot in safety. A few miles brought us to the route, when the Bee's men returned by a less hazardous path. We continued our ride to the aoul in the great gorge, and a little before dark I was welcomed by the young chiefs.

CHAP. IX.

A MOUNTAIN LAKE DRAINED BY AN EARTHQUAKE.

The difficulties and dangers that lay in the route I proposed to take were so formidable, that the only man who knew the country refused to accompany me; but on showing as a reward a flask of gunpowder and a few balls, his eyes sparkled with delight, and his objections vanished. All arrangements for the ascent having been completed, and a party sent back with our horses to the great water-course, we left the aoul. Turning our steeds towards the south branch of the pass, we rode up to the base of the basaltic cliffs, whence the view down the gorge was savagely grand.

While looking on this scene I could not avoid contrasting the puny efforts of man with these stupendous works of nature. How marvellously small the pyramids and temples of the Egyptians, and the great works of the Romans would appear, if placed at the foot of these towers of basalt, or near the shelving masses of trap, forming mighty stairs leading into the great recesses of the mountains, that in some parts are riven asunder, and horrible chasms seem to penetrate far towards their centre. Here was a place in which a legion of robbers might hide, or defend themselves against an army.

My company consisted of the two young chiefs, who had requested leave to join me; the old guide, three Kirghis, myself, and my two men. The young Kirghis were dressed in rich Chinese silk kalats, highly ornamented tchimbar, and richly embroidered silk caps turned up with fox-skin; they were mounted on splendid horses, which they sat with a firm and graceful seat. After riding more than two hours, sometimes between high precipices, at others rocky slopes, we arrived at a part of the pass so abrupt, that it was impossible to ascend on horseback; even on foot we found it no easy matter to scramble up. At last we reached a small level space, about twenty yards in length and four in width, when a scene was presented to us that few could look down upon without a shudder.

We were standing on the brink of a precipice, and looking into a fearful abyss, with dark overhanging crags, that gave the place a most terrific aspect. The rocks were of dark purple slate, with a few shrubs hanging from the cliffs; yellow and green moss covered the upper ledges, and at the bottom was a small lake, the water appearing of inky blackness. To the north, crags rose far above us: I climbed these, and got a better view into the Tartarian gulf below. To the south the mountain was so steep that it appeared impossible to find a path in that direction. This, however, was our only chance; but it was a route never taken by the Kirghis on their migrations.

We began our ascent by going in slanting lines, gaining but little at each tack, and turning our horses with great difficulty. As we ascended higher, each turning gave us a deeper view into the terrible abyss, with nothing to stop man or horse should either slip. After extraordinary toil and no little anxiety, we reached a part more easy to ascend, and riding on, in due time gained the crest of the mountain, where we turned towards the west, and saw that the day was fast declining. The old guide rode by my side, pointing out the peaks and crags near which we were to pass, proving that he possessed a good knowledge of the region, that for some reason he had wished to conceal. I was equally anxious to know something more about him, and inquired how he became so well acquainted with this wild country.

After a few questions to ascertain whence I came, and finding he had nothing to fear from me, he acknowledged that he had once belonged to a strong band of robbers, commanded by a celebrated chief, "Kinsara," whose name alone was sufficient to make the women and children tremble. The Kirghis quailed as he led on his wild bands; even the Russians, on the frontiers, dreaded his marauding expeditions. He had been the scourge of all the tribes, whom he often plundered, carrying off their camels, horses, men, women, and children. Indeed, his daring acts had so intimidated the Kirghis that no one dared to follow him into the mountains, amidst scenes so terrible that they believed them to be the veritable residence of the enemy of man.

We proceeded along a mountain ridge, sometimes at the base of high crags of dark igneous rocks, at others over parts covered with moss and short grass. Then we came into a labyrinth of rocks, through which it appeared impossible to find our way; but our robber-guide led on without once being at fault. We presently obtained a magnificent view of the snowy chain of the Ac-tau, stretching to the east and west. Its vast glaciers and high peaks were sparkling like rubies in the setting sun, while beneath several bold rocky ridges rose out of the haze; nearer to us we beheld a lower chain of mountains, and valleys covered with vegetation. This is the region where the Kirghis find their summer pastures.

A short ride brought us to the bank of a torrent, which we followed down into the valley, where we found a fine clump of birch and picta trees, and there we took up our night's lodgings. It was indeed a quiet spot, for not a sound could be heard, save the murmuring of the stream and our own voices. Near our encampment another narrow valley branched off to the southward, running up between high mountains and rugged precipices. At the end of the ravine rose some high cliffs, and far beyond these one of the highest peaks of the Ac-tau reared his mighty head, where the last rays of the sun were shining, lighting it up like a crimson beacon, while a gloomy twilight was creeping over us. The effect was singularly beautiful. Around us luxuriant summer vegetation was growing, intermingled with flowers blooming in all their glory. As the valley ascended both vegetation and flowers gradually diminished through every grade, till the moss on the rocks disappeared. Then came a scene of utter desolation, where the effects of the thundering avalanches are palpably visible, the wreck of which cut off the view of the glaciers, while the high peak, clothed in his cold wintry garb, looked inexpressibly ghastly and chilling.

Wishing to get a peep at my companions, I walked to a short distance, and beheld the group sitting around our camp fire. As the valley was shrouded in deep gloom, the strong red glare of our fire gave a peculiar character to the scene. The young chiefs, with their richly-coloured costumes, were sitting, surrounded by their followers, in anxious discussion, forming a picturesque group. At a little distance sat the old guide and my two Cossacks, in strong contrast with their neighbours: from the difference in garb of these men, they might have been taken for banditti guarding their prisoners and a rich booty. On the branches above them our arms were hanging and gleaming; and beyond these the horses were picketed, their heads just appearing in the blazing light. Having jotted down a few notes of this scene, I joined my companions. Our saddle cloths were presently spread on the ground, and very soon all, except the sentinel, were fast asleep.

Just as day dawned, I was roused by the neighing of one of the horses close to my ear; the Kirghis had turned them loose to feed, and this fellow had taken a fancy to some tufts of grass near my head. On looking round, I observed that my companions were still sleeping soundly. As yet the sun's rays had not touched the snowy peaks, and the entire chain beneath was enveloped in a grey misty haze.

Presently the people were roused, and each man was attending to his duties. The young chiefs spread their kalats on the grass and offered up their devotions; their example was followed by the other Kirghis and my men, each in his peculiar way. Leaving our encampment, the guide led the way across the valley to the southern branch: along this we rode for about three miles, and several of the scenes through which we passed were truly grand. The valley was covered with grass intermingled with flowers; among them several varieties of the anemone, that gave the place the appearance of a garden. In parts the precipices rose from 800 to 1,000 feet, their summits split into various-shaped turrets and pinnacles, and round many dwarf cedars were twining their branches, while shrubs and creeping plants were hanging from the clefts, covered with flowers of various hues. At one point huge buttresses jutted far out into the narrow valley, appearing, as we approached, to close up the ravine and stop all further progress. In these rocks I found great masses of a beautiful red jasper, from which I obtained some fine specimens. Having passed these, and ascended the valley about a mile, we had a magnificent view of the snowy chain of the Ac-tau.

Near the source of the Bascan, there was one very high peak, that had evidently been conical in form, and this had been torn asunder. One half only was standing; the rent was curved, and the upper part overhanging considerably. No snow could rest on this precipitous face, and the rocks appeared of a dark purple colour. The snow that had been accumulating on this mountain, probably for thousands of ages, was riven into perpendicular cliffs, 700 or 800 feet high, appearing like pentelic marble. This was a stupendous precipice, but the whole height could not be seen from our position: my impression, however, is, that it is more than 2,000 feet. I was most anxious to explore this region, and visit the ruins of the mountain; but my old guide declared it was impossible to continue our route in that direction.

Having reached a point where he changed our route, we turned towards the west, up a narrow and abrupt ravine, by which we were to ascend to the top of the cliffs. Here we

Ac-tau.

had to dismount, and lead our horses over places even difficult to pass on foot, and in about an hour we stood on the mountain slope, about 500 yards from the brink of the precipices. We had now ascended to about 1,000 feet above the valley, and this small difference in elevation had effected a wonderful change. Instead of fine grass and luxuriant herbage, short mossy turf and stunted plants covered the surface. I found the rhododendron chrysanthemum creeping among the rocks, with its dark shining green leaves and large bunches of beautiful yellow flowers. Even in sheltered situations, this plant never exceeds three feet in height; and is often found spreading over a large space, and covering the rocks with its ever-green foliage. A dwarf cedar was also trailing its branches among the masses of granite, extending to the length of fifty paces; the stems and branches twisted about the rocks like huge serpents coiling round them.

Our guide now led the way towards the crest of the ridge. After riding more than an hour, we left vegetation behind us, and began to pick our slow and toilsome way over a rough and stony region. At length we reached enormous masses of green slate, shooting up into high pinnacles, so smooth and perpendicular that they never can be ascended. Passing round to the southward of these, we came upon a scene of terrible disruption and desolation, where rocks had been uprooted and hurled down into one chaotic mass, of a most fearful aspect, extending to the brink of a vast rent that had cut the mountain asunder.

A terrible convulsion must have taken place here. I had felt the heaving of the ground during an earthquake when in a valley to the westward, and had listened to an awful sound, as it approached, deep in the bowels of the earth, that had apparently passed beneath me. I had heard the appalling subterranean thunder as it rolled through the mountains, and now I beheld the terrific effects of one of these fearful visitations. I had read of the destruction of cities, of cathedrals being overthrown, and the most solid works of man strewn about like reeds. But what was the power that laid those in ruins, in comparison with that which had rushed through this region?—rending the mountains in twain, and forming chasms, wherein the boldest man cannot look without feelings of dread.

Having spent a short time contemplating this wonderful scene, we left the spot and rode along the edge of the fallen rocks for about two miles. At length we arrived on the brink of the terrible chasm, where it descended in a series of deep precipices. Beyond this point our horses could not proceed, and here we had to part with our friends. Before separating we sat down at a little spring, and ate our simple dinner,—a few small pieces of hard Kirghis cheese, washed down by water from the rill. Game is not abundant in this region: during the whole of our ride we had only seen two small herds of argali, and in both instances they were far out of the range of our rifles.

Our guide did not permit us to sit long; he urged our speedy departure, knowing the difficulties we had to encounter. After saying "aman-bul," the young chiefs and their followers sprung into their saddles and rode away, intending to sleep at our last night's encampment. We watched their retiring forms till they were lost behind the rocks, and then commenced our descent into the fearful gulf. The way down was in an oblique direction for about 200 paces, after which we turned the steep rocks—clinging as well as we could to the projecting points. Having gained a narrow ledge, extending along the top of a high precipice, the Kirghis led the way onward till we came to a break in the rocks.

Here a part of the precipice had fallen, forming a stony slope, both steep and dangerous, with another perpendicular cliff at its base, where huge masses were overhanging, that appeared ready to topple into the gulf at the slightest touch. We stood for a few minutes looking at this rugged and dangerous spot with dread, fearing, if we attempted to descend, the stones would give way and carry us into the depths below. As there was no other path, the guide stepped on to the stony mass, when all followed. It was no easy matter clambering over the huge blocks, nor was it without many slips and some bruises that we reached the terrace, which I found ten to fifteen paces wide, and covered with bushes and plants. From this point we could discern the fearful depth beneath us.

We proceeded along the terrace, that gradually descended to the westward, narrowing to a mere ledge, and ultimately forming a most rugged staircase, not more than three feet wide, and in some parts even less. This had a most ugly appearance; but, by the aid of the bushes, we let ourselves down over many fearful places, and reached a steep part covered with fallen rocks, where poplar and birch trees were growing, with numerous shrubs concealing the cavities, and rendering our progress both slow and dangerous. We next came upon another narrow terrace covered with luxuriant vegetation, in some parts reaching above our heads. From the edge of this nearly level space, a slope descended to a great depth, and so abruptly that it was impossible to find a footing there.

The guide led us along through beds of plants, in which we lost sight of each other. We had not, however, gone far when we discovered a well-trodden track made by a large animal that the Kirghis at once pronounced to be a barse. Our rifles were instantly examined, and creeping cautiously along, we reached the lair of the beast, where we found positive evidence that a tiger had recently been. As the Kirghis declined leading the van, I walked beside him, rifle in hand, the other men close behind us. We followed the animal's track along the terrace about 200 yards, and then found he had turned down into the gorge, among rocks and thick bushes we could not penetrate.

Leaving his path we pushed on through the thick vegetation, and came to a point beyond which it seemed impossible to proceed. The place was formed of granite rocks, descending nearly perpendicular, with a few bushes growing from the clefts — the mass presenting numerous jutting points and fissures, our only aids in overcoming the difficulties of our descent. At length we arrived in safety on another grassy slope, that led us to the brink of the last precipice. Having reached this place, we all stood looking at the wild scene before us, lost in wonder. The opposite side of the gorge was equally rugged and abrupt with that we had descended. We beheld stupendous precipices with large trees growing at their base; shrubs and creeping plants were hanging from the fissures, that gave a softer, but a more sublime character, to the scene than when viewed from above.

As the eye wandered over these vast and rugged cliffs, scanning the various forms they assumed, they reminded me of the battlements Milton makes the fallen angels scale, after leaving Pandemonium. At one part a line of stony turrets was standing on this vast wall, receding into hazy distance; in another, a huge mass, 700 or 800 feet high, was quite isolated from the precipice by a great chasm, having around its base large trees covered with green and yellow foliage, contrasting beautifully with the red and purple rocks. Beneath these was a slope composed of débris fallen from the cliffs above, now covered with moss of almost every hue, and extending to the bottom of the pass. The ground appeared covered with grass, but the great depth made it look intensely gloomy. Looking up the gorge towards the south, I saw several of the snowy peaks of the Ac-tau gleaming in the sun, while all around us was in deep shade.

Having transferred this scene to my sketch-book, we continued our march downward, scrambling over many difficult spots, and reached the bottom, to our infinite delight. Close to the foot of the rocks we found the bed of a torrent, in which a small stream was leaping and bubbling over the large stones heaped up in its channel. Following the stream down this tremendous defile for about half a mile, we saw a track, by which the wild animals come down to drink,—the footprints of the argali, large deer, and the wild goat, were found; but no trace of the tiger. We were certain that he was in the gorge; but having no time to spare for hunting, he was left to his own devices.

Proceeding onward, we presently came to a part where

The Great Gorge.

the water disappeared beneath the rocks. The defile here became narrower, and the precipices were riven into numerous fissures, with large cavities extending into the rocks. Down one of these rents a small waterfall was pouring; its upper part being invisible to us, but the last leap was from a cliff between 500 and 600 feet above our heads. Soon after bounding over the ledge of rock, the stream was wafted about by the breeze, like fine gauze floating in the air. As it descended lower the water was dispersed in white spray, that fell upon us as we passed like a Scotch mist, and quickly produced a similar effect. I deeply regret not having seen this fall during a storm in the mountains; it would then be sublime.

After passing this the gorge became narrower, till we could not see 100 paces before us. At length it became a mere fissure, in some parts only twenty-two paces wide, in others twenty-five, varying from 1,000 to 1,200 feet in height. On one side the rocks were overhanging, on the other receding, having all the appearance of being able to fit into each other, could any power be found to reunite them. The bottom was strewn with gigantic blocks of granite, slate, and jasper, that had been rolled on and rounded by the torrent. Sometimes the water rushes down this place, filling it to the height of thirty-five feet, as was clearly shown by the lines on the face of the rocks. At these times no pencil could delineate the impetuosity of the water, or pen describe the thundering of the flood, as it must have rushed through this fearful chasm.

After proceeding about half a mile, which occupied more than an hour, climbing over large stones covering the bottom of the gorge, we emerged from the terrible cleft into an enormous oval-shaped valley. Scrambling up the side of a channel, cut by the torrent to a depth of sixty feet, caused us much trouble and some risk. On reaching the top of the bank I found we were on luxuriant pastures, covered with flowers. As our guide recognised the spot his eyes sparkled with delight,—we were on one of the encamping grounds of Kinsara, and no doubt it recalled to the old man's mind many scenes of festal enjoyment after successful barantas. He pointed to a place on the north-west side of the valley, near some high precipices, as the locality of the Sultan's yourts. Farther to the west, he indicated the position of the aoul of his band, and directed my attention right across the valley, to a point near the bank of a torrent, as the spot where a party had always been stationed to guard the pass.

We were now in a deep valley, from four to five miles in width, and nearly twenty in length, and surrounded by mountains, varying from 5,000 to 7,000 feet in height, from which there appeared no outlet. The sun was shining brightly, and we found it intensely hot; still, the grass was green and the flowers blooming beautifully,—proving that they received plenty of moisture. So great was the change on leaving the deep and gloomy gorge, and entering this sunny spot, that it entirely removed a sense of oppression created by the rugged scenes I had passed. Standing for a short time on one of the heaps of stones the torrent had piled up, I examined the view around, and clearly perceived that this had once been a mountain lake of vast depth.

Going towards the base of the cliffs on the eastward, I passed several scattered heaps of large rounded blocks of granite, with patches of sand and shells around them; but none perfect. Had I possessed the necessary implements for excavation, I should no doubt have found good specimens. On reaching the cliffs, I saw large masses of light-green slate, washed down from the strata above, that had been thrown up, at this point, nearly perpendicular. The line was also distinctly visible along the face of the cliffs, where the action of the water had smoothed the rocks.

Having, with much difficulty, climbed the precipice, about 560 feet, I observed great cavities formed by the water; and the slate broken away and rounded. Above this part there were no cavities, and all the rocks were angular and sharp. Thus a line was distinctly marked along the face of the cliffs, indicating the water-level.

During the time I had been thus engaged, the guide had become impatient, frequently assuring my men that we should not be able to get through the pass before dark, and that it would be impossible to proceed in the night. I therefore ordered our march to be resumed, and proceeded in the direction of Kinsara's old encampment, apparently about six miles distant. We shortly reached the dry channel of the torrent, and found it no easy matter descending and ascending its steep and rugged banks. Our way was over a thick grassy turf, with occasional patches of sand and pebbles, among which I found several beautiful agates. Here I again discovered numerous shells, and, after digging up a few inches of sand with my dagger, came upon a bed containing several kinds.

Having gone about three miles, we reached another deep channel coming from the south-west, in which a rapid stream was running over a rocky bed. The guide led the way up the bank to a point where he knew we could ford it without difficulty. Here the stream was about twenty yards wide, and deeper than agreeable, for in one part it was near five feet, and exceedingly cold,—proving that it came from a snowy source at no great distance. My old robber-guide informed me that this river was swallowed up in a cavern in the mountain,—a most horrible place; and that no one dare approach, as Shaitan had his dwelling there.

Shortly after passing the river we found the head and horns of a large stag, the body having been devoured not more than two days before; most probably by a tiger. The old man said that these beasts had sometimes killed their horses here. A little further on we found the well-known footprints on the sand: by these we judged he was a fine large animal, and one who would give us some trouble should we encounter him. We hastened onward, as the sun was lengthening our shadows fast, and he would soon be lost behind the purple mountains to the west. Just at dark we reached our resting-place, where we found a comfortable berth under some overhanging masses of granite, that had been scooped out by water; and here we lost no time in taking our glass of tea, with a few scraps of soaked ai-ran. Few Europeans would have envied us either our frugal supper or the stony couches on which we were to rest. The first, however, appeased hunger, and on the latter we slept soundly.

When darkness spread its mantle over the valley, shutting out of view the mountains to the south, we had nothing to look upon except the river and serrated cliffs rising above us. These were partly lit up by the flickering light of our fire, that gave a spectral appearance to their singular forms. Our little party was scarcely sufficient to break the solitude of this lonely spot, that had often rung with the wild shouts of a lawless band. This was the place on which Kinsara had lived and held his daring associates in subjection. My guide told me that no one of the band ever dared to disobey his orders, as doing so would have been certain death. He had acquired unbounded power over the minds of his followers, by his indomitable courage. If a desperate attack had to be made against fearful odds, he led the van, and was ever first in the fight,—shouting his war-cry with uplifted battle-axe, and plunging his fiery steed into the thickest of the battle. This gave confidence to his men, and was the secret of his success; but the Kirghis thought he was in league with Shaitan, and that no steel could touch him.

At the foot of these rocks many a man had rested before being sold into slavery, often seeing his wives and children divided among his captors. The guide told me that the band consisted of more than 300 men, many of whom were desperate characters,—convicts, escaped from the Chinese penal settlements on the Ili. As we sat around our little fire, watching the red glare upon the rocks, we were suddenly startled by a vivid flash of lightning, that for a moment illumined the whole valley and adjacent mountains with a pale blue light. We were almost blinded, and the next instant left in thick darkness. A heavy roll of thunder now echoed among the mountains on the opposite side of the ridge under which we were encamped. Several other flashes followed, all equally grand; but the storm passed along the chain, and did not reach us in the valley. Having piled a quantity of bushes on the fire, and placed our rifles at hand in case of need, we turned down on our stony couches, and were shortly revelling in the land of dreams.

A little after midnight our slumbers were broken by a tremendous clap of thunder, that caused every man to spring up. For a few moments we were lost in amazement, fancying that the rocks were falling. Nothing, however, could be seen; it was impenetrable darkness, and our eyes tried in vain to peer into the black canopy that hung over the valley. Before the echoes of the first peal had died away, there came a flash, rending the black pall asunder, and showing the fearful billowy clouds above us, receding in endless perspective, while it filled the valley for a few moments with a blaze of reddish light, far more intense than the meridian sun, making every surrounding crag visible. Nearly at the same instant there were three or four quick reports, like guns, and then a fearful crash, that seemed to make the rocks tremble. Before this had rolled off there came another, and another, till it was one incessant roar, and the flashes followed each other in quick succession.

Presently another sound was heard—the roaring of the wind, and the approaching storm of rain; this caused us to retire farther under the rocks: gradually the sound came nearer, which to me was more appalling than the crashing thunder. In a few minutes the fearful blast swept past;

then came the rushing rain, that was shortly changed into a terrific storm of hail, quickly covering the ground; while every few minutes streams of lightning darted around us, calling to mind that sublime scene where "fire, mingled with hail, ran along upon the ground." In about two hours the storm had passed; but it left an indelible impression on my mind.

The night, with its fearful storms, passed over, and morning dawned with a serene sky; and long before the sun cast his rays into the valley, we had left our granite beds. While tea was preparing, I rambled along the base of the cliffs, and found additional indications of this basin having once been a lake. About half a mile to the west of our encampment, there were heaps of rounded granite blocks, strewn over a sandy shore; also several isolated masses, varying from 100 to 300 feet in height, were standing about sixty yards from the base of the precipices. The sharp angles of all these masses had been worn away by water, and the cliffs at this part were much undermined, in some places forming recesses forty and sixty feet deep.

At one place I found a great triangular-shaped mass, 130 yards on its sides, and about 450 feet high. This was pierced through by natural arches, formed on each face, thirty-two yards wide, and of greater height, leaving the upper part standing on three great abutments. The scene was strikingly grand; and while sketching this beautiful object, the sun rose, and I beheld part of his crimson orb through one of the natural arches, giving quite a magical effect to the landscape. Nature had completed this structure thousands of ages before the monks of Crowland built their triangular bridge. It was to me a matter of deep regret, that time did not permit me to extend my rambles along this shore still farther to the westward, as I perceived many other isolated masses and some beautiful scenes in that direction.

Having returned to my companions, our morning meal was soon dispatched, when the old guide led me to the very spot on which his daring chief had lived: this was sacred ground to him, and his eye moistened as we turned away from the spot. We visited several other places which he examined with intense interest, and then came to the spot where his

A Mass of Granite Rocks, with Natural Arches.

yourt had stood. There were the black ashes of his own hearth: he looked at these for a few minutes, and then led the way to the eastward. As he strode along he often looked back, evidently lingering affectionately over a locality that had called up many pleasant recollections.

We continued our march along the base of the granite

cliffs, in some places along patches of sand and broken shells, and in others over a fine grassy turf. After going about two miles, we reached a deep circular indentation, extending into the mountain about a mile. The bottom was strewn with blocks of granite, and the precipices rose to an enormous height, some to more than 1,000 feet. Crossing this bay, we reached the opposite headland, and then beheld the rent in the mountain through which we expected to make our exit, and join our friends on the steppe.

A walk of nearly two hours brought us to the bank of the torrent we forded yesterday, and not far from its entrance into the great ravine. The guide informed me that there were two tracks by which we could cross the mountains. One was down the gorge and much shorter, but was both difficult and dangerous; the other was a little way to the east, and over the mountains: by this route Kinsara's band always rode their horses. I at once decided to follow the ravine at all risks, as it would take me to the cavern so much dreaded by the Kirghis, and into it the torrent plunged. The entrance to the chasm was about 120 yards wide, covered with fallen rocks, over and among which the torrent went leaping and foaming with great fury.

Our way was a rough and dangerous one over fallen rocks, sometimes 200 and 300 feet above the stream, and often nearly perpendicular down to the level of the water. These we were compelled to descend by clinging to the shrubs and rocks as best as we could: a tumble or a slip here would have sent us into the raging torrent. Having proceeded about two miles, and that with great toil, we arrived at a part of the gorge where the slate was heaved up into nearly a perpendicular position by the granite, and both kinds of rocks were lying about in the wildest confusion. At this point the torrent rushed down a steep rapid more than 500 yards in length, and then bounded over a fall of about sixty feet. Looking up the rapid, the water appeared like flakes of snow, as it dashed over and against the dark rocks in its bed. This was a sublime scene: the high towering crags rugged and picturesque in form, and tinted with the most brilliant hues; the chaos of rocks piled up in the gorge, with trees of enormous size growing from the cavities, but reduced to dwarfs by contrast with the mighty cliffs; and then the surging and roaring water, combined, formed a picture of unsurpassed grandeur and beauty.

Continuing our way onward, we reached a spot beyond which, to all appearance, we could not proceed. We were now a little above the torrent that was hidden from our view, and immediately before us the cliffs rose up like a wall to an enormous height. Their tops were riven into pinnacles, some of them leaning so far over the brink as to excite our wonder at their stability. A loud roaring of water was heard near at hand, and it induced me to suppose that the stream was rolling over a fall. Passing along huge blocks of red and purple porphyry, straight towards the base of the cliffs, we came to some enormous masses it was impossible to climb. After scrambling round the end of one of these, we stood before a cleft formed in the fallen mass. This looked a dark and dismal place; still the guide led on, groping his way through the gloom. I followed close at his heels, and our two companions were immediately behind me. Having threaded our way through this fissure for about fifty yards, we emerged into daylight upon a narrow ledge overhanging the torrent.

What a terrific scene burst upon me! I was standing before the portal these wild people say leads into the regions of Tartarus. In front a dark jutting precipice almost closed the chasm: it rose nearly perpendicular not less than 1,800 feet. A few small bushes were growing in the crevices near its summit, with scattered plants on the upper ledges, and in this Cyclopean mass was the terrible cavern swallowing up the river. All were silent with astonishment, and we stood watching the torrent rush on into the fearful abyss, producing a sound that created such a feeling of dread, I ceased to wonder at the convictions of the Kirghis.

The entrance to this cavern is formed by a vast and rugged archway, about fifty feet wide and seventy feet high. The various-coloured mosses on the dark rocks give them a bronzed and metallic appearance, quite in character with the scene. Through this dismal opening the river passed in a channel thirty feet wide, and apparently ten feet deep. A stony ledge about twelve feet wide formed a terrace along the edge of the stream, just above the level of the water, and extended into the cave till lost in darkness.

When my amazement had somewhat subsided, I prepared to explore the cavern, by placing my packet of baggage and my rifle on the rocks, and the two Cossacks followed my example. The guide watched these proceedings with great interest, but when he beheld us enter the gloomy cave, he was horrified. Having proceeded about twenty paces, the noise caused by the falling water became fearful, and a damp chilling blast met us. Beyond this point the cavern extended both in width and height, but I could form no idea of its dimensions. We cautiously groped our way on; and as my eyes gradually became more accustomed to the gloom, I could distinguish the broken floor and the rushing water. Having gone about eighty yards from the entrance, we could see the river bound into a terrific abyss, "black as Erebus," while some white vapour came wreathing up, giving the spot a most supernatural appearance.

It was an awful place, and few persons could stand on the brink of this gulf without a shudder, while the roaring of the water was appalling as it resounded in the lofty dome over our heads. It was utterly impossible to hear a word spoken, nor could this scene be contemplated long; there was something too fearful for the strongest nerves, when trying to peer into these horrible depths. At last we turned away and looked towards the opening by which we had entered. For a short distance the sides and arch were lighted up, but the great space and vast dome were lost in darkness.

Shaitan's Cavern.

I sat down on a rock about fifty yards from the entrance, and in the twilight made a sketch of the cavern.

After remaining more than two hours in this dismal place, I was not sorry to be once more in the light of day. The old man was delighted when he saw me leave the abode of Shaitan, and urged our instant departure, saying the way was long and difficult. We quickly shouldered our arms and baggage, passed round the jutting rocks, and entered the narrow chasm beyond. Its bed was covered with large and small rounded stones, proving that water had once flowed through this part of the gorge, and I have no doubt it does still during the great storms in the mountains. As we proceeded onward, the ravine narrowed into a mere rent with overhanging rocks, rendering the place dark and dismal. Through this part our progress was slow and tedious; but in about an hour we came to a place where the gorge divided into two branches, one going towards the north and the other to the north-east. The guide said the latter, which was the widest, did not extend far into the mountains; but on proceeding up this branch, I found it a very picturesque ravine. The bottom was strewn with masses of dolomite fallen from the high and overhanging cliffs, and a small torrent was rushing down the middle, forming many beautiful cascades. Numerous flowering shrubs and bushes were growing among the fallen rocks, and many creeping plants were hanging from the clefts.

We continued our march by the side of the torrent: sometimes it was bridged by huge masses that had been hurled from their beds above. In one place our passage onward seemed completely stopped, the whole gorge being filled with fallen rocks to the height of 200 feet, over which we found it no easy matter to climb. This mass of débris extended about 500 yards, and the torrent found its way beneath. The precipices on both sides of the ravine had recently fallen, apparent by the shrubs with their withered green leaves strewn over the rocks. We crossed this chaos with much difficulty, and not without considerable apprehension, caused by the appearance of several huge blocks that were hanging on the cliffs, as if ready to fall with the slightest shake. Having gone about two miles, we arrived at another rent in the mountain. This chasm extended to the westward, down which came a rushing stream, hissing and boiling, on its course.

From the loud roaring in this great fissure, I was certain that there was a waterfall at no great distance. The guide could not be induced to enter, so one Cossack remained with him, and the other accompanied me into the chasm. It was not more than fifty feet wide, with precipices rising 1,000 to 1,200 feet above us. Having proceeded about 100 yards, I came to a sudden turn in the cleft, where the rocks closed over so much that the sky could not be seen. It was indeed a gloomy twilight and a dismal-looking place, in which all objects were but dimly shadowed forth; even the sparkling water, that was dashed into spray as it broke over the rocks, had a strange supernatural appearance. It now required care in stepping over the green and slippery stones, that rendered our progress slow; but the roaring of the fall became louder every few minutes, adding much to the fearful effect of the place.

After groping our way on about 300 yards without getting a gleam of daylight, we entered a wider part of the chasm, and beheld the sun shining on the crags. They were fringed with bushes and plants, that were swinging about with the breeze more than 1,200 feet over our heads. Looking up at these from the dismal depth, their foliage appeared bathed in glorious light; this, and the glowing sky above, would have made a poet fancy that he was gazing from the shades of death into Elysium. From this point we hurried onward, and the noise of the waterfall became deafening. Presently we caught a glimpse of white vapour, and in a few minutes stood before a sheet of falling water, that came bounding from a rocky ledge

300 feet above us. It fell into a deep basin, out of which it came seething as from a cauldron.

Looking upwards, the scene was sublime: three successive falls were visible, leaping from rock to rock, and flinging their white spray into mid-air. The precipices have been worn by water into pillars and columns, and round them the spray and vapour were curling in wreaths as the wind wafted them upward. In front of the middle fall stands an enormous mass of dark rock quite isolated, and from sixty to seventy feet in height. The falling water strikes upon the head of this, and is thrown off in innumerable jets, forming a crystalline crown for the stony monarch of the chasm; while thin sheets of water descended over his sides, clothing him with a liquid garment through which his gigantic form was indistinctly visible. From behind this mass a cloud of vapour rises, that covers the rugged crags above as with a veil, gently wafted up by the breeze. Still higher there were other falls, but invisible to us; and, unfortunately, we could discover no part by which it was possible to climb the tremendous precipices.

Here was a fine study for a geologist—the rocks having been riven asunder, and their formation exposed to the depth of 1,500 feet; while to the lover of the savage and sublime, it was worth a pilgrimage. After retracing my steps, the guide led on down the gorge at a brisk pace. Our march was now by the side of a roaring torrent, over which we were compelled to pass several times; and it could only be accomplished with great difficulty and considerable risk. On one side of the chasm dark frowning precipices rise up to a great height, and from these prodigious buttresses project, crowned with huge pinnacles. Facing these are deep recesses in the cliffs; clearly indicating that these enormous masses have been torn asunder by some colossal power.

In about an hour after leaving the waterfall we reached a wider part of the gorge, less abrupt on one side. Farther down, I saw that the rocks rose from the edge of the torrent, without even a ledge whereon to set our feet. To proceed onward down the ravine was impossible, and to climb the rocks before us appeared equally so. The guide pointed to a place at the top of the cliffs, at least 1,500 feet above, to which we must ascend; but to do this required both good heads and strong hands. Having rested a few minutes, each man strapped his package firmly on his shoulders, and then I gave the word "march."

The old man led on to a mass of débris: up this we clambered to a ledge, and gradually ascended to the base of some perpendicular rocks, rising to a great height. On reaching these I found some were torn from the precipices, and standing quite isolated; in other parts fissures were rent in their sides, and in one we began to scale the towering cliffs. We had not ascended far when I had proof that the guide was on the right track, for some pieces of wood had been driven into the bed of the rocks, to hold on by in this perilous path. Our progress was slow and laborious. As each new point was gained we scanned the crags above, to which it seemed almost impossible to climb. At length we reached a grassy ledge, about 500 feet above the torrent, whence we could look into the gorge and see where the water filled up the whole space.

After resting a short time we commenced toiling our way up in many a zigzag line, often swinging ourselves past jutting rocks by the aid of bushes we found growing in the clefts. Having reached the base of some rocks that formed a complete bar to our further progress, our guide for a moment looked bewildered. He soon, however, discovered that we had taken a wrong track, and quickly descended about fifty feet and found the right one. We joined him, and then proceeded onward to the foot of some lofty slate crags of a deep red colour. Round these we had to creep along a narrow ledge with a perpendicular wall of rock, nearly 600 feet beneath us. This was a most dangerous-looking place, and fearful to pass along. Our packs and rifles were taken from our shoulders, and we prepared to push them on before us. After crawling on in this way for about thirty yards, we turned round the rocks and reached a grassy terrace about twenty feet wide; greatly comforted with the assurance that we had passed the worst part of the ascent.

Looking down into the dark and yawning chasm, with the foaming and roaring torrent 1,200 feet beneath, tried the nerves severely, while the opposite cliffs were so near that the Cossacks and myself threw stones across that struck the rocks. A little further to the north I saw that the chasm became a mere rent; in one place the upper slaty masses projecting so far that a stone dropped from their edge would have struck the opposite side before reaching mid-way down; and so little had the hand of time affected these masses, that each projection would have fitted into the recess in front. Having rested a short time to breathe, we began our last ascent with fresh vigour. As we turned away, the precipices seemed to unite, forming a most stupendous archway.

The path even now was sufficiently abrupt: sometimes we had to climb the almost perpendicular cliffs, clinging to the bushes, by the aid of which we reached the small terraces that led us upwards. From one of these we beheld a group of Argali about 100 yards from us; but before any rifle could be unslung, they galloped past some rocks and were lost to our view. In a few minutes they appeared again on the top of some lofty crags, but far out of our reach; they stood watching our movements for several minutes, and then scampered off.

At last, after much toil, we stood on the summit, having been two hours and forty minutes making the ascent. What a savage and desolate scene was now before me! To the south the crest of the mountain rose up nearly 4,000 feet above us, riven into lofty crags; enormous rocks were lying tumbled about into a wild chaotic mass, extending from the brink of the gorge several miles to the westward. To the east were similar confused masses, and the ridge terminated in a rugged and lofty peak. The view to the northward was over vast plains, but no signs of

Looking down on to the Kirghis Steppe.

either man or animal were visible. It was a dreary solitude, over which the last rays of the sun were shedding a golden light, and casting long shadows from the objects around us.

From this point the chasm turned slightly towards the east for about 500 yards, and then it ran in a northerly direction till lost to my view. After carefully examining the precipices during our march through the ravine and our last ascent, I became fully convinced that this stupendous chasm had been formed at once by a fearful earthquake that had rent the mountains asunder, and let out the water of the lake.

The guide was not satisfied with my delay; he was impatient to be gone, as we had still a long march to the steppe. Proceeding in a north-westerly direction, and leaving the gorge considerably to our right, we soon reached a grassy turf, among which numerous flowers were growing, some of great beauty, particularly a deep crimson variety, that was trailing its delicate branches along the grass. The grey tints of twilight, however, told me there was no time for botanizing, and we hastened onward. In little more than an hour we attained a very abrupt part of the mountain, from which we looked down on the last low ridge. This appeared about three miles across, and at a short distance beyond we saw the fire of our companions blazing brightly. From here the descent was steep; but we proceeded at a good speed, as night was rapidly advancing. In about an hour and a half we reached the crest of the last low hill, and now it was quite dark: as we descended darkness rendered the track difficult, and no signs of our friends were visible. When near the bottom, we turned past some rocks, and saw the fire about half a mile distant. We instantly fired a volley from our rifles: in a few minutes a bright flame rose up, and the ascending sparks told that our signal had been heard. Shortly afterwards I was comfortably sitting at our camp, not sorry at having safely concluded an adventurous day's journey of sixteen hours.

Immediately after breakfast next morning, the old guide, two men, and myself, started for the ravine. We rode our horses as far as possible; but before reaching the mouth of the gorge, large stones compelled us to proceed on foot. Leaving our horses in charge of one man, we scrambled on and tried to penetrate farther. As we approached the mountain, the channel became narrower, and the whole bed covered with stones. A few of vast dimensions were heaped up, showing the tremendous power of water when rushing through these narrow gorges.

Near the outlet from the mountain, rocks have been piled up to the height of 100 feet, extending 200 yards in width, and more than 400 down towards the plain. Here are materials for a vast pyramid, quarried by nature and ready for the builder; they have been torn from the heart of the mountain, and thrown upon this spot, by "water power." Both mason and sculptor would find material in this mass on which to employ their chisels for ages to come. Here are blocks of granite, marble, jasper, slate, and porphyry, with various other rocks, some of them of enormous dimensions and beautiful colour, and the whole heaped up in the wildest disorder. This great mass has turned the stream a little to the westward, after which it has ploughed its enormous channel through the steppe.

We proceeded up the bed of the torrent; here it is about 120 yards in width, but becomes gradually less, till it is reduced to eighty yards at the mouth of the gorge. This was not formed by grassy slopes, as in many other passes: perpendicular rocky banks rose up, increasing in height as we came nearer the mountain. After going about half a mile the ravine had narrowed to about forty yards in width; and here were slate cliffs 500 to 600 feet high. The bottom of the gorge was heaped up to a considerable height with fallen rocks, from beneath which the stream gushed forth. Having climbed to the top of this mass of débris, we had a rough path over the huge blocks, and then descended to the bed of a torrent that frequently changed its course from one side to the other, and rendered it extremely difficult to proceed.

At this part the gorge made a turn to the eastward, and appeared quite closed; but on passing a projecting mass, we had a splendid view. Another high barrier crossed the ravine, over which the torrent was falling. A few hundred yards beyond, white cliffs were seen rising to a great height, with numerous small picta trees growing on the narrow terraces and slopes. On reaching the rugged embankment, I found that this was also a mass of débris, that dammed up the torrent, and formed a small lake that stopped all further explorations in this direction. I had, however, convinced myself that the water that had burst from the mountain lake had formed the enormous channel through the plain. In other regions of the steppes there are dry beds of former rivers, nearly equal in width to this, but not more than twenty feet deep. I am inclined to believe that they have also been formed by similar causes, as great disruptions have occurred in these mountain chains.

After I had sketched the wild scene we returned to our friends, when I gave the old guide his well-earned reward, making it two pounds of gunpowder, in a leathern bottle, fifty rifle balls, and a small piece of lead. He was in an ecstasy of delight, and insisted on accompanying me to the aoul, along with the two men of his tribe who had brought our horses: most reluctantly I was compelled to consent to this arrangement. While we had been exploring the ravine, one of the Cossacks had been hunting, and had brought back a deer—parts of which were already cooked. As our appetites were sharpened by the mountain air, we fell to with a good will; and no alderman ever enjoyed his venison better.

Ascending the high and abrupt bank from the great water-course caused us some trouble; but we succeeded in leading our horses to the top without accident—gave them a short breathing, and then rode on at a good pace. The Kirghis belonging to Djani-bek said that he intended removing his aoul to other pastures the day after we left him. I therefore ordered our march in the direction to where it was expected we should find his tribe. Our way was along the foot of the mountains, over rough ground, consisting of coarse gravel, with numerous masses of large stones strewn over the surface, and without any vegetation. In some parts the mountains to the south rose up in shelving precipices of dark purple slate, in others the granite appeared, having caused great disruption.

After proceeding over this stony desert for more than four hours, we reached a grassy steppe just as the sun was sinking below the horizon. As in these regions there is little twilight, we lost no time in ascending one of the low ridges, to enable the Kirghis who accompanied me to look out for the aoul of Djani-bek,—my present destination; but no sign of habitation on the vast plain, or of life, was visible before us. We continued our journey at a rapid gallop, but in less than an hour it became too dark to distinguish objects at a short distance. This compelled us to slacken our speed, after a ride of about five miles. Though our guide thought the aoul was at hand, no fires could be seen in any direction, nor the voice of a dog heard.

A halt was ordered; some of the men dismounted and laid their heads on the ground, hoping to hear a bark, but were disappointed. The Kirghis being completely at fault, I suggested that we should extend our lines and proceed slowly, by which means we might probably stumble on our friends. But after having continued our progress a considerable time without the desired result, I called a council to determine our course. After due consideration we again extended our line, proceeding in a northerly direction. A light was at last observed at a great distance to the eastward. At once the men were called in, we turned our horses, and rode towards it at a brisk pace. More than an hour had elapsed when the fire we had descried gradually decreased, and finally went out. I now ordered a volley to be fired from our rifles, and the vociferous barking of dogs at no great distance to our left, proved that the experiment had not been unsuccessful.

Presently we reached a Kirghis encampment, where, as before, we caused a great commotion; but the usual explanation was quickly followed by the customary welcome. In a few minutes I found myself standing close to several sleeping children, and near two young maidens, who were just unrolling themselves out of their voilocks. It is unpleasant to enter a Kirghis abode that has been closed several hours. The strong scent of the koumis bag, mingled with various other odours from biped and quadruped, makes the intruder start back with horror, as plague and other deadly maladies are instantly suggested. One of my Cossacks threw open the top of the yourt, and the fire carried off the noxious effluvia, otherwise it would have been impossible to endure them.

The great cauldron was quickly placed on its iron tripod, when a goodly portion of brick tea, clotted cream, and the other ingredients were thrown into it. Looking at the size of the vessel, I thought there was sufficient to feast a multitude. The people now crowded round to gaze at the stranger who had so unceremoniously entered their abodes. A Cossack was standing near the fire preparing my little somervar, while the inmates watched him with intense interest. During these operations I had time to examine the dwelling, with my host and his family, and a strong flickering light from the fire enabled me to scan each individual.

The chief's name was Kairan: he was a man about fifty years of age, had a dark swarthy or dirty complexion, with broad and heavy features, a wide mouth, small and deeply-set black eyes, a well-formed nose, and a large forehead. His head was shaved, and he wore a closely-fitting blue kanfa cap, embroidered with silver and coloured silks. His neck was as thick and as sturdy as one of his bulls; he was broad-shouldered and strongly built: taking him altogether, he was a powerful man. His dress was a Kokhan cotton kalat striped with yellow, red, and green, reaching down to his feet, and was tied round his waist with a red and green shawl.

His two wives had on sheepskin coats, in which they slept, and high pointed cotton caps. I cannot say that their night gear was particularly clean or interesting, still it may have a charm for a Kirghis. The heads of four children were peeping from their fur coverings, and one, a girl about six years old, crept out, showing that they were not troubled with night-gowns. Near to the children there was a pen in which three young kids slept, and on the opposite side of the yourt four young lambs had a similar berth. These were the inmates of a dwelling twenty-five feet in diameter; besides which, the space was still farther curtailed by a pile of boxes, carpets, and other chattels.

Having seated myself on a carpet spread in front of the boxes, the Cossacks placed my tea apparatus before me, and possessing four glasses, I was enabled to serve my host and his wives with the beverage. Several of the chief's followers were sitting in the yourt, intently watching my proceedings. When I handed tea to the women they evidently thought me a barbarian, as no man with any breeding among their tribes would serve a female until every man and boy had been satisfied. Before Kairan went to sleep he informed me that many tribes were on their march towards the mountains, and that great numbers were encamped to the westward. After receiving this news I turned down without ceremony on the place where I had been sitting; a Cossack spread a carpet over me, and then rolled himself up in another. A Kirghis put out the fire, and let down the top of the yourt, shutting us up in utter darkness; but a long ride over these dreary plains is an excellent promoter of sleep. My Cossack was soon snoring, and in a few minutes I was lost to either sound or scent.

CHAP. X.

KIRGHIS EMIGRATION TO THEIR SUMMER PASTURES.

In the morning I beheld a scene that can only be witnessed in these pastoral regions. The aoul consisted of thirteen yourts, in which there were twenty-nine men, thirty-four women, and twenty-six children. They had encamped here only two days before, and the remainder of the tribe were far to the northward. The yourts were put up in a temporary manner, and the voilocks were hanging in picturesque folds. Near us there were several other aouls. At a short distance in front of the yourt, Kairan was seated on the ground, with several chiefs around him, in deep consultation. Not far from them the women were at their morning's occupation, milking their cows, sheep, and goats, and the men were preparing to drive the herds to their pastures. When the latter began to move off, the plain around seemed one mass of living animals; while Kirghis, dressed in their gay costumes, and mounted on spirited horses, were galloping to and fro, separating their different charges. More than 35,000 animals were in motion.

Having ascended one of the numerous tumuli, that afforded a clear view over the vast steppe, I observed long lines of dark objects extending far into the distance. These were horses, oxen, and camels, belonging to other tribes, now on their march towards the pass. In every direction great herds of cattle could be seen — some so far away that they appeared like specks on these interminable plains. To the south, the snowy peaks of the Ac-tau were glittering in the sun, while the lower ranges of the Ala-tau were lit up, showing their varied colours in all their splendour. My attention was riveted to the scene, as it forcibly suggested the exodus from Egypt.

While thus employed, Kairan and the chiefs broke up their council, ascended the tumulus, and told me that three Kirghis had returned from the mountains, whither they had been to examine the upper passes; a necessary precaution to ascertain if the herds could cross the high ridge, and descend into the valleys beyond. They had reported favourably, and the intelligence had already been sent on into the steppe to the other Kirghis, by whom it would be communicated from one tribe to another, and set the whole on the march.

After quitting my host, and riding about an hour, I came upon an aoul, belonging to another chief, "Urtigun," whom I found standing at the door of his yourt. He was a tall, well-built man, about forty years old, with the audacity of a captain of freebooters; indeed, he would not have disgraced the illustrious robber chief whose region I had just left, by claiming descent from him. It was obvious that we were to each other objects of interest, while to his followers, who had crowded into the yourt, I appeared a great curiosity. He inquired whence I came, and where I was going; and to satisfy his curiosity, my maps were opened, when I showed him his own region, and then mine. I also pointed out Bokharia, Tashkent, and Kokhan, towns known to him, and to which he had, most probably, sent captives. This information interested him greatly, and he desired to see Pekin and Kulja on the map.

I spent more than an hour with this chief, and then departed with the usual salutations. When outside the yourt, I observed a fine bearcoot chained to his perch, and several splendid dogs ranging about; they were of a particularly fine race, somewhat like the Irish wolf-hound, were powerful animals, and exceedingly fleet. Urtigun held my horse, and gave me his hand to the saddle; he then mounted his own steed, and accompanied my party to a small stream about a mile from his aoul. Here we parted, when he expressed a wish that we might meet again in the mountains, and hunt deer with his bearcoot. From this place a fine grassy steppe extended to the west, over which we were soon galloping at a good speed.

My old guide through the great gorge was in ecstacies as we bounded over the plain. He obtained a long lance from one of the men, and showed me how well he could wield it. Having pushed his horse in advance, he put him into a gallop, turning the lance round his head on his fingers; in an instant he brought it down to the side of his horse, placing the butt in the stirrup, and levelling the weapon for a charge. Giving a wild shriek, he bent low on his saddle, and went off at full speed. He had his horse in perfect command; and throwing him on his haunches, turned suddenly round, and, with lance levelled, charged towards me, passing close by my side. My Cossacks, who could use the weapon well, were delighted with his dexterity. It was evident that his leader, Kinsara, had not failed to drill his men. Indeed, I was assured that it was their proficiency in the use of the lance and battle-axe, that had made them so formidable among the Asiatic tribes. If these men are ever trained under good officers, they will become some of the best irregular cavalry in the world, unequalled for long and rapid marches. They possess all the qualities that made the reputation of the wild hordes led on by Genghis Khan.

As we travelled along, vast herds of cattle were seen in every direction, all drawing towards the mountains, and after a ride of nearly six hours, we reached the aoul of our friends. When my people saw us they were greatly delighted, and my host Djani-bek seemed pleased to see me again.

On the following morning, looking up towards the

mountains, I perceived the sun just gilding their snowy peaks and glaciers with his glorious rays. It was a lovely sight: one crest after another received his golden tint, till at length all were lighted up with the full blaze of day. The beautiful and continued changes that passed over the scene, and the pure mountain breeze, gave me new vigour. I quickly forgot hunger and toil, and desired nothing more

Ala-tau from the Steppe.

than to penetrate their mighty passes, scale their snow-capped crests, and wander amidst the scenes in the valleys beyond.

Our first duty was a thorough cleaning of arms, and putting everything in order for our migration with the Kirghis, as we had not passed through the robbers' haunts scatheless. Djani-bek and his friends assembled and remained seated around, watching our operations, and drinking their favourite beverage. They were greatly astonished at seeing me take my rifle to pieces, wash the barrel, and spurt the water from the nipple, examining with much care and interest the different parts, exclaiming "yak-she," (very good,) as they passed them from one to another.

Suddenly we observed a cloud of dust rising on the plain at a considerable distance; and it was not long before we discovered a party of horsemen advancing towards us. Djani-bek gave some orders to his people, and at once several mounted and rode out to meet these visitors, and welcome them if friends. In about an hour one of his men and a stranger galloped up, and announced his approaching guests. They were followed almost immediately by their companions. The visitors proved to be a young chief, betrothed to Djani-bek's daughter, accompanied by five of his tribe; and it was his first appearance at the aoul of his bride, whom he had not yet seen.

Djani-bek rose to receive him, taking hold of his bridle, and giving his hand to aid in dismounting. He then led him to a yourt, which had been moved bodily to a new site by eight or ten matrons and damsels. When seated, koumis was handed to him in a large Chinese bowl, containing about three pints, which he quickly drained with much gusto. This accomplished, he inquired about the health of his future father-in-law, and received Djani-bek's assurance that he never was better. His next inquiry was after the health of Djani-bek's sons; then after the camels, horses, oxen, sheep, goats, bearcoot, and dogs, and, lastly, about his mother-in-law and his bride. This is the usual mode among the tribes of Central Asia.

Among the Kirghis, the young lady has no voice in her own nuptials; her father places a certain value upon her, and whoever is able to pay it may become her husband.

Some of the Sultans put so high a price on their daughters, it is difficult to find a partner for them: this occasionally leads to most tragic results, one of which nearly resembles the fate of the young Babylonians.

The first point to be settled is the "Kalym," or marriage portion, to be given for the young lady; which consists of a number of camels, horses, oxen, and sheep. These must be handed over to the father, who retains them for the benefit of the daughter, in case the husband returns her to her parents, which does sometimes happen. When this preliminary is arranged, the Mulla is called in to ratify the marriage contract. He asks the fathers and mothers of the young couple if they are satisfied with the match, and all the arrangements: if the reply is satisfactory, it is announced to the relations on both sides for their approval. Sanction has sometimes to be obtained by bribes, where (as is quite common in these regions) family feuds exist.

After this the Mulla reads several prayers for the prosperity and happiness of the bride and bridegroom. This part of the ceremony is performed in the presence of two or more persons, who are chosen by the parents as arbitrators, to settle any dispute that may arise before the marriage is completed. Such is a Kirghis betrothal. When the matter has proceeded thus far, the father of the bridegroom pays a portion of the kalym, and the father of the bride must prepare his daughter's dowry as agreed upon. The young lover is now permitted to visit his bride in private, and even to remain with her in the same yourt.

My host's intended son-in-law had come to see his bride, bedecked with all the finery suitable for the occasion, with a determination to make a favourable impression, both on the young lady, and on her family. His age was about six-and-twenty; I cannot say that he was particularly handsome, at least according to European ideas,—to Asiatic ones it might be otherwise. He was neither tall nor stout, but had a graceful figure when mounted on his splendid horse. His seat was perfect, according to Kirghis notions, and he managed his champing steed well; he was evidently quite at home in the saddle.

His costume was a richly-coloured yellow and crimson kalat, with a pair of black velvet tchimbar embroidered in various-coloured silks. He wore a valuable green shawl round his waist, and a pair of madder-coloured high-heeled boots, but so short in the foot that walking was difficult. On his head was a crimson kanfa cap, turned up with black fox-skin. His leathern pouch was decorated with iron, inlaid with silver; in this he carried his flint, steel, tinder, and snuff bottle. A knife, pipe, and a whip, stuck in his sash, completed the outfit of the Asiatic lover. The horse he rode was one of the best from his father's stud, and was a splendid dark iron grey. His pedigree could be traced up to one of the finest races in the steppe, which are highly valued by the Kirghis. They have a decided passion for rich and costly horse trappings, and this the young chief had indulged.

The bridle was decorated with small plates of iron, inlaid with silver, and wrought in a beautiful pattern—work for which the Kirghis are justly celebrated; several of the Sultans keeping their own armourer to execute it. The martingale, the saddle, and all straps attached thereto, were beautifully embellished; even the voilock saddle-cloth was ornamented with a pattern worked in several colours. His battle-axe, with the iron rings on the handle, was also inlaid with the precious metal. Thus adorned, and mounted on his fiery steed, few Kirghis maidens could have rejected him. His followers were all young men, dressed in rich costumes, having good horses, and some splendid accoutrements.

When on horseback the group had an imposing appearance, but on foot their high-heeled, short-footed boots gave them so hobbling a gait, it was plain that they might be easily knocked over. They were, however, the admiration of the Kirghis, and the women were visible peering from the different yourts, casting scrutinizing glances at the visitors, as they paraded about the aoul. The young lady was quickly informed of the arrival of her future husband, when she retired into one of the yourts, remaining under the care of the females, who concealed her from all intruders. Her swain was anxious to behold her, but all applications to that effect met with a flat denial from the young lady. He was,

Kara-tau and Aouls.

therefore, obliged to adopt the usual course, and seek the aid of her married female relatives. By bribes they were induced to persuade her to visit his yourt: after a display of much coyness, she consented, and was led there by her friends. She was left with him, and they remained together undisturbed.

In the meantime, the usual banquet was being enjoyed, and the mirth of the festal party had become "fast and furious," which induced me to seek quiet on the steppe. Accompanied by three of my people, I started for a ride over the plain, going to the northward, in the direction of a small lake which was visible in the distance. After proceeding more than an hour, I beheld a large aoul three or four miles off, and towards it I turned. Two Kirghis presently met me, and led me to their chief, whom we found sitting at the door of his yourt, like a patriarch, surrounded by his family, having in front his poet singing the great deeds of his race. He rose to receive me, gave me a seat on his own carpet, and then the bard continued his song.

This family group, the glowing sky, and the vast plain, with the thousands of animals scattered over it, formed a charming picture. Homer was never listened to with more attention than was this shepherd poet, while singing the traditions of the ancestors of his tribe. Whatever power the old Greek possessed over the minds of his audience, was equalled by that of the bard before me. When he sung of the mountain scenes around, the pastoral habits of the people, their flocks and herds, the faces of his hearers were calm, and they sat unmoved. But when he began to recite the warlike deeds of their race, their eyes flashed with delight; as he proceeded, they were worked up into a passion, and some grasped their battle-axes, and sprang to their feet in a state of frenzy. Then followed a mournful strain, telling of the death of a chief, when all excitement ceased, and every one listened with deep attention. Such was the sway this unlettered bard held over the minds of his wild comrades.

As I sat watching the group, I saw there were many sturdy fellows sitting round their aged chief, all of whom appeared quiet and calm; but a word from him would rouse their passions, and change the scene into one of the wildest excitement. The uplifting of his battle-axe would send them on a plundering expedition, when they would spare neither age nor sex. If the baranta was a successful one, the poet would add one more stanza to his song. I listened long to these wild strains, which delayed my departure till the sun was casting his last rays over the steppe. Nor was it without reluctance that I said "aman-bul" to the old chief, mounted my horse, and galloped over the plain.

Night was drawing on fast, and our steeds were not spared; but darkness caught us before we had gone half the distance. Soon all objects were lost in gloom, and it was not till past midnight that we reached our temporary home. The aoul was perfectly quiet, and all the revellers were sleeping; there was not a sound excepting the challenge of the watchmen, and the bark of their faithful dogs. I sat down at the door of the yourt while the horses were being turned loose, and observed several meteors dart across the sky.

When the first pale yellowish streaks were seen breaking over the steppe, and extending in narrow lines along the horizon, each few minutes added light and depth to their colour, till they changed through all the shades of orange to a deep crimson, far more brilliant than the ruby. Still the plain was a dark purple grey, and all objects upon it were indistinct and almost lost in gloom. As one group of cattle after another rose out of the dusky vapour that shrouded the earth, they appeared magnified, which caused the head and neck of the camels to assume the proportions of some mighty antediluvian monster stalking over the plain, while the huge forms of the other creatures aided in the illusion. Gradually the whole scene changed, and the commotion in the aoul began; the bulls were up and bellowing, as if calling and marshalling their herds together for the march. Turning in another direction, the horses were seen with their heads thrown aloft and snorting; others were plunging and kicking furiously, while the sheep and goats, with their kids and lambs, seemed just rising into existence. A little later, as the sun rose, the plain was seen covered far and wide with myriads of living animals.

Soon after daylight long lines of camels and horses were seen wending their way in a south-westerly direction, followed by herds of oxen. The sheep and goats were innumerable; they stretched over miles of country, and were following slowly in the rear. With each herd and flock there were a number of Kirghis mounted on good horses; these, galloping to and fro, added greatly to the general effect.

At the aoul women in their best attire were taking down the yourts and securing them on camels. Their household goods were being packed up by the girls and boys, after which they were loaded on camels, bulls, and cows. These children of the steppe are not long in making their preparations to depart in search of new homes. In less than three hours all were ready, when we sprung into our saddles and rode away.

The camels formed a most curious portion of the spectacle, with the willow framework of the yourts hanging from their saddles, giving them the appearance of huge animals with wings just expanding for a flight. Others were loaded with the voilock coverings, placed across their backs, piled up high, and crowned with the circular top of the yourt. The poor creatures had burthens far larger than themselves, under which they evidently walked with difficulty. Then followed a string of bulls with bales of Bokharian carpets slung over their saddles, and boxes and other household utensils placed above. Then a refractory bull was seen similarly loaded, with the large iron cauldron on the top. The furious beast went rushing on; presently the straps gave way, and the cauldron went rolling down the declivity. Seeing this he became frantic, leaping and plunging, and at each bound a part of his load was left behind. As the bales rolled over he charged at them vigorously, and soon got rid of all his encumbrances. He now rushed at every horseman who happened to be in his course, and several had narrow escapes; at last he took refuge among the herd. The koumis bag, with its contents, so precious to a Kirghis, was secured on a grave and careful bull, who moved along with stately dignity.

After these a number of cows joined in the procession, having two leathern bags secured on their backs, with a young child sitting in each, watching the crowd of animals as they bounded past. Mingled with this throng were women dressed in their rich Chinese silk costumes, some crimson, others yellow, red, and green, and the elder females in black velvet kalats. A few of the young girls had fox-skin caps, and others silk caps, richly embroidered in various colours. The matrons wore white calico head gear, embroidered with red, hanging down over their shoulders like hoods. Many were mounted on wild steeds, which they sat and managed with extraordinary ease and skill. Girls and boys were riding various animals according to their ages; some of the elder ones horses, others young bulls, and some were even mounted on calves, having voilock boots secured to the saddles, into which the young urchins inserted their legs, guiding the beast by a thong secured to his nose. This was a cavalcade to be seen only in these regions.

A ride over the plain of somewhat more than two hours brought us to the foot of the mountains; we crossed a low hill, and beheld the entrance to the pass, which appeared filled with a mass of animals moving slowly onward. Turning towards the north, vast herds of cattle were seen extending as far as my vision could reach, marching from various points in the steppe towards their pastures in the mountains; and through this pass the enormous multitude must ascend.

Having stood a short time watching the living tide roll on, I rode into the valley, and joined the moving mass.

The mouth of the pass was about 300 yards wide, between grassy slopes, up which it was impossible for either man or animal to climb. The whole width, and as far as I could see, was filled with camels, horses, and oxen; Kirghis were riding among them, shouting, and using their whips on any refractory brute that came within their reach. At length we plunged into a herd of horses, with camels in front, and bulls and oxen in our rear. We presently passed the grassy slopes to where the gorge narrowed to about 100 yards in width, with precipices rising up on each side to the height of 600 or 700 feet. From this mob of quadrupeds there was no escape on either side, and to turn back was utterly impossible, as we were now wedged in among wild horses. These brutes showed every disposition to kick, but, fortunately for us, without the power, the space for each animal being too limited. This did not, however, prevent them using their teeth, and it required great vigilance and constant use of the whip to pass unscathed.

As we rode on the scene became fearfully grand: the precipices increased in height at every hundred yards we advanced. In one place there were overhanging crags 900 feet above us, split and rent into fragments, ready apparently to topple over at the slightest impulse, while higher in the pass the scenery became more savage. Then we had the shouting of men, the cry of the camels, the shrieks and snorting of the horses when bitten by their neighbours, with the bellowing of the bulls and oxen in our rear—a wonderfully savage chorus, heightened by the echoes resounding from crag to crag, accompanied by a constant drone in the distant bleating of an immense multitude of sheep.

The bottom of the gorge ascended rapidly, which enabled me to look back, when I saw, about fifty paces in our rear, a phalanx of bulls, which no man would dare to face—even the Kirghis kept clear of these. They came steadily on, but the horses near them plunged and reared when the sharp horns gored their haunches. Another danger presently beset us. The Kirghis said that a little further on, the bed of the gorge was strewn with fallen rocks and small stones, and that riding over these would require great care, for if one of our steeds fell, it would be fatal to both horse and rider. Shortly we came to a recess in the precipice, and here two children mounted on young bulls had taken refuge: having escaped from the crowd of animals, they had clambered up among the rocks, and the four were looking down at the passing mass in perfect calm. Poor creatures, it was impossible to reach them or afford them the least aid; the only thing that could be done was to urge them to remain still where they were.

The rough ground that had been mentioned by the Kirghis was now distinctly seen by the motion of the animals before us. Hitherto the stream of heads and backs had ran smoothly on; now, however, it became a rapid, where heads and tails were tossed aloft in quick succession. We were approaching some jutting masses that formed a bend in the gorge. On reaching these, a terrific scene burst upon us. The pass was narrowed by huge blocks fallen from above, one of which was thirty-five to forty feet high, and somewhat more in width, standing about twenty paces from the foot of the rocks, and about 200 yards from us. The prospect was fearful, for as we rode on, the horses were being wedged more closely together between the frowning cliffs. All looked with anxiety at the pent-up tide of animals struggling onward, till they burst over the rocky barrier.

Each few minutes brought us nearer the danger: not a word was spoken, but every eye was fixed on the horses bounding over the rocks. Several fell, uttering a shriek, and were seen no more. Instinct seemed to warn the animals of their impending danger; they were, however, forced along by those behind, nor was it possible for us to see the ground over which we were riding. At length we came among the

March through the Gorge.

crowd of leaping horses; our own made three or four bounds, and the dreaded spot was passed. The gorge opened out wider; still it was filled with camels and horses, moving slowly onward. To stop and look back was impossible, as the living stream came rushing on. Although accidents are often fatal to the people on this spot, and many animals belonging to each tribe are killed on their journey to and from the mountains, such is the apathy of these Asiatics that they never think of removing a single stone. After the herds have passed, whatever remains of camel, horse, or other animal, is gathered up, and feasted on by the people.

We had been more than four hours ascending this mountain gorge when we reached a part less abrupt. Here we got out of the throng, and, guided by a Kirghis, began to ascend a narrow ravine that brought us to the foot of some high crags. These compelled us to dismount, and ascend on foot, leading our horses with difficulty through a great rent in the rocks. Everything below was hidden from our view, still the sounds were heard as they rolled up to our position. In about an hour we emerged from the chasm, nearly at the top of the precipice. A Kirghis led the way to some elevated rocks, from which we had a view into the gorge, where we saw the vast herds still struggling along. My guide said it would take them three hours to reach the head of the pass. Having looked down upon this singular scene for a short time, I mounted my horse, and shortly reached the plateau. From this point a ride of about three miles brought me to the top of the gorge, and here I found a stream of camels and horses pouring towards the high plain.

We had reached a point just beneath the snow-line, about 7,000 feet above the sea, and presently it began to rain, while the higher ridges became shrouded in vapour. At a short distance from the head of the pass some Kirghis had pitched their yourts. Here we sought shelter from the pelting storm, and dined, remaining a couple of hours, in the vain hope that the shower would cease. During this time the stream of countless animals still passed on, attended by the wet and shivering herdsmen, bent on reaching a sheltered valley, in which to pass the night. Finding that waiting was useless, I proceeded in search of another aoul, where we could find pastures for our horses and obtain shelter for the night.

The wind had increased to a gale, with an accompaniment of rain and sleet that soon penetrated our clothing, and made our teeth chatter. Occasionally a break in the dark canopy of vapour gave us hopes of better weather, and showed us the snowy crests of the Ac-tau, far above the clouds. It was the snow and glaciers of this region that rendered the blast so cutting as we rode along the elevated plateau. Our route was towards one of the higher ridges to the south, leaving the track followed by the Kirghis with their herds. The guide led the way to the eastward. We rode along the base of the ridge for more than an hour, to a point where we began to ascend over a very stony track, towards some high crags, near which, the guide said, we must cross to the valley beyond. Having ascertained that these crags were nearly due south, we passed on, but before we reached the summit a dense fog came over us, obscuring everything even at a few paces distant. This added greatly to our difficulty and danger, as we were not far from the top of some high precipices that extended along on our left.

In a few minutes we were brought to a standstill, as the guide refused to proceed further. After a few minutes spent in consultation, I decided on going forward, as preferable to the risk of remaining on this bleak spot in such a night, without either shelter or a bush to make a fire. Rain and sleet were beating upon us heavily, and the wind was nearly in our teeth. Taking out my compass, I led the way to the south-west, riding slowly on, till we came to patches of snow lying among fallen rocks. We soon reached large masses that rose up on our right, but their summits were lost in the billowy clouds. On our left, at a few paces distant, we beheld black crags jutting out of a sea of vapour; these told plainly that danger was near. The guide, however, thought they were the landmarks he had pointed out to me; if so, he said, we were near the precipices at the eastern end of the crags.

After examining our position, I dismounted, leading the way, guided by my compass, towards the west, and in a short time found the track. Our difficulty was the fog, or rather clouds, that were driving past, sometimes in dense rolling masses, and then in thin veils of vapour, through which we got a glimpse of lofty crags extending far above us. The descent was steep, but not difficult; at times over beds of hard snow, whereon we found the footprints of cattle. These were pleasing tokens, as we felt assured we were in the right direction. After going what seemed a considerable distance, we heard dogs on our left; turning our horses, we rode carefully on, guided by the sound, and shortly found some Kirghis yourts.

My wishes were soon made known, and one of their temporary dwellings was given up to us. The people were part of a tribe who, like us, had been caught in the fog, and were compelled to remain and encamp for the night. My finding them was fortunate, as the clouds enveloped all around in one dense mass: the rain poured down in streams, and the night soon set in. Even the frail yourt on such a night became a comfortable dwelling. We learned that it would take two hours, even in daylight, to descend into the valley, but in this weather, I was assured, that no man could accomplish it. They also informed me that one of their camels had fallen over a precipice not far from our path.

It is only those who have been exposed to a pelting storm for many hours, and been surrounded by such dangers as beset me, who can fully appreciate the security and comfort afforded by a strip of voilock spread over a few willow rods.

During the early part of the night the wind swept up the narrow valley with great fury, at times almost tearing up the yourt. This and the heavy pattering of the rain, that forced its way through every chink, made all feel thankful to Providence for having guided us hither in safety.

Just as day was breaking I turned out to examine our position, when I found the clouds still covered all the higher summits to the south. Our little encampment was in a small, narrow valley, on the east and west enclosed by rocky cliffs of no great elevation: on the south the ground descended rapidly for about 300 yards to the brink of a precipice of enormous depth; while on the north the little valley extended about 200 yards up to a ridge of serrated rocks. Towards these I directed my steps, hoping to get a view of the surrounding region.

When I had gained the summit, a prospect opened out to the north that greatly astonished me. I was standing on some rocky pinnacles, rising over a precipice not less than 1,500 feet deep, from which it appeared possible to send a rifle-ball into the gorge we had ascended yesterday; but the purity of the atmosphere in these regions renders distance most deceptive, as I have often proved at the cost of a long and solitary ride.

From my present elevated position the steppe appeared boundless, and extending till earth and sky were blended in misty air. Notwithstanding the vast number of cattle that ascended yesterday, immense herds were scattered over the plain in all directions, preparing to ascend the pass. While I sat contemplating this scene, the clouds were gradually rising from the mountains to the south, when one rugged ridge after another started into view. At length the base of the snowy chain of the Ac-tau became visible, but the crest remained shrouded in the misty veil. Wishing to see something of the route that had led me to this spot, I proceeded along the ridge, following our track for about half a mile, when I beheld the dangers we had escaped. We had ridden along the brink of a great precipice obscured by the fog. I found the spot over which the camel of our friends had fallen, and on looking down observed a party of four wolves at breakfast.

On my way back to the aoul I had a splendid view of the great chains running to the westward, and along a magnificent valley lying between the Kara-tau and Ala-tau mountains. Some parts of this valley afford good pasturage for numerous herds of cattle, that now appeared like swarms of flies at the great depth beneath me. As the eye wandered over the Kara-tau to the vast plain, several rivers were seen meandering along till they were either lost in the sand or formed morasses, while far beyond these the Balkash was glittering in the sun like polished silver.

When I joined my friends, they were preparing for the descent into the valley. The women had already taken down the yourts, and were placing them on camels; in a short time, each beast having got its burthen, we mounted our horses and left the spot. Our way was along the serrated ridge of granite for several miles, after which we turned towards the east, and began to descend into a small valley. The track was rugged and difficult for the camels to travel over; in parts the mountain was abrupt, and the ground rendered slippery by the rain. This was rather unpleasant, as several of our horses fell, and some of the people had a flounder in the mire.

After consulting with the Kirghis, I proposed that we should cross the valley by a much shorter route than that taken by the shepherds with their herds, ascend the high chain to the east, and then find our way into the valley beyond. One of the men with whom we had remained the night thought this would be impossible, as none of their tribe had been able to find a track in that direction. I determined that this information should not prevent me from making the attempt, seeing that it would take us through some splendid scenery, and into a new region. One of our last night's companions wished to accompany me, to which I made no objection. All being arranged, we separated; the Kirghis, with their camels, horses, and oxen, turned in a westerly direction, and we rode towards the south-east.

As we descended into the valley, I found the ground covered with flowers—large patches of gentiana, some with beautiful dark blue blossoms, and others almost white, with blue stripes. Several varieties of iris were just bursting their buds, while our horses trampled over beds of forget-me-not, which caused my thoughts to wander homeward. We soon crossed the valley, and ascended a steep spur running up to the higher ridge, that extended to the south-west for many miles. As we rode up the hill, we had to pick our way between great masses of greenstone, that I also found formed the rugged crest above. Having reached the top, we looked down into a deep ravine, extending into the mountain and terminating in a precipice, over which a small torrent leaped that formed many cascades before it reached the bottom.

Looking from this point, it seemed doubtful whether we should be able to descend and cross to the opposite ridge. Still, having overcome difficulties that at the time appeared insurmountable, I determined not to give this up without an effort. After examining the declivity, it was decided that we should try to descend a little more to the south. The Kirghis who accompanied me thought the attempt would prove useless, as the ridge on the opposite side rose to a much greater height. He also said that beyond the mountain before us there was a terrible ravine and a great waterfall, that some of his people had seen from a distant mountain. This information had a contrary effect to what he expected, as it increased my desire to visit the place. I gave the word "forward," and on we went, seeking a spot by which to descend.

We had not gone far when a herd of argali were found browsing among the rocks. They were first seen by a Cossack, who leaped from his horse, and the crack of his rifle followed instantly. I then beheld a fine male bound high, tumble over the brink, and roll down the declivity. No one now thought of difficulties, all being anxious to follow the ram: a track was soon found made by the wild animals descending to the water, and down this we rode our horses; when presently we observed the Cossack with his game; two Kirghis were sent to his assistance, and they were speedily engaged in helping him to dress it. Leaving this party to follow, we continued our course downward by many a zigzag turn. At length we reached the bottom, and ascended the opposite side without any great difficulty.

On gaining the summit, I found the Kirghis had not exaggerated the depth of the ravine, and the roaring of a waterfall was heard, although it could not be seen. We saw at a glance that it was utterly impossible to take our horses into this gorge. I therefore started with two men, and determined to descend on foot till a sight of the waterfall could be obtained. The way was rugged and difficult; perseverance, however, brought us to a point where we beheld the water take its first leap, but we could not see the bottom of the fall. At a great depth beneath us some rocks jutted far out into the gorge, and from these I felt assured that I should get a splendid view. How to reach them was the question; but my men were resolute, and we set about it with a determination to succeed. After clambering over crags and down fissures, aided by the plants and shrubs growing in their riven sides, we gained the desired spot, when I was well rewarded for my toil.

We were standing upon a mass of red porphyry that

rose perpendicularly from the bottom of the gorge, not less than 800 feet. The opposite side was equally abrupt,

Waterfall.

and the width of the chasm about 400 yards. Looking up the ravine, there was nothing to interrupt the view: the falls were before us in their full grandeur, at about 600 yards' distance. The water bounds over a ledge of rocks formed into a crescent, down which it leaps in one broad sheet for about 600 feet. Then it was seen dashing and foaming over fallen rocks for about another 150 feet, whence there was a second fall of 350 feet; after which the water rushes down the ravine for about 100 yards, and then leaps over a third fall, apparently higher than the second. From the bottom of this it tumbles and boils, appearing like snow among the dark masses beneath, and then the torrent rolls on down the gorge. At some distance beyond the top of the fall, high precipices and crags rose up, and over these were seen the snowy crests of the chain.

The great depth beneath, the towering cliffs above, and the tremendous roar of the falling water, gave a peculiar character of savage grandeur to the scene, while wreaths of white vapour curled up and were wafted across the gorge, producing apparently magical effects. Having added this scene to my folio, I collected some fine specimens of porphyry, and then began to ascend. On reaching the top we dined on chops from the wild sheep, which proved excellent fare.

It was long past mid-day when our meal was ended, and we started up the slope that extended for more than two miles to the foot of the high chain, forming a plateau running east and west. From this the higher summits rose abruptly, far into the region of eternal snow, some of them terminating in pinnacles of bare rock. The only way of continuing our journey in this direction was by crossing the torrent before it leaped into the ravine. After riding about a mile with this object in view, we found ourselves close to the top of the fall. It was a wild-looking place, and a considerable body of water was rushing over into the abyss. At this point there were blocks of the finest green jasper I had met with in any region, unequalled by those either in the Oural or Altai.

The idea of being carried over the fall by the rushing torrent, seemed to be suggested to every one, and we determined to ford the stream as far from it as possible. We continued our ride over the grassy slope, where masses of green and purple jasper jutted out in many places, while the foaming water that rolled along plainly indicated the danger awaiting us. On reaching the bank, we found the bed of the stream filled with large stones, over which the water was rushing with such force that it would have swept both horses and men away in a moment. Proceeding up the bank of the stream, each place that seemed to afford the smallest chance was scanned with intense interest; but not one could be found that we considered safe, and every one began to think our case hopeless.

We had now reached within a few hundred yards of the entrance to the gorge in the higher mountains, where we could hear the water thundering loudly. The Kirghis urged me to give up the attempt, and return by a new route over which he would guide us; but on proceeding a little further, I found the stream somewhat wider and not so deep, and every man saw at a glance that we had reached the only practicable ford. We were eight in number, all well mounted: I knew the Cossacks would run any risk with me, and if we decided to go, the Kirghis must. After examining the place carefully, that was about twenty-five paces in width, I resolved to try the experiment, by the whole party riding into the stream wedged together.

We formed into close line on the bank, and as one of the Cossacks and myself had the strongest horses, it was decided that we should take the upper end of the line, and receive the full force of the torrent. I gave the word, when we rode slowly into the stream, intending to cross obliquely, as there seemed better landing a little higher up. For the first few paces we found no difficulty; after this the Cossack and I got into deeper water, when it rushed up the sides of our horses and over our saddles, sending each against the other with great force. All, however, kept their places, and the horses bravely breasted the torrent. They moved each foot slowly and with care, feeling one secure before making another step forward.

We had just passed the middle of the stream, when the horse next to me stumbled; the Kirghis did all he could to save him, but unfortunately he fell. Both horse and rider were now floundering in the torrent, with the water rushing over them. The man kept his seat, and remained perfectly collected; his comrade on one side, and I on the other, got hold of the reins, lifted the horse up, and held him till his rider obtained a secure footing. As we went on, other horses stumbled on the slippery stones; fortunately, however, no one went down, and we reached the bank in safety.

This was more than any one expected when the Kirghis was down, and it was a great relief to all when we stood on the rocks, and looked back upon the rushing water. I think we should have ridden far before again risking this small passage. Indeed, the Kirghis said that fording this torrent was so dangerous, that nothing should induce them to travel by this route. These, in fact, are the difficulties and dangers of a mountain journey; there is also the certainty of a wetting, which in this instance was a good one.

We did not remain long contemplating the dangerous ford, as the sinking sun suggested that this high plateau, so near the snow line, would prove a cold lodging in wet clothing. We took a last look at the rushing torrent, thinking what might have been our fate had the water been only a few inches deeper, for neither the Cossack's horse nor mine could have withstood the force of the stream, and our line once in disorder, all must have perished. Turning from the spot, we rode to the eastward, wending our way among huge masses of dark purple and red slate, rolled down from the summits above. Having ridden along the plateau for more than three miles, anxiously looking for some sheltered spot in which our horses could find grass, we turned more to the southward, and in less than an hour reached the head of a ravine.

This was a welcome sight, for here we observed dwarf cedars coiling their branches round the rocks, and plenty of juniper bushes that would afford food enough for our fires. Descending lower, we found a snug berth beneath some porphyry cliffs; nor was it long before two fires were kindled. Not far from us abundance of grass was found for our horses; these were first cared for, and then commenced a busy scene at our little camp. While two of the men prepared our evening meal, four brought in fuel, which a Cossack and myself applied scientifically, when the fires soon produced a cheering influence. Shortly our camp had the appearance of a great washing establishment, so numerous and varied were the garments steaming around the fire.

We were awakened in the morning by the crash of an avalanche, which caused every man to start to his feet; it was in the higher regions, so that we saw nothing of its terrible effects. Ascending to the plateau, we continued our ride in a south-easterly direction for several hours. Some of the slate cliffs in this region were exceedingly interesting, as they varied much in colour. First a deep purple stratum, forty or fifty feet thick; above this a bright red one of equal thickness, and then a light green of similar dimensions: when seen from a distance, the effect was singular. Having ascended some lofty granite masses, we turned to the south, and shortly reached a point that gave us a view into the valley; when we observed several large aouls scattered about, and vast herds of camels, horses, and oxen were spread over the pastures, while immense flocks of sheep were browsing on the hill-sides.

From this place we began to descend. At first this was not difficult, till we reached some granite precipices, and then our progress was slow. In one part the place was a perfect chaos of fallen rocks, as if a mountain had been hurled down; the blocks were grey granite, containing fine crystals of black shorl, which seemed abundant here. Had I possessed the necessary implements, and had had time, some fine specimens might have been obtained. In another part were found lofty crags of syenite, of a beautiful pink colour; around their base huge blocks were lying in heaps, proving that these had been tumbled down by some powerful agent, and not by the slow process of time.

After passing this labyrinth we had a most difficult, and in some parts a dangerous, descent. Several times we were brought to a stand by deep precipices that compelled us to retrace our steps and seek another path where we could lead our horses down, often no easy task. At last, after a three hours' toil, we reached the lower range. Here we were on good turf, and our horses were put to their speed, when we soon came upon the great track by which the tribes had descended with their herds. We had not gone far when we met a group of Kirghis, who informed us that many disasters had occurred during the fog. At one spot three camels had fallen over a precipice, at another several horses had shared a similar fate. Kirghis were engaged skinning the animals, and preparing to carry the flesh to the aouls.

Proceeding onward, along the edge of some high cliffs, we beheld at every few hundred paces, groups of men collecting the dead cattle. Unfortunately these were not the worst accidents, for I was afterwards informed that several people had been killed, which made me reflect on our escape through such dangers. After riding about ten miles we reached the valley, and just at dusk arrived at the Kirghis aoul, when the chief received me kindly. I had now reached their summer pastures, at the foot of the snowy peaks of the Ac-tau, in Chinese Tartary, and about 7,000 feet above the level of the sea. This is the highest point at which the Kirghis obtain food for their cattle. They remain here a month or five weeks, and then gradually descend, eating up the different pastures on their way back to the steppe, which they usually reach about the first week in September.

CHAP. XI.

CARAVAN AND COSSACK ROUTES.

I HAVE taken my readers through some of the most sublime scenery in this portion of the globe, and given an account of the pastoral habits and migrations of the Nomades; but it would, I fear, be tedious were I to add a description of my route from the summer pastures into a more westerly region, where Russia has established her power. I shall therefore describe those by which the caravans carry on their commercial intercourse with the towns and people of Central Asia, mentioning the names and positions of all the places on the Russian frontier where these routes begin, and stating the time occupied in crossing these vast steppes, with a short account of each journey.

The most westerly point to which the caravans proceed, and the nearest to the great fair at Nijne Novgorod, is Orenburg, in lat. 51° 46′ N., and long. 55° 4′ 45″ E. The others are Troitska, in lat. 54° N., and long. 61° 20′ E.; Petropavalovsk, in lat. 54° 30′ N., and long. 69° E.; and Semipalatinsk, in lat. 50° 30′ N., and long. 80° E.

From Orenburg to Khiva, in lat. 41° 40′ N., and long. 59° 23′ E., there are two routes; one traverses the country between the Aral and Caspian, the other along the eastern shore of the Aral. On leaving Orenburg the former runs in a south-easterly direction to the river Ilek, which it crosses, and then continues up the western bank of the stream till it reaches the Isan-bai. This river is followed far up towards its source; then the way is over the mountain Bassa-gha, whence it descends to the river Kooblei-li-Temir, following this stream to its junction with the Emba, or Djem. From this place it turns in a south-westerly direction, down the river bank, till it joins the old route of the Nogais (from Khiva to Suratchikoff, on the river Oural), at the ancient cemetery, Bakash-aoul. It now turns in a south-easterly direction, and strikes on the shores of the Aral, near the Bay of Ktchou-Kool-maghir; thence it runs along the shore of the Aral to Kara-Ghumbett, passing round the Bay of Sara-Massat. Shortly after leaving this it turns directly east, towards the Amoo-Daria, which it reaches at Khodji-Terek, and thence continues up the western bank of the river to Khiva. The journey usually occupies twenty-five or thirty days.

Most of the way, after leaving the Emba, is over arid steppes. General Peroffsky met here a terrible disaster, having lost nearly the whole of his army in the attempt to cross the region and chastise the Khan of Khiva. From one of the officers engaged in the expedition, I obtained many particulars of the sufferings the men endured without a murmur; and, from my own experience, can fully comprehend the effects of bourans upon troops on the march. When enveloped in the dense clouds of snow the men became bewildered, falling by hundreds, and were speedily frozen to death. The horses also died in great numbers, and every camel perished.

From Orenburg to Bokhara, in lat. 39° 40′ N., and long. 64° 45′ E., is a sixty days' journey, and frequently travelled by caravans, being the great road from Central Asia to the fair at Nijne Novgorod. On leaving Orenburg the route is the same as that to Khiva, as far as the river Isanbai; but after crossing the stream it continues south-east, over the Mongodjar Mountains, to the source of the river Koundjour, and then follows this stream down to the plain, to a point where it falls into the lake Tchi-lar. Thus far both fresh water and herbage is abundant; but beyond this lake a sterile region commences, on which there is little grass, and the water is salt and bad. It extends for about 200 miles, and to within thirty miles of the Syr-Daria, where good grass and water is plentiful, which renders green pastures delightful to look upon after a long ride on a sandy desert. The route now turns more to the south, round the head of the bay Sari Tchaganak, and along the eastern side of the Aral, passing the lakes Kamish-li-bash, Ag-hi-rek, and Djil-tir; hence to the Syr-Daria, where the river is crossed about forty miles from its mouth.

Shortly after passing the river it enters the desert of Kara-Koom (Black Sand), and at about thirty miles distant in the desert it crosses the Kouvan-Daria, where but little herbage is met with. The distance between this river and the Djany-Daria is sixty miles, still over the desert of Kara-Koom, but occasional pastures and water are found. This brings the traveller to the desert of Kizil-Koom, which extends 170 miles, to the wells of Jous-Koaduk; in some parts water and a little grass can be obtained, but reeds and salt lakes are more abundant. Hence the route crosses the desert of Batak-Koom, about 100 miles in breadth, also sterile, till it reaches the mountains Kara Sou-souk, and here are both water and pastures. Beyond these there is a saline steppe, that extends about fifty miles, to the wells of Odoon-Koudook; thence to Bokhara it is cultivated country. The whole distance from Orenburg to Bokhara is about 1,100 miles.

From Troitsk to Bokhara is a journey of sixty to sixty-five days. The route commences in a south-easterly direction, and continues through a fertile country as far as the river Tog-ouzak. After crossing this, it turns nearly south, and passes between numerous freshwater lakes, till it reaches the river Aiat. Beyond the route winds more to the east, crosses the river Djol-Koamar, and enters the wooded region Aman Kara-gai, between the lakes Hèbèlai and Ouba-gan-Denghis. It continues onward in the same course, and crosses the upper Ouba-gan, follows this river to its source beyond Lake Noor-zoom, and leaving Mount Kizil to the west, passes over some low hills, that form the watershed between the rivers flowing north and into the Arctic Sea, and those running south, to be evaporated from the lakes in the steppe. On the west of the route is the lake Sarie Kapa; having passed this, it turns in a westerly direction for about thirty miles, and then due south, till it crosses the Kara-Tourgai.

Hence there are two routes. One turns to the south-east, and follows the river Djél-an-chik, crossing several of its branches. Here the pastures are good, and the banks of the streams are wooded. The next river is the Kar-gali, and then the Boolan-dei, that rises in the Oulou-tau, and from here the picturesque summits of the chain are distinctly visible. Beyond this river the route enters on a vast plain, that extends to the Syr-Daria, and after riding about 100 miles the traveller reaches Kara-Koom, where the route joins the road from Petropavalovsk. The other turns a little to the south-west, for about 100 miles, and then passes to the east of the lakes Tchubar-Tenaze and Oulk-Tenaze, then over the bed of a dried up lake, covered in most parts with high reeds. Again it turns due south through a sterile region on which little grass grows, and where bad water is mostly found. Having passed this, the wayfarer and his camels enter the desert of Kara-Koom, and cross the Syr-Daria, about 100 miles east of the Orenburg route. He then continues onward along the desert, and passes over the branches of the Kouvan-Daria, going east of the numerous lakes of Arali-Kouliar. Beyond these the route enters the Ac-kyr Mountains, and passes the ruins of Kouven-Kala, going to the west of the mountains Bala-tau and Ouch-Tuba. It now enters the desert of Kizil-Koom, and at about sixty miles beyond the Yanè-Daria it joins the route from Orenburg.

The journey from Petropavalovsk to Bokhara usually occupies sixty-five or seventy days; the whole distance is about 1,200 miles. The route runs due south, passing to the east of lake Terane, and between the lakes Zaranda and Kap-tchi. The first is the source of the river Tchag-li, that runs east, and falls into the lake Tchag-a-li, about 100 miles distant. The second lake is the source of the river Badoun-Boulac, that falls into the Ischim. Beyond these the route passes to the east of Kokchi-tau, and near the mountain and lake Yakshi-Yagni. It then crosses many of the streams that fall into the upper Ischim. A little farther on it enters among the numerous ridges that separate this river from the Noura, and passes over the western end of the Ildi-ghis Mountains. This chain extends to a considerable distance to the south-east, and rises much in elevation in that direction. The whole region is exceedingly rich in minerals. Silver, copper, and lead are found; here also that beautiful mineral, ashiret (copper emerald), was first discovered. Mines of great value will, ere long, be worked in these mountains by the Russian miners.

About thirty miles beyond this ridge the route reaches the line of Cossack piquets, that extend from Djar-gam-nagatch to Ac-molenskoi. It passes the Ischim at Tchan-gar Piquet, and immediately, on crossing the river, enters the Mus-Bel steppe, that extends nearly 100 miles from east to west, and fifty from north to south. Here the grass is good in many parts, but fresh water is not abundant. Having crossed this plain, the traveller enters a region of lakes, many of which are salt, and about twenty-five miles beyond this labyrinth is the Yakshi-Kon. After crossing the stream, the route turns up its western bank, and follows the river near to its source in the Oulou-tau. This is a most interesting and picturesque group of mountains, and the route crosses them in a south-westerly direction as far as the Kara-Kingoar. Hence it turns more south, and after passing all the high ridges, descends to the great valley of the Toorma, north of the Kara-Koom.

To the south of the river Bel-goosh, a sterile region commences, that stretches out more than 120 miles to the edge of the "Black Desert." Then the Kara-Koom, on which not a single well of water exists, has to be encountered; it

Sand Pillars on the Desert.

is eighty miles across, and its sombre colour presents a most dreary aspect.

The woodcut represents a phenomenon I have often witnessed on these sandy plains of Central Asia, which accounts in some measure for the innumerable sandy mounds that are found in some regions. When seen at a distance for the first time, it made a strong impression on my mind; about twenty pillars were in view, wheeling round and licking up the sand. As they passed along a cloud of dust was raised on the ground, apparently eight or ten yards in diameter. This gradually assumed the form of a column, that continued to increase in height and diameter as it moved over the plain, appearing like a mighty serpent rearing his head aloft, and twisting his huge body into contortions in his efforts to ascend.

The pillars were of various sizes, some 20 and 30 feet high, others 50, 60, and 100 feet, and some ascended to near 200 feet. As the whirlwinds began gathering up the dust, one might have fancied that antediluvian monsters were rising into life and activity. The smaller ones seemed to trip it lightly over the plain, bending their bodies in graceful curves as they passed each other; while those of larger dimensions revolved with gravity, swelling out their trunks as they moved onward, till the sandy fabric suddenly dissolved, forming a great mound, and creating a cloud of dust that was swept over the desert.

Having passed the Kara-Koom, there is another hundred miles of sterile region, where grass is rarely found, and seldom fresh water. Salt lakes are numerous, and appear beautiful with their fringes of salsola, but these afford neither food nor drink for man or beast. About forty miles from the Syr-Daria, bushes are found scattered over the steppe, and among them both grass and water. As the traveller proceeds, the country becomes more fertile, till he arrives on the banks of the river, where the route crosses it about seventy miles below Ac-Mastchet. Hence it continues onward over the desert of Kara-Koom, crosses the branches of Kouven-Daria, passes near the ruins of Koven-Kala, and joins the route from Orenburg in the desert of Kizil-Koom.

There is another route from Petropavalovsk to Bokhara and to Tashkend, in lat. 43° N., and long. 69° E., which on leaving Petropavalovsk runs nearly parallel with that to Bokhara for about 150 miles, and then it turns in a more easterly direction to Ac-molenskoi. This place, like Ayagus, is the seat of a local government, whose power extends over a large district in the Middle Horde. Hence the route runs along the western bank of the river Noura more than 100 miles, and not far from the Cossack piquets that are placed on the eastern side of the river, extending to the fortress of Ac-tauskoi, more than 500 miles south of Omsk. It then leaves the Noura, and turns in a more westerly direction, crosses several of the sources of the Yakshi-Kon, and over the high ridge of Souk-bash-tau. Beyond there are two routes: one turns to the south-west, and follows the Sara-Sou for more than 450 miles, till it reaches a group of lakes into which the river runs. It passes the western end of Saou-mal-Kcol, then it turns due west, and goes to the north of Kabous-ten-Kool, and round to the fortress of Ac-Mastchet on the Syr-Daria.

This is a large and strong fort, more than 400 miles from the Aral Sea; it gives Russia the complete command of the Syr-Daria and the regions around. Her steamers can pass up the river beyond this fortress to within twenty miles of the town of Turkestan, and to within thirty miles of Tashkend, and boats can ascend the river Tchubar-sou nearly to the town. Vessels of a small draught of water will be able to reach Khodjend, and even near to Kokhan. Thus steam has placed these States under the control of Russia, and her will must be their law.

After leaving Ac-Mestchet, the route passes through a wooded region to the desert of Kizil-Koom; when this dreary spot is passed, the caravans reach the Arolan Mountains, and beyond them is a cultivated country to the end of the journey. The distance from Petropavalovsk to Bokhara by this route is above 1,400 miles.

I now return to the point where the second route branches off, after passing the Souk-bash-tau, and this forms the direct one between Petropavalovsk and Tashkend.

Shortly after crossing the ridge of the Souk-bash-tau, it turns to the south-east, towards the fortress of Ac-tau-skoi, running in that direction for thirty-five miles to the river Maneka, whence it takes a course south-west, and passes over the Kish-tau. From this point it continues over numerous hills, where grass and water is abundant, as far as the Kok-tash. Beyond this river it crosses the mountains Sasarloi and E-dalnin-aki-dingul. After passing these, it enters the sterile steppe of Bad-Pak-Dala, that extends for 160 miles to the river Tchui. This is a dreary region, affording but little food for either horses or camels; the water is also bad. Kol-sol-Boulac is the first spring found on the route, and this is good water. The other springs are Sol-Baksi-sor, Kol-Buru-Tusken, Kol-Oubanas-Koudook, Kizee-Emask, and Sol-Atch-Kazanee; they are all brackish; both man and beast often suffer severely before reaching the Tchui.

After passing this river the caravans enter upon the desert of Ous-Kokchan-nin-sara-Koom; it is only about twenty-five miles broad. The route passes the western end of Djooban-tau, to the spring Kol-oush-ouzen-Koudook; it then turns to the south-east, along the foot of the Kara-tau, and passes within a few miles of the fort Sou-zak. Thence to fort Chald-Koorgan, where it crosses the mountains to Tchem-Kesh, and then about fifty miles to Tashkend over a good track. From fort Sou-zak a route crosses the Kara-tau to Turkestan.

The routes which start from Semipalatinsk are very important in connection with the commerce of Central Asia, there being considerable intercourse between this town and Tashkend, Kokhan, Samarkand, Kashgar, and Yarkand. I shall commence with the one from Semipalatinsk to Tashkend, a journey of fifty to fifty-five days; which, after crossing the Irtisch, turns in a south-westerly direction as far as the river Astche-sou, that runs from the south and falls into the Irtisch at Dolouskoi. It runs nearly west for about fifty miles after passing this river, and then turns in a southerly course, passing to the north of the Argali mountain, and round the north-western end of Tchingiz-Tau. From here it proceeds over the mountains Yakshi Arolie, Yeman Arolie, and Tchul-par, after which it descends to the river Dogan-del; this stream runs south, and falls into the Balkash. About thirty-five miles beyond this river the road divides, one branch going due west, towards Tashkend, and the other south-west, for Kokhan.

I shall follow the western one first, that passes over the upper end of the valley of Tarlaou, and onward to the river Kou-sak; whence it continues over the Siegalia-Kizil-rai Mountain, where it turns more to the south, crossing the Korgen-tash, the Djag-tash, and several large streams that have their sources in these mountains, and are afterwards lost in the steppe. Leaving the Ac-tau group to the north, the route proceeds over two of its southern spurs, Yakshe-bot and Kizil-siga. After crossing two other ridges, Tai-gat-Kaa and Boulat, it descends to the Bed-Pak-Dala, about 300 miles distant from the Tchui. Up to this point good water and pastures are found along the whole route; but now it enters a sterile region, in which, although not a desert, there are many sandy plains, with tracks of rough grass separating them, that afford indifferent pastures for the caravans. In some places the sand has been whirled into thousands of hillocks, some forty and fifty feet in height, and others of smaller dimensions. These give a most extraordinary aspect to the region, and compel the traveller to make almost double the distance by winding his way among them. For about 100 miles beyond Boulat the route passes through a country in which a few springs are found. There are wells at Kol-Tash-Djargan, at Kol-Bish-Bakier, and others at Keze-Kazan, and the last at Tok-Koom-Tik-Kau.

Hence to the Tchui it is a painful journey: mirage and sand-storms frequently await the traveller; the former tantalizes his thirst, and the latter may form his grave. Many of my readers know nothing practically of the mirage, and thus they can neither appreciate the beauty of this deception, nor estimate the disappointment it creates. I fear my pencil fails in rendering its magical effect, and my pen cannot give an adequate idea of its tantalizing power on the thirsty traveller. It has, however, often fallen to my lot to witness it, when an apparent lake stretched out before me, tempting both man and animal to rush on and slake their burning thirst. Even after years of experience I have been deceived by this phenomenon, so real has it appeared, and many of its peculiar and magical effects have been preserved. Sometimes vast cities seemed rising on the plains, in which a multitude of towers, spires, domes, and columns were grouped together with a picturesque effect that neither poet nor painter could depict. And these were reflected in the deceptive fluid with all the distinctness of a mirror; at times a slight breeze seemed to ruffle the placid surface, destroying the forms for a few minutes, and then they reappeared.

Sometimes I have been almost induced to believe that vast tropical forests were before me, where palms of gigantic size, with their graceful foliage, overtopped every other tree, and that beyond were mountain crests, giving a reality to the scene that caused me for the moment to doubt its being a phantom. At last I have passed over the spot where the lake, the mighty city, and the vast forest had appeared, and found nothing but small bushes and tufts of grass growing on the steppe.

Having left the wells, after a long ride the caravan reaches Tess-Boulac, the sparkling water having been visible over a distance of thirty miles. The sight of shining liquid and the burning sun constantly adding to the thirst of the traveller, at last the wished-for draught is reached. But, alas! it is too briny for even the animals to taste, and man and beast turn away in despair. The next lake is Tosg-Boulac, but here is no relief. Another long ride brings the caravan to a group of three conical mounts, Kara-Kea, Kazaa-gap, and Tan-tau, and to brackish water. From here the route passes the eastern end of Koksha-tau, and then turns westerly to the ford on the Tchui, at Kazangau-out-Kool. Hence it crosses the desert Ous-Kokchau-nin-sara-Koom, and then the sandy steppe Koksha-Koom, pass-

Mirage on the Steppes.

ing the western end of Kara-gol, to the fort Chala-Koorgan, where it joins the route to Tashkend.

Returning to the head of the valley of Tarlaou, I now proceed to trace out the route from that point to Kokhan. From here it runs down the valley that extends for about 140 miles to the Balkash. There are many isolated mounts in this valley, some of considerable elevation and exceedingly picturesque. The route passes between two of them, Asan and Tchou-lak, and then it strikes on the shores of the Balkash, at Zalave-Tchag-a-nak, passing the head of the bay of Bala-Dersen, and a conical hill, Djar-Tash. It continues close to the shore, passes another mount, Tar-gil, and proceeds round the bay of Kal-mak-Kargan to Sarim-sakti. It then leaves the shore for about twenty-five miles, till it reaches the bay of Djed-il-Toubek, which it also encircles, and turns to the south-east, close along the shore, till it reaches the southern end of the lake at Ac-taga.

A few miles beyond the end of the lake it crosses the river Djar-Tashnin-Karalou, and goes due south. After proceeding over a steppe for about twenty-five miles, it ascends the Arkarle chain, to the summits Djar-e-leeau, Koi-Djar-e-leeau, and Khau-tau. It then descends into the valley of the Tchui, crossing the river Dala-Kai-nar about fifteen miles east of the fort Sale-Koorja, and continues southward, passing over the Tchui and the Kare-Tche-too, to the fort Saroi-Kodja, at the foot of the high chain of Koonge-Ala-tau. Leaving this place, it advances along the chain over some difficult passes, and descends to the Keez-Koort-Ata, proceeding over the sources of the river Sou-Sara. It then crosses a part of Kader-tau to the source of the river Ac-sa-tchi, and continues along this valley to the Syr-Daria and Kokhan. The whole journey from Semipalatinsk to Kokhan occupies seventy days.

I shall now give the routes from Semipalatinsk to the Chinese town of Tchoubachak, in lat. 46° 15′ N., and long. 83° 5′ E. There are two: one by the new fort of Kokpektinskoi, the other by Ayagus. On leaving Semipalatinsk, both go due south as far as the first Cossack piquet Ouloogoosky. From this point, the one for Kokpektinskoi turns over the steppe towards the south-east, crosses the river Tchor-Gourban, and passes along at the foot of the Sara-Tau. It then continues over the great steppe that extends to the south, as far as the Kaude-ga-tai, and east to the

Kaden Mountains, which it crosses, to the fort at Kokpektinskoi. After leaving this place, it proceeds on towards Nor-Zaisan, keeping to the east of Sand-dik-Tash, and having passed this chain, enters the great plain lying between the Tarbagatai and Nor-Zaisan.

On this part of the route the caravans occasionally meet with some difficulties from the numerous small streams that cut deep channels in the sand. Beside these they have to cross the river Bougaz, the Ac-sou-at, the Kaberga-Bazar, a deep and dangerous stream, and then the Salde-roma. All these rivers have their source in the Tarbagatai, and fall into Nor-Zaisan. After passing them, the route ascends the Sarte-Tologui, and crosses the high ridge Dju-bau-Tube; thence descends the southern slopes of the Tarbagatai, within the Chinese frontier, and proceeds along the plain to Tchou-bachak. This is a ten days' journey over a region where good pastures and water abound throughout.

The other route to Tchoubachak goes due south from Semipalatinsk for nearly 200 miles, following the military road, along the line of piquets, till it reaches Ayagus. On leaving this place, it turns to the south-east, passing over the plain to the southern side of the Tarbagatai, where it crosses several hills that extend from the chain. Numerous streams descend from the mountains on this side, and the route passes over the sources of the Kara-Kal and Our-djar, also over the rivers Katen-sou, Kok-terric, and Ash-boulac. Shortly after getting beyond the Katen-sou, it enters on a sandy plain, on which there is but little herbage, extending for more than fifty miles, till it reaches several small lakes, some of which are surrounded with reeds. At the western end of one of these lakes there is a Chinese piquet, close on the Russian frontier, and eight miles beyond is the town of Tchoubachak. It stands on a level plain at the foot of the Tarbagatai, that rises abruptly from the plain for about 3,000 feet. This journey occupies fourteen days.

From Semipalatinsk to the Chinese town of Kulja, in lat. 42° 46′ N., and long. 82° 48′ 15″ E., there are two routes: both follow the line of Cossack piquets, and pass within fifteen miles of Ayagus. For about ninety miles beyond the fort the road runs to the south-west, to Ourotch-ac-Togai, where it branches off. The first route turns to the south-east, passing over a sterile region for about 100 miles, till it reaches the river Djel-a-nash, that falls into the Sasuk-Kool. It follows this river up to its source in the Kara-tau, and then passes over the chain into the upper valley of the Tin-tek. After crossing this river it ascends to the Chinese piquet on the north side of Kouga-tau, thence over the Chinese frontier to another high ridge, Doual-Yannin-Bate, and then descends to the piquet on Konoa-tau. From this place it follows a small mountain torrent to the Kara-boulac, and subsequently ascends the mountains Our-tak-sara and Byan-Djooruk to the river Kang-e-ga. Here it turns to the south-east, and joins the line of Chinese piquets at the northern end of Syram-Kool. From this point it turns to the south-west, along the shore of the lake, and thence by the line of piquets to Kulja. This journey is usually performed in thirty days, but it is not always safe crossing the mountains.

I shall now trace the westerly route, beginning at the junction at Ourotch-ac-Togai. This branch follows the river Ayagus, passing the eastern end of the Balkash, at about fifteen miles distant. It then crosses the Mai-Bieruk-Kool, a large dried-up lake, and proceeds over the small ridge Arkarale. Hence it runs along the edge of the great sandy plain Et-djep to Kok-terric, where it turns to the south-west over the sandy steppe. After crossing the Lep-sou it winds its way among a vast multitude of sandy hillocks to Baskau-Kool, and thence to the Ac-sou in its deep sandy bed. Beyond this river it passes the numerous lakes formed by the river Bean. In spring, when the snow-water comes from the mountains, this part of the route is both difficult and dangerous. Again the route runs along the edge of the sandy plain to the deep ravine Kizil-a-gatch, and a few miles beyond crosses the river Ala-Djeda.

Its course is now towards the mountains, on reaching which it ascends the Boura-Kol, the most westerly point of the Kara-tau. Hence it goes due south to the river Terek-te, and here begins the ascent of the Soroi-a-kin chain. After passing this it turns to the south-east, up the valley of the Kok-sou, and then proceeds into the valley of the Kou-tal. At this place the caravan begins to ascend the highest and most difficult part of the route, the Ugen-Tash; still loaded camels are able to cross, except in the depth of winter, and then all travelling ceases. Having crossed this high, rocky ridge, the traveller passes the frontier into China, and soon reaches the first piquet; then it is only a short distance to the town of Ak-kent. On leaving this town the route crosses several streams that fall into the Ili; it then passes through Kourgan, where the Chinese have a garrison; beyond this there is a good road to the town of Kulja, about twenty miles distant. The caravans usually make the journey from Semipalatinsk in thirty-five days.

It now only remains to trace the route towards Kashgar, in lat. 39° 25′ N., and long. 74° 5′ E., which branches off at Boura-Koi, and crosses the several streams that form the Kara-tal. Then it continues onward to the Sara-tau; beyond here it passes two branches of the river Beja, the mountain Molpai-sara, then goes round the western end of the Tchoulac Mountains into the valley of the Ili. It crosses this river at Ourotch-Tamgalee-out-Kool, and turns south-east into the valley of the Tcharin. Following this river nearly to its source, it passes a little to the west of the Khan-Tergee Mountain, along the crest of which Russia has for the present set her boundary. Hence it turns to the south, crossing the lofty chain of To-boulgee-assan, and descends into that extraordinary basin of the Issa-Kool to Sara-Tologui, near which there is a Cossack piquet.

From this point the route continues along the north-west side of the Mus-tau for about 100 miles, and then crosses this great chain, over a pass said to be 14,000 feet above the sea. The crest of this chain is indicated by Russia as the boundary of her empire. About eighty miles from this the route joins the Chinese road to Kashgar. These are all the routes by which commerce is carried on between Russia, Siberia, and this part of Central Asia.

The Cossack one extends along the southern frontier for about 800 miles from Kopal, on the east, to Ac-mastchet, on the Syr-Daria. In a previous chapter I have described the founding of Kopal, but the aspect of the place has been completely changed. At the present time it contains 11,000 inhabitants, and will gradually increase as commerce extends into these regions. Notwithstanding the defective position of the place, wealth will be acquired here, and population is sure to follow. A considerable number of Tatar merchants are established in Kopal, and carry on a most profitable trade with the nomade tribes, as well as with China.

Such has been the sudden rise of Kopal, and its prosperity has induced the people to form another settlement on the Almatee, or "Apple River," about 200 miles south-west of the former fort. The new town of Vernoje is rapidly springing up on this spot. Russia is thus surrounding the Kirghis hordes with civilisation, which will ultimately bring about a moral revolution in this country. Agriculture and other branches of industry will be introduced by the Russian peasant, than whom no man can better adapt himself to circumstances. He is ingenious, can turn his hand to any occupation; indeed, by the aid of his axe and saw alone he will build his dwelling, and be his own cabinet-maker. He is his own tailor and shoemaker, grows his flax, and his wife and children spin and weave their linen. In short, there are few necessaries which these people cannot prepare. Generally he is a good hunter, and understands the use of his rifle; he can thus procure food wherever game is found. This gives him confidence in his new position, and makes him formidable to an enemy if molested. When once made a free agent his natural capabilities will be developed, and then he will not be behind any European, either in genius or industry. He has my best wishes for his freedom.

It has been stated that "Vernoje would become a manufacturing town, that extensive cotton mills were about to be erected, and were to be worked by the nomades." I doubt this having been contemplated, unless in the brain of an enthusiastic speculator, who knows nothing either of the region or of its inhabitants. From my own experience among the Kirghis, I know the utter impossibility of converting nomades into industrious mechanics. Their pastoral habits and love of a wandering life have been formed during several centuries, and it will take many generations to change them. Their chivalrous spirit disdains the idea of manual labour in every shape, except with the flocks and herds. They will long remain as free as the wild steeds of the plains. Another important article is wanting—viz., fuel, to render this a manufacturing district, and there is little probability of coal being found in these mountains. There is wood in some of the valleys and ravines, but not in sufficient quantities to supply more than the ordinary wants of the people.

It is true that water-power to any amount could be obtained on some of the mountain streams—that is, during the summer season. But when winter stops the snow melting, large torrents become small rills in a few days, and then water-power would cease for several months. Even if this difficulty did not exist, that of machinery and artisans would be insuperable. The cost of transit from Europe into these distant regions would be ruin to any person or company who engaged in such speculations. Besides which, either English or Russian manufacturers could supply both plain and printed calicoes cheaper than they could be produced at Vernoje.

While on this subject I shall mention a circumstance that occurred during my sojourn here. In 1849 a considerable quantity of English calicoes reached Yarkand, Kokhan, and Tashkend. They were printed in the two latter towns in patterns to suit the taste of the people: from their superior quality and price, the Tatar merchants were induced to purchase the goods and carry them in their trading expeditions among the nomades of Central Asia. They also found a ready sale, and the people were delighted with their new garments. Several of these kalats were shown to me, and their superior quality commented on by their owners. All were anxious to possess them: thus the articles had at once established a character and a trade.

The following year, when the merchants visited Kokhan and Tashkend, they obtained similar goods, and these were still more appreciated by the Kirghis. In 1851 the Tatar traders bought their goods as usual, which in appearance resembled those of the former years. These were taken by the caravans into distant regions, and they also met with a ready sale. But, alas, the purchaser soon discovered that he had been victimised; the material proved to be complete trash, and the discovery caused a great reaction. It was a fact well known in Siberia that agents for English houses were in Kokhan, and, from all I could learn, they were natives of India. This was not only a disreputable transaction, but a most foolish experiment, which has done considerable injury to trade among these tribes.

From personal observation I am induced to believe that the best mode of opening a trade into Central Asia will be by establishing fairs. These should be at one or more points near to the passes in the Himalaya, or, perhaps, one great fair as far up the Indus as possible, would be best. This I deem preferable to the English plan of consigning goods to agents either in Yarkand, Kokhan, or Tashkend. Once these fairs are established the Tatar and other merchants will attend and purchase the necessary articles for the people among whom they vend their wares, and this would soon be felt in Nijne Novgorod, as the distance from the Indus is but little more than half of that from Semipalatinsk to Novgorod.

If agents for English houses were located in any of those towns it would create jealousy; the Tatar merchant would fear that an attempt might be made to push the trade into Central Asia and deprive him of his legitimate profit. Besides, these men are thoroughly acquainted with the tribes, and know all their wants; they are industrious and energetic in their calling, travelling over thousands of miles with their caravans. They know every part of the country, and where to find the tribes at all seasons of the year: it is by them that Russia distributes her merchandise over Central Asia. The following are some of the most important articles required by the Kirghis.

Plain calicoes.
Printed calicoes of particular patterns, vivid colouring, and highly glazed.
Good silks are obtained from China, but a common kind might sell.
Velveteens are much in request.
Long shawls, for tying round the waist, are greatly valued; some of the Sultans have them from Cashmere. The Paisley shawls would be highly prized.
Woollen cloths, of a bright scarlet, light blue, yellow, and green, would find a market; but none of a sombre shade could be sold.
Red and green baize.
Handkerchiefs, Turkey red.
Ribbons, in one shade, of either red, blue, yellow, or green.
Fringes.
Sewing cotton, white and red.
Thread.

Gilt, glass and fancy buttons.
Imitation pearls.
Coral beads are highly valued.
Imitation coral beads.
Glass beads, crimson and yellow.
Birmingham trinkets, such as ear-rings, rings, and bracelets.
Cheap watches.
Small looking-glasses.
Knives, large and small.
Scissors, large and moderate size.
Needles of various sizes.
Thimbles, brass and steel.
Padlocks.
Axes.
Stirrup-irons.

Sabres. Guns, single barrel. Rifles. Pistols. Gunpowder and shot. Percussion-caps.	Russia will not supply any of these articles. A few bad rifles are brought from Persia with matchlocks.

Tea; that from the Himalaya would supersede brick-tea, if brought in cheap.
Loaf sugar; that brought from Russia is sold at 3*s*. 2*d*. per lb.
Rice, common, which is brought from Kokhan, is sold at 6*d*. per lb. If this article could be obtained cheaper, great quantities would be consumed.
Tobacco and snuff.
Opium.

The distance from the Indus to Vernoje and Kopal is about one third of that from these places to the great fair on the Volga. This is of no small importance commercially, as these towns will become the centres whence the Tatar merchants will send forth their agents to disperse their goods among all the Kirghis of the steppes. From these points they will also go to the Mongolian tribes on the north of the Gobi, and this region contains a vast population. I have no doubt, should this trade be established, that the merchandise will find its way through the country of the Kalkas into Daouria, and to the regions beyond the Selenga and the sources of the Amoor, where it may advantageously compete with goods brought up the latter river. Nor will the

Siberians fail to avail themselves of its advantages. Whenever there shall be fairs on the Indus, the Kirghis will send into India vast numbers of good horses annually; silver and gold is plentiful in their country, and their other resources will be rapidly developed.

By a reference to my map, the position of the forts on the southern frontier and on the Syr-Daria will be seen. I think it will be obvious to every one that they are so placed as not only to command the whole of the Kirghis hordes, but to exercise a great influence over the countries to the south. It may, indeed, be said that they virtually command the region as far as the thirty-ninth parallel of north latitude, and we may ere long expect to see Cossack piquets near Kashgar.

The whole regions around the Issa-Kool and the Mus-tau Mountains beyond, are occupied by the descendants of those Kalmuck tribes who left the banks of the Volga with their Prince, Oui-bach, to return to the land of their ancestors in Chinese Tartary. This modern exodus of 600,000 people has been so graphically described by De Quincy, that I dare not attempt to follow him, and, although the march route and its termination, which he has described, is not geographically correct, I shall only state a few facts.

The priests and Zebeck-Dorchi, a relation of the Prince, decided the time for departure, and on the 5th of January 1,771, Oui-bach began this exodus with his vast multitude. After leaving the Volga they had a march of about 370 miles before reaching the river Yaik (Oural), the boundary of their own territory. Having passed the river they were in the Kirghis steppe, among hostile tribes who used every means to harass them on their journey. At length they encamped for a time on the river Oulou-Irghis, after which they proceeded in a south-easterly direction, and crossed several sandy plains. Here they suffered many disasters and frequent defeats.

From experience I know something of the difficulties and dangers to which these people were exposed on their march. The elements often prove disastrous and fatal in their consequences, both in winter and in summer. The bourans at the former season bury the people in snow and ice, and in the latter the sand storms smother them. These are not unfrequent on the deserts of Asia over which the Kalmucks marched, and where the caravans still pursue

A Sand Storm on the Desert.

their way. The illustration here given is but a feeble representation of a sand storm and its terrible effect. I have seen one extending over four miles in width, and if travellers or a caravan are caught in them, the consequences are often fatal to man and beast.

Their approach is seen at a long distance, and when they are of moderate breadth it is not difficult to escape; but should they extend over many miles in width, there is real danger.

At a distance a dense black cloud appears rolling over the desert, rising 700 or 800 feet above the ground, and sweeping on with fearful velocity. This causes the people to watch its advance with considerable anxiety, as it is impossible to say which way to turn for security. Instinct tells the animals that danger is approaching, when they too become uneasy, and attempt to escape. Horses and all other animals, when free, rush off at the top of their speed. It is a most exciting scene when these storms reach the pastures: a herd of several thousand horses, with camels and oxen, are seen rushing madly on before the tempest, and the herdsmen are trying to lead them out of its course. On these occasions many fall from exhaustion, and perish as the storm rolls over them.

In every region they passed through, continued attacks were made upon them by the Kirghis, till they reached the southern end of the Balkash, when a final effort was made by the Kirghis to annihilate them. A little beyond this they reached a country prepared for them by the Chinese Emperor, Kien Long; this was on the banks of the Ili, and near the mountains to the south.

From that period to the present, these people, now named Mountain Kirghis, have occupied this region, and long ago the Khans have made themselves independent of their previous benefactors.

During my sojourn in this part of Asia, efforts were made by Russia to form amicable relations with these daring mountaineers, as they were by far the most formidable people to be encountered in any advance southward. It was also feared that they might resist the establishment of forts so near their frontier. Nothing particular arose out of these negotiations, but the works proceeded.

After the fort at Kopal was completed, the Kirghis of the Great Horde awoke out of their lethargy. They collected a great body of men, made an attack on the garrison, and received a severe lesson. The Kirghis had no leader to command them, nor were they aware of the range of the guns, or the terrible effects of grape-shot on their dense masses. A troop of Cossacks was sent out to reconnoitre, and had several skirmishes with the advanced parties, when some were killed on both sides; but the Kirghis so far outnumbered them that they were compelled to retire to the fort.

A great body of Kirghis had been observed advancing along at the foot of the mountains about four miles distant. Those who had been engaged with the Cossacks followed them to within a mile of the fort, and waited the arrival of the main body; this seemed sufficiently numerous to devour the garrison, that did not exceed 500 fighting men. As the Kirghis advanced their numbers were estimated at from 6,000 to 7,000. Having passed a low ridge, they turned on to the plain, and advanced in two divisions, one intending to cross the river and approach on the north. Captain Abakamoff knew the range of his guns, and quietly waited the advancing masses. They came slowly on, and at length reached the fatal ground, when several rounds of grape-shot were poured into them with terrible effect. Each discharge made a gap through their masses, and caused all who could to retreat in the greatest consternation.

Having galloped to a place where they deemed themselves far out of danger, they drew up in a mass, when Abakamoff pitched several round shot into their midst, that killed some and scattered the others like chaff. After this they returned to their aouls, subdued.

The terrible effects caused by the guns was spread far and wide, and soon became known to the Mountain Kirghis. They now wished to renew the negotiations, and sent some of their chiefs to the commander in Kopal to offer their allegiance to "the Great White Khan," from whom their forefathers had fled. This was accepted, and the Mountain Kirghis, it is said, are now the subjects of his Imperial Majesty.

CHAP. XII.

SULTAN TIMOUR AND DJAN-GHIR KHAN.

SULTAN TIMOUR, the father of my hero in the following tragic but well-authenticated story, was the representative of the most ancient and distinguished family of the steppe. His genealogical tree had its roots in the family of the great Genghiz. His poet traced the pedigree through a long line of ancestors, extending to the period when the mighty and cruel conqueror left his capital of Kara-Korum, near the sources of the river Orkhon, marching westward with his vast hordes, and leading them onward to plunder and to conquest.

The countries through which these legions passed were turned into a desert, the inhabitants barbarously murdered, and the cattle driven onward to provide food for the ravagers. As these savages proceeded, the news of their atrocities was spread far and wide, causing the utmost consternation. Some of the tribes escaped across the Irtisch into Siberia, and constantly retreating before the bands sent in pursuit, they ultimately reached and settled in a region beyond Yakoutsk, where their descendants are still found, having retained the language and customs of their ancestors to this day.

A tinge of the blood of the savage conqueror being in the veins of Sultan Timour, made him proud of his descent and imperious in his conduct. As chief of the Great Horde he had unlimited power, would brook no opposition to his will, and many have felt the effects of his cruel temper. His position was an important one, he being the acknowledged head of the Kirghis, and occupying one of the most interesting regions in Central Asia, that contained vast steppes and several mountain chains. The country is bounded on the west by Tashkend, Kokhan, and the Desert of Kisil-koom; on the south by the most northern province of China, that of Ili, in which the Chinese have their penal settlements. It extends eastward to the rivers Ac-sou and Sarcand, while on the north the boundary has never been properly defined between the Great and Middle Hordes, and thus a continued warfare is carried on all along this frontier. In fact, the Great Horde contains within it nearly the whole of ancient Songaria.

To the south-west, commencing towards the upper valley of the Ili, is a vast mountain region, extending around and far beyond the Issa-kool. This country is inhabited by the "Kara Kirghis," so named on account of the dark colour of their skins. They are a brave and warlike people, the men athletic and well-proportioned, with fine faces, large black eyes, and jet black hair; quite a distinct race from the Kirghis who inhabit the plains. I was assured that if the chiefs combined they could muster 40,000 cavalry. Having associated much with these Kirghis, I can safely state that if they were engaged to ravage a country, I know of no force likely to commence their work more willingly, or to accomplish its object with greater effect.

These mountaineers are greatly feared by the Kirghis of the steppes, and not without cause, as they frequently descend from their mountain pastures in great numbers, and commit terrible ravages on all the tribes within their reach; sometimes even carrying their marauding expeditions far into the Middle Horde, and then skilfully retreating with their captives and plunder. I have no doubt whatever that these people and the Kalmucks are at the present moment the subjects of His Imperial Majesty, and when under proper command they will be the most formidable body for mischief of any in Central Asia.

At the commencement of the present century a celebrated chief, Djan-ghir Khan, ruled these tribes, making his power felt in all the surrounding regions. Even the Chinese Governor and their Generals on the Ili found him a dangerous neighbour, and one with whom it was necessary to be on friendly terms. He had often given them a taste of his power for mischief by sweeping down upon their frontier and carrying the people into captivity. Besides which, he frequently plundered the caravans passing through or near his country, while from his mountain fastnesses he bade defiance to the whole Chinese army.

Sultan Timour had his pastures in the southern part of the region inhabited by the Great Horde, frequently feeding his flocks and herds close up to the frontier. This circumstance often brought him in contact with Djan-ghir Khan, and as both were men of undaunted courage, neither liked to be the aggressor: thus a friendly compact sprung up between the two chiefs; probably on the principle which I found governed the Siberian wolves — they never eat each other as long as other food can be obtained, which they hunt for in packs. These two friends followed their example, occasionally uniting their bands of lawless marauders, and then no tribes could resist them. How many Kirghis were sold into captivity, and their wives and daughters made the slaves of these men, it is impossible to say; but the number must have been very great, whole districts having been made desolate.

The arrangements necessary while planning their barantas caused interviews between the chiefs; sometimes at the pastures of one, and then at those of the other. The Sultan's eldest son, Souk, at this time a young man about twenty-eight years old, always took a part in these proceedings. His personal appearance was prepossessing, and he was already distinguished for his valour. He had been the leader in several great and successful barantas where the number of his opponents far exceeded his own band; but his cool courage always gained the victory. He had also engaged in some hand-to-hand conflicts with distinguished warriors, some of whom had been slain and others unseated. These deeds of arms had gained him a renown throughout the Great Horde, and all the tribes looked up to him as their future chief, while by his own people he was almost adored.

Sultan Timour had great confidence in the sagacity of his son, especially in all matters connected with their expeditions. Nor would he enter upon one without consulting him, when the Sultan frequently gave him the command. Thus his presence was necessary at all the interviews between the two chiefs, and this had frequently taken young Souk to the aoul of Djan-ghir Khan, where he became intimate with the family.

The Khan had a daughter possessing great personal charms. Her beauty and kind disposition had made a great impression on the young Kirghis, and being thrown much together, a mutual attachment had grown up between them. After several visits Souk determined to make her his wife: the high rank of his family, and his father's wealth, placed him in a position to demand the hand of any lady in the region; therefore he had no reason to fear any opposition from the Khan.

Having communicated his wishes to Sultan Timour, the old man made no objections to the match; on the contrary, he thought it would be highly advantageous, by cementing a strong friendship between the tribes. In the course of a few days the Sultan sent three of his most distinguished chiefs to the aoul of Djan-ghir Khan, a ten days' journey distant, to make a formal offer for the hand of his daughter. These men were received with marked attention after their long journey, and when the object of their mission was stated, the Khan expressed his great satisfaction.

After calling a council of his chiefs, he gave his consent to the marriage, saying that he was delighted that his daughter should be the wife of so brave a man as the son of his friend. The chiefs were detained at his aoul several days, when the event was celebrated by feasting and various amusements, after which they returned, carrying several presents to their master.

When the result of their mission was made known, the Sultan, his family, and chiefs were delighted, as it was expected the union would prevent all further feuds between the two tribes; but another important matter had yet to be settled between the two families—the kalym. It was feared this might create a difficulty, as the Sultan thought that the honour of an alliance with him ought to weigh heavy in the scale against flocks and herds. On the other hand, it was known that the Khan set a great price on his daughter.

No Rowland Hill has yet sprung up in these regions to organise a post-office, nor would it avail, as none save the Mullas can read or write. A Sultan would, like a baron of the Middle Ages, have deemed it an insult to be thought capable of such an unaristocratic accomplishment. It will be long before the schoolmaster is abroad among these people. Under these circumstances no epistolary correspondence could be carried on between the lovers, and a ride of ten days through such a region was attended with no little risk, so that their chances of communication were difficult and doubtful.

The distance and dangers that separated the couple had no terrors for the young Sultan; they only added to his determination to encounter them, and visit his bride. His father possessed a celebrated stud of horses, powerful and fleet, and one of the best of these was his constant companion. A Kirghis, like an Arab, loves his horse, and they live together like members of an affectionate family. When on a journey, the animal is piqueted at night beside his master's earthy couch, and then he acts the part of a faithful watch-dog. Nothing can approach without his giving notice, and by the snort or the tone of recognition his master knows whether friend or foe is at hand.

Noble and faithful animal! if civilised man as well understood your qualities as the savage or semi-barbarian, how different would be your lot! No spur would be used to lance your heaving sides, no lash applied to cut your glossy flanks. No powerful bit, with its torturing inventions, would be needed; in truth, the curb ought to be put into the mouth of the civilised savage who applies it. Rarey has proved that the horse often possesses more intelligence than his master, and if the animal becomes vicious it is caused by bad or improper treatment.

Souk and some of his young companions possessed steeds on which they could fully depend; they were trained to carry their riders into battle, and by bounding give additional force to the uplifted axe, which, when thus wielded, no sabre can parry. If outnumbered they can retreat at a speed that their pursuers cannot attain. A portion of the region through which Souk must pass to reach the aoul of Djan-ghir Khan was exceedingly dangerous, being inhabited by wild tribes who lived by plunder. They were formed into bands, and elected the most daring men for their chiefs: the mountainous nature of the country, and the difficult passes, rendered this district a safe asylum; and desperate characters from all the surrounding tribes sought refuge and employment here.

This being the month of June, Souk knew that Djanghir Khan would be at his pastures, in the Mus-tau, and to reach him it would take a ride of seven or eight days. He therefore selected a little band of his often-tried companions, eight in number, all of whom he knew would stand by him to the last. The marauders usually hovered at some distance around the regions in which the Kirghis were pasturing their cattle. They were more likely to be found during their first or second day's ride, and again when approaching the pastures of Djan-ghir Khan.

With a light heart and pleasant anticipations, young Souk prepared to lead his companions. Taking leave of

A Valley in the Mus-tau.

his family and tribe, they started on their perilous journey, each man taking two horses, as they intended to ride hard. The first day's journey was towards the Ili, through his father's domain, and evening was fast closing in when they reached the bank of the river. Here they encamped for the night, deeming it prudent to sleep before crossing the stream, as the opposite bank belonged to the Kalmucks.

Besides which, there might also be some of the plundering bands prowling about; if so, it was better to have the Ili flowing between them, at this point about 400 yards broad, and it could only be crossed by swimming.

Their camp was quickly formed under some bushes on the bank of the stream, and their horses were piqueted to feed, attended by two men as guards. Other enemies besides the Kalmucks had their haunts in this region, who might take a fancy to their horses. Tigers were numerous on the shores of the Balkash, near the mouth of the Ili, and these animals often prowl far in search of prey. This rendered the Kirghis cautious, and when night came on the horses were secured near the fire, not far from the men. Two sentinels mounted guard with their battle-axes, with fire-brands close at hand.

They were not disturbed, and morning dawned on a busy group preparing for their march. Having taken their morning meal, they stripped, secured their clothing, mounted their steeds, and plunged into the stream; carrying their garments high above their heads, they breasted its flowing current, and reached the opposite bank in safety. They were now on hostile ground, where it required caution in clearing the belt of shrubs that grew along the bank, and extended half a mile in breadth, for here an ambush might have been effectually concealed. This passed, they were in the open country, and after riding over the plain they began to ascend the first low hills, the offshoots of the chain.

As they rode along the ground was scanned in search of trails, by which they might learn if any bands were in the neighbourhood. Such signs should never be overlooked by travellers among these wild tribes; they are like finger-posts pointing in the direction of danger, and by carefully observing them it may be avoided. On the other hand, a trail as often guides the plunderer to his victim, and thus a man is constantly compelled to make good use of three of his organs here,— brain, eyes, and ears.

The route was in a south-westerly direction, which led them over a fine hilly country, almost destitute of wood except in some of the narrow mountain valleys and deep ravines. The sun had long passed the meridian, the horses had rested, and the travellers had taken their mid-day meal, but as yet they had seen nothing to indicate that man was in this vast region. This was a favourable circumstance, and they hastened onward, intending to stop at a good encamping ground, well known to several of the party.

Having reached the summit of a high ridge, a magnificent scene burst upon their view, lit up and tinged with a golden hue by the setting sun. A Kirghis, as I have said, is a lover of nature, and not without poetry in his soul.

The scene before them was one fitted to call forth poetic feelings; they were standing on a rocky ridge, whence they looked down into a deep valley, clothed with luxuriant vegetation. A large stream was meandering through its centre, fringed with tall cedars, picta trees, and underwood, consisting of a variety of flowering shrubs. Behind these the river was partly hidden from their view, but only to burst forth again, and receive the reflection from the glowing tints of evening, that gave it the appearance of liquid gold shining between banks of emeralds.

The opposite ridge far overtopped that on which they stood, while the sun was lighting up its riven crags, and casting long shadows of the deepest purple over its rocky masses. Beyond this were many other crests receding into a purple misty haze, till they were almost lost in blue ethereal vapour. And still more distant rose the majestic summits of the Mus-tau, wrapt in their coverings of eternal snow, now glowing with a rosy hue, like a pale pink flame flickering over their lit-up sides, rendered still more beautiful by its strong contrast with the cold wintry tone of those in shade.

Leaving this spot they descended into the valley, and before reaching half way down, turned in a southerly direction; continuing their ride along the mountain side to a point where another deep and narrow valley opened towards the south-east. Having reached a shoulder of the mountain that descended abruptly down into the deep ravine, they were suddenly brought to a stand by two objects. One, a great mass of rock, that completely barred their path; the other, which they regarded with no little apprehension, was a column of smoke curling up in the valley at about two miles distant. From their present position they could not observe the fires whence the smoke arose. But the sight of the vapour caused them instantly to dismount and lead their horses under the shelter of the rock, fearing they might be discovered.

Two advanced on foot to reconnoitre, creeping cautiously round the base of the rocks, and then onward among some fallen masses, that completely screened them. At length they reached a point, about half a mile from the encampment, and two thousand feet above it. From their elevated position they looked down into the valley, unseen by those below, and beheld three large fires blazing. A considerable number of men were sitting around each, and many others were engaged piqueting the horses. This scene they understood at a glance; here was a band of more than one hundred men going out on a baranta,—above ten times their number, and in the act of encamping on the very place on which Souk intended to sleep. Had they reached this spot an hour earlier, their fate would have been sealed: for every man would have been either killed or captured.

The two scouts had not been long in their observatory when they saw three men riding towards the camp at a gallop, having come up the valley in their direction. It was evident that these people had seen Souk and his men, and were conveying the news to their chief; beside which, it was not improbable that an advanced party of them was encamped lower down in the valley. The approaching horsemen were watched with much anxiety: they soon reached the fires, when by their gestures, and pointing towards the high cliffs, Souk's men knew that they had been discovered. In a few minutes several groups assembled around the riders, no doubt to learn the news, and presently were engaged saddling their horses, as if they had been ordered to reconnoitre.

There was no time to lose, and the scouts left their hiding-place to hasten to their companions, and inform them of what they had seen. The intelligence proved that their position was somewhat dangerous, as their enemies greatly outnumbered them. A council was held to decide what was to be done. Souk asked his friends if any of them wished to abandon the journey, and if so, he recommended them do it at once, while the route was open. All exclaimed "No," and assured him that they were ready to go into the marauders' camp if he would lead them.

He then told them that they had to deal with a dangerous and cunning enemy, who knew every pass and route in the mountains, while only one route was known to him. Notwithstanding this, he said that he was determined to proceed at all risks, and felt quite sure that by caution, and the superior speed of their horses, he could baffle their pursuit. He advised a return down the valley for about two miles, then to cross the ridge and descend into another, running more to the south-east, as this would lead them to the only pass by which he knew they could ascend to the upper lands.

Without waiting to discover the intentions of the marauders, they started back at a brisk pace, hoping to cross the ridge, and reach the valley before night closed in. The ascent was abrupt, although not difficult, but before they attained the summit the dusky shades of evening filled the deep hollow in which their enemies were encamped. On looking back no living objects were visible beneath, although it was possible they might be seen from below, as the crest was still glowing with the last rays of departing day. Pushing onwards they crossed the ridge, and descended into the gloom, which rendered their progress slow; but the coming darkness had one advantage—it would prevent their trail being discovered till morning.

Fortunately, Kirghis horses are safe animals when descending a mountain, even in the dark, as I have often proved; but it is necessary to place implicit confidence in them, to throw the reins on their necks, and give them their own time. They appear to snuff danger before they reach it, and turn away. On this side of the mountain, however, there were no precipices to avoid, but they had another danger. Tigers have their dens among the rocks.

On a former journey through this valley one of Souk's men had a narrow escape; a tiger sprung upon one of his horses, and severely wounded the man, who, however, succeeded in releasing himself, by leaving the horse to the beast.

Souk was the only person in the party who had any knowledge of this route, and after descending he led the way to the south, riding sharply on towards the gorge. In about an hour and a half they came to a small stream that flowed down the ravine; turning up its bank, they shortly reached the mouth of the pass, and here prepared to encamp. Bushes were speedily obtained, when a fire was kindled, that lighted up the base of the cliffs near them, while everything else was lost in darkness. Their horses were piqueted to feed near at hand, and soon the little party were seated at their evening meal, discussing their position. They had no fear of being surprised during the darkness, but knew that men would be on their trail with the dawn; consequently it behoved them to proceed with as little delay as possible. Two sentinels were placed, and urged to be vigilant on their watch, and the rest were soon sleeping soundly.

The night passed without any cause of alarm, and before day dawned they were in their saddles, being determined to get a good start before their trail could be discovered. In

A Kirghis attacked by a Tiger.

these regions, where man hunts man, following his footsteps with the sagacity of a bloodhound, it requires a thorough knowledge of the country, great prudence, and no lack of courage to effect an escape from such pursuers, especially if the chase promises to be a long one.

The robbers, by their intimate knowledge of the country, possess advantages they are not slow in turning to account. In this instance it was feared that men had been sent on during the night to give notice to their associates in the more elevated lands, that a prize was in the country. Thus the young chief might have to run the gauntlet against numerous bands of plunderers who would be watching for his approach.

The travellers pursued their march at a rapid pace, frequently changing their horses to enable them to push on. The country over which they rode was highly interesting; rich valleys, extending between mountains, that rose up into bare and rugged crests; beyond these several snow-capped summits were visible in the distance. But no tribes with their cattle were found, they being further to the south, at their summer pastures. During this day's ride they crossed several mountain ridges, but no men were seen following on their trail.

After a long ride they stopped for the night in the entrance of a great ravine, through which lay their onward route for the morrow. Before lying down to rest every precaution was taken against surprise.

All was quiet in the camp, the guard had been several times changed, and their companions slept on in security. About two hours before daybreak several of the horses gave an alarm that caused the sentinels to rouse up the men instantly. From this circumstance it was believed that other horses were in the neighbourhood, and every one thought that the robbers were coming; but it was still exceedingly dark, and the high cliffs added to the thick gloom that rendered objects invisible beyond the glare of the camp fire. Though all were certain that it was not a false alarm, as nothing more was heard, they turned down and slept.

Soon after daybreak, while the horses were being saddled,

two Kirghis walked out of the ravine, returning a short distance on their old track, in the hope of discovering the cause of the alarm; but they found nothing indicating that either man or beast had been there. Presently all were in their saddles and rode away, wondering what had disturbed the animals.

It was a magnificent morning when they left their camp, the sunbeams were tipping the tops of the lofty crags with golden light; but it would be long ere his slanting rays penetrated to the bottom of the rocky gorge, which was still enveloped in deep grey shade, making the place look cold and gloomy. Here and there huge blocks were strewn over the bottom of the pass, that had fallen from the granite cliffs above. Both summer sun and winter frost had aided in hurling these rocks from their lofty beds, and in some places they were piled up into mighty heaps, reaching quite across the gorge.

About 300 yards from the camp they came upon one of these confused masses, over which they found it exceedingly difficult to lead their steeds. The first man who passed discovered the footprints of horses. When the young Sultan and the others joined him, he pointed to the numerous footmarks: several men instantly dismounted to examine them, and quickly ascertained that two horses had been piqueted at this place, and that they had not left the spot more than two hours. The cause of the alarm was now evident; the men had walked down the gorge, approaching near enough to see what was passing at the encampment, but, finding the sentinels on the alert, had returned.

Could it be possible that a party had already reached the pass and were waiting for them higher up, or were these two men scouts sent to follow on their trail? Having considered the matter for a few minutes with some anxiety, the party inclined to the last supposition; nevertheless, it was deemed necessary to proceed with caution. Souk now ordered the spare horses to be strung together and to be led by one man, leaving the others at liberty to use their weapons in case of need.

He also resolved to push forward through the pass at all risk, and without delay, knowing that there were fine open valleys beyond, that would afford a much better chance of escape than their present resting-place. To prevent a surprise, one man rode on about fifty yards in advance, and others observed the trail. After proceeding about two miles, they reached a point where the gorge made a turn to the south-west. Having passed the jutting angle about 200 yards, the man in advance reined in his horse, and signalled to his companions, who rode rapidly up. They had scarcely reached him when three men rode into the gorge, about fifty paces from them, and both parties were surprised. The new comers gave a signal to others, when Souk and his men heard the clatter of hoofs among the rocks above, that led them to suppose another group was descending a steep ravine.

The young Sultan saw in an instant there was not a moment to lose; he gave the word "charge!" and dashed on at the three horsemen before him. Before he reached them a fourth sprung out into the pass, calling him to surrender; but as Souk's steed rushed on, the battle-axe was swung with terrible force, and with unerring aim it fell on the head of the man who attempted to oppose him, causing instant death, and inflicting a severe wound on the neck of the steed, which plunged forward and fell. Two of the man's associates fell by the axes of Souk's followers, but the fourth leaped his horse into a narrow ravine, down which a numerous body now appeared descending, uttering shouts of vengeance on seeing their leader and comrades fall; but they were too high up in the chasm to afford assistance to their friends.

Souk ordered the spare horses to be separated; the thongs were slipped in a few moments, and three men dashed off with the steeds up the gorge, the others following close at their heels. Before any number of the banditti had reached the gorge, Souk and his friends were several hundred yards from the ravine; but soon a terrible shout

The Charge.

was set up, and a large body followed in full chase. The rough and stony pass rendered galloping dangerous, and retarded the pace of the pursued; still the latter maintained their distance—the young Sultan and one of his most daring companions bringing up the rear, and occasionally glancing back at their enemies. After riding about an hour, they emerged from the gorge on to a high plateau. During the last half mile they had gained in the race, and having cleared the pass, Souk ordered his people to dismount and change their horses. This was quickly done, and when their pursuers had reached within fifty yards, they sprung into their saddles and scoured over the plain. The latter, finding that they lost ground on the plateau, in about half an hour gave up the chase.

In an open country like this no ambush could be formed to take them by surprise, and with their fleet steeds they felt safe even if ten times their number were in pursuit. This plateau was known by some of the Sultan's men, who also were acquainted with a route to the eastward, leading through a series of valleys, by following which they might reach Djan-ghir Khan's summer pastures in three days.

To the south-west, at the distance of a few miles, thickly-wooded mountain slopes rose about 2,000 feet; and beyond these were rugged crests appearing far above the line of vegetation. To the east and north the chains were somewhat lower, but not less savage in character; and the people inhabiting some of these valleys partake of the wild nature of their country. The place over which the men were now riding was one vast solitude, unbroken by any living sound except the scream of the eagle as he soared aloft. Two months later and these valleys, with their luxuriant pastures, would be covered with herds of camels, horses, and oxen, with vast flocks of sheep, and with the aouls of the tribes scattered over their surface in every direction. They, however, made a long day's ride, without either a sight or sign of man, and encamped on the wooded bank of a little rivulet, where they passed the night in perfect security.

It was not, however, until the evening of the seventh day after leaving his father's aoul, that the young Sultan was greeted by the father of his bride, who received him with a most cordial welcome. It is not my intention to describe the meeting of the young lovers, or tell of the tender scenes that passed between them during the short time the young chief remained at the aoul.

Souk found the Khan in one of the upper valleys of the Mus-tau — a most lovely and romantic spot. It would be difficult to discover one more attractive, as summer vegetation was in its prime. The valley was about fifteen miles in length, and four or five in breadth, apparently surrounded by lofty mountains, some of whose summits pierced far into the region of eternal snow, where sparkling glaciers are seen, and the thundering avalanche heard as it rushes down into the valley, shaking the mountains with its mighty crash, and forming a chaos of ice, rocks, and snow, terrible in effect.

Not far from these ruins of the mountains the ground was covered with rich pastures, and flowers of almost every hue were intermingled and blooming in tropical luxuriance, forming a carpet of unsurpassable beauty. On the mountain sides thousands of horses were grazing, while camels and oxen were feeding along their base. Sheep and goats were seen browsing high up in the mountains; the goats were scaling the loftiest crags in search of the short and velvety herbage found near the summits.

Several aouls were dotted over the valley, and Kirghis in their gay and various-coloured costumes were galloping to and fro, while groups of saddle horses were seen piqueted near the yourts. Here was the temporary home of an Asiatic chief, surrounded by his followers and his living property. This is a summer phase in nomade life.

In front of one of the yourts a number of men were seated in a circle on the turf, quietly surveying the scene around them, and quaffing their favourite beverage, koumis. These were Djan-ghir Khan and his followers, who now appeared in pastoral and pacific guise. They, however, were unscrupulous men, whose ideas on right are governed by those of might. They deem slaughter no crime, and plunder obtained by prowess an honourable acquisition.

The young Sultan had gained the esteem of Djan-ghir Khan by prowess and successful barantas, and his account of his encounter and defeat of the robbers in the pass raised him greatly in his favour.

During this visit Souk became still more captivated by the beauty and courage of Aï-Khanym. She had taken a part in some of their sports, and proved herself a perfect horsewoman, easily managing the most fiery steed in her father's stud. She could wield the lance, and her richly-decorated battle-axe would have proved no toy in any encounter. She carried the hawk on her wrist, and followed recklessly in the chase. Such are the accomplishments of some of these daughters of the steppe.

At the end of a week the young Sultan and his friends left the aoul of the Khan on their homeward journey, and by his advice they returned by a route far to the eastward of that which had nearly proved fatal to them. This was somewhat longer, but over a most interesting region, and gave them a ride of nine days. As the Khan anticipated, no great dangers beset their path, and they reached home without any particular adventure.

Summer and autumn had passed, and young Souk had again visited his intended bride. Snow had covered the upper valleys, and extended far down the lower mountains, and a severe frost had driven both families to their winter pastures, only a three days' journey from each other. Sultan Timour determined to avail himself of this opportunity, and make the final arrangements with the Khan, more especially as his son was constantly urging him to have the marriage completed.

The time had now arrived when the Sultan must pay

the kalym, and great tact was required to bring this part of the business to an amicable conclusion. He selected his Mulla and two chiefs to arrange the amount with the Khan, at the same time limiting them to a very moderate sum. They were accompanied by young Souk with several of his followers, and after a rough and stormy ride reached the aoul of Djan-ghir Khan.

Like all diplomatists, these people move slowly in their arrangements. Hours, nay days, are sometimes spent in conversing on indifferent subjects, without once alluding to the matter that has called them together. This case was no exception, and several days were spent with the Khan before the Mulla announced his mission to the family conclave. Djan-ghir had called his Mulla to his aid along with two of his chiefs; some members of his family and the young Sultan were also present.

Sultan Timour's Mulla opened the conference by a speech, in which he expatiated on the distinguished ancestors and noble descent of the Sultan, his power and sovereignty over the tribes constituting the Great Horde, and his prowess in battle; adding, that the son was worthy of the sire, possessing great prudence as a leader, undaunted courage as a warrior, and all other gifts that qualified him for the high position of the chief of the Great Horde. He concluded a long oration by demanding of the Khan the fulfilment of his promise to give his daughter to young Souk, and requested him to state the amount of the kalym.

The chiefs followed, reiterating the Mulla's request, and extolling the high positions of both the Sultan and his son. To give more weight to their arguments, they stated that several of the most distinguished Sultans in the Great and Middle Hordes had made overtures to Sultan Timour, being anxious to form a matrimonial alliance with his family and its powerful chief. They finished their laudatory speeches by expressing a hope that the Khan would bear in mind, when deciding on the kalym, the honour that his daughter would attain when she became the wife of the chief at the head of the Great Horde. The conference was then adjourned till the following day, to give the Khan and his advisers an opportunity for consideration.

Next morning the Khan, his Mulla, and several chiefs, assembled in a yourt placed apart from the aoul, sending a messenger to invite Sultan Timour's friends to join them in the council. They shortly repaired to the yourt, and seated themselves in front of the Khan. He opened the proceedings by expressing his satisfaction at the proposed union between the distinguished family of the Sultan and his own, but regretted that his friend was not present to take a part in the arrangements, adding, "as he is not here, neither must I remain. I have therefore intrusted the Mulla and my chiefs with the arrangement, and they have full power to settle it." He then retired from the yourt.

After the Khan's departure his Mulla commenced an address, sitting in the usual position, cross-legged on the ground. He expressed his great admiration for so renowned a chief as Sultan Timour, referred in appropriate terms to his wealth and power, as well as to his sagacity and courage. He also bore testimony to the prudence and valour of the young Sultan, whom he styled "the brave son of a great father."

He then spoke of the warlike deeds of the Khan in terms of high panegyric, and intimated that an alliance of two such powerful chiefs might bring all the regions into subjection. The Mulla next touched on the beauty and accomplishments of Aï-Khanym, asserting that she was a bride worthy of the great conqueror, and that in giving her in marriage to the young Sultan, her father was parting with an inestimable jewel. He assured the other party that her hand had already been sought by the Khan of Badakshan, and that several other great families had desired the alliance, but that these offers had been rejected by the Khan, that she might be united to the son of his friend. Lastly, he said that the kalym demanded was 200 camels, 3,000 horses, 5,000 oxen, and 10,000 sheep.

Other chiefs addressed the assembly, one and all expatiating on the beauty of Aï-Khanym, and intimating that the Khan showed his desire for the union of the families by his generosity in the amount of the kalym. And more especially so, as another suitor of great distinction had already offered double the price named. They therefore hoped that the generous friendship displayed by the Khan would be fully appreciated by the Sultan, and the marriage secure a lasting peace between the tribes.

The amount named for the kalym startled the friends of Sultan Timour, their instructions being for about one third, to offer which, however, would now have been an insult. Thus ended the conference.

The following day the Mulla, the chiefs with young Souk and his attendants, prepared to return after an unsuccessful attempt to induce the Khan to reduce his demand. When all were assembled to take leave of the Khan, he gave the Mulla some valuable presents for Sultan Timour, and saying "aman-bul," they departed. Young Souk had painful forebodings, and left the aoul with a heavy heart; but he had pledged his honour to return to his fair mistress before his tribe left their winter pastures.

The journey homeward was a rapid one; being bearers of evil tidings, they carried them quickly, though they felt assured that the news would put their chief into a fit of anger. On reaching the aoul they gave an account of their mission. On hearing the amount of the kalym the Sultan broke out into a great rage, saying that such a demand was an insult to his family and the Great Horde, for which he would be avenged. After a time the first outburst of his passion subsided, ending, however, in a determination not to pay what had been demanded. Still he deemed it prudent to avoid an open rupture with the wily Khan, hoping that circumstances might arise which would enable him to have his revenge.

Many secret councils were held between the Sultan and his chiefs, and numerous plans of vengeance were suggested. Some advised a junction with the robber tribes of the mountains, and then to make a great baranta upon Djan-ghir Khan during the winter and carry off his daughter. Others were more prudent, believing that he had friends among the bandits who would give him notice, when it was probable he would be able to bring the whole force upon the Great Horde, and the tribes might suffer severely.

Time passed. The winter was nearly over, still the grass was crisped with hoar frost, making it sparkle in the morning sun as if powdered with brilliants, while in some of the warm and sheltered nooks white and purple crocuses were springing into bloom. This was the signal for the departure of young Souk on a visit to his intended bride. He selected three of his companions to accompany him; but before leaving the aoul his father gave him a present and a message for the Khan, saying that he would visit him in the summer.

It was a splendid morning when the young men started on their mountain journey, and the rays of the sun soon began to tell on the snows in the upper regions. This was apparent from the numerous small waterfalls that came leaping from the lofty precipices near them, frequently covering them with misty spray. When they had proceeded for several hours, and ascended to the higher valleys, the sun had passed his meridian, and every little rill was becoming a torrent, rushing along with fearful rapidity. Streams which a few hours before they could have crossed without the water reaching to the knees of their steeds, were now from six to ten feet deep, rolling on with a deafening roar, tearing huge rocks from their beds, and tumbling them onward with a kind of muffled reports, like a battery fired under water. One of these torrents brought the little party to a stand two hours before sunset. A ride through such a region is attended with many hardships and some dangers, nor was it till the evening of the third day that they reached the aoul of the Khan.

Souk was received by its chief most cordially; but on his first interview with Aï-Khanym she intimated treachery, telling him that the Khan of Badakshan had sent several of his chiefs on a visit to her father, and that arrangements had already been made for her marriage with the Khan, which was to take place when they went to their summer pastures. She also warned Souk to tell this to no one, or appear to have the least suspicion, assuring him that she would fly to the mountains and perish amidst their eternal snows sooner than become the wife of another. Her lover was satisfied, and determined to rescue her. Having given her this assurance, he departed, after spending a few days, and on taking leave of the Khan announced his intention of visiting him at the Mus-tau.

During Souk's journey homeward he had time to reflect on his position, which gave him no little anxiety, but he dared not show it to his companions. He knew, if the circumstance became known to his father and the chiefs, some plan of vengeance would be adopted, and then all his hopes would be destroyed. That Aï-Khanym would prove true he had no doubt, and he determined to carry her off unaided; but how this was to be accomplished he could not imagine.

Many and anxious were his forebodings during the dreary months of winter, but this season was his security. To travel in the mountains before May was utterly impossible, so that Aï-Khanym was as safe as if shut up in a fortress. Long before the snow began to melt on the plains his plan was formed.

The few dreary months of winter appeared to him five

times their usual length, but in this region he was greatly favoured, as spring commences early; indeed, I have seen the ground covered with a carpet of flowers before the middle of February. When the snow had disappeared on the plains, young Souk determined to attempt a journey

A Mountain Torrent in the Mus-tau.

over the mountains, accompanied by only one companion. On his next visit to the Khan he wished to avoid suspicion; and did not risk his favourite steed, knowing the ride would be both difficult and dangerous to man and horse.

Some of the mountain torrents forced them to ride far out of their route, and in two instances they were in great peril of being carried away by the flood. Notwithstanding they reached the aoul of Djan-ghir on the fourth day, and found him still at his winter quarters.

He was greatly astonished to see his guest, believing the mountains impossible to cross at this season. Souk was received with every mark of friendship, the Khan even inquiring when the Sultan intended meeting him to complete the preliminaries of the marriage. Souk said that his father proposed deferring his journey till the end of May, when he would visit the Khan at his pastures; but messengers would be sent on to announce his arrangements.

As Djan-ghir and his tribes intended moving to another valley in a couple of days, the young Sultan's stay was cut short. Still he found an opportunity of communicating his plans to the Khan's daughter, and prepared her for his next visit. She communicated to him that everything had been settled for her marriage with the Khan of Badakshan; that the kalym would be brought by his chiefs to her father's summer pastures in the Mus-tau, and that she was to return with them to his encampment.

When the Khan broke up his aoul to proceed to other pastures, Souk started on his homeward journey. Three months had yet to pass before he could make an effort to carry off Aï-Khanym, for he was fully convinced that it would be madness to make the attempt before the first week in June, as the mountain torrents and the snow in the passes might retard or even stop their progress, and thus the speed of their fleet horses would be of no avail.

Souk had watched the spring glide on, and the summer approach; he had seen the snow melt on the lower mountains, while the serrated crests of a still higher chain were protruding their dark masses through the wintry covering, and each clear sunny day was dissolving the white patches on their rocky heights. These were indications that told him the passes would soon be free. May had arrived, bringing glorious weather, and this was highly favourable to his project.

As the days rolled on his anxiety increased. He trained his steed for the task he was about to undertake. He had not breathed his intentions to his most intimate friends, fearing, if it became known to his father and the chiefs, they would adopt severe measures and frustrate his plans. In order to allay suspicion he announced his intention of spending two or three weeks with some friends near the Ili, to join in a hunting expedition after wild horses, which at this season are found in great herds near the foot of the mountains beyond that river.

This animal is not like the wild horse of South America, which undoubtedly sprung from those taken into the country by the Spaniards. He is of a distinct race from the Asiatic horse, very small (not so large as an ass), beautiful in form, having a small head and short ears, and varying in colour from black, bay, grey, and white, the latter being the most rare. He is called "muss" by the Kirghis. His sense of smell is very acute, which renders him most difficult to approach. He is exceedingly fleet, and few horses can run him down.

I will describe the mode of hunting him:—A great number of Kirghis assemble, and when the scouts have found the herd, the horsemen form an extended line at a considerable distance towards the steppe. When so much has been accomplished they gradually ride up, forcing the herd towards a pass in the mountains. As they approach near to the ravine the hunters draw closer, forming a crescent, and proceed with extreme caution till the stallions enter the pass. While this has been going on, another party of hunters have made their way into the pass, taking their stand in the narrowest part, and waiting till the herd appears. Having signalled to the hunters on the plain that the pass is secured, the whole body close up and the poor animals are in a trap. They are now driven onward till stopped by the hunters above, when the work of slaughter begins, and vast numbers of these beautiful creatures are killed by their battle-axes. The Kirghis consider their flesh the greatest delicacy the steppe affords.

Joining in this hunting expedition would not take Souk far out of his route; he therefore started, taking two horses, riding one and leading his own to save him for his mountain gallop. The mountain streams were forded with ease, and he found the snow lying in small patches in some of the passes. The aoul of his friends was reached on the second day. Having spent two days there, he started with his two steeds for the pastures of Djan-ghir Khan. He knew the region in which the tribes were feeding their herds, but not the exact locality. As they never remain more than eight or ten days on the same spot, it is often no easy matter to find them on such vast spaces. The Khan had stated to young Souk on his last visit that the Sultan would find him in some of the upper valleys of the Terric-sou until the end of May, but that after that time he should be far to the south-west, in the Mus-tau. And this was all the information on which he could rely.

CHAP. XIII.

A KIRGHIS ELOPEMENT.

THE young Sultan pursued his lonely way, intending to strike upon the Terric-sou far up towards its source, where he felt sure Aï-Khanym was anxiously watching for his arrival. A solitary ride over such a region would have terrors for most people, especially Europeans. Even Kirghis seldom make such journeys alone, the risk by flood and mountain being too great. Tigers are often found here, and bands of marauders are always hovering about in the neighbourhood of the encampments.

To avoid falling in with any of these, Souk followed a route to the eastward of the region in which the tribes had pastured their herds. Two days passed over, and no living being was seen; on the third he came upon trails, but they were several weeks old, and four days and nights passed without any adventure worth recording.

About two in the afternoon of the fifth day, he crossed a high ridge whence he had a view into the valley of the Terric-sou, but neither aoul nor cattle was visible. He passed on towards the river, and soon found traces of the herds; continuing his ride, he came to the place of their encampment, when he perceived that it had been long deserted. He was now fearful that he should not find them at their next resting-place, and this induced him to hasten onward. As he proceeded up the valley he had no difficulty in tracing out their route, and a little after dusk piqueted his horses and spread his saddle cloth for the night on one of their encamping grounds. The following morning he started early, and continued his journey up the valley. At length, after a long ride, he arrived at a part where another narrow rocky valley opened to the westward, and here there was also a Kirghis trail.

Black clouds had long been rolling up behind some high snowy peaks to the south-west, and he perceived that a storm was gathering. The sun was setting when he came upon this spot, and now a great difficulty arose as to which trail would lead him to the Khan. This could not be solved in the dark, nor was it possible for him to proceed further that day.

While occupied examining the trails, and speculating on the route, he had not observed the storm advancing towards him; but a roll of distant thunder caught his ear, and then he saw that the high peaks were enveloped in a black mass of surging vapour, from which fiery shafts were darting in thick streams, and the thunder became louder at intervals of a few minutes. The Terric-sou was rushing over its rocky bed with a great noise at about a mile distant, but this was soon lost in other sounds.

A little brook ran through the middle of the narrow valley, its banks covered with thick bushes and a few stunted trees; these, however, could afford him no cover. He turned hastily towards the precipices, hoping to find a nook which would shelter both himself and his steeds. Having arrived at some deep recesses, no time was lost in securing his horses under their projections; but this was scarcely accomplished when the bellowing thunder and the big drops told him the warring elements were near; while a sable pall was rapidly spreading over the valley, rendering all objects indistinct except when lit up by the electric flash.

Another sound was heard approaching, like the roaring of the sea when its mighty billows are breaking on a rocky shore. Louder and louder it became, till the fearful hurricane swept down the valley, tearing up trees and bushes, and scattering them like chaff. Then came rain, not in drops but in streams, while the red lightning shot forth incessantly. The thunder now became one continued roar, causing the horses to crouch and tremble, as one explosion after another rent the clouds asunder and shook the solid rocks.

Suddenly the rain changed into hail, cutting down the herbage, and quickly changing a summer landscape into a wintry one. These are terrific phenomena, but when witnessed by a solitary traveller in such a region they have (as I can vouch) a most appalling effect. In about an hour the fearful storm had passed, leaving a serene and calm twilight, with a chilling temperature, while the rippling brook had become a torrent, that rushed forward with great force. The flood rendered it quite impossible to obtain fuel, and the traveller went supperless to his stony couch.

Before the grey dawn began to streak the eastern sky the horses were piqueted to feed, and Souk was preparing for his departure. The difficulty which beset him before the storm had not been removed, but after due consideration he decided on following the trail leading to the westward. Having ridden through the narrow winding valley for several hours, he reached a part where it opened into another of considerable extent, with high mountains to the south, and a lower chain to the north. Nature had distinctly marked out his route, and he continued his ride westward to the upper part of a valley, that ended in a granite region. This was picturesque and beautiful, uniting savage grandeur with luxuriant vegetation. He pushed on his way through a labyrinth of stupendous objects,—isolated masses of granite formed into most fantastic shapes. Advancing onward, the precipices became more lofty and rugged as the pass narrowed, and its bed rose rapidly. This led him to a mountain slope, whence he saw the sun sink below the horizon, compelling him to seek a resting-place and pastures for his steeds. Darkness quickly following as usual, he was once more shrouded in gloom.

The night, however, passed without either man or animal being disturbed, and when morning came he examined more closely his position. He was now on a high mountain plain, extending to the base of a very lofty ridge running far to the south-east, some seven or eight miles distant. After leaving his night quarters he had not gone far when he discovered that the herds had pastured on this spot. A new difficulty now beset him. Here was a vast space not less than seven miles broad and twenty-five in length, over which the herds had grazed, leaving tracks in all directions. He scanned the country around him, but neither man, animal, nor landmark was visible to guide him to the tribes. Which ever way he turned a vast solitude was before him, while the characters stamped on the plain were so numerous, crossing each other to all points of the compass, that they only added to his perplexity.

He knew the Kirghis would be engaged in their domestic duties, and he gazed anxiously over the plain in the hope of seeing smoke rise from some of the aouls; but without success. The young Kirghis felt a painful sensation, and pushed his horses into a gallop, riding westward, and drawing nearer to the base of the mountain. Having gone on for a considerable distance in that direction, he reached an elevation that gave him a view far over the plain; but neither Kirghis, their dwellings, nor their cattle were visible. His only chance was to proceed quickly onward, and two more hours were nearly passed when he reached the edge of a great depression.

Beneath him aouls and herds lay scattered over the valley. The sight caused him to push forward at a rapid pace, and he speedily came up to several herdsmen; they recognised him, and one offered to guide him to the Khan.

The man turned towards the south, leading the way up to the mountains. Souk now learned that the tribes had been encamped five days at these pastures, that the Khan left them only two days ago, and that all the aouls would move westward shortly.

As they proceeded he acquired much valuable information from his guide, who pointed out a short route to the Terric-sou. By crossing the mountains to the north, one of the lower valleys of that river could be reached in less than two days; the only drawback to this route being the upper part of the pass, which was so difficult that few men would attempt it a second time. The young Sultan noted down in his memory the several points by which he could be guided in this direction. A great chasm was cleft in the ridge, forming a landmark that could not be mistaken, and this, his companion said, was the pass by which he was to cross the chain.

Having ridden seven or eight miles they reached the crest of a low ridge, whence they looked down upon the aoul of the Khan, standing in a lovely nook, sheltered from every blast save the south. As they descended, several men rode out to meet them. They recognised the young Sultan, and told him the Khan was absent, and would not return for a few days; but that Aï-Khanym and her mother were in the aoul. In a few minutes he was in their yourt, when he met with a most affectionate reception.

Souk had arrived at a favourable moment, when several of the chiefs were absent, having been sent on a mission by the Khan; but Aï-Khanym told him that her father would return the following evening, that the aoul would be moved to another valley in a few days, and that all the tribes were to assemble three weeks hence in one of the higher valleys of the Mus-tau, where the chiefs from the Khan of Badakshan were to meet her father with the kalym and to take her away.

The young Sultan thought that, being unattended, neither the Khan nor any of his people would suspect his intentions, and that therefore Aï-Khanym would be free from restraint. He lost no time, however, in making his plans known to her. After she had heard them it was agreed that they should leave the aoul at daybreak on the morning when the tribes moved, as the herdsmen would then be busy preparing for the march. This being settled, they had little more to arrange excepting how Aï-Khanym was to get possession of the Khan's favourite steed, the fleetest in his stud. This animal was so highly prized by her father that he never permitted him to travel from one pasture to another except in his train. On these occasions Aï-Khanym often rode him, and he was always piqueted near the yourt at night.

Souk knew that his own horse was fresh for his work, and that if they could escape with the two, even with only an hour's start, no other horses in the Khan's stud could come up with them. With most of the people he was a favourite, indeed many of them looked upon him as belonging to the tribe. Some of the chiefs, however, were thoroughly acquainted with the Khan's plans, and knew that the time was not far distant when the two families would be at deadly feud.

The Khan returned at the appointed time, and received his young guest most kindly, inviting him to accompany the tribe to their other pastures, that he might return home by a different route. During the three days' visit the young couple went out hawking twice, once accompanied by the Khan, and once attended by his people. The sedgy banks of a small lake a few miles distant from the aoul, had supplied abundance of game for their sport. The last evening of the stay of the tribes at the present pastures had arrived, and the Khan had given instructions for the march. Part of the people were to leave with the herds at daybreak, pitch the mid-day encampment, and wait there till the chief and the rest of the tribe joined them. He had also ordered the favourite steed to be saddled for his daughter: thus all promised well.

The hours of this night were passed in a state of great anxiety by the confederates, who were convinced that if their plan failed it would be fatal to their hopes; the young lady, moreover, was fearful for her lover's liberty, if not for his life. Souk was out before the morning dawned attending to his steed, which presently was saddled for the journey. Aï-Khanym now appeared with her saddle and trappings; she handed them to a Kirghis, telling him to prepare her horse, while she brought out her favourite hawk. In a few minutes she returned fully equipped.

The herdsmen were already driving off their different charges; some were tending the camels and horses, others the oxen and sheep, and numbers of horsemen were galloping to and fro to force them into their right position. While this was going on, the maiden had mounted her steed; a Kirghis then placed the hawk on her wrist, to whom she left a message for her father that she was going to the pastures by another route, intending to fly her hawk on some of the small lakes. Souk left his spare horse under the charge of one of the Khan's attendants, to be taken forward with those accompanying the chief.

Before the men had succeeded in getting the mass of animals fairly on their march, it was daylight, and when the young couple left the aoul to follow in their rear, the sun was tipping the icy peaks of the Mus-tau. The progress of such vast herds keeps the herdsmen in constant motion, as some are frequently refractory, and lead the others from their route; the men had therefore little leisure for observation.

A bright sun was flooding mountain and valley with his glorious light, when the lovers reached some low hills about two hours distant from the aoul. From these they had a view of a small lake in the valley to the north. Aï-Khanym told some of the herdsmen that she should try for game, and meet them farther up in the mountains. The herds moved slowly on their way as the young couple cast their last look after them, and then turned towards the lake. Before they had reached half-way to its shores, both men and animals had disappeared beyond the hills.

Fortune had favoured them greatly; they were now in

Aï-Khanym sets free her Hawk.

a valley four or five miles broad, but exposed to full view from the ridge on the south, immediately beneath which, on the opposite side, was the aoul of the Khan, not more than four miles distant from them. Reining in their horses, they looked around, but no one could be seen. Aï-Khanym took the hood and shackles from her hawk, when he soared aloft and wheeled around in freedom, never to perch again on the hand that had so often caressed him. After watching his flight for a few minutes she gave her steed his head, and in a gallop across the valley endeavoured to hide her painful feelings.

Before reaching the northern summit their eyes were often turned in the direction of the aoul, but nothing was seen to indicate that their flight had been discovered. They hastened onward, and shortly came upon the route by which Souk had travelled to the aoul. Now they must decide upon their course. Far to the north was seen the mighty cleft the Kirghis had pointed out to the young Sultan, and he told Aï-Khanym of its dangers, though he believed it to offer the surest means of escape. She knew the difficulties, and thought the risk too great to incur, because the pass had proved so fatal to several of her father's tribe that it had been abandoned. Only two summers ago, as she stated, seven of their people travelled that way, when three, with their horses, fell over a precipice and perished; the other four found it impossible to return and struggled onward, but only succeeded in taking two horses over, the others being killed in the pass.

She then informed her lover that there was another route not far distant to the westward, by which the tribes sometimes passed, but it was unknown to her. Souk gave up his intention, and determined to follow his route to the Terric-sou; for doing this he entertained hopes that their flight would not be discovered till evening, when the Khan reached his pastures; and as their trail could not be followed in the night, they would have a start of twelve hours in the chase.

Their ride onward was rapid, without distressing their steeds, and it was about an hour past noon when they rode into that wonderful labyrinth of rocks through which Souk had passed. He led the way to a spot where there was pasture and water for their steeds; a spring supplied drink, and some slight nourishment they had carried with them, refreshment.

They presently resumed their flight, and arrived where the young Sultan had slept. Here they supped, and sat conversing on their prospects till long after darkness had warned them it was time to sleep.

Their morning meal required little preparation, and was soon dispatched. The hurricane had swept down this valley with terrific force, uprooting the trees that fringed the river, and laying them prostrate in all directions. Their ride now was a long one, for darkness shrouded the valley before they stopped on the bank of the river, where a pleasant sheltered spot was found for their bivouac.

On looking around the next morning Souk recognised their position, and knew that it would take eight hours of rapid riding to reach the path by which he had descended to the Terric-sou. He feared that if Aï-Khanym was right about the pass to the westward, the Khan's people might reach it before them. This contingency caused them much anxiety; finally, he decided on seeking another route more to the eastward, in the hope of escaping any men that might have been sent to cut them off in front, and trusting to the speed of their horses to keep far in advance of those in their rear.

They rode down the bank of the stream, and its course being exceedingly rapid and over a rocky bed, they were obliged to ride seven or eight miles before they found a place to ford; even then it was not accomplished without great risk.

Souk scanned the rugged slopes with the practised eye of a mountaineer, and soon selected a path. Both steeds were accustomed to climbing, and the dread of capture gave their riders courage for any risk. The mountain they were going to scale was not more than 5,000 feet above the valley;

lower down it was considerably less, but their enemies were there. An hour's ride brought them to the first acclivity—a grassy slope, rather steep, reaching to the base of some rugged rocks that formed a series of terraces rising several thousand feet.

The first part they rode up with ease, but the rocky terraces gave them much trouble; for in some places it was like a gigantic staircase, up which it seemed impossible for horses to climb. The maiden, however, took the lead, riding over portions that would have severely tried the nerves of many of the stronger sex. Her light weight enabled her horse to hold on and scramble over places, where Souk's steed could not (with his weight) maintain his footing.

Each new difficulty that arose in her path as she ascended from crag to crag only added to her courage,—sometimes riding along a narrow ledge with her foot dangling over a precipice, and her keen eye scanning a more dangerous part above. Higher and higher she ascended, riding up places over which Souk was compelled to lead his steed.

Each new terrace gained gave them a more extended view over the valley that was spread out like a map at their feet, while the Terric-sou appeared like a band of silver as its waters fretted over its rocky bed. After much toil and great risk they had nearly reached the summit, when they were suddenly brought to a stand by some objects far away in the valley below. They were so small that, at first sight, it was doubtful whether they were cattle feeding, or bushes. The figures were those of horsemen, and they presently separated into two groups, one going down the valley, and the other coming towards the fugitives.

They both dismounted, leading their horses upwards to prevent discovery, and speedily reaching some fallen crags that concealed them from view. Leaving Aï-Khanym on the watch, Souk led the horses up the ascent and piqueted them in a sheltered spot far out of sight. On his return the party were distinctly visible. They were the Khan's people, a part having gone forward, probably in hopes of securing the pass lower down, while the others anticipated meeting the fugitives in the valley.

Souk had thrown the remains of his fire into the river, as a wreath of smoke would point out their trail. The riders came on at a rapid pace, and in about an hour were passing near enough to be recognised; among them were three of the Khan's chiefs. They were twenty-three in number, and several were looking for the trail. Souk knew that they had ten or twelve miles to ride before they could reach its first indication, unless they should turn to the bank of the stream; this, however, they seemed to avoid.

While he had been gazing at them beneath, Aï-Khanym had scanned the upper part of the valley, and there discovered other horsemen approaching. The young Sultan's attention was quickly turned in this direction. This group was also in motion, and he knew that in little more than an hour the two parties must meet, and would soon be on the trail.

Aï-Khanym was convinced that her pursuers were led by her father's chiefs, who would spare neither man nor steed in the chase. Her only hope lay in the dangerous crags they had just ascended, which men even on foot could not scale in the dark.

After casting a last look up the valley they mounted their horses, rode up the mountain crest, and shortly gained the summit. It was nearly flat, extending about 300 yards in width, and was covered with masses of quartz and granite, that rendered it exceedingly difficult to ride over. They presently came to the brink of a fearful slope, forming a vast crescent scooped out of the mountain; so steep that scarcely a vestige of herbage was visible on its surface. Souk examined this mighty curve as far as his eye could reach, and found it utterly impassable. They rode along the crest to the north, where it descended rapidly, forming a high plateau, whence several spurs ran down into a deep valley, that extended for many miles to the north-east.

By descending here many dangers would be encountered, but there was no alternative; and they turned to the north-west. Here they had to pick their way among the ruins of mountain summits that time is constantly cutting down and disentombing their long-buried mineral treasures. In some parts of the chain large veins of lapis-lazuli are found, as well as splendid nephrite of a dark green colour, with large blotches of orange marked with dark veins, surpassing in beauty any specimens I have ever seen from China. Silver and lead are also here; and the Kirghis say that splendid stones which sparkle like flame have been found in the region,—probably rubies.

The lovers, however, thought neither of silver nor gems. Painful was their toil among the masses of wreck. As they descended they were compelled to watch each step of their steeds, to prevent an accident that could not fail of being instantly fatal.

Having reached the bottom they were in rich pastures on the shore of a small lake, upon whose glassy surface thousands of waterfowl were feeding and sporting, apparently without any dread of the strangers,—man had probably never visited their haunt before. It offered a resting-place as pleasant as it was secure. When the horses were piqueted and the fire blazing, the fugitives walked along the shore, examining it with care. They found that neither man nor savage beast had preceded them, for they could discover only a few footprints of deer and argali. On their return the last rays of the sun flooded the upper end of the valley; and presently all around them was in shade. Gradually the grey gloom crept up the mountain sides, till one summit after another lost its golden hue. A little longer, the snowy peaks and glaciers of the Mus-tau flashed forth their rosy beams.

Though the speed of their horses had hitherto availed them little, the valley they would now have to cross would give them an opportunity for trying it further. They started shortly after sunrise, and rode along the shores of the lake, when they disturbed vast multitudes of waterfowl and several groups of deer. Their steeds were presently put into a gallop, and having proceeded several miles, they reached a point that afforded a view of the chain they had passed. No living object was visible there, nor in the opposite direction, with the exception of some herds of deer and antelopes. The valley extended in a north-easterly course, but they could not see its termination; still, toward this point Souk proceeded. A few miles carried them into the broadest part of it, that appeared to be about ten miles in width, enclosed by picturesque mountains—those to the south-east being the most lofty, some few peaks rising above the line of eternal snow, while in many parts of the lower range their northern faces were covered with dense forests.

The mountains to the north-west were lower, having a more sterile aspect; they were principally slate. Most of the upper ridges were a dark purple, and this sombre colour had given the name of Kara-tau to the chain. Some of the precipices presented a peculiar appearance, having strata of different colours,—a cream-coloured band 150 to 200 feet thick; above that a pale green stratum of nearly equal thickness. Over this another bed of about 50 feet in depth, of a fine Indian red, that towards its upper surface changed into vermilion: then came a light bluish purple, probably 100 feet thick, and above that a dark purple, almost black, of equal if not greater dimensions.

These strata were occasionally horizontal, extending for several miles. In other parts great disruptions had taken place, and the beds had been heaved up into nearly vertical

Falls near the source of the Kara-sou.

positions. In another part a vast dome-shaped mass was

thrown up, of a deep crimson colour, on which scarcely a blade of grass had taken root; while the range beneath was covered with a thick sward of the brightest green.

After going about eight miles further it was observed that the valley branched in two directions; one running up into the mountains to the south-east, and the other turning to the north. Towards this opening the lovers galloped, and in half an hour had passed the jutting rocks, and entered a small hollow, with a rapid stream running down its centre; they were obliged to follow it some distance before it could be forded. They then proceeded onward, and found that the torrent entered a narrow ravine. In many parts the cliffs rose from the water's edge, rendering it impossible to find a route in that direction. This forced them to ascend the mountain and seek another path. There were few difficulties in their way, and in about an hour they reached the summit.

From here their ride was down into one of those high mountain valleys which at this season are clothed with a carpet of flowers and luxuriant herbage. On reaching a spring the fugitives pulled up their horses and let them feed, while they partook of their own simple fare.

It required but a short time to reach the opposite summit, whence they had a view into the lower ground, which Souk recognised as an opening he had passed through on a former journey. Once in this valley he knew his route, and this would disarm the chase of half its terrors. He, however, saw at a glance that the descent would be a tedious one, and could not be accomplished before night.

As the sun began to tip the snowy peaks the lovers were in their saddles and riding in a more northerly direction. Having travelled about an hour they saw smoke rising from behind a mass of rocks several miles distant, and not far beyond the point where their route turned into a pass leading to a high plateau.

Souk led the way to the left, riding close to the foot of some precipices to conceal them from view. Should they be seen before they could arrive opposite to the pass, they would have to make a dash for it, and trust to the speed of their horses.

Having reached some masses of granite that jutted far out into the valley at about two miles from the pass, completely hiding everything beyond, he deemed it necessary to dismount and reconnoitre. He had not climbed far when he obtained a view of the encampment, which caused him to descend instantly. Great was his astonishment when he discovered that a large party were riding cautiously up the valley, and were already nearer the pass than themselves, while those at the camp were busy saddling their horses. Some of the scouts must have discovered their approach, and it was evident that the men were now preparing to take them. In a few moments he explained their danger to his companion, leapt into the saddle, unslung his battle-axe, and urging her to ride hard, dashed out into the valley. In a few moments the Kirghis discovered them, and setting up a terrible shout, started for the pass, with the great advantage of a quarter of a mile in point of distance.

Having gone about half the distance, Souk perceived that they had gained considerably, but three of their opponents had drawn far ahead of their followers, and were intent on securing the pass. The fugitives knew how much depended on the speed of their horses for the next mile, for they had determined not to be taken alive. As they drew near their enemies, Souk told his companion to give her animal his full speed while he checked the foremost pursuers, two of whom were trying to cut them off.

On they came at a furious speed, their battle-axes in hand, but Aï-Khanym shot past them when they were within a few strides of her. At this moment Souk, calculating his distance well, touched his steed, causing him to bound forward; as he passed, his battle-axe flashed aloft and fell on the head of the first horse, bringing him dead to the ground, and sending his rider rolling over on the grass. The second man seeing this, swerved on one side, and saved his steed from a similar fate, as the young Sultan dashed at full speed into the pass by the side of his fair companion.

The Race and Escape.

The lovers heard the shouts of their baffled pursuers, but proceeded without attempting to look round.

At length they emerged from the pass on to a fine undulating plain, and Souk pointed out the last blue mountains, immediately beyond which was the valley of the Ili, while Lake Tenghiz was shining like a mirror, and extending so far into the steppe that land, water, and sky were mingled in misty haze. He felt almost at home as he gazed on the land of his birth. Aï-Khanym looked intently towards the plains that were to be her future home, and contemplated them with pleasure.

The fugitives kept about a mile in advance; sometimes a few of their pursuers approached nearer, but they were soon distanced whenever greater speed was expedient. In the afternoon the band pulled up on the bank of a small stream, finding it necessary to feed their horses. On seeing this Souk turned to a little brook, and both parties were soon refreshing themselves on the same stream, within little more than half a mile of each other.

The horses having rested, the lovers were the first to move. After riding on at an easy speed for several miles, on looking back they noticed half-a-dozen men separate from the main body and go in a north-westerly direction, three having spare horses. Suspecting their design the young Sultan continued his course, inclining a little to the eastward. The two leading steeds kept increasing their distance from their pursuers without putting forth their full power, and many of the Khan's people were falling behind.

Souk still kept inclining to the east, and rapidly increasing the distance, till it was too dark for the Kirghis to observe the trail. Then letting his companion follow, he led the way towards the mountains on the north-west, at full speed. Aï-Khanym was at his side in a few moments, and they rode rapidly for several miles. At last they stopped and stood still, listening for their pursuers, but no sound reached them. The young Sultan dismounted, and laying his head on the ground, presently heard the distant roll of hoofs. They gradually approached nearer for about ten minutes, and then died away. After regaining his saddle, the horses were walked quietly, as other ears were likely to be on the ground listening.

They rode on, occasionally stopping to listen: while thus engaged a sound was heard approaching that caused the horses to snort and become restive. It suddenly ceased when at no great distance from them, and Souk knew it proceeded from a herd of deer that had been disturbed, most probably by a party of the Khan's men. He was therefore certain there were scouts out in that direction, and not far distant.

This was a warning not to be neglected, and they proceeded onward. More than two hours had passed, when they reached a stream which Souk was aware was not far from the pass. Here they stopped for the night.

As daylight spread over the country the young Sultan examined their position, and found that they were near the base of the mountain, and not far from the pass. He also scanned the country around them, and ascertained that scouts had been sent out in the night, as the smoke of their fires was curling up, though at a long distance.

They started, riding up a low ridge that afforded a view over the vast plain, and Souk observed the smoke of their enemies' camp at some six or eight miles' distance; but neither men nor horses could be seen.

The pass was formed in a mountain of granite by a sudden and great convulsion, making one of those vast chasms that shows the mighty power at work beneath the earth; and wild goats were seen feeding and springing from ledge to ledge, where it seems impossible to find a footing. The argali looked down from the lofty crags, and the large-bearded eagle reared his young among the pinnacles of basalt.

It is a splendid sight watching this feathered monarch as he soars aloft, or swoops down upon his prey. The young of the argali and the kids he clutches in his terrible talons, carrying them to his eyrie with ease. Even the larger animals are not safe from his attack; he has been seen to force them from a dangerous ledge by his powerful swoop—

following their fall through the air like a shot, ready to strike his prey before it reached the bottom. He is by far the most dangerous and daring of the feathered tribe that I have ever encountered.

The wanderers wended their way through this gigantic rent, proceeding with caution, carefully examining the windings in the gorge, and fearing at each turn to behold an

The Bearded Eagle and Steinbock.

enemy. The frowning cliffs cast so deep and sombre a shade over their path, that Aï-Khanym could not shake off her dread of danger. Yet they went on undisturbed, and after a ride of near four hours, emerged into a narrow valley running to the eastward. A bright sun was shining on the green turf, causing a cheerful change, and from this point the broad and glittering surface of Lake Tenghiz was seen, with some of the branches by which the Ili empties its flood.

The sight of places so near his home urged the young Sultan to greater exertions, and the horses were put into a sharp gallop. Having gone along the valley some four or five miles, they were suddenly surprised by seeing a small party galloping over a low hill about two miles distant to the westward. It appeared doubtful whether these men had observed them; nevertheless here was cause for alarm, as Souk knew that no tribes were in this region. From the course taken by the horsemen they appeared to be travelling to the north-west, the direction Souk and his bride must proceed.

On reaching the point of exit, the country was well scrutinised, but nothing in the shape of an enemy could be seen, yet the men that had been observed on the hill could not be far distant. Pushing on at a brisk pace they soon reached another opening that led into a lower valley, extending about twelve miles to the north-west in the direction of their route. Along its south side precipices of limestone rose up from 100 to 150 feet, pierced by several ravines ascending the higher chain. They had not gone further than a mile when a party of horsemen sprung out of one of these gorges not more than three hundred yards from them, as several well mounted men galloped across the valley to cut off their escape in that direction; while others spread themselves out in front, and two dashed out from their line, riding straight toward the fugitives, and calling on them to surrender.

At this moment Aï-Khanym observed that other horsemen were closing up in their rear. Souk directed her to pass the men on her right, then to gallop along the valley till he joined her. She followed the suggestion, and seemed to be riding into the midst of her enemies. This caused several of the band to dash up, thinking to surround her; but in doing so they left a considerable break in their line. Seeing this she suddenly wheeled round within a few yards of the men, and dashed past them like a swallow.

Her lover singled out the foremost of his pursuers, caused his horse to swerve slightly, and bound forward, giving room for the full swoop of his battle-axe. It severed the handle of his enemy's uplifted weapon, inflicting a terrible wound on his breast, and struck him to the ground, while his horse started away at full speed.

The fall of one of the chiefs caused some confusion in the band, and Souk galloped through their line, not one of the men having courage to meet him; but as soon as he had passed, they were like hounds in full cry. His attention was fixed on his companion, who had shot far ahead, followed by one of the chiefs and by several men. Souk soon passed these and had left them behind, when the horse belonging to the wounded chief dashed up to his side, gave a snort, and rushed on after his companion.

The young Sultan saw that he was a Turcoman of great value, and that the chief before him was equally well mounted. So intent was the latter in the chase of the fair fugitive, that he had not looked back. Not so Aï-Khanym; she had frequently cast a glance backwards, and when she saw Souk within a few hundred yards of her, she made a sweep and rode round her pursuer. This soon brought her to the side of the young Sultan, when he and the chief reined up their horses and stood face to face at no great distance from each other; and the riderless steed rushed up to his companion.

It was obvious to the chief that his comrade had fallen. Souk commanded him to take the horse and return to his band, or he would cut him down before any of his people could come to his assistance. The tone and manner were impressive, and the man thought it wisest to turn his horse and ride away. The lovers, putting their steeds into a gallop, went over the plain at a speed that put pursuit out of the question in an open country. Souk determined to strike on the river several miles below the place where it was usually crossed, fearing an ambush might be concealed in the thickets. Having ridden onward till long past mid-day, the pair at length stopped for an hour to refresh their horses; but this was on an open plain where they could not be surprised.

The nearer they approached the Ili, the more anxious the young Sultan became; still he hoped that a few hours would place them out of danger. The sun was sinking fast as they neared the belt of willows, reeds, and bushes that extended for miles along the river bank, and rose far above their heads. Proceeding cautiously along the edge of the copse, they had not gone far when Souk observed a fresh trail, made by a number of horsemen. This warned him of danger, and they rode slowly on, fearing the sound of their hoofs might be heard. Having ridden several miles Souk led the way into the thicket, and after some trouble, they reached the bank at a bend in the river.

After fording the stream he told her that they were now in the Great Horde, and another day would take them to his home.

Not far from the bank an open space was found, with abundance of grass, and the horses were soon piqueted to feed. A sheltered spot was selected for their resting-place, and Souk collected "argolls" for a fire, as these give out neither smoke nor flame. While the young Sultan was thus engaged, his bride walked back to the river; he watched her turn along its bank, and in a few minutes she was lost to his view. The fire was soon lighted, and Souk was busy making preparations for their evening meal. While thus engaged, he was suddenly startled by a fearful shriek at no great distance.

Seizing his battle-axe he rushed towards the spot: he saw no one. Calling out the name of his bride, he dashed forward through the thicket, but nothing could be seen; he then stood still, and again called her name loudly, but there was no response. The suspense became agonizing, and he listened for several minutes with intense anxiety, till he heard the crashing of branches in the distance; he rushed frantically towards the spot, but his career was quickly stopped by an object on the sand—the torn and bloody garment of his beloved! The fearful mystery was at once explained. She had retired to this secluded spot to offer up her devotions, having, as is customary, taken off her outward garment and spread it on the sand. On this she had prostrated herself in prayer, when a tiger had sprung forth and killed her before she could utter a second cry. His huge paws were deeply printed on the sand, and the trail was visible along which she had been dragged. Souk seized the rent and reeking garment, and with uplifted battle-axe dashed into the jungle.

He crossed the thicket in several directions, but in vain. Night having at last compelled him to give up the search, he returned to the encampment, where he sat down in fearful agony. A firm resolve had taken possession of his soul, to track the savage beast to his lair, and kill him or perish in the conflict. Hours passed on, and he waited with impatience the return of day.

At last a narrow streak of light appeared in the east and began to extend along the horizon, but he thought that daylight would never come. Then the eastern sky became a reddish grey, gradually increasing to a deep crimson just above the horizon. A little longer, and the under edges of the clouds were tinged with the glowing colour, that spread rapidly and gave out the light of day. Before the sun appeared Souk had prepared for the conflict. Knowing that his kalats would afford no protection against the claws and fangs of the tiger, and might impede his action, in a few minutes they were thrown on the ground; he then eagerly seized his battle-axe and started forth.

He reached the blood-stained spot, and saw the lair

The Tiger and his Victim.

whence the beast had sprung and the deep footprints made in the sand when he struck his victim. By daylight the trail was distinctly marked, and he followed it. Pieces of her garments were left on some of the bushes, and where the beast had crossed the sand, other marks were imprinted. The tiger had gone nearly half a mile to the edge of a bed of reeds without once stopping with his burthen.

Souk started on the tiger's trail across a sandy waste extending for several miles. Beyond this was a jungle, in which he tracked him for some distance, till the trail was lost in the bed of a stream; unwilling to relinquish his object, he continued the search, but without success, and after hours of painful toil was forced to return.

He mounted one horse and led the other, and started at full speed, nor did he check their career. It afforded him some relief as he left the place behind. Before night closed in he stopped on the Kara-tal, more than fifty miles from the Ili, and on the following afternoon reached home.

CHAP. XIV.

CARAVAN ROUTE AND MAI-MA-TCHIN.

English merchandise will sooner or later find its way into the northern provinces of China, through the Tatar merchants engaged in trade among the Kirghis hordes. I shall, however, point out another and more direct route by which commerce may be carried into these regions, if a fair were established on the Indus. During my wanderings I became acquainted with several merchants who had frequently visited Yarkand, Kashgar, and Cashmere. Between these places caravans often pass, so that various wares are constantly being transported through this country without any extraordinary difficulty. It may, I think, be taken for granted that wherever trade can be carried on with profit, all natural obstacles have been surmounted. It is a well known fact that the caravans that travel from Kulja into some of the interior provinces of China, encounter greater dangers than will be met with between Yarkand, Kashgar, and the Indus.

From Yarkand there is a caravan road going to the north-east, in a direct course into Mongolia; numerous routes branch from it into the tea provinces, and to various parts of the Chinese empire. Yarkand is a large town, which, I was informed, contained nearly 14,000 houses; and the population was estimated at from 85,000 to 90,000 in 1852; by some of the merchants, at 100,000. There is also a Chinese garrison of 5,000 men. It is a place of considerable trade, and a great number of Chinese, Tatar, Bokharian, and Cashmerian merchants reside here. Formerly Persians were also numerous, but now there are but few to be found in the city. The bazaars are three miles and a half in length, and on market days present a busy scene. Rich silks and porcelain are conspicuously displayed,—also embroidered Kanfa kalats, for which the Kirghis chiefs give twenty and thirty horses in exchange—brick tea appears in vast quantities — as well as printed calicoes from Kokhan. The loom of Cashmere contributes its quota to the mass of manufactured goods.

Jade abounds in the vicinity; some is found in the rivers; other kinds in the mountains. Notwithstanding that the Emperor claims the right over such treasures, it is largely sold, and the merchants succeed in obtaining it both in the rough state and in ornaments. Vegetables and fruit are abundant, and of excellent quality; the grapes are particularly fine both in size and flavour. Apricots, peaches, pears, apples, and water-melons are grown in every garden; and the people are excellent horticulturists.

Shortly after leaving Yarkand, the route crosses the river of that name, and then proceeds to the north-east, and passes the Kashgar at the small town of Bar-tchuk, after which it follows this river for more than 200 miles over a fertile country, till it reaches Kara-tal, where it crosses the Ac-sou. Hence it takes a course towards the Syan-Shan Mountains, passing the small towns of Yeil-gan, Dja-ban, and Sha-yar, crossing the river Sha-yar, whence it turns due north to Koutche.

This town contains between 5,000 and 6,000 inhabitants besides the Chinese garrison. To the north of this place is the Moussoor-Daban (or pass), on the route to Kulja, and the great volcano Pe-shan is on the east. Iron and copper are abundant in this region, and the latter mineral is worked. Sulphur and saltpetre are also found, and chloride of ammonium. Some fine specimens of this were brought to me that had been obtained in a large cavern near the Moussoor-Daban. To the south of Koutche a considerable quantity of rhubarb is produced. It is taken by the caravans to Mai-ma-tchin on the Siberian frontier.

After passing Koutche the route runs due east to Tokanai, along the foot of the Youl-douz Mountains, passing through Bugur or Youg-gur and several other small towns, till it reaches Kalga-man, at the western end of Bosteng-Noor, and thence proceeds to the town of Kara-shara. About forty miles to the north rises the Bogda-Oula, the highest summit in this part of Asia. It is a stupendous object, its dark precipices rising 7,000 or 8,000 feet above all the surrounding summits; and its canopy of ice and snow seems to pierce the skies. Kara-shara is a large town. One of my informants stated its population to be 30,000; another made it less. The whole region to the north is densely populated with nomades, who possess vast herds of cattle.

The next town of importance through which the route passes is Tourfan, and then Pidjan. About twenty-five miles north of Tourfan is the volcano Ho-theou, which was in violent action in 1852, and had been so for many years. On leaving Pidjan the route ascends the first ranges of Kongor-adzirgan, then crosses the chain and joins the route coming from the Tarbagatai and Tchoubachak, and thence to Barkol or Tchin-si. This is a large town, having a population of 10,000 and a garrison of 5,000 men. Numerous caravans pass through this place on their way to Tchoubachak and Ourga.

On leaving Barkol the route turns more to the north, and passes for more than 200 miles over a grassy steppe, on which the Mongol tribes find good pastures for their herds of horses and cattle.

It then enters on the sandy plain of Tchagan-Tala. Water is found here, but very little pasture. Having passed this dreary waste, the traveller reaches the southern slopes of the Khangai-Oula, where pasture and water are abundant. It then crosses the chain by a pass in the Koukou-Daban, at a point about fifty miles west of Kara-Korum, on the river Orkhon. Here is the town once so famed when Genghiz held his court. A friend of mine, a Cossack officer, with a

Tombs and Tumuli.

party of his men and two mining engineers, explored the Orkhon twenty-five years ago in search of gold, when they visited the site of the ancient capital of the Mongols. I ascertained from his description that there are few remains left to mark its magnitude, and nothing to indicate any former splendour.

Some of the summits of the Khangai-Oula I have seen covered with snow in August. The north-eastern face of these mountains give rise to a great number of rivers that fall into the Selenga, which collects nearly all the water on the south and west of the Baikal, and becomes the great affluent of that mountain sea. The route then descends into the valley of the Orkhon, crossing several torrents before it reaches that river, and passes some ruins on the shore of a small lake.

It then follows the north bank of the Orkhon for more than 100 miles to its junction with the Tola. This river runs from the east, having its rise on the western side of the Khin-gan Mountain, and on the eastern face of the chain is the source of the Keroulun, the longest affluent of the Amoor. After crossing the Orkhon, a little below the junction of the rivers, the route turns due east for about 130 miles, till it joins the road between the Chinese towns of Mai-ma-tchin and Ourga. It enters the road at a post-station, Kountsai, about sixty miles from the latter town and 120 from the former. From this point the caravans follow the post-road, going north-west over the mountains, and passes eight post-stations before reaching Mai-ma-tchin.

This town is what its name implies, "The place of trade," and stands on the edge of a plain that stretches out to the south to a chain of wooded hills, extending to the east thirty or forty miles, nearly to the river Kiran, which falls into the Tche-koi, while to the west it runs up towards the Selenga. At a few hundred yards to the north of the Chinese town is Kiachta, the Russian town, and three miles beyond this is Troitska-selo, standing among hills. From those to the north-west of the town I obtained an extensive view over the country to the southward. The plain on which these towns stand is said to be about 2,500 feet above the level of the sea; snow seldom falls here in the winter.

My visit to this place was at the time of the great Chinese festival, "The white month," which commences on the 4th of March. The Governor-General of Oriental Siberia provided me with letters to the officials, and other friends commended me to the merchants. During my stay I was the guest of the Director of the Customs, an officer holding a most important position, particularly as regards all mercantile transactions with the Chinese: in fact, he is the only official recognised by the Sargootcha (Chinese Governor), and at this season visits of ceremony take place between the two.

For the first time since the establishment of the trade with China, Russia had appointed a Civil Governor, to reside at Kiachta; and he had arrived at his post three weeks before the festival. This circumstance created some difficulties, as he expected to take precedence of the Director, and that all communications between the Chinese Governors and the Russian government should pass through his hands. The Sargootcha, however, thought otherwise, and declined to hold any official communication with him. He was willing to receive the Governor as a Russian officer of high rank, and give him a Chinese dinner in that capacity, but would recognise him in no other way. This was a most unexpected circumstance; and the Russian, who had just left the Chancéry of Count Nesselrode, gave vent to expressions in nowise flattering to the Chinaman. They were overheard, and rendered the breach still wider. The Director of the Customs and the resident merchants, through whom all the trade between Russia and China is carried on, tried to bring about a reconciliation. After some days they were successful, and the Sargootcha consented to receive him as Governor, but would give no pledge as to future communications.

A day was appointed for the reception, and the Governor,

intending to make an impression, had ordered all the Russian officials and the merchants to be in attendance. Every carriage and droshky in the place was held in requisition for the important event, and a guard of mounted Cossacks preceded the procession and brought up the rear. As this cavalcade passed over the neutral ground that separates the towns, both Russians and Chinese gazed with astonishment at the display of uniforms. Chinese streets, however, are not calculated to give an imposing effect to any procession, and the carriages were obliged to be left at the gates. In this instance it was difficult for even a small number to find standing room; and it was remarked that the gates into many of the courtyards were closed, which were always filled with spectators when the Director made his annual visit of ceremony.

At length the procession reached the dwelling of the Sargootcha, and entered the court-yard, where it was formed according to rank, and proceeded along a covered gallery to the house. A number of Chinese officials were in attendance to receive the Governor and conduct him to the Sargootcha. The meeting was characterised by a bland politeness on the part of the host, and an extraordinary degree of hauteur on the part of the guest. The presents which the Governor had brought for his host were tendered and received with cool politeness. The dinner, of near sixty courses, passed without producing any change for the better, and they separated with mutual feelings of distaste. A few days later the Governor performed the office of host, when the Sargootcha returned the ceremonial visit, and presented some of the choicest products of the empire, partook of his hospitality, and left without having excited the slightest approach to cordiality. The amiable politeness with which the Chinaman treated his host only exasperated him the more, and rendered him irritable towards the other officers.

It was not my first acquaintance with the Governor,

and on my visits he once or twice showed that a strong prejudice had taken possession of his mind with regard to some of his colleagues: this soon became apparent in his intercourse with the Director and some of the other officials,—even the merchants were not exempt. I must state that at this period the circulation of gold was strictly prohibited, so much so that on my first visit to Kiachta the Director inquired if I had any gold with me. Having assured him that I had only sufficient for the expenses of my journey, he desired me to deposit it with him, and he would send an order for me to pass the gate without being examined. He also informed me that I was not to pay for anything, and sent to one of the merchants, Mr. Igoumnoff, to procure whatever I wished. Although I was taken into the town in the Director's droshky, and was driven by his coachman, both the man and vehicle were searched each time they passed.

Having called to pay my respects to one of these wealthy merchants, he and his family received me with great kindness, and we were sitting talking of acquaintances in Siberia and Moscow, when a party of Cossacks marched up and surrounded the house. Three police officers entered, with ten or twelve men at their heels, and having stationed a man at each door with orders to permit no one to leave the room, they announced that they had come to search him and his house for gold, as it was known that he had both coin and gold from the mines on his premises.

My friend remonstrated, and assured them that he had no gold in his possession. He also inquired why they had surrounded his house with Cossacks, and entered it as if they were after a common thief. At last, having demanded to be taken to the Governor instantly, one of them showed him that high functionary's order for the proceeding that had excited his indignation. They therefore commenced their search, rummaging every part of the house, even examining his papers and letters, and his wife's and children's wardrobes, without permitting her to be present; in short, explored every corner, but not a single coin was found.

This circumstance created a great sensation in the little town, and the merchants, feeling that no one of them was safe from suspicion and outrage, refused to hold intercourse with the Governor. Mr. Trepaznikoff having in vain endeavoured to obtain information as to his accuser, or redress for the wrong he had suffered, announced his intention to break up his establishment and leave Kiachta, which he shortly afterwards fulfilled.

The town of Mai-ma-tchin is composed entirely of wooden buildings, and is surrounded by a wooden palisade having two gates: one on the north facing Kiachta, and the other opening to the south on to the plain. A narrow street runs straight through the town from one gate to the other, the distance being between 500 and 600 yards. Parallel to this are other streets on each side, and a space of about thirty yards in width extends from the houses to the palisade. Other streets run at right angles, and thus they divide the town into numerous blocks. At the intersection in the centre of the two principal streets there is a square edifice, standing on four square pillars, that form openings into the four streets. It contains three stories, and the upper ones diminish in size like a Chinese pagoda. The angles of the roofs are ornamented with Chinese dragons and other monsters; in each face of the upper stories there are openings filled in with highly decorated trellis work, cut in wood, with balconies and an ornamented balustrade beneath. The walls are curiously painted in red with green monsters, and other allegorical figures. A small staircase winds up in one of the pillars, and this leads into the observatory of Mai-ma-tchin.

On my first visit to the town a group of twenty people, or perhaps more, were assembled near this tower, playing at a game quite new to me. They were formed into a circle, having a small shuttlecock, which they were kicking up with the side of the foot. Some of them tossed it twelve or fifteen feet high for twenty times together, then it was tossed to the opposite side of the circle, and if the man near whom it fell missed kicking it up, there was a great shout and a forfeit. This seemed to be a favourite game.

A little beyond the tower is the residence of the Sar-

A Man at his Trade.—From a Chinese drawing.

gootcha, which is entered, like all other Chinese dwellings, through a pair of folding doors. These lead into a covered gallery or colonnade, its roof standing on pillars, and extending across the court-yard about 125 feet in width. It was intersected in the centre by a similar gallery that extended to the right and left; the left led to the Sargootcha's residence and the right to the theatre: the distance between the fronts of these buildings is about 180 feet. The house of the Sargootcha, like all the others in the town, is one story in height, and that not lofty, the rooms not being more than nine feet high; nor are any of them of large size. The covered colonnades render them somewhat dark and gloomy, the windows not affording much light, as they are small and formed of mica, placed in wooden frames; some are of curious pattern. Several divans and small tables were placed in the rooms, on some of which stood magnificent porcelain vases and a few Chinese bronzes.

On leaving the house of the Sargootcha, the Temple of Fo stands on the right hand, and on the left the court of justice. The temple is a small quadrangular building, with an opening in the centre that affords a view into the interior. The other parts of the front are constructed of curiously-formed lattice-work, in which are two doorways giving entrance to the side aisles of the temple. Rich Kanfa curtains separate the aisles from the centre, where stood a table with a considerable number of small images placed upon it, among them numerous silver and brass cups containing offerings. Near the end of the centre part of the temple there were four statues the size of life, painted with various colours, that gave them more the character of demons than gods. Several musical instruments were hanging on the walls: among them were two somewhat like clarionets, one about seven feet long, and the other five feet; there were also several gongs ready to add their sonorous sounds to those of the monster clarionets. Numerous flags and banners were suspended from the roof, forming a canopy of the most brilliant colours. These, with the elaborately embroidered and beautifully coloured curtains, produced a charming effect. Here the Chinese artist had displayed his thorough knowledge of colour, in which he excels almost every nation. The effect was perfect.

Opposite the temple was the court of justice, over which a red flag was fluttering; on the walls were various implements of torture and several bamboos piled up in front, perhaps as a warning to any refractory Chinese. At the further end of this building, and against the wooden fence of the court, was a large room with a number of small lattice windows in its front, and a doorway near the end. From this place there issued a most terrific volume of sound, and my curiosity led me to ascertain its cause. The interpreter whom the Director had ordered to attend me said it was a concert. I therefore lifted the latch and walked in. The room was about twenty-five feet long, and fifteen feet wide; its height was not more than ten feet; and numerous benches ran from side to side. Near the centre of one side of the room a tall Chinese was standing, with two small sticks in his hand. On the benches about thirty performers were sitting and standing, each having a gong, on which he was plying two thick sticks with all his might. As the master waved or clattered his wands the volume of sound was regulated, and the din of gongs became deafening. This, however, seemed to add to their enjoyment; and as the thundering increased, each performer appeared absorbed in the harmony he believed he was producing. At length they reached the climax: the wand dropped; every hand ceased wielding its stick; the men looked at each other with evident satisfaction, and then burst into a fit of laughter. They had produced one of the most thundering performances to which it was ever my lot to listen.

Afterwards I proceeded along the centre colonnade to the theatre, that stands at the opposite end to the Sargootcha's dwelling. This is a small building, and immediately in front is a recess on each side of the colonnade, which form rooms about twenty feet long, and fifteen feet wide. In the centre of these were two pictured groups considerably larger than life; and the moment I saw them it was obvious to me that they were subjects from Greek history. That on the right hand represented a wild horse rearing on his haunches, held by two slaves. Although rudely executed in sandstone, there was much spirit and character in the composition, and the story was well told. In the left-hand recess the group consisted of a horse, probably the same animal, being led by a single figure, after his fiery temper had been subdued. I recognised the story of Alexander and Bucephalus. Without giving any hint of my own views on the subject, I desired the interpreter to inquire from the Chinese officer sent with me by the Sargootcha what these figures meant, and the literal translation of his answer was, "Philip of Macedon." I could obtain no information as to when and where they were executed, but they are supposed to have been brought from China shortly after the building of Mai-ma-tchin.

The theatre was a building of little importance; the stage small, having seats in front for the Sargootcha and his officers, the other part of the audience having to stand in the colonnade. The walls were covered with Chinese paintings, but none of any interest; and the performances almost invariably take place in the daytime.

During my numerous rambles in Mai-ma-tchin I visited the dwellings of most of the Chinese merchants; they resemble each other so much that a description of one will be sufficient. Each has its courtyard, and is enclosed within its own fence. The wealthier merchants have their abodes along the line of the principal streets; those of a lower grade are in the narrow lanes nearer the palisade. The courtyard is entered by a pair of folding doors from the street; and immediately the visitor has passed the threshold he finds convincing evidence that the establishment is kept with great care and cleanliness. The courtyard is twenty-five feet wide, and forty feet deep; on the right hand are several private apartments, about ten feet square, and in the centre of this front there is an altar to Fo. The windows are filled in with mica; some are highly ornamented. On the left hand are the kitchens and rooms of the domestics.

At the end of the court is the magazine, with a doorway in the centre; and the roof over this part of the establishment is decorated with dragons and other monsters of Chinese invention. It extends to the width of the courtyard and the rooms on each side; is twenty feet in width, and divided in its length into two rooms,—one being about twenty feet by fifteen feet, and the other thirty feet by twenty feet, with a large opening between them. At the extremity of the large room there is a raised platform ten feet wide and two feet nine inches high. A small stove is constructed beneath this in brickwork, with an opening in the centre for the fuel; the other part forms a large air chamber, heated by the stove, that maintains a warm current which is diffused through the rooms. This platform has a boarded floor, extending the whole width of the room; and on it the inmates sleep.

The walls are tastefully decorated with silk and Chinese paintings, and here the merchant has his choicest wares; silks of great variety and beauty, embroidered Kanfa kalats, jackets, and various other articles of costume; porcelain vases of most exquisite workmanship and great value—various dinner and tea services, some of them exceedingly costly—ornaments in jade—and groups of flowers formed in various-coloured stones, showing the patience of the Chinese workmen. Window screens are articles on which they bestow great labour; some of them are most minutely carved in ebony, on others they execute foliage and flowers in green and white jade. One piece of wood-carving was shown to me, about six feet high and four feet wide; the centre was covered with a multitude of flowers and fruit in amethyst, beryl, chalcedony, and jade. The price of this was equal to £600. It had remained several years without a purchaser, and now was about to be returned to Pekin.

Almost all the merchants have adopted the Russian somervar, and the teapot seems in action from morning till night. At whatever hour I called, the tea was ready. It is presented with a great variety of sweetmeats, for which the Chinese are justly celebrated; dried fruits they also have in great abundance. Very little tea is offered for sale in these magazines; it is taken from the caravans into the government warehouses in Kiachta, and then it is removed by the Russians to the custom-house at Troitska.

Chinese dinners have been so often described that I shall only say that the Sargootcha afforded me the opportunity of appreciating his hospitality in its fullest extent. No one is allowed to reside in the Russian town Kiachta except the merchants through whom the trade with China is conducted, a number of custom-house officers, an officer of Cossacks with 200 men, and a considerable body of workmen with their families.

Free intercourse is permitted between Kiachta and Mai-ma-tchin from sunrise to sunset; after that hour the Chinese shut their gate, and the Cossacks stop the egress from Kiachta. The resident merchants have become exceedingly wealthy by acting as agents for those in Moscow and in other parts of the empire. Several of their dwellings are spacious and built of brick, and some are furnished with taste. They contain many articles of Chinese production, and some of great value. These men, like all the commercial class of Russia, possess the true spirit of hospitality. A visitor in these far-off regions who can give them news of what is going on in Europe is quite a godsend.

My abode was in Troitska (as no one would have dared to give me a night's lodging in Kiachta). Here is the custom-house, where all merchandise, whether from China or Russia, must be deposited in the government warehouses, and where the barter is actually carried on. It is thus a place of much commercial activity while the various wares are passing through. Hitherto Mai-ma-tchin has been almost the only town whence Russia has received her tea. The importation has now reached near six millions of Russian pounds, no portion being cheap or common tea. Until within the last few years the whole of this, as well as other Chinese merchandise, was paid for in Russian goods, the value being decided by the authorities in Troitska, Kiachta, and Mai-ma-tchin. Now a portion is paid for in money, greatly to the advantage of the merchant.

Beside the trade in tea, that in rhubarb is important. I was informed that 360,000 lbs. pass through Mai-ma-tchin annually. Silks of various kinds are imported, but these are principally purchased in Siberia.

The merchants from Moscow and a few other towns in Siberia usually reach Troitska and Kiachta in the beginning of February; and before the middle of March their transactions are completed, and long caravans are on their march towards Irbit and Nijne-Novgorod.

The custom-house and warehouses in Troitska are on an extensive scale; they stand in a good position, a little removed from the town, and employ a vast number of people. Nearly all the custom-house officers are sent from different parts of Russia, and think this a banishment. During my stay a gentleman and his family arrived from Odessa; he had received the appointment as second in command, and when he reached his destination and knew that he was to remain in this region for ten years, he was in terrible distress.

With Russian and Chinese merchandise the transit trade through Siberia is of considerable importance, affording employment to a vast number of horses and men. The best time for conveying the goods is in winter; beside, the sledge being of easier draught, the rivers, the passage of which often occasions great losses, are crossed without risk. The merchants engaged in the tea trade always try to send their purchases by the winter roads; and as these are formed six weeks or two months before the Baikal is frozen, the caravans have to pass round the western end of the lake.

It is seldom that the tea can be sent on sledges from Troitska to Oust-Kiachta at any period during the most

Ancient Remains.

severe winter, as snow rarely remains on the ground near Kiachta. It has to be taken about twenty-five miles in telagas and then placed on sledges. The country over which the tea caravans have to pass by this route is exceedingly difficult. On leaving Oust-Kiachta it turns to the west at no great distance from the Chinese frontier, and crosses the Selenga. This river has its source far to the westward in the lake Tsa-gan; on its shore there are some remains of a very ancient date. The people have no tradition in connection with them, but their appearance inclined me to think them Druidical.

After passing the Selenga the route is over a country inhabited by Bouriats. After continuing about 100 miles, it reaches the mountains that rise on the south-western side of the Baikal. These, although not of great elevation, offer serious obstacles, and at some periods of the year the road is really dangerous. Before reaching Sne-jinoi it enters the mountains, and ascends the steeps of the lower range of Amar-daban.

This route was made by the Cossacks and hunters when endeavouring to penetrate into the region beyond the Baikal. The pursuit of game and sables first led them in this direction; but even these daring men never succeeded in riding their horses over Amar-daban, which is the highest summit in the region. It rises in rugged precipices and abrupt rocky slopes so steep that the early attempts to scale it often proved fatal, tradition having handed down many accounts of the fearful disasters that befell the pioneers in this region. At last, after many years, they succeeded in forming a horse track, by which it was possible to cross the chain, though only for a short time in summer, from the middle of June to August; so that this was almost useless as a means of communication even for hunting.

When the tea trade was opened with China, a road became a matter of the first importance, and as this was the only direction by which the caravans could reach Mai-ma-tchin, the Russian government sent an order to the authorities in Irkoutsk to make a good one round the western end of the Baikal. The best engineer at their disposal (a peasant) was sent to direct the operations, and by perseverance and the aid of a sound judgment he succeeded. It was, however, a work of immense labour. The trees were carried up by Bouriats to the top of the highest summit in the chain, and the road passes over its peak, that being the only part practicable. The abrupt face of the mountain had to be scaled by zigzag lines, running along the edge of deep precipices, which are protected by wooden pillars and rails.

Having passed Amar-daban the road descends into numerous ravines, and after travelling over these rugged places, the caravan reaches Sloudenka. Even here, near the shore of the Baikal, the path descends like a staircase, broken into many flights, and the small wooden rails seem but a frail protection. When the caravans commence their first winter journey, it is attended with great danger. The snow is often from six to eight feet deep, and in some places the road is covered to four times that depth, and has to be cut through. But in ordinary cases of six feet deep, a good track is formed by drawing empty sledges with broad runners over the snow. I believe not a winter passes without this operation proving fatal to both men and horses. Even in spring I have known the post be two days in travelling over a station of thirty versts.

From Sloudenka to Koultouk the distance is only twenty miles, but a part of this station is very bad, till the road descends to the shore of the Baikal, which it reaches near a mass of rocks named Shaman Kamen. Formerly these religious fanatics executed their criminals here. Their religion and its ceremonies are founded on sorcery; they believe in good and evil spirits, and sacrifice parts of the maral to their god, whom they name Bour-Khan. They give themselves little trouble about the good spirit, but for the evil one they have a great reverence. They believe him an inhabitant of our earth, that he has his abode in dense forests and rugged mountains, and that he is ever active in the midst of terrific storms. They also think that he has the power to transform men into whatever shape he pleases.

With the Shamans the priesthood is hereditary; it is a rare instance that a stranger is admitted into it.

Not far from this place there is a beautiful natural arch; its effect at a short distance is like a deep moulded and richly decorated Gothic portal.

The road, after leaving Koultouk, ascends some high ridges which bound the Baikal to the north; they are

A Natural Arch on the Baikal.

covered with a dense forest, where large game and bears are numerous. The forest on the north shore of the lake is a famous hunting ground for the Cossacks and peasants; here they obtain venison in abundance, and many valuable skins. There is very little open country on this route; but small patches have been cleared around the stations sufficient to feed the horses. In summer they seek their food in the forest, where they occasionally become victims to Bruin. At length the route descends the steep and wooded hills to the bank of the Angara, which at this point spreads out to near 600 yards in width, and on the opposite bank stands Irkoutsk, the capital of Oriental Siberia.

This has always been an important town, as the Governor-General exercises authority over a country more than ten times the size of England. Within the last few years its consequence has increased by the great acquisition on the Amoor. The plan and preparations for effecting that object emanated from the present Governor-General Mouravioff, who has well earned his title of Count d'Amoor. He has my good wishes for a long life to enjoy his honour.

My first approach to Irkoutsk was by the post road from Russia: it enters the valley of the Angara at Polovinnia station, about seventy miles to the north-west of Irkoutsk; hence it runs along at a short distance from the river. On the west side of the valley densely wooded hills arise, and on the east are seen the cliffs at the foot where the Angara is rolling on its rapid stream. Along the bank and on other parts of the plain fine clumps of trees are growing, between which the sparkling water is seen, and then lost behind thick foliage, till, by a bend in the river, it bursts forth into a wide expanse. Several views on this route made a strong impression on my mind; they were really beautiful: indeed, many charming subjects for the pencil may be found here.

At last, at a turn in the valley, I caught sight of a dome and several tall spires rising over the tops of a forest of birches and pines. This was the monastery of Saint Irkout, which stands in a very picturesque position on the bank of the Angara. I was surprised to find an architectural edifice possessing so much taste, in these far-off regions. Having passed the monastery, Irkoutsk was before me at about two miles distant. This was on a Sunday afternoon—a beautiful day, and a sky without a cloud; the Angara was seen in its full width, stretching up to the walls of the town, where it made a great bend to the westward and appeared like a lake. The gateway formed a striking object: it was massive and imposing. Beyond the walls numerous towers, domes, and spires were visible, rising far above the dwellings. As these objects were scattered over a considerable space, it gave the place the appearance of a large city. I shortly afterwards reached the river, the Yemstchik, drove on to the ferry-boat, and I passed through the gate.

Having spent two winters in Irkoutsk, and two summers in the regions to the south, I necessarily saw the preparations which were in progress for the annexation of the Amoor, and had an opportunity of judging of their efficiency. I beheld the chests of arms for the new regiments of Cossacks, as they passed through; and some of my friends received important appointments on the Trans-Baikal; one has since been made General, and now commands from 30,000 to 40,000 Cossacks,—fine daring fellows they are. He has also several batteries of Cossack artillery, thoroughly equipped, and competent for any service; he could march to Pekin in a month.

Irkoutsk stands in a curve of the Angara, on its eastern bank, at the western edge of a plain, in lat. 52° 40′ N, and long. 104° 20′ E, and 1, 360 ft. 6 in. above the level of the sea. Wooded hills extend on the east and north-east, also along the western bank of the Angara, till the latter joins the valley of the Irkout. The small river Ouska-kofka runs from the eastward, and is crossed by a wooden bridge near 300 yards in length: this stream divides the town from the prison and the workshops in which the convicts are employed, as well as from the Admiralty and dockyards on the eastern bank of the Angara.

The principal part of the town stands in an angle formed by the Angara and the Ouska-kofka. The streets run nearly parallel with the river, and are crossed at right angles by others. There are many good houses, and some with considerable architectural pretensions; each has a large courtyard; many have gardens. There are but few shops, and these are in the Gastinoi-Dvor: they are large and well supplied with almost all necessary European goods that find their way through the fair at Nijne-Novgorod, and with Chinese articles from Mai-ma-tchin.

A fine broad road runs along the bank of the Angara; towards the upper end of this is the residence of the Governor-General. It is truly a magnificent mansion, and was originally built by a merchant who realised an enormous fortune in the Chinese trade. Here, on the confines of China, he surrounded himself with European luxuries, and did much, by example, to change the rude habits of his countrymen. At his death the family left to reside in Moscow, and the house was bought by the Government. Several merchants have built good houses fronting the river; and my friend Rosguildaoff is doing much to improve the taste of the people, and at the same time adding to his architectural fame.

Several of the merchants here might vie with our commercial princes,—their wealth being enormous. One has a taste for the fine arts, and I was greatly surprised to find his folios filled with proofs of every important engraving from Landseer. He is also a book collector, and has built an excellent library, in which he has stored upwards of 5,000 volumes. His collection of Chinese ornaments is both choice and valuable; besides, he is a great horticulturist, and spends large sums in procuring plants from Europe. I might instance several others who are also aiding in the work of refinement.

The Cathedral is a large building on the Great Parade, and near it are two other churches: on the opposite side are the courts of justice and other Government offices. The different churches are all well placed, with fine open squares around them. Many were designed and built under the superintendence of two Swedish engineer officers, who were made prisoners at the battle of Pultava, and were banished hither by Peter. They must have made architecture a study, for they have left monuments that few Europeans have surpassed. I must not omit the name of Kouznetsoff, a merchant who died during my stay. He has been a great benefactor to the town and people. He built a very large house, containing magnificent rooms, with every accommodation, and furnished it without regard to cost; even including plate and a grand piano. This he presented to the town, as a residence for its civil governors. He endowed some of the schools, and left a sum equal to £50,000 for various purposes and improvements; besides leaving more than half a million to two nieces. His own mansion, which was far advanced, was on a princely scale; but I fear its present possessor will never complete it.

I have mentioned these men to show that there are enterprising and energetic minds in this part of Asia. Their descendants will find a new field for commercial enterprise down the Amoor, and into the Pacific. A time is not distant when a mercantile fleet will be moored in their harbours, in the Gulf of Tartary and the Sea of Japan.

Irkoutsk has a population of near 20,000, and the number of its buildings has increased considerably of late years. The transit trade between China and Russia has made many wealthy; but accidents sometimes cause great losses in tea, one of which I witnessed. Large quantities are conveyed to Pasolsky by the sledge roads and put on board a vessel, called a "Soudna." One, having taken in 1,200 chests, crossed the Baikal and reached the Angara; while descending the river, she struck on some masses of ice that had grounded, was nearly cut in two, and had the greater portion of her cargo washed out of her. Though this entailed a loss on the carrier of £20,000, it was deemed a matter of little moment. The Angara is the last river in Siberia to close and the first to open; the former occurring on the 13th of December, the latter on the 11th of April.

The markets are well furnished with all kinds of provisions except mutton; beef is good, and is principally supplied by the Bouriats beyond and on the north of the Baikal. I have bought a live calf, six weeks old, for a rouble (3*s.* 2*d.*); so that veal is both cheap and good. Game of all kinds is abundant and cheap, and so is fish; in short, all the necessaries of life which are produced in the country are exceed-

Part of Irkoutsk.

ingly moderate in cost; but European articles, and other foreign produce brought from Russia, are very expensive. Sugar is 2*s.* 7½*d.* per lb.; coffee, 3*s.* 2*d.*; rice, 6*d.*; lemons, 3*s.* 2*d.* each; oranges, 2*s.*; sardines, 4*s.* 9*d.* per box; English porter and Scotch ale, 11*s.* 1*d.* per bottle; French brandy, 11*s.* 1*d.* per bottle, (mostly made in Russia). Wine equally dear; Champagne, 16*s.* 10*d.* per bottle, and more of it is drank than of any other wine. Those who can dispense with these luxuries will find living cheap in the capital of Oriental Siberia. When communications are established between the Angara and the Amoor, and merchantmen discharge their cargoes in the latter river, a great change will be effected throughout Siberia.

At the time of my visit to Irkoutsk there were six of the exiles still living in the town, viz., Prince Volkonskoi, Prince Troubetskoi, and Colonel Pogge, with their families; the others were, Mokhanoff, and two brothers Barrisoff. These formed the best society in Irkoutsk, and some of the most agreeable days which I spent in Siberia, was in enjoying my intercourse with them. They were now living in comfort, mixing in society, and gathering around them all the best that Irkoutsk afforded. The Princess Troubetskoi had spent several of her youthful years in England, associating with the highest families in the kingdom. She was a clever and highly-educated woman, devoted all her energies to the education of her three daughters and a young son, and was the first lady who followed her husband into Siberia. I heard from her own lips an account of her journey through those dreary regions, when she was attended only by a maid-servant, as well as of her reception and treatment when at the mines of Nerchinsk. The Princess Volkonskoi was the next to follow: she had a son and daughter; the latter one of the most beautiful girls I ever beheld. Both these families possessed everything they could desire, except liberty to return to their homes; with the others it was different, and with two of them it was indeed a hard struggle for existence.

CHAP. XV.

TRANSBAIKAL AND THE SOURCES OF THE AMOOR.

My way on leaving Irkoutsk was along the bank of the Angara. I had travelled it once before, but then on a stormy day, and my errand was a melancholy one. It was to select a block of granite on the shore of the Baikal, to be placed over the grave of a friend, Basil Mouravioff, who died in Irkoutsk the year before my visit. The last time we met was on the road more than 3,000 miles from his final resting-place, where we breakfasted together at the post station. He was on his journey to Irkoutsk, full of hope, and delighted with his new position. He was a nephew of the General of Kars, and a cousin and aide-de-camp to the Governor-General of Oriental Siberia. In less than two years his career had terminated. A contusion caused by a cannon ball passing near his head during an engagement in the Caucasus was the cause of his death.

Shortly after leaving Irkoutsk the road enters a wooded part of the valley of the Angara, and runs along at a considerable elevation above the river. I observed that both sides of the valley were clothed with timber down to the water's edge. Sandstone crops out here and forms high cliffs, rising from the water, and the flood was rolling on at a rapid rate. About ten miles from the town I came upon a line of twenty horses towing a soudna up the stream to the Baikal. This vessel had conveyed a cargo of 600 chests of tea and 25,000 bricks of tea to Irkoutsk, and was on her return in ballast. Although the distance from Irkoutsk to the Baikal is only forty miles the current is so strong that it takes three days to draw the vessels up the river to within four miles of the lake, and then it required another day to draw her up the rapid, even with double the number of horses.

As the road winds along the valley, it passes many points that present magnificent views. In some parts enormous cliffs arise crowned with dark pines and cedars; in others the thick forest descends to the river's brink, and the broad sheet of water is seen rolling onward. Shortly after passing Pash-kou-a station the valley becomes more rugged, and the rocks rise in huge masses, with deep ravines running up into the mountains. Beyond this the road has been formed along the edge of a cliff, at a considerable elevation above the river. Both sides of the valley show that this part of the earth's crust has been much disturbed, and that here great disruptions have occurred.

About five miles before reaching the Baikal a scene is presented that causes almost every traveller to stop. The valley becomes wider, and the mountains rise abruptly to a much greater elevation. The Angara is more than a mile in width, and this great body of water is seen rolling down a steep incline, forming a rapid nearly four miles in length. At the head of this, and in the centre of the stream, a great mass of rock elevates itself, called the Shaman-Kamen. Beyond is the broad expanse of the Baikal, extending about fifty miles to where its waves wash the foot of Amar-Daban, whose summit is usually covered with snow, even in June. The mighty torrent throwing up its jets of spray, the rugged rocks with their fringes of pendent birch overtopped by lofty pines, and the ethereal colouring on the mountains, produce a picture of extraordinary beauty and grandeur.

A few miles further and the Baikal is seen spreading out like a sea, and its rolling waves are heard lashing the rocky shores. The Shaman-Kamen is more distinctly seen. As I stood gazing at it, I could not help recalling to mind some of the scenes that have been enacted there. It is held sacred by all of the Shaman creed, and they never pass it without offering up their devotions. Rude figures have been sculptured upon its surface, and formerly both men, women, and children have been offered up on its summit, or hurled into the flood.

The steamboat station is not far distant, and I was

Kolo-kolnia, on the Baikal.

not long in reaching Listvenitz, when I found that both the steamers were on the opposite side of the lake; the larger one taking in a cargo of tea at Pasolskoi, and the small one searching for a convenient harbour—the navigation usually closing at the end of September.

As she would not be ready for her return voyage to Pasolskoi before the fourth day, I had time to explore the neighbourhood.

The danger and delay in crossing the Baikal in boats was

very great; it was no uncommon occurrence to be detained three weeks on the voyage without being able to land on either shore; and accidents were frequent. This induced an enterprising merchant, Menchnikoff, to place a steamer on the lake; but it was done at a great cost: the engines, boiler, and all the machinery were made in Petersburg, and had to be transported by land more than 4,000 miles. Mr. Baird, the mechanical engineer, sent a competent person to the Baikal to build the hull, and this, under his superintendence, the Russian peasants accomplished. With their aid the mechanics put in the engines: after a few trials the vessel steamed across to the Mongolian shore, and the dangers of the Baikal had vanished. Both the Siberians and Mongolians gazed with astonishment when they beheld the steamer make her way across in a heavy gale.

Without wasting time I arranged to explore the shore going to the eastward, and to be taken up by the steamer at Golo-oustnaia. A crew of five men and my Cossack were my companions in the boat. Shortly after leaving Listvenitz the shore of the Baikal becomes exceedingly abrupt; the rock — a coarse-grained granite — has a dense larch forest growing on the mountain above, which rises considerably to the north. This formation continues for more than twenty miles, and many picturesque and striking scenes were presented to me. It then changes to conglomerate exceedingly coarse-grained, the shingle on the shore being entirely composed of it. Several torrents have cut their channels through these precipices, forming, in some, beautiful waterfalls.

The north shore is by far the most lofty; in some parts the precipices rise 800 and 900 feet, and a little beyond the river Anga, to 1,200 feet. I shall not attempt to describe the strata, which are here exposed for more than 400 miles in length, as my description would interest the geologist only, and would take a much larger space than I can afford. Beyond the island of Olkhon basaltic cliffs appear, sometimes rising from deep water to an elevation of 700 feet. At little more than a boat's length from their base, soundings have been taken to the depth of 900 feet. After passing these the shore becomes somewhat less elevated, but exhibits unquestionable evidence of volcanic action. In some of the ravines were great masses of lava, which, unfortunately, I was unable to trace to its source. No doubt it has been ejected from a crater in the Baikal chain to the north, and probably from near the sources of the Kerengha. Hot mineral springs are also found in several parts of the chain.

Between the shore of the lake and the Baikal chain an elevated steppe, extends for about 130 miles in length, and in some parts it is twenty-five miles in width. Here are numerous aouls of Bouriats, who possess large herds of cattle, and the plain gradually descends towards the mouth of the upper Angara. This river falls into the Baikal at its most northerly point, and is exceedingly valuable to the Siberians for its fishery of omula (*Salmo omul Pall*), which is caught here in enormous quantities, salted, and then sent to all parts of Siberia. Thus preserved, they equal the best Dutch herrings, and when fresh are the most delicious fish I ever tasted. A great number of men are engaged in the fishery. They leave Irkoutsk about the first week in July, and the fleet of soudnas usually reach the upper Angara before the 1st of August, when the omula ascend the river in such vast shoals that the fishermen speedily obtain their cargoes, and make several voyages to Listvenitz before the season closes. The river is not navigable much beyond the village of Upper Angarsk, and can never be made a means of communication with the Amoor, as some persons have supposed.

Instead of meeting the steamer at Golo-oustnaia, I continued my explorations, and on my return visited the south shore of the island of Olkhon. It is about sixty miles in length, in some parts fifteen miles in breadth, and is separated from the north shore of the lake, called by the natives "the Little Baikal," by them considered the most sacred part of this "Holy Sea." The island is about eight miles from the north shore, excepting at its western end, where a great mass runs out into the lake for several miles, and forms a magnificent entrance to the sacred sea. A little farther to the west the rocks rise to about 1,200 feet, forming a stupendous object when seen from the water.

The people have a tradition in connection with this region which they implicitly believe. They say "that Christ visited this part of Asia and ascended this summit, whence he looked down on all the region around. After blessing the country to the northward, he turned towards the south, and looking across the Baikal, he waved his hand, exclaiming, Beyond this there is nothing." Thus they account for the sterility of Daouria, where it is said "no corn will grow."

The south shore of the island is exceedingly abrupt, and very few points are presented where it is possible to land. We had been rowing on for many hours without finding any place on which to sleep; night was drawing on apace, and a stiff breeze springing up. In the cliffs opposite I observed numerous caverns, and in front a promontory of high rocks jutting out into the lake, containing several others, and in some places it was pierced by galleries.

We had noticed the indication of a squall to the south-east, and the boatmen wished to land in one of the caverns, there to pass the night. To this proposition I decidedly objected, fearing we might be detained for some days. Our prospect was a bad one, unless we could pass the headland, and reach shelter beyond; but a streak of white was observed approaching, and all were aware what it foreboded.

Knowing what effect example has on these men, I threw off my jacket and took one of the oars, the Cossack seized another, and this induced the men to pull with a hearty good-will. Before we could round the point, the squall caught us and covered us with spray: at this moment the steersman called to us to pull for our lives, or we should be driven against the rocks. It was a struggle I shall never forget; at last we shot out beyond the rocks, that were then only a

Caverns on the Baikal.

few boat's lengths from us, and the thundering of the waves, as they rushed into the caverns, was truly appalling.

Having passed this danger, a sandy beach was seen about a quarter of a mile distant; towards which we pulled with all our might. The waves rolled in and a great surf was thrown upon the shore; presently we dashed through it, but the boat was nearly half filled before we could run her up the beach. This was a narrow escape; and we were kept prisoners here for three days.

After spending nineteen days in exploring the northern shore, I reached Golo-oustnaia, where the steamer picked me up. When I got on board, the captain stated to me, in English, that my long absence had excited some apprehensions of my safety. I was not a little astonished to hear my native tongue spoken in the Baikal, and my look of surprise must have been evident; the captain explained, by informing me that he was a Swedish officer, and had served in our navy under Admiral Codrington. He had been eight years in his present occupation; sometimes steaming across the lake when it was smooth as glass, at other times in fearful storms,—which he declared were worse here than in the ocean; more especially when the garra (or mountain gale) came rushing from the mountains. I inquired if he had sounded the lake, but learnt that he knew the depth only by running out his cable when trying to anchor. Once, during a gale, he ran out 200 sagènes (1,400 feet), within 100 yards of a sand-bank, and on another occasion 300 sagènes (2,100 feet), without finding a bottom. This proves the great depth of the lake, and such prodigious abysses are often found close to places where the rocks are not ten sagènes under water.

The day was calm, and the steamer ran across in three hours and a half, when I left the worthy captain, and landed at Posolsky.

There is a monastery here of the Transfiguration of our Saviour, that possesses some claims as an architectural composition, for its numerous turrets formed picturesque groups, and the whole building had a pleasing effect when viewed from the Baikal. It was founded by Abbot Feodosayi, about the year 1682, to commemorate a tragic event that occurred on this spot. In 1650 a Russian ambassador, Zabolotsky, and his retinue, were murdered here, either by the Bouriats or Mongolians. Hence it is named Posolsky, or the Monastery of the Ambassador. The building and the village stand on a low plain that runs along the shores of the Baikal, commencing about four miles to the south-west of the landing-place, and extending north-east to the mouth of the Selenga. From Posolsky the road crosses the Delta, following the shore of the lake for about eight miles, and then turns eastward, to the post station at Stepnoi, near the mouth of the western branch of the Selenga. The river divides into eight branches before it falls into the Baikal; and from the north-west to the south-easterly channel is a distance of twenty miles.

This delta undoubtedly occupies what has formerly been a portion of the lake, which in the course of ages has been filled up by matter washed from the Mongolian Mountains. It is named by the people Kounderenskoi Steppe; like all such deltas, it is a most fertile spot, and well cultivated. This contradicts the tradition I have quoted, as an abundance of rye and wheat grows here. After leaving Stepnoi the road continues along the western bank of the Selenga; the hills to the right rise considerably, and are well wooded. On reaching Kabanskoi the river makes a great bend towards the north-east for about thirty miles, to Ilenskoi, and the mountains to the south-west become higher.

The first monastery established on the Transbaikalian shore, that of Troitska, stands in a picturesque spot at some ten miles before reaching Ilenskoi. It was founded by Abbot Feodosayi, who settled here in 1681, accompanied by a few monks from Moscow. The selection of this spot and the style of the building prove that those ecclesiastics, like their brethren in all ages, were men of taste. Though the structure must have produced a striking effect on the minds of the Bouriats, whom the abbot intended to convert, they could not be induced to change their faith.

After passing Ilenskoi, a route turns still more to the north-east, and approaches the shores of the Baikal. It leads into a most highly interesting region, where the mountains have been tossed up and broken into precipices and deep ravines. This route affords many extraordinary scenes on the Baikal, and, when the traveller looks down upon its vast expanse, reflecting on the terrible phenomenon that caused such a rent in the earth's crust (if rent it be), he will cease to wonder at the superstitious dread of the ignorant people who inhabit its shores. I have heard the subject reasoned upon by some of the most eminent mining engineers and geologists in Siberia, who have visited almost every part of its shore, examining the structure of its precipices, and have observed the composition of the strata laid bare. They differ widely in opinion from one German author, who, after a "gallop across the lake" of seven German miles, in about two hours, by moonlight, settled this difficult problem. I am in hopes of seeing it elucidated by one thoroughly acquainted with this singular region, for which the materials have been collected during many years of patient investigation.

On this coast there are several hot mineral springs,— that of Tourkinsk is the most accessible, and has become the Buxton of Oriental Siberia. Many families from Irkoutsk spend part of their summer here, and people go more than a thousand miles to take a dip in its waters. Between this place and Oust Bargouzin there are other springs, in which the gushing fluid scalds the hand if placed in it. About forty miles beyond there is proof that volcanic agency has once been active, for here is an extinct crater, from out of which vast quantities of lava have poured. In the vicinity of Bargouzin, naphtha and bitumen are constantly rising in the Baikal, and earthquakes are not uncommon.

Some of the exiles of 1825 were sent to live in Bargouzin, after undergoing a severe part of their sentence in the mines. One only was living there when the present Emperor recalled them to Russia, and he, having married a peasant's daughter, chose to remain, rather than return with his family into a society where he felt they would be out of place. He had served as a midshipman in the British navy, on board the same ship as young Codrington; they passed their examination together, and a strong intimacy had sprung up between them. He desired me to wait on the admiral on my return, and give him an account of his old

Boklau, on the Baikal.

messmate, who had turned sable hunter. I arrived in England too late to fulfil my promise.

Bargouzin is famed for its sables; no skins have yet been found in any part of the world equal to them. The fur is of a deep jet black, with the points of the hairs tipped with white, and this constitutes their peculiar beauty. I have seen a single skin for which the hunter demanded the sum of eighteen pounds.

Leaving the sable hunters, I return to Ilenskoi, and follow the Selenga up the valley, near the station of Polovena (or half way), where the prospect is very picturesque, for high cliffs, fringed in parts with trees and huge granite rocks, diversify the scenes as far as Verknoi Oudinsk. This is a small town, prettily situated, and many of its houses, and three of its churches, are built of stone; the green domes and spires have a pleasing effect when seen at a distance. Many of the inhabitants have become wealthy through the fisheries and the transport of tea to the Baikal.

After leaving Oudinsk the scenery on the river becomes exceedingly beautiful. Granite rocks rise to a considerable elevation; they are rent asunder and piled up into pinnacles in every variety of form. No one can pass through this valley without being struck by the beauty of its scenery, portions being equal to anything on the Rhine. I saw these masses in the setting sun and under the influence of a young moon, and then passed through them for some hours in the darkness, to Selenginsk.

It was some time after midnight when the Yemstchik drove into the town, and I desired him to take me to the house of the brothers Bestoushoff, two exiles. I was the bearer of letters from some of their comrades in a far distant part of Siberia, and of a watch for one of them. At last the driver pulled up his horses in the middle of a large yard.

I instantly stepped out of the tarantas, but the night was so dark that objects were scarcely visible. The Yemstchik turned me in the direction of the house, and I saw a dark mass before me, but neither window nor portal was visible. Having reached the wall, I passed along and found a door. Knowing that neither bar nor lock guards the Siberian chambers, I opened the latch and walked in. Not a sound was heard; I groped my way onward, and opened a second door. The moment the latch was lifted a female voice called in Russian, "Who is there?" I asked for Nicholai Bestoushoff. I was directed to seek him in another part of the building—the wing. Bidding the voice good night, I departed, and shortly found the persons I sought, from whom, on presenting my credentials, I received a hearty welcome, and remained enjoying their hospitality and answering their questions till daylight.

The following morning I was introduced to their three sisters, when I found that on entering the house I had opened the door of the room in which two of them were sleeping. These gentlemen were also naval officers, and had been trained in the British navy. One of them spoke English, and I managed to converse with the other in Russian and German. Their history I had heard from their comrades, but I was not aware that their sisters had sacrificed all their prospects in life, and had, after many difficulties, succeeded in joining them; an order, however, had been given that they were not to be permitted to return. I then left them with regret, and for ever.

Selendinsk was the residence of two English missionaries, who, from all I heard, were most estimable men; nevertheless, they were unable to make converts among the Bouriats.

My next point was Petropavlofskoi, a Zavod on the south side of a small chain of mountains which separates the Ouda from the Khilok. Here are iron and machine works, and since the acquisition of the region of the Amoor they have become of vast importance. They had also another interest for me, as this was the place where the exiles of 1825 worked out their last five years of hard labour. In the summer they were employed in making roads. The Princes Volkonskoi, Troubitskoi, and also all their comrades, used the pick-axe, barrow, and spade on several of the roads around this Zavod. In winter they worked in a mill, grinding corn like the mill horses.

The engines for the first steamers that Russia placed on the Amoor, were made here. Guns have also been cast and bored here; and now there is a good machine shop under the control of a very clever superintendent, having several intelligent subordinates. Under the present enlightened and energetic Governor-General of Oriental Siberia these works will be organised on a great scale. Good efficient officers and practical men will be selected to superintend the mechanical operations, and then the place will become of vast importance in connection with the Russian steam fleet on the Amoor.

Hence my route was southward to the Tchikoi, and into the Khingan Mountains across to the source of the Onon, which, with the Ingoda, forms the Schilka. Bouriats are numerous throughout this region, and they possess fine herds of cattle. The Keroulun has its source on the south side of the Kentai, or Kente mountain, about forty miles from the source of the Onon. I believe it to be the longest affluent of the Amoor; and some of my friends, who were engaged many years as mining engineers in Nertchinsk, confirm this supposition. Two of them ascended more than 200 miles beyond Lake Koulun, into which this river falls. In some parts of its course it is exceedingly picturesque, and at one place they found it rushing through a deep and narrow gorge. Having re-crossed the chain, over a very difficult route, and descended into the valley of Onon, we proceeded onward, passing along the lines of Cossack picquets to Akchinskaia. After this the route goes nearly north, passing through a number of Cossack villages, and crosses the chain which separates the valleys of the Onon and Ingoda. At about thirty miles beyond the mountains I reached Tourinskai, on the road to Nertchinsk. The route follows the Ingoda, passing over some sandy hills that descend to the steppe; and here the Cossacks hunt the badgers. Before reaching the station of Kaida-lovskaia, a large Cossack village, the country is slightly wooded. Between this place and Knaz Bere-govia there are Toungouz tribes, governed by one of their Princes Gantemouroff, who formerly served in the Russian army. The road passes over high hills, and the Ingoda runs between elevated cliffs, fringed with dwarf elms. Here the country is sandy, and granite rocks crop out along the bank of the river. There is very little change in the aspect of the country, or in the banks of the river for the next forty miles, till it joins the Onon, and the united streams form the Schilka. Shortly after the junction there are several islands, and in some parts the bed is rocky, producing rapids. The country on the right bank of the Schilka is marshy, but on the left it is hilly, with very little wood except the willows. The Nertche falls into the Schilka from the north; it runs through a pretty valley, where the river is thickly shaded with elms and willows, and its banks are but little above the waters.

To European travellers the view of Nertchinsk, with its churches, must have a pleasing effect, as it recalls home views, and, for the moment, creates a forgetfulness of the various Asiatic tribes through which he has wandered to reach this distant spot. Nertchinsk has, however, other associations, and its name is known by, and has been the dread of almost every peasant. It was not, however, the peasant alone that had felt a dread of it; many a noble has shuddered when its name has reached his ear. The convicts from every part of the empire are marched towards this spot, and have ample time for reflection during their journey of eleven months. Nertchinsk has had within its district some of the most daring and desperate characters any community could produce. On the other hand, vast numbers of serfs have been sent hither, who have been driven to resistance by the bad treatment of their masters; and several touching stories of the kind have come to my knowledge.

The climate is not so horrible as many have supposed; nor is the earth a perpetual mass of ice at a few feet below the surface, as I have seen it stated. The summers are not so long as in Europe; but they are very hot, and the country produces a magnificent flora. Both agriculture and horticulture are carried on successfully, and vegetables of almost every variety can be grown here. Tobacco is extensively cultivated, for which the people find a sale among the Bouriats and Toungouz.

The town is in lat 51° 58′ N., and in long. 116° 40′ E., and stands on the left bank of the Nertche, about three miles from its junction with the Schilka. The first settlement was formed nearer the mouth of the river; but the constant risk from inundations caused its removal to the present site—nor is it always safe here. An officer, who has resided in the place many years, informed me, that in the summer of 1840 the lower part of the town was seriously injured. It was under water for several days, and at one time he expected that it would be entirely destroyed. The Ingoda and Onon poured down such vast floods, that the Schilka rose twenty-two feet above its usual level, thereby damming up the water in the Nertche, which caused great losses to many of the inhabitants. Small inundations are frequent.

The churches, the hospital, and a few houses are built of brick and stone; the others are of wood, and the population is about 5,000, many of whom are engaged in trade, purchasing and bartering furs for tea, powder, lead, and other necessaries required by the hunters; some of them are engaged in the Chinese trade, and convey their merchandise to the fair at Irbit, where they exchange it for European produce. Nertchinsk is an important place in connection with the government, and with the distribution of the convicts who are sent to work in the different mines.

Its mining district extends over a considerable area, and for a long period of years produced a considerable revenue to the crown, besides employing vast numbers of convicts who would otherwise have been non-productive. The mines were worked under the supervision and direction of a clever and experienced chief, having a numerous staff of officers, and many of the most distinguished mineralogists and geologists in Russia have commenced their career here. Up to the year 1847 silver and lead formed the principal products; of the former 250 poods, and of the latter 35,500 poods, were produced annually. All the lead, excepting 500 poods, was transported to Barnaoul, where it was used in smelting the ores of the Altai. The lead of Nertchinsk never found its way to the Russian arsenals; it would have cost six times the price of English lead delivered either in Petersburg or Moscow. This supply, so essential to the mining operations in the Altai, suddenly ceased, from the fact of the greater part of the population on the Trans-Baikal being made Cossacks when the annexation of the Amoor was decided upon in 1848.

Tin and zinc ores are found, but neither have as yet been much worked, and I am not aware of the existence of quicksilver, though it is said to be found in these regions. An engineer officer of my acquaintance was engaged from the year 1825 to 1830 exploring many of the valleys of the Khingan and Yablonoi in search of gold, but the indications of this metal were not of such a character as to induce the director to carry on the works. The wood-cut represents a singular formation lying between the limestone and granite found on a small lake in the Khingan. Up to the year 1837 the quantity obtained never exceeded 4 poods, sometimes not 3 poods. In 1838 a captain of engineers discovered gold near the mouth of the Kara, and obtained in that year $11\frac{3}{4}$ poods; and this gave a zest to the operations.

It was not, however, till the year 1850 that the gold in this district began to be largely developed, when a certain Captain left his service in the Oural, and proposed to the Minister of Finance to work the mines in some of the valleys running from the Yablonoi to the Schilka. The Captain pledged himself to the Minister to produce 100 poods a year if he was permitted to organise the men and carry out the operations. It was too tempting a proposal to resist, and the order was given. As an inducement to exertion, he obtained his colonelcy before he left Petersburg.

He arrived at Nertchinsk in the autumn, and during the winter organised parties to commence exploring the valleys;

A Curious Geological Formation.

for early in the spring of the following year his great operations would be proceeded with. There was no lack of convicts for his purpose. Several valleys were thoroughly explored, and this proved that nearly all those of the Yablonoi running down to the Schilka contained gold. Other parties discovered the precious metals beyond the junction of the Schilka and the Argoun on the Amoor, and it was ascertained that a rich auriferous region extended far to the east.

The Colonel commenced extensive operations in the spring of 1851, having a large body of the "unfortunates" at his disposal. They were marched to the mines under a guard of Cossacks, divided into several parties, and the works began in the different valleys. Whenever gold mines are first opened, sickness is sure to ensue, for which preparations are always made beforehand by all who desire to save the people. Temporary hospitals are prepared, and a medical officer is engaged to remain during the whole period of washing. I ever found this the case throughout the Oural, the Altai, and at the mines on the Yenissey. Besides these precautions, proper dwellings for the workmen are invariably provided.

In this instance, however, nothing of the kind was done. The people had to throw up huts of earth, and roof them with either grass or bark; and in such habitations were so thickly stowed that many preferred sleeping in the open air. As the works proceeded, sickness began to spread among the men, and numbers were confined to their damp, earthy couches. Added to this, the food was said to be both bad and deficient. In a short time many died, but their places were immediately taken by others sent to keep up the requisite number of hands. The work of excavating and washing went on, and gold was being accumulated. No one was allowed to neglect his work; and it was only when quite struck down by disease that they were permitted to retire to their damp and smoky dens.

The deaths became so numerous, that it was found absolutely necessary to separate the sick from those who were able to work. Temporary hospitals were raised, having berths formed like those in a ship's cabin, with this difference, that there was only just room for a man between the tiers, and these were four in height. As men could not be spared to act as nurses, such as were able to move were compelled to attend to their comrades. The more the works were opened, and the men exposed to wet and a burning sun, the more malignant the disease became; and great numbers died. Yet fresh detachments were sent, and the works pushed on incessantly. The Colonel determined that the 100 poods of gold should be obtained, at whatever cost of life; nor did he once relax his exertions. More than half the season having passed, and not half the quantity obtained, it was evident that greater efforts must be made.

Additional hours of labour were insisted on, and the birch applied if the duty was not fulfilled. The poor creatures laboured till they sank at their barrows.

A short time before the close of the season it was discovered that some of the Nertchinsk merchants had been engaged in smuggling a large quantity of brick tea, and that the officers had been bribed; some serious charges were also made against the officials in Nertchinsk. In consequence, the Governor of Irkoutsk sent one of his officers to investigate the matter; and circumstances connected with this affair took him to the gold mines, where he had to examine a number of men said to be implicated in the transaction. Some named on his list were dead, and others were in their berths unable to be moved. This compelled him to enter the gloomy place. He found the odour horrible, and as he described it to me, it was worse than the black hole in Calcutta. He was preparing to rush out, when several feeble voices begged to be removed into the open air, or they should die. He stopped and spoke to them, and, as his eyes became more accustomed to the gloom, he distinguished the objects that surrounded him. But his horror was intense when he saw that the berths contained both dead and dying; and some had been left so long uninterred, that it was impossible to approach the spot.

He called in a number of men, and all the living were removed into the huts, and then ordered that the rest should be instantly buried. The object of his visit was not accomplished; but he had the satisfaction of knowing that he had released many poor creatures from their misery. I saw his report, but its details were too horrible to be repeated.

The season ended by a sharp frost, stopping all the operations at the mines, and seventy poods was the produce to set against the misery many had endured, and the terrible sacrifice of life. This was the most costly gold that ever entered his Imperial Majesty's treasury; for it has been stated, and on good authority, that every pood cost him thirteen lives. This circumstance created a great sensation throughout the Altai and in all the mining districts, and every one expected it would be a matter of serious consequence to the officer who had shown such utter disregard for the lives of those under his charge.

By the first winter roads a caravan left Nertchinsk, carrying the produce of the mines to Petersburg. The Colonel accompanied it as far as Irkoutsk, where I saw him several times before his departure; but the extent of the calamity was not then generally known. He preceded the caravan to the capital, and by some means prevented the circumstances of the case reaching the ear of his Imperial master, or a pension would never have been granted for extraordinary service.

I must say a few words about some of the exiles who were banished to this distant spot.

Erman says, Vol. II., p. 183, "The 'unfortunates' of the 14th of December, who had been condemned to hard labour, were confined to the settlement at Chità, which lies beyond the Baikal, on the road from Verkne Oudinsk to Nertchinsk. There are no mines there, so that, in order to carry out the sentence of the convicts to the letter, they have erected a polishing mill, in which to employ them."

Whoever has read this paragraph will have concluded that the exiles never were employed in the mines; but such is not the fact. My informants were the " unfortunates" and their wives, all of whom were living in Irkoutsk, and in other places that I have visited. I was on terms of great intimacy with these people, and retain many pleasing recollections of them.

They were taken from the capital in chains, each man in a telega, attended by a gendarme (this is an especial corps under the command of the secret police), but not by the usual route through Moscow: they were sent by Yaroslav and Vatka. This was through a part of the country but little travelled, and they entered on the great Siberian road before reaching Perm. Orders were given that no time should be lost on the road, nor any stoppage allowed except for refreshment. Their journey was a long one, 7,029 versts, and they were hurried onward night and day. On the evening of the thirtieth day they reached Nertchinsk, and were handed over to the authorities. Here they slept, and the next morning started for the mines, at a distance of 279 versts. They reached them in the afternoon of the following day, having travelled over 7,308 versts in thirty-two days. Here was their prison and place of punishment, and they quickly found themselves in the hands of a man who determined to carry out their sentence in its utmost rigour.

They arrived on the Wednesday, and on the following Monday morning Prince Volkonskoi, Prince Troubetskoi, and four others began their mining labours. This was hard service; wielding the pick-axe and hammer was a new occupation, and their keeper made their toil severe. The others, as they arrived, were divided into gangs and sent into the mines. Each was known only by his number, and here they worked for two years. Others were banished to a solitary life in the forests of Yakoutsk, and of these exiles I could also give a few incidents that would not say much for the "leniency of the Government or its servants," of which Mr. Erman speaks.

I am not one of those who acquit these men of blame,

or think their banishment unmerited; my allusions are directed only against the agents who made that banishment a torment.

Several of these exiles (convicts he calls them) were advanced in years, and had left grown up sons and daughters; others, their juniors, were torn away from young children, and mothers, with infants in their arms, had pressed up to the telegas to give the father a last look at his child. Some had been but recently married, many were single, and a few had not reached their twentieth year.

The first lady who followed her husband was the Princess Troubetskoi: she was young, and determined to share the fate of her partner, and, if possible, sooth his years of banishment. It was with great difficulty that she obtained permission; and when it was granted, it was coupled with a condition that "no lady who followed her husband to his place of exile should ever return." Even such a condition did not change her resolve, and she started, accompanied only by a faithful maid-servant, who determined to share her danger and her exile. She narrated to me an account of her adventurous journey of near 5,000 miles, made during a severe winter, when she often encountered the fearful storms so frequent in Siberia. Nor were they the only dangers—she had seen the wolves running on each side the sledge ready to pounce on the horses if they slackened their speed or fell. These were not slight trials for a delicate female to encounter; but some of the incidents of her adventure are among the most touching I ever heard.

She, however, reached Nertchinsk in safety, and a mining engineer officer, who was returning to the Zavod, kindly offered to escort her to her destination. Her inquiries of this gentleman were numerous. She wished to know the fate of her husband. He gave her an assurance that he was well, but evaded all other questions. On their arrival she was taken to that officer's home, and his wife offered all the comforts their dwelling afforded, while he sent her passport to inform his chief of her arrival, and expressed to him her desire to see the Prince.

Presently a police officer arrived, and told her that he had received instructions to conduct her to her quarters, and that she would be permitted to see her husband on the morrow. A single room was assigned to her and the maid, bearing all the aspects of a prison, and it was announced that she was not at liberty to visit any one in the town without permission. Next morning she was taken to the house of the chief, when she urged her request to see the Prince, and also to be permitted to spend some hours each day in his society. The first part of her request was granted, but the latter was refused; and this man said as she had come to share her husband's exile she must submit to prison discipline; adding that she was not to be permitted to write a single line without its passing through his hands.

After this he ordered the police to conduct her to the Prince, giving his number—but not his name—and then to her dwelling. A sledge was waiting for them, and the man drove them several versts to one of the mines, when she was conducted down and along the gallery to where the exiles were working. For a few moments they all gazed on her in amazement, thinking it a vision; and the spell was only broken when she rushed into her husband's arms. I dare not attempt to paint this interview; but the clanking of his chains recalled her to a knowledge of his position, and the police officer proved that he possessed a better heart than his chief, by removing her from a scene heartrending to all.

The chief placed her on prison fare, nor would he permit her to have tea. After this she saw the Prince once a week, but not in the mines. In about a month two other ladies arrived, and went through the same ordeal. Eighteen months passed without any change, when this brute was called before a tribunal from which none can escape. I can only hope that he possessed some unknown good qualities that would recommend him to more mercy than he extended to those under his charge.

After his death another officer was appointed, who received the ladies and treated them as members of his own family. He did everything consistent with his duty to relieve the unfortunate exiles, and through his intercession at the end of two years they ceased to work in the mines, and then were removed to Cheta and the Mill.

CHAP. XVI.

THE KEROULUN, THE PRINCIPAL SOURCE OF THE AMOOR.

In my last chapter the Keroulun was traced from its source in the Khingan Mountains to Lake Koulun, or Dalai-Noor. I shall commence this with the Argoun, where it issues from the north-eastern end of the Lake. Between its outlet and

Bouriat Encampment.

the river Kailar there are several rapids, and numerous small lakes are entered along its banks.

The Kailar falls into the Argoun from the eastward, by two branches, and this river has its source in the Khingan chain, which runs nearly due north, and ends in a low hill near the head of the Amoor. This chain forms the eastern side of the valley of the Argoun, and portions of it have been slightly explored by the mining engineers of Nertchinsk, who believe that this region will, some time or other, afford another profitable field for mining operations.

In some parts the Argoun presents a peculiar character; its bed is rocky, and its banks are strewn with numerous pieces of red and white chalcedony and agates,—while dark rocks rise into picturesque cliffs. On its western bank there is a line of Cossack piquets, extending near 300 miles, and the men keep up a strict guard against the flight of convicts in that direction. Notwithstanding their vigilance escapes are frequent; but each week throughout the year fills up the vacancies they occasion. Proceeding downward the river approaches the mountains, receiving in its course many small streams from the east. It is celebrated throughout Siberia for its carp, which are carried in the winter several thousand miles, when they are produced at the tables of the wealthy as a great delicacy. One of my friends, who had spent seventeen years in Nertchinsk Zavod, believes that this fish abounds in the Dalai-noor, whence they descend the river. The carp is not found in any Siberian river.

There are numerous encampments on the east side of the Argoun, where good pasture exists on the steppe extending up to the Khingan chain. None of these summits rise to a great elevation, but they become more lofty to the southward; some of them rising far above the snow line. The Gazimoor falls into the Argoun on the west side; it has its source in one of the best mining districts of Nertchinsk. About twenty-five miles below the mouth of the river is Oust-strelka, a post of Cossacks, who, like those on every part of the Russian frontiers, are traders. In January they ascend the Argoun, and meet the natives on different parts of it; these places become little yermaks (fairs), and commerce is at once established among them. The Cossacks carry with them, for barter, flour, powder, and lead—these articles being much in request—receiving furs in exchange.

The Shilka below Nertchinsk increases considerably in size, as numerous streams pour into it from the Yablonoi Mountains, and in most of them gold is found. Islands are also numerous—they have been formed by the alluvial soil washed from the mountains; many are covered with willows, and others with cheromika. There are also several villages; some of the older ones being occupied by convicts, and many new ones have been formed by the Cossacks since 1850, when it was decided to add the region of the Amoor to the empire. These men are ever the pioneers in the advance of Russia, and they accomplish their object well. One of these villages, Byan-keno, is large, and contains two churches, one of wood and the other of brick: at this place the banks of the Shilka are frequently inundated, as a few days' rain in the Yablonoi raises the river twelve feet above its usual level.

The Aradi falls into the Shilka further down, and the valley runs far up into the mountains to the northward. Auriferous sand is carried down by this stream, and it is expected that a profitable gold field will be discovered here. At a considerable distance beyond, the river Motankana falls into the Shilka on its south bank; it has its source in the mining district of Nertchinsk. A part of its course is between granite cliffs of no great elevation; but these, where they are fringed with wood, afford many picturesque scenes.

Stratenskoi, on the south bank, is another ancient village occupied by these hardy pioneers; here they cultivate European vegetables, and the Cossacks show that they are an industrious race by the comforts they contrive to gather around them. At a short distance to the south there is a lake where thousands of water-fowl congregate; while snipes and woodcocks are found in great numbers. The

Cossacks never use shot; both animals and birds are obtained by them with the rifle. As a woodcock is too swift and erratic, when on the wing, to be dropped by a bullet, they have adopted a small whistle, with which they imitate his call, when he pops on to a tuft of grass to look round, and is instantly knocked over.

Between Stratenskoi and Shilkinskoi the left bank of the river is well populated; the country is good, and most of the necessaries of life easily obtained. Fish and game are abundant, both in the Shilka and in the numerous small streams that come from the mountains. Granite rocks mostly predominate on both banks of the Shilka as far as the village of Botie; beyond this limestone prevails. A great change takes place here—the cliffs become lofty, and their summits are riven into numerous picturesque turrets, while beneath are openings leading into many caverns. In some, considerable quantities of bitumen are obtained by the people of the villages of Tcha-boo-tche and Oule-getche.

A few miles beyond these villages, the valley of the Shilka opens out, and the rocks recede to a considerable distance till they reach the valley of Tchal-bou-tchenskoi, which runs to the north-west towards the Yablonoi,—and down the centre of it flows the river Tchal-boo-tche. On the space formed by the receding rocks stands Shilkinskoi Zavod; the houses are built of wood, and extend along the bank of the Shilka as far as the mouth of the Tchal-boo-tche. On the opposite side of this river is the smelting works; they were formerly used for lead and silver; but iron will now be found a more profitable commodity.

Several of the barges were built here for the first great expedition on the Amoor, in 1854, which my friend Colonel Korsakoff commanded; and here his party were fitted out with all the necessaries and military stores for the voyage. The Government have also a glass manufactory; and a very large tan-yard is an important part of the establishment at Shilkinskoi. The leather made here has a great reputation among all the tribes beyond the Argoun and in Mongolia. It is famed even among the Russians in Siberia. The cause of its superiority, I was told, was its being tanned with birch bark; but this cannot be the only one, as I have known other tan-yards in Siberia where the material used and the process were exactly the same, and the leather from the two tan-yards could not be compared.

There is a considerable tract of meadow land along the bank of the Shilka, and good pastures are found in many parts of the valley of Tchal-bou-tchenskoi, where the cows and horses of the peasants feed, and wood for fuel is close at hand. Game is plentiful in the forest. There are many small lakes, which swarm with water-fowl, and wild geese come in vast numbers. Since the acquisition of the Amoor, Shilkinskoi has become a most important establishment. The Shilka is navigable for small craft to the Amoor; but the barges and other vessels could not descend fully laden, and the voyage up the stream is both long and tedious. There is plenty of iron ore in the vicinity of this Zavod, and the present General-Governor knows the advantage to be derived by making it the great mechanical establishment on the Trans-Baikal. As commerce extends into the region on the south of the Amoor, steam will be required to aid in its transit, and here both steamboats and their machinery can be advantageously constructed.

General Anosoff used to say that he would make the valley of the Tom the Birmingham and Sheffield of Siberia, and then he could supply the whole of Central Asia with rifles, cutlery, needles, and other useful articles. His ideas may in some degree be carried out; at Shilkinskoi all the materials are near at hand, and Russia may thus employ some of her convict population to a greater and more permanent advantage than at the gold mines. No industrious population has ever sprung up where gold seeking has been their employment; nor has the establishment of convict villages in different parts of Siberia been successful: wherever I have found them, squalid misery has predominated. These men can only be induced to work by a strict supervision, and this could easily be given in a mechanical establishment and cutlery workshops. An industrious and rising population is sure to be the result.

The river Kara falls into the Shilka on its right bank, at about ten miles below the Zavod, and here are the most extensive gold priesks yet discovered on the Trans-Baikal. Lately gold seeking parties have been exploring the country on the left bank of the Shilka, to the north-west, and have found the precious metal in many places between the mouth of the Kara and the Gorbitza. Beyond the Kara several small rivers fall into the Shilka, before reaching the new Cossack station on the Great Koularke. This is also an important position, and several barges were built here for the Amoor expedition. Opening that river has caused a great change; for thriving villages are rising where the bear, the elk, and the maral were almost the sole inhabitants. Further down the Tchornoi falls into the Shilka by two channels. The former has its source among the higher summits of the Yablonoi Mountains, and runs through a well wooded and picturesque valley. Near its mouth there is another Cossack station.

Shortly after passing the Tchornoi the scenery changes on the south side; perpendicular cliffs of limestone, with groups of birch and larch growing on their tops and in the small ravines. Over these rounded summits appear, and a long chain of hills stretches out towards the Argoun. The left bank is also well wooded, and many islands occur in this part of the Shilka, and prove a serious obstacle to its navigation, more especially when going against the current.

All through this limestone formation the scenery possesses a similar character till it reaches the Cossack station of Gorbitza. Here the valley of the Shilka becomes considerably wider, forming extensive meadows along the shore. On this flat place stands the village of Gorbitza, with its wooden church, and cottages nestling in its sheltered nook, which seems to invite the traveller to quiet and repose. The high ridge to the south continues beyond, and is frequently intersected by deep ravines that bring their streams to swell the flood of the Amoor.

The river Gorbitza was the boundary between Russia and China until the acquisition of the Amoor, and has its source in the lower hills of the Yablonoi, and at no great distance from its mouth. Not far distant a yermak is held annually at a mineral spring, Bogdoi. A few Russian merchants and Cossacks assemble to meet the Manjours who come to barter. They ascend the Amoor from Aigoon in large boats, bringing printed cotton goods, silk, tobacco, and Chinese brandy, which they exchange for glass ware, soap, and the horns of the maral. In this place, and all along the Chinese frontier, the Cossacks provide the Chinamen with an article so much prized in a Chinese pharmacopæia.

Leaving Bogdoi, which to this little gathering of traders is regarded with as much importance as freighting a ship for any distant port, the river enters a part where the cliffs become considerably higher than in the limestone formation. Here it is granite heaved up into huge masses, which time, frost, and sun have riven and shattered into curious forms. Ravines are also rent far into the mountains, and down them these clear streams descend gushing into the river. A little further down the stream the shores become wooded; pine trees are growing along the banks, but on the upper slopes are black and white birches, with occasional clumps of larches, while the dwarf elm is growing from the clefts in the rocks.

Mineral springs are frequently met with on the banks of the Shilka, and some are resorted to by the natives. One is found in a beautiful and romantic spot near two small waterfalls, Moshen-dakhan and Moshen-da. If this place was within reach of Europeans it would prove a dangerous

A Mangoon in his Fur Coat.

rival to Matlock and the German Spas. The natives in their fur clothing, and the Manjours in their curious costumes, would give variety to the usual society found at the

Brunnens, while sportsmen would find occupation for their rifles in the Yablonoi.

At a considerable distance below the mineral spring is the mouth of the river Djel-tou-gee, one of the principal affluents of the Shilka. It has its source far to the north-west in the Yablonoi, and collects the contents of many rivulets in its course. During the heavy rains it pours a great torrent into the Shilka. At other seasons its water is pure and transparent, nor does it mingle with the turbid water of the Shilka, for the two streams are seen running side by side for a long distance, and the Cossacks say that the fish of the Shilka are never seen in the other stream. Again, the river enters a granite gorge; in this part it is rapid and free from islands. At the end of the gorge is one of the best fishing grounds in the Shilka. The Cossacks from Gorbitza, from the banks of the Gazemoura, and the inhabitants from very long distances, come here to fish, and the supply seems to be inexhaustible.

Further down are several islands, on one of which, named Sable Island, pine, larch, and birch trees are growing. Beyond this is Bere-zoom, a long, low wooded island, and the country on both sides the river is covered with a forest, consisting principally of larch and pines; the latter of great size. At the river Bankova, that has its source in the mining district near the Argoun, and falls into the Shilka from the south, there is another place where a yermak is held by the Cossacks of the Argoun and the Toungouz of the Yablonoi. The latter bring skins, horns of the maral, a few sable skins, and those of the fox. These they barter with the Cossacks for flour, wodky, powder, and lead. It is somewhat curious to see these people collecting from such great distances, and the punctuality with which they assemble. They meet under the shade of some trees on the bank of a stream, and there, with all the gravity of men engaged in vast mercantile transactions, exchange their commodities, and at the end of the third day depart for their homes.

The next point of interest is a deep valley that opens from the Shilka and extends northward towards the Yablonoi. Along it is the road to Bouch-tens-kene gold priesk. On leaving the upper part the track enters into a wild part of the mountain range. On the second day's journey the traveller reaches the Amagar, and then commences the most difficult part of the route, where it follows the river towards its source, and crosses the summit of the chain. It is a journey of five or six days from the Shilka to the priesk. This mine is on the north side of the mountains, and near the source of the principal branch of the Olekma. Gold is found here in a sufficient quantity to render the working profitable; but lower down, Solavioff discovered a priesk which has proved immensely valuable, although at a depth of seventy feet beneath the surface. The great drawback to the mines in this vicinity is the short time that they can be worked. The people cannot commence operations before the 20th of May, and the works are closed by the frost on the 1st of September. Notwithstanding such a long winter the frost never penetrates into the ground more than five feet, even in lat. 55° N., and long. 123° E.

One of my Siberian friends explored the southern slopes of the Yablonoi range, in 1828, as far as the source of the Zeya, or in lat. 54° 30′ N., and long. 126° E., and in several parts he discovered gold. He believes that valuable gold mines will be found on most of the streams that flow from the north into the Amoor. Thus another source of vast wealth will open out to Russia as the region of the Amoor begins to be developed.

For more than twenty miles below the Ban-kova there is little or no change in the country; it is only after passing Perc-valnia that the river assumes a more picturesque appearance. Its shores become abrupt near the mineral spring of Bonde-Kova, on the south bank of the Shilka. The inhabitants and the Cossacks have a tradition in connection with the ravine in which the spring has its source. They say that a great robber, named Bonde-Kova, had his dwelling among the sandstone recesses that are found here; that he used to make long journeys, and plunder the people in the villages, carrying his spoil to his gloomy abode in the glen, whither none dared to pursue him. His scouts were always on the watch, and if any persons approached the district they were sure to become his victims. At length none dared to pass within several miles of it. Finding that all shunned his domain he became bold, made an attack on one of the Zavods, and carried off some silver. This closed his career; Cossacks were sent in search of him, and after a long chase he was hunted to his lair and secured. His trial was short. When brought before the chief he admitted his guilt; the Cossacks were ordered to put him in irons and give him a berth among the convicts.

Beyond this robber's dwelling the river runs on between the sandstone cliffs till it reaches a bend in its course that forms a whirlpool, by the water striking against the jutting rocks; and this renders the navigation dangerous. A little further on, the Son-ghe-noi enters the Shilka from the south; not far distant there is a salt lake, from which the Cossacks and the Orotchons obtain their supplies. They assemble here in considerable numbers in the month of August.

A few miles below the Son-ghe-noi there are two islands in the Shilka, and a little beyond these the sandstone rocks rise abruptly from the water, affording one of the best scenes on the river. The rocks recede to the southward, and a small delta has been formed extending to the mouth of the Argoun; on this, a lake, stretching along at the foot of the cliffs, abounds with carp. About a mile beyond is Oust-Strelkoi Karaoul, which stands close to the junction of the two rivers, in lat. 53° 19′ 45″ N., and long. 121° 50′ 7″ E., and here the Argoun and Shilka form the Amoor.

Some geographers say that the Onon must be considered the source of the Amoor, which, when united with the Ingoda, forms the Shilka. But I am inclined to give the Keroulun the honour of being parent to this great river of Asia. The same opinion is held by many eminent mining engineers who have lived long in Nertchinsk, and have thoroughly explored the country. The Keroulun and the Argoun have a course of about 1,000 miles, whereas the course of the Onon and the Shilka does not exceed 750 miles. It was on the bank of the Keroulun that Genghiz first saw the light; many historical events are associated with its name, and great battles have been fought in the valleys.

From 1689 to 1854 the junction of the Argoun and Shilka was the most easterly point of the Russian empire in the region of the Amoor. But, during all this period of 165 years, the frontier Cossacks were constantly penetrating into the country on the north of the Amoor; and many wild stories have been handed down of the contests these hardy hunters had with the Manjour race. Besides which, many convicts have escaped from the mines, and descended the Amoor only to be captured by the people on its banks. An exile escaped this way and succeeded in passing all the Chinese posts in a canoe, or small boat, by keeping to the north side of the river. He lived on the produce of his rifle, enduring great hardships, and finally reached the mouth of the Amoor, in the hope of getting away in some vessel. In this he was disappointed, and after all chance of escape had vanished, started on his return. He fell in with a party of Toungouz sable hunters, and spent the hunting season with them. After which they crossed the country towards the upper part of the Zeya, and ultimately brought him to one of the fairs attended by the Cossacks. He was recognised by his countrymen and carried back to the mines of Nertchinsk, after an absence of more than eighteen months.

The information which he had acquired was considered of so much value that the chief got his sentence remitted, on condition of his taking another journey to gain more knowledge of the region. At the season of the yermak he was provided with powder, lead, and a few other necessaries, and accompanied the Cossacks to the fair, in the hope of meeting his old companions, the Toungouz. They were there, delighted to see him, and he having been provided with a packet of powder for each man, was again admitted as a brother, and invited to accompany them to hunt the sable. At the end of three days the fair broke up, when he said goodbye to his countrymen, and started with the Toungouz on their homeward journey. This time he acquired a knowledge of the southern side of the Yablonoi, and discovered a short route to the sable-hunting ground far down towards the mouth of the Amoor. Having spent another season sable-hunting, he returned with his companions to the fair, and then to the Zavod, bringing much valuable information about the different people dwelling on the banks of the Amoor, and opened up a road into a valuable fur-producing country.

This exile was sent a third time with instructions to penetrate into the regions on the south side of the Amoor, during the sable-hunting season, and return in time to accompany the Toungouz to the fair. They, however, arrived, but he was not with them, nor was he ever heard of afterwards. After him several convicts escaped down the river, but no one returned to tell his story, and it is supposed that they were killed.

In 1848 it was decided to explore the Amoor, when an officer, with four Cossacks, were sent in the spring of that year on an expedition down the river in a boat; they were armed and provisioned, and it was hoped that this small party might be permitted to pass unmolested. He also carried instruments for making observations, a telescope, and a quantity of gold coin. It was well known that great jealousy existed among the Chinese authorities; that they always endeavoured to stop the Cossacks pursuing game into their territory, and it was only the dread of their deadly rifles that enabled them to escape from superior numbers. The officer was instructed to avoid coming in contact with the authorities, if possible; to examine their towns and villages from a distance, but not to enter them. He was desired to conciliate the people on every opportunity, and he carried various articles for presents. It was expected that this party would accomplish the object, if permitted to proceed, in about nine months, and, if stopped, that they would speedily return.

Time passed on, and nine months had elapsed; but there were no tidings of the officer and his men. During the winter the Cossacks inquired from all the Orotchons who attended the fairs, if these men had been seen; but no one could give any tidings about them. The Tongouz sable-hunters were promised a reward if they could find them, or learn if they were detained by the Chinese; but all efforts proved fruitless. In 1852 an application was made by the Governor of Kiachta to the Chinese governor in Ourga, stating that an officer and four men had deserted, carrying away with them a large sum in gold and several instruments; that they had descended the Amoor, and it was believed that they had been captured by the Chinese officers, and were detained in one of the towns. If so, the Russian Government desired that they should be delivered up, either at Kiachta, or at any of the forts on the frontier. This produced no results, and I have good reason to believe that they have never been heard of.

The Governor-General of Oriental Siberia determined to

explore the Amoor, and in 1854 a great expedition was organised by him for that object. It was on such a scale that the Chinese could neither check his progress nor prevent him taking possession of the north bank of the river. In less than six weeks the whole of this vast region, including the country between the Amoor and the Russian frontier to the north of the Yablonoi, had changed masters; it had now fallen into strong hands, and before the end of the year the entire Chinese army could not have dislodged the small body of Cossacks placed in position. General Mouravioff had seized on all the points which his keen eye and practical experience told him were necessary for the security of the new acquisition.

Russia has now got possession of the great water-course, and the only one through which access from the sea to the vast plains and mountain districts of Central Asia can be obtained; the Lena, the Yenissey, and the Ob being sealed in the Arctic Ocean. This is a great water-way, extending more than 2,200 miles into the eastern portion of the empire, with its outlet into the Pacific. It will also open up a water communication into the vast region bordering on the Sea of Japan, and up to the great deserts of Gobi. It is the commencement of a new era for Siberia: foreign produce will flow in by this channel, and Siberian products will pass through it to the ocean, and thence to other nations. Many of the resources of the country that have long lain dormant will now be called into active operation, and an industrious and intelligent population will spring up where ignorance and indolence have long held sway.

Immediately after the junction of the Argoun and Shilka, the Amoor enters a narrow valley, with lofty slate crags extending along the shore, and sometimes rising from the water's edge. In other places these rocks recede, leaving rich meadow land stretching out between the river and their base. After passing these rocky cliffs, the Mou-koon-doi enters the Amoor from the north: it is a broad stream, and pours a considerable body of water into the river. The hills slope down to the valley, and form meadow land stretching along the bank; many small rivulets flow from the hills and cross the level tracts, in which the anglers would find plenty of sport.

Some miles further down is the small river Koude-khan: the country is wooded in the vicinity; pines and larches predominate, and various shrubs are growing along the bank. Here is stationed the first Manjour frontier guard. The men have not a very formidable appearance, and a pointed pole, with a bow and arrows, are but poor weapons against a Cossack rifle. The flat meadows along the bank produce excellent hay; many of the small valleys could be used for pastures, and some for agriculture. The valley of the Amoor becomes wider near the river Yapan, and is covered with clumps of white birch, pine, and larch trees. Along the foot of the slopes several lakes extend for a considerable distance; these are probably formed by inundation.

The next river is the Mon-gholia; this falls into the Amoor from the north; and here begins a great stretch of meadow land on both banks: in some parts it is covered with long grass, and many wild boars are found in this portion of the valley. To the sportsman it will afford great excitement; but boar hunting is attended with some risk, as many of the animals are of large size.

The Ama-zara is a large river that falls into the Amoor from the north, having its source high up in the Yablonoi chain; near its mouth there is a village of Orotchons. Beyond this the north bank of the Amoor is formed by lofty and picturesque slate cliffs, and these extend as far as the Aou-khan. This river has its source in the high summits of the Yablonoi, and along the bank of this stream the Toungouz have made a route to one of the affluents of the Oleckma and the Alda-noo — their favourite hunting grounds for the Alain. After passing the Aou-khan the valley of the Amoor becomes wider, and the shores are flat, with several islands in the river covered with shrubs.

The Elin-tchnoi falls into the Amoor on the south: the Cossacks have given it this name from the red pine growing on its bank, which produces a resin that gives out a strong aromatic scent when burning — they call it the "holy oil." A few miles below is the mouth of the Ouran-tche, that comes from the north; the country through which it runs is flat and well wooded, and in parts fine open pastures where cattle might graze. Beyond, the valley of the Amoor changes; the hills on each side rise higher and are overtopped by conical mountains, wooded to their summits; and these the Cossacks have named "Med-vajaya Sopkas," on account of so many bears being found here. It is a great hunting ground for both the Orotchons and Cossacks: the latter come here from the forts on the Argoun. Below this place the valley opens out wider, and islands are formed in the river; one extends four miles in length from the mouth of the Koude-khan to the Monas-tirke rivers. The latter takes its name from a monastery built on its banks by the Cossacks, in 1671. The district is famed for its sables and squirrels.

Many Orotchons and Manyargs live in this part of the valley. The meadows extend for three miles in breadth, up to the foot of the wooded slopes on the north and south, and numerous small lakes are scattered over the surface. These tracts of meadow land stretch along the water for many miles, to the mouth of the Oldoi-ya, and a little above this there is a Cossack post. This river is of considerable magnitude; it has its source in the Yablonoi Mountains, near to some of the affluents of the Oleckma. Below the Oldoi-ya the Amoor makes a considerable bend towards the south-east, where the valley becomes narrower, and the river is divided by islands into three streams, which take the names of Tchar-pel, Daunon, and Gonau.

The Gonau branch makes a great curve to the northward, extending over fourteen miles, and at its lower end stands the Cossack post, at the mouth of the Koto-mang-da. The Bour-gatche is nearly opposite the Cossack post; and from this point the Amoor turns more to the southward: the banks are high and abrupt, and the mountains recede on each side, giving a broad expanse to the valley. Looking downwards, the river assumes the appearance of a lake studded with islands, and in the distance high mountain summits are visible.

A few miles further down the river is Albazin, 103 miles from Oust-Strelkai-Karaoul; this was the first Russian fortress and settlement on the Amoor. It stands on the site of an ancient Toungouz town, and derives its name from Albaza, a Daourian Prince who lived there. Several attempts were made to penetrate into the region beyond the Yablonoi by these pioneers—the hunters and Cossacks—and some of them had reached the Amoor, and others the upper branches of the Zeya. Each party found an almost inexhaustible supply of animals, such as were valuable for their fur, as well as those proper for food. It was not, however, till the year 1643 that a party of Cossack hunters crossed the Yablonoi, reached the Amoor, and descended to the sea. After their success, and the reported wealth of the region, it was decided that a settlement should be made on the Amoor. In the year 1650, Khabaroff was dispatched from Yakoutsk, with a body of Cossacks, to select a position on the Amoor, and fortify themselves in it. After a difficult march these warriors reached the river; and having made a careful examination of several localities, Albazin was chosen, as affording most of the requisites for such an establishment—wood, water, and good pastures.

In 1551 the fort was completed, and its position commanded all the approaches. A numerous body of hunters followed the Cossacks, and took up their abode here. Thus the town sprang up rapidly, and before the hunting season, sufficient dwellings were erected to shelter all the inhabitants. This additional force of well-armed men rendered their post quite secure, and no body of Chinese troops could dislodge them. When the hunting season came round, these men dispersed in every direction, and game was found in abundance.

Manyarg Boy and Girl.

Orotchons, Manyargs, and some other tribes, who live by the produce of their forests, deemed this an intrusion on their domains. But the Cossacks and hunters looked upon the territory as their own, and wherever sables could be obtained, there they followed their pursuit. As the animals became less numerous in the forests around, they descended the Amoor, and drove the natives from their hunting grounds, often committing other depredations.

Year after year these men oppressed the people, and others of a worse character sought here escape from the punishment which awaited them in Siberia. Thus a number of daring and desperate characters were ever ready for mischief; and when the hunt failed them, they did not hesitate to appropriate any property at hand. At length they became more daring, crossed the Amoor, pillaged the villages, and set the Chinese authorities at defiance. Remonstrances were frequently made by the Chinese, but without any avail; and each year, as the hunters had to proceed further to obtain the animals, their labour became more severe. Even by great exertion they could not always obtain a sufficient supply to satisfy their rapacity. When this happened, a large body scoured the country and plundered every tribe on their route.

These proceedings roused all the ire of the Celestials, and in 1657 an army from the Central Flowery Land sat down before Albazin and summoned the garrison to surrender the fort and leave the country, taking their arms and property. To this they sent a defiance; and the Chinese general commenced operations by erecting batteries on an island fronting Albazin. The ruins of these works still exist, and they are of considerable extent. I shall not attempt any description of the siege, or repeat the traditions that have been handed down, and which may be still heard when sitting around a Cossack camp fire. It is only necessary to say that the siege lasted till late in 1658, nearly two years, to prove that the defence was a determined one, and that want of provisions alone compelled the Cossacks to surrender. They marched out, however, with their arms, and returned into Siberia, the Chinese army attending them across the frontier; and Albazin was destroyed. All the prisoners taken during the siege were sent to Pekin, and hence in after years Russia stipulated to send a mission to give spiritual instruction to the Cossacks of Albazin.

The valuable furs that were obtained in this region and were constantly being bartered at the different Yermaks on the frontier, were too tempting to many of the wild spirits who had been driven out. In 1665 a number of hunters descended the Amoor to Albazin, and some of them restored their old habitations. This time they were more prudent, avoiding the hunting grounds frequented by the natives; and thus they were left in peace. In 1670 Nekifir Tchernigovsky organised a small body of men at Kerenska, and descended the Amoor. On his arrival at Albazin he found it occupied by the few hunters, but they were living among the ruins. As he knew that in its present state he could not hold it if the Chinese came to dispute possession, he set about restoring the fort. The works went on without molestation, and in due time were finished. It was soon made known in Siberia that Albazin was restored, and this induced numbers to join the little garrison.

In about two years Tchernigovsky had more men under his command than were engaged in the first siege, and he kept them under control, avoiding as much as possible all intercourse with the Manjours. Under his command the place flourished, and the Chinese perceived that it would endanger their power. This induced them to build the town of Ai-goon on the Middle Amoor, to counteract its effect, and, if possible, force the Russians to leave their territory.

On the 4th of June, 1685, the Chinese army appeared before the town, and took up their former position on the island. The general had a large force, and, as the batteries had not been destroyed, he was soon ready for the attack. Tolbouzin was appointed to the command in Albazin; the place was put in the best possible state for defence, but the Chinese outnumbered his men ten to one. On the 22nd the enemy made an assault, when Tolbouzin and his garrison defended the town with the utmost bravery for several days; subsequently however, perceiving that it was impossible to hold it against such numbers, he withdrew in the night. The Chinese entered the fort the following day, and again levelled the works; having accomplished this, they retreated to Ai-goon.

Tolbouzin left scouts to watch their movements, and when informed of their departure, he marched back to Albazin. On the 7th of August he began restoring the fort; and before the winter set in, was in a position to defend the town. During the cold season he made preparations for another struggle, and endeavoured to render his post impregnable. The snow and ice stopped the return of the Chinese, but he learned that their next campaign would be on a greater scale, as they were determined to destroy the Muscovites.

Early in the spring of 1686 the Celestials commenced their preparations; the whole of the Amoor flotilla was collected to take a part in the coming struggle and aid in the complete annihilation of the Russians. Long before they sailed Tolbouzin knew that the Chinese general had collected an overwhelming force, but, great as was its numbers, he was not daunted, and his officers and men determined never to yield. When the ice broke up on the Amoor, supplies were sent from Nertchinsk, and his little garrison were soon provisioned for the siege. It was the last week in June when the Chinese land forces marched into their position before the town; their naval expedition arrived a few days later.

On the 2nd of July the enemy began his operations against the town, using both his land and naval forces; but without making any impression on the besieged. Both the attack and defence were conducted with the utmost bravery for several weeks, and Tolbouzin was killed. This was a great loss to the Cossacks; but it gave hope to the Chinese, and they pressed on the siege with more vigour.

The command in Albazin now devolved on an officer named Beaton, and he continued to hold the place against the Celestials in spite of all their efforts, till severe losses and the approach of winter compelled them to retire to their encampment. This determined defence had not been maintained without loss, as many Cossacks were killed: the survivors were, however, left in peace throughout the winter.

In the following spring Beaton received reinforcements and provisions from Nertchinsk, and prepared for another obstinate defence. The siege was again renewed as soon as the season permitted, and was continued throughout the summer; but the Chinese gained no advantage. Notwithstanding the great superiority of the latter in numbers, winter found Beaton and his Cossacks still unconquered and in possession. He held Albazin for a period of two years, until the winter of 1688, and then retired, after having defended the place against ten times his force. Beaton gave the Celestials many proofs of his bull-dog courage, showing that it does not evaporate even in the wilds of Asia; and I have the best authority for saying that he was an Englishman.

On the 27th of August, 1689, a treaty was concluded at Nertchinsk between the Russians and Chinese, by which Russia was compelled to surrender all her settlements in Manjouria; it was stipulated that neither power should occupy Albazin, and a boundary was defined from the Baikal to the Sea of Okhotsk. Other disputes arose, and as it was found impossible to prevent the Siberian hunter from pursuing his avocation beyond the prescribed limits, a second treaty was concluded from Chinese dictation, in June, 1728. At that period Chinese authority predominated, and Russia was subjected to numerous insults, and his Celestial Majesty believed that she was his vassal.

What a change has come over the scene since Khabaroff and his Cossacks were apparently imitating the old buccaneers! and tradition has handed down to the present races on the Amoor an account of the plundering and piratical conduct of these men, whose names even yet cause a dread. In this year of grace 1860, Russia's power in these regions is not in idea, but in fact. One hundred and thirty-two years have elapsed since her Cossacks, after performing prodigies of valour, were compelled to retreat from their settlements on the Amoor. In 1854 the descendants of these men took possession of this great river, from its commencement to the sea, and added nearly half of Manjouria to the Russian empire; and this was accomplished in less than six weeks. Were it now either necessary or politic, Mouravioff, with his Cossacks, could pitch his celestial-born Majesty, mandarins, pigtails, and all, into the Gulf of Pe-tche-lee.

Albazin will, I have no doubt, assume a new importance: its situation is good, surrounded by rich pastures where great herds of cattle can find food, and agriculture may be introduced into some of the valleys. Sables and squirrels are numerous in the vicinity. The forests assume another aspect here; the Siberian character has given place to a more European type. Oaks clothe the mountain slopes, elms stretch forth their branches, and the ash pushes out her graceful foliage, while the hazel and wild rose cover the forest with underwood : all these objects will recall to the mind of the emigrant his European home.

CHAP. XVII.

THE UPPER AMOOR.

The Amoor expands in width immediately below Albazin, and the islands become numerous, rendering the navigation extremely difficult. When settlements are established at and near Albazin, the Russian peasant will soon make himself acquainted with the difficulties of the navigation, and become a pilot in the river. In fact, it will be a wise arrangement if the Government were to direct attention to this subject.

There are many villages of Manyargs in the country between Albazin and the Pango—the latter falls into the Amoor from the south—and again about the river Semelke. The principal occupations of the men are fishing and hunting; the first is usually performed with a spear when taking large fish, and the latter with a very rude Chinese rifle. Still, with these implements they obtain both fish and sables.

Although horses are not numerous among these people, they treat them as do the Kirghis, leaving them to provide their own food in winter by scraping the snow from off the ground. They have no idea of making hay. Their conduct towards the women does not differ from that of their brethren in the steppes. All the hard work, putting up the yourts, making clothing, cutting the wood in the forests, and drawing it home, devolves upon the female, and is never ended; whereas, when the man returns from either fishing or the chase, he puts down his weapons and remains at rest.

Before reaching the Koukou-khan the Amoor turns to the south, and then makes a great bend towards the north. In this part there are many islands covered with cheromika, and the sandstone rocks form in many places a bold shore. The valley of Tchal-bouet runs from the Amoor to the northward, where the river of the same

A Manyarg Overseer.

name has its source among the lower hills at the foot of the Yablonoï. Some twelve or fifteen miles below this is the place where Admiral Pouteatine was obliged to leave the steamer in which he ascended the Amoor, in August, 1855: it was found impossible to proceed higher, as this part of the river is obstructed by a bar. There is a large mass of sandstone here, which rises to a considerable elevation, and juts far out into the Amoor. Under the shelter of this rock the steamer was moored, and for the protection which it afforded their "Little Hope," the Russians have given it the steamer's name, "Maloi Nadejda."

The bar will prove a great obstacle to the navigation hereabouts, as there is only three feet of water for the summer months; in the spring it has ten feet, but this is only for a short period, while the snow-water is running from the mountains, when every river and stream is pouring down its contents to swell the great Amoor. Below Nadejda the banks disclose their sandstone formation, but no striking features are exhibited before reaching the mouth of the Bou-renda, which enters the Amoor from the north. It is a fine valley, in which the Cossacks, under Khabaroff, formed a settlement, and this, like their other positions, shows that it was selected with judgment. The post here commands a fertile valley, stretching far up among the hills, and affords good pastures, as well as access into a region abounding in game; while in the river they could obtain an unlimited supply of fish.

Leaving the Bou-renda, the river still runs on between its sandstone banks, above which are seen forests of poplars, elms, and the black birch, with broad spaces of what appears good pasture land. There are many Manyargs living on the banks of the numerous small rivers which fall into the Amoor; also on the banks of the Bour-gali, that comes from the south; shortly after passing which it makes a great turn towards the north-east, and islands appear, some of them thickly covered with willows. For about twenty-five miles below Bour-gali the Amoor runs in a more southerly direction, and then it makes a great curve towards the south-west, receiving many small rivers coming from the south. Below this place the Amoor expands considerably; where it has scooped out its course in the sandstone cliffs, several islands have been formed, which are covered with cheromika and other shrubs. The country is also well wooded, and produces a luxuriant vegetation.

At the lower end of the curve the Bou-sou-lee enters the Amoor from the north-east: on the opposite, or now Manjourian, side of the river there are high cliffs, extending for many miles, and numerous islands are dotted over the broad stream, giving it the appearance of a lake. The scenery on this part of it is better than higher up, but there is nothing particularly striking excepting the broad stream flowing slowly on. Further down is the Gerbel-yak, another broad stream flowing from the north-east, having its rise in the mountain chain which divides the upper affluents of the Zeya from the Amoor. The country is more open, with clumps of trees dotted over the valley, and several Manyarg families dwell in the vicinity.

Beyond the Gerbel-yak the Amoor takes a course due south to the mouth of the second Bou-sou-lee, and here the country greatly improves. Broad valleys extend far to the north-east, and vegetation assumes a new aspect. The trees of Siberia have become nearly extinct, and everything be-tokens a more genial clime. The valley of the Augan is of considerable extent, is rich in pastures and beautiful woodland scenes. It is a favourite spot of the Manyargs, who have adopted more pastoral habits than any of their race higher up the river. Great numbers of ponies are bred by these people, and the country is well adapted for grazing.

The Cossack and Russian will not be slow in taking advantage of this locality, and, ere many years are passed, the hill-sides will be seen waving with fine crops of corn, while the valley will be covered with herds of cattle. It is true that the animal whose furs make their present wealth will disappear before civilisation and agriculture; but a settled population will rise up and aid in developing its resources. The hunter will then have to seek his furs in the upper region of the Zeya.

As the wild animal disappears wherever man takes up his abode, so will it be with the present races; and their means of obtaining a livelihood will be rendered ten times more difficult than at present. They will have to seek it in a wilder district, subject to many vicissitudes which they

A Manyarg Woman.

now escape; the introduction of wodky will accomplish the rest.

Between the Angan and the mouth of the Onon the river runs through a granite region for about thirty miles. There are but few islands in this part, and the water rolls on in one great stream about half a mile in width, and in some parts seventy feet in depth. The Onon is a large river, running in a very wide valley that stretches out into meadow land of great extent, and several Manyarg villages are scattered over it. This is another fine position which an industrious population will speedily render valuable. The natives remain here through the winter, living in their settlements, about three miles above the mouth of the Onon, and in summer they take up their abode in yourts on an island, of which there are several close at hand, and all are covered with cheromika.

After passing this river a broad strip of meadow land stretches out on both banks of the Amoor; that on the north-east slopes down to the water's edge, and on the other the granite crops out in low cliffs. The meadows are dotted over with clumps of elm, black birch, and poplar, giving them a park-like appearance. About eight miles below the Onon is Tsa-ga-yan, a succession of granite masses that rise up close to the water, having a flat shore at both ends covered with timber. These are named by the Chinese Tcha-kha-yan-Khada, or the "boundary cliffs." The river is more than half a mile in width at this place, and becomes rapid, which proved somewhat dangerous to the expedition in 1854. Some of the barges got into a strong current, and one was carried ashore, where she was in danger of being broken up. Fortunately the commander had a strong force at his disposal, and 400 Cossacks were set to work to discharge the cargo, when they got her off without much damage.

The shores of the river continue low for a long distance, as far as Cape Ele-Khan, which the Russians have named Cape Kosekavitch in honour of a naval officer of my acquaintance, who is now Governor of the Amoor. The summit of the hill that forms this cape is covered with fine trees that descend in patches down its slopes, more like the work of an Asiatic gardener than Madame Nature, who has here produced some beautiful bits of woodland scenery. On the opposite or west side the rocks rise into high cliffs, named Van-yan; after passing these the river turns to the south-west and forms two great curves, in both of which there are the mouths of small streams. Then it takes a course nearly due south through a more fertile region, where the valleys stretch out into plains, extending for many miles up to the foot of the mountains. A luxuriant vegetation covers the ground, and clumps of trees are scattered over the valleys, while the hills are clothed with oak and other timber.

It may be said, and with truth, that this country has charms for every class; the agriculturist and the grazier would look upon it with delight in anticipation of the crops and herds of fat cattle it would produce; the horticulturist would view its sloping hills, and think of the clusters hanging on his vines and the vintage which would ensue in a country where the grape is indigenous; and the florist would be charmed with the variety and beauty of its flora; the miner would scan the mountains and think of the mineral wealth they contain; and the sportsman could indulge in his favourite pursuit of almost every kind of feathered and large game, from a woodcock to a tiger; while the lover of nature would gaze on the great stream and its accompanying scenes with admiration.

Below Van-yan the river has a moderately straight course for a long distance, and then makes a sudden turn, after which it expands, and then runs among a complete labyrinth of islands formed near the mouth of the Koomar. On reaching this spot the scene changes; great numbers of Manyargs are seen skimming over the water in their light boats, and Manjour merchants are observed plying their trade.

The Koomar is the greatest affluent of the Upper Amoor, which falls into it from the Daourian side. It has its source in the Eke-gou-Kooda Mountains, near their northern end, that abuts on the Amoor, to the east of the Argoun. Some of my friends from the mines of Nertchinsk have visited these mountains, and have descended into the upper valleys of the Koomar, and thus they have obtained a knowledge of the mineral wealth of this region, which will never be productive in the hands of the Chinese. The river is little short of 600 miles in length, more than one-half of which is navigable, and the upper part of the valley is inhabited by Daourians, who are engaged in agricultural pursuits and in the breeding of cattle.

There are two yermaks held near the mouth of the Koomar; one begins on the 1st of December, and the other on the 10th of March. To the first of these fairs the Manjour authorities go to receive the tribute of furs that the Manyargs have to pay. Manjourian merchants from Daouria also attend to barter their wares for the produce of the hardy hunter's rifle. They bring Chinese goods, consisting of coarsely-printed or dyed dabi, common silks, tea, salt, rice, millet, tobacco, powder, and lead; also that abominable stinking stuff, Chinese brandy. Lead and powder are the essentials for the hunter; but the merchant tries to tempt him first with his other wares, and, if possible, obtain all his skins before he has supplied himself with the means of obtaining more. If he succeeds in this, the man is in his power, and no usurer in civilised life could fleece him better. Although professing great benevolence, and a parental affection for the poor fellow, he does not fail to read him a severe lecture on his improvidence. After this his conscience permits him to demand two sable skins for the hunter's ammunition; more than one hundred times its value.

The Daourians from the valley of the Koomar attend the fair with their agricultural produce, and the Cossacks from the Argoun go there in March, carrying powder and lead, with a few articles of Russian produce, which they barter for sable and squirrel skins. The latter pass current among these people as money, and anything can be purchased with them. The tax which the hunter pays to the Manjourian authorities here is the same I found them paying on the southern slopes of the Altai, viz. a sable skin annually. None of the Manyargs under twenty years of age is called upon to contribute to his Celestial Majesty's coffers; after that age no excuse is permitted—every person must deliver his sable skin, and those who do not hunt barter for them with the Manjourian merchants at the rate of seventy squirrel skins for a sable. Nor are the people taken as soldiers before the age of twenty or after forty; having attained the latter age, they are free.

The religion of the Manyargs is Shamanisim. They are exceedingly superstitious, and the priests possess great power over them, influencing all their actions, even in their domestic and family intercourse.

Some of the islands at the mouth of the Koomar are of considerable extent; a few are covered with willows, and many others with cheromika. One is meadow land, with good pastures: on this were the Manjourian guard, consisting of three officers and a body of Chinese troops. They are stationed here in summer, and in winter they return to Ai-goon. Khabaroff was here in 1652, and built a small fort on one of the islands; some of the remains still exist. This was after his establishment at Albazin.

The banks of the river opposite the mouth of the Koomar attain a considerable elevation; and one part is remarkable both for its appearance and name. This is a mass of volcanic rocks thrown up in rugged crags, but in most picturesque forms, and it bears the name of "Long-tor" among the Manyargs. By the Manjourians it is called Da-o-she-Khada. Long-tor has no connection either with Daourian, Manjourian, or any other Asiatic language, and thus it seems strange to find it here. The only way in which I can account for it is this:—Beaton (whose name I believe was Beatson) was here on the 12th of March, 1686, and it is probable that he remained some time in the fort which Khabaroff had built, standing directly opposite this singular rocky mass. He may have thought that it resembled some of the rocky cliffs in his own land, designated by the word "Tor," not uncommon in Derbyshire, and thus, as a re-

Long-tor.

membrance of his native home, he may have called it "Long-tor" on account of its extent. At all events, the name is significant.

Unfortunately, like many others, this appellation has been changed, for that of a young man who accompanied the expedition. Now it is Cape "Bibikoff;" I much fear that this case will be no exception to the rule, "that a bad name requires no care," and thus Long-tor may be lost. From the lower end of these cliffs a strip of meadow land extends for about six miles along the bank of the Amoor, till it reaches the mouth of the Bele-yan, which runs from the high land dividing the Zeya and the valley of the Amoor. It is a small river running in a broad valley, where pastures, covered with rich herbage, extend far up among the hills; but at present there are no cattle to crop the luxuriant grass.

Below Bele-yan it runs for some distance between rocky shores, with a wooded country on each side, and islands are still found, covered as usual with cheromika. Before reaching Ouloo-sou Modon it turns to the west, making an enormous curve. In fact, it encloses a great space, leaving only a narrow neck of land between the commencement and the end of the curves, and on this the Karaoul of Ouloo-sou Modon is placed. This is another Chinese military post, where the Manjour frontier-guard perform duty during the summer, usually arriving from Ai-goon in May.

This Karaoul consists of three small dwellings for the officer and his men, and near them a small Temple is built, fronting the river. It is a Temple of Confucius, and close to its entrance were two yew trees, with flags suspended from their branches. The curve encloses a space of about twelve miles in length, that forms a large area, and a number of Chinese live here, who are engaged in cutting wood to float down to Ai-goon. From this place the Amoor runs nearly due south, and both its shores are covered with forest, wherein a great number of Chinese were engaged cutting their winter fuel. The Kerleu falls into the Amoor on the right bank; here, larch trees are scattered over the narrow valley through which this river runs, and a few conical yourts were seen in the distance.

Below this part it becomes broader, islands are less frequent, and the country is more open, with extensive tracts of meadow land, that continue with but little change to the village of Amba Saghalian. Here was a group of poor dwellings, built of clay and roofed with wood; and everything indicated that the people understood little either of cleanliness or comfort. A little further is the village of Dag-ega, which consists of about forty dwellings, scattered about under clumps of elms, maples, and acacias, each cottage having its garden. From this point the Amoor runs through a broad expanse of meadow land, uninterrupted on the left shore as far as the Khingan Mountains. The character of the country now changes; the mountains are no longer covered with dense forests as on the upper part of the Amoor: here is a fertile region of vast extent, on which groups of elms, birches, maples, and acacias are dotted, giving it an appearance, very pleasant to the eye, while everything indicates that population, under a proper government, is alone wanting to make this part of Asia as valuable as the best portions of Europe.

The Zeya has its outlet on this broad tract, affording a good means of communication into a vast region on the north-east. This is by far the largest affluent that falls into the Upper Amoor; and from its source in the Yablonoi Mountains, to its mouth, it has a course of more than 700 miles. A river flowing over such a distance presents varied aspects: the lower and middle regions are capable of sustaining a great population, with vast herds of horses and cattle; while the upper valleys are clothed with immense forests abounding in wild animals; and here the hunter obtains valuable skins. The early Russian explorers of the Amoor, under Poiyarkoff, in 1643, descended by this valley, and several Cossack posts were afterwards formed in the upper region.

At a short distance from the mouth of the river, Zenovioff commenced building a fort; but the Chinese stopped it, and drove the Russians from all their posts in this country before the fall of Albazin. Although their forts were destroyed the hunters paid their annual visits to the upper forests and hunting grounds, whence they derived a considerable amount of valuable furs; and thus the route was kept open.

In the meantime the Manjours formed permanent settlements on the Zeya, villages were established near its mouth, and some of the people were sent higher up. Many of these settlements remain at the present time, and are inhabited by Manjourians and Daourians, who are occupied in agriculture and in breeding cattle. This is destined to become a place of commerce in the hands of the Russians, who will develop its resources, and before long its mountain chains will be explored by intelligent engineers. Its mineral wealth will then be ascertained, and whatever is valuable will be extracted, to add to the other resources of this enormous territory. Iron was discovered while the Cossacks occupied the country; it will be of vast importance to the settlements on the Amoor.

The mouth of the Zeya, at its junction with the Amoor, is about 1,100 yards in width, and pours in a vast flood to swell the already great river. On the right, or Chinese bank of the Amoor, stands the Manjourian villages of Khona-Khour-Kha and Tong-don; below these is the village of Ovour-Toxso, opposite to which is a large island, separated from the Manjourian shore by a narrow arm. Beyond, the bank becomes more elevated and rocky, and here are the settlements of Bordo and Nertchu. In short, lower down the country is thickly populated; villages and dwellings may be observed nestling under woods and clumps of trees as far as the eye can reach, while cattle and horses are seen grazing on the pastures. These people live in a fine climate and a fertile region.

Blagovestchinsk is intended to be the chief town on the Amoor. The site selected is a short distance below the mouth of the Zeya, on the left or Russian bank of the river. This is an excellent situation, in the midst of a numerous population, occupied tilling the ground, on which they have been long established. The Governor-General has made a wise selection, as here he secures an industrious people already prepared to his hands, who, I hope, will be better treated by their new masters than they were by their Manjourian rulers, who are notorious for their cruelty and extortion.

When Khabaroff descended the Amoor in 1651, he found three towns, each having a fort, about twenty miles below the mouth of the Zeya. They were governed by three Daourian Princes—Tou-roon-ga, Tolga, and Omou-tae. These men tried to stop his descent, but it was unavailing; he took the fortresses, destroyed them, and burnt the towns, after which he proceeded on his voyage. On the place where the first of these forts stood is the village of Djoue-aikho, and this is the ancient site of Ai-goon, or "Saghalian-Oula-Khoton." In 1685 this was deserted, and the new town was erected on a more eligible situation, four miles lower down, on the right bank of the river. On approaching Saghalian-Oula-Khoton numerous villages are seen on both banks of the river, each house having its garden, and agriculture seems to be the occupation of the inhabitants. Before reaching the town the village of Sir-khan-tse-toxo is passed on the left bank, and almost immediately opposite is El-dijo Tadea.

This is the harbour, and immediately below is the town of Saghalian-Oula-Khoton, or Ai-goon, the head-quarters of the Chinese Amoor fleet, which consists of thirty-six boats of various sizes, some of them able to carry five tons, the others considerably smaller. These will do but little should they ever enter into a contest with the Russian armed steamers. Ai-goon is the seat of government for the whole of the Upper Amoor, from the commencement of the river at the mouth of the Argoun, to the Khingan Mountains. Its influence extends over a distance of more than 800 miles; indeed, until recently reached beyond the sources of the Zeya to the boundary on the Yablonoi. It is now terribly curtailed in its dimensions and population.

The town stands on a flat piece of land, which stretches along the bank of the Amoor for a considerable distance, and the buildings occupy a space of about two miles in length and 600 yards in breadth. A large space is enclosed in the centre of the town, that forms the fortress; within this enclosure stands the Amban, or Governor's house, several Government offices, the courts of justice, and numerous small temples. The other streets run parallel to each other, and are crossed at right angles, dividing the town into numerous quadrangular plots, occupied by the dwellings of the inhabitants. The houses are built of wood, and are nearly similar to those I have described in Maima-tchin. As in almost all Chinese towns, the buildings are only one story in height; and although there are many temples to Confucius here, there is no remarkable feature to attract the attention of the traveller.

The river is about one mile in width, with an island opposite the lower part of the town, on which a fortress formerly stood. This was built after Khabaroff had destroyed those higher up. Immediately below Ai-goon there are villages scattered over the broad belts of meadow land that extend along the banks. In this region vegetation assumes a more European character; elms, limes, and poplars are seen growing among the villages, with occasional clumps of oak and black birch, while among the bushes that fringe the banks of the river, hazel, briony, and dogwood are found mingled with others of Daourian type.

The flat plain on the right bank is bounded by a small mountain chain, called Bal-Khada, branching from the Khingan, and which runs nearly parallel with the course of the stream. About twenty miles below Ai-goon the mountains turn to the northward, and terminate on the river in a high conical mount rising abruptly from it. The Amoor turns to the left, and has scooped out a deep indentation in the mountain, forming a natural harbour, which the Chinese have improved and turned into good docks for their war boats. Here is the large Daourian village of Khor-mol-djend, and several others are seen at a little distance from the river. A large island has been formed nearly opposite these villages, on which the wild grapes of the Amoor were found flourishing most luxuriantly, and my friend Colonel Korsakoff, who partook of them, assured me of their excellent flavour and sweetness. The cork tree was also growing on this island, the only spot on which it had then been found on the Amoor. The ground was covered with the lilies of the valley in full bloom, filling the air with their fragrance.

After passing Bal-Khada, a mountain chain is seen to the south, but so far in the distance that at times it is lost in haze, while the great plain that extends in that direction seems like a sea of herbage waving to and fro in the breeze. On the left bank there are no elevations visible; it is one uninterrupted plain, stretching out till it appears to dissolve into vapour. Here are rich pastures, on which tens of thousands of cattle can find food, and where corn and other agricultural produce can be grown to an almost unlimited extent. Such is the nature of the country nearly as far as the mouth of the Numan.

This river is one of the great affluents of the Upper Amoor, and it falls into it by two mouths on the left side; it has its source in the most northern part of the Khingan Mountains, and receives many affluents in its course. A little to the west of the Numan low hills appear, in which there are a few ravines thickly wooded, but no trees grow on the hills. The mouth of this river was selected by the

Governor-General for one of the first settlements on the Amoor, and now a Russian town is rising on the site. Timber for building purposes is obtained in the upper valleys of the Numan; an inexhaustible supply of fire-wood can also be floated down the river. The water and the climate is good, — the vegetation luxuriant; the place is surrounded by good pastures, and the entire country well adapted for agriculture. There is every requisite on this spot to render the population comfortable and even wealthy.

Shortly after leaving the Numan the stream becomes studded with islands, and on the right bank rises the Marma chain, which extends along the river, sometimes close to the water, and then the hills recede, leaving extensive plains well suited for cultivation. On the left bank there are several lakes, some villages and small settlements, and the people are engaged in tilling the land and hunting. Still farther down on both sides the hills rise up into slopes, which are covered with a rich vegetation; and here the people follow their agricultural pursuits. These elevations continue along the river till they terminate abruptly at a high cliff, named Cape "Sverbeef."

Here is another folly of the Russian geographer; he has robbed a rugged cliff of its characteristic name, and has substituted one of perfect insignificance. Who in after years will care to know that this was named after a stripling who accompanied the expedition? I sincerely hope that His Imperial Majesty will issue an order to stop this desecration of ancient names, or few places in his new acquisition will remain unappropriated.

Beyond Cape Sverbeef the Amoor runs in mountain channels, sometimes between high cliffs, and then again between slopes covered with dense forests. There are many inhabitants in the small valleys; they are chiefly of the Daourian race, and occupy themselves in cultivating the soil and in killing animals for their skins. Having passed through the hills, the river continues its course along a channel near two miles in width. The mountains recede on each side, and form extensive tracts of meadow, which terminate in a wide valley. At the end of this the Oubera falls into the Amoor on the right bank, and here is stationed the Manjour frontier-guard. Shortly after passing this place it enters the gorge in the Khingan Mountains, in which its bed is reduced to about half a mile in width, but its pent-up flood now attains a depth of 70 feet, and rushes on with increased rapidity. The cliffs on each side are not of great elevation, except at a few points, but this enormous body of water rolling onward for more than 60 miles and dashing against the rocks, has a sublime effect.

Although the cliffs are not high, the mountain slopes rise very abruptly to a great elevation, and many of them are covered with larch and pine, while oak, elm, and birch form extensive forests. At a short distance from the end of this rapid are two islands; one is a mass of red rock, fringed with shrubs, and the other is lower, and covered with trees. A few miles beyond the gorge of the Khingan the river turns to the eastward and expands in width, and here is presented one of the most characteristic views on the Amoor. A vast multitude of islands lie scattered over the river; many are thickly covered with trees, others would afford good pastures for herds of cattle. These masses are strewn so thickly over the flood, that the water seems to be encircling them in a network of silver; nor does it appear an easy matter to guide a barque through these intricate mazes.

On both sides of the river a vast steppe stretches out till the sky and the horizon seem blended into one. The plains commence from the south-eastern slopes of the Khingan chain, forming an immense area of country, which appears never to have been cultivated. The soil is composed of sand and clay, with a stratum of rich dark mould above, created during a succession of ages by decayed vegetable matter, that has produced a crop of the most luxuriant grass and plants, —only to be cut down by the frost, and add their portion to the earth. The bend of the river on this plain is the most southern point of the Amoor; it is in lat. 47° 42′ 18″ N.; under this parallel it runs about sixty miles to the mouth of the Soungaria, and beyond it turns to the north-east. The temperature on these plains is sufficiently warm to produce almost any vegetation. On the 25th of June the thermometer stood in the tent at 31° Reau. (102° Fahr.); out in the open air, in the shade, 27° Reau. (93° Fahr.); and in the sun at 41° Reau. (125° Fahr.) On these plains many birds are found, which come from Java, Sumatra, and the neighbouring islands.

About twenty miles below the most southern point the Amoor divides into several arms, and these run in deep beds, the banks being from twenty-five to twenty-eight feet above the water, and in many parts they were covered with a dense forest of black birches, oaks, and aspens. Lower down, on the right bank, Russia has established a Cossack post; it is near the large river Bi-djan, which flows from the Bi-djan-vodze chain, having a course of more than 200 miles; it has cut a deep channel through the plain.

A few miles beyond, the Bi-djan unites into two great arms; one runs to the south-east and receives the Soungaria. The united streams flow on for a short distance, and then join the other arm, when they form the great Amoor. Two small mountain chains bound the valley of the Soungaria; looking up the valley, the river is seen winding its course towards the mountains on the left, and running some distance along their base. It then sweeps across the valley till it reaches the mountains on the right, and gradually approaches the Amoor. On the left bank of the Soungaria, and near its mouth, stands the village of Djang-djoon, containing a strong guard of Chinese soldiers and their officers.

An immense plain commences at the mouth of the Soungaria, which extends along its bank up to the mountains; it is covered with high grass. Numerous lakes are formed upon it, and many of them are surrounded by a belt of bamboos, while others have a clear shore. From the great quantity of drift-wood that is strewn over the plain, there can be no doubt of its being covered with water during the high floods in spring, when this will appear a mighty

A Manjour Officer and a Lady.

stream. When the Soungaria and the Amoor meet, they do not mingle; they run on, each in its course, for many miles. The water of the latter has a deep tinge of burnt sienna, but is bright and pellucid; that of the former has a deep tint of green, caused by minute particles of vegetable matter, giving it a semi-transparent appearance.

The same phenomenon occurs in some of the large Siberian rivers at the latter end of June and in the early part of July. The whole body of the water becomes thick with plants so exceedingly small that they give the water the appearance of a pale green soup. The Siberians name this "the flowering of the water." They cautioned me against drinking it at this period, as it might be attended with serious consequences. Horses will not touch water when in this state.

The Soungaria is about a mile and one-third in breadth; it joins the Amoor by one, not, as it has been supposed, by two streams. It runs sluggishly on till it flows into the rapid current of the Amoor, where a considerable commotion is raised by the meeting of the waters. The Soungaria has its source on the north-eastern side of Tchan-bo-shan, "the great white mountain," as the Chinese name it. Its course, according to Manjour authority, is not less than 1,000 miles in length, before its junction with the Amoor. It has five great affluents, one of which, the Noun, has its source in the south-eastern side of the Eke-gou-Kooda Mountains to the eastward of the Argoun; and this river has a course of near 500 miles before it joins the Soungaria.

The valley of the Soungaria and those of its affluents are said to be the most densely populated portions of this part of the Chinese Empire. Besides the people settled in the numerous towns on the banks of the river, there is a great nomade population engaged in breeding cattle, and the river opens up a water-way for Russian commerce. There is, however, here a great drawback to the success of Russia, in the distance which her European products have to be transported, and the long winters which close up her inland navigation. Either the Americans or the English can deposit their manufactures in the warehouses on the Amoor at one-third of the sum it costs the Russians. Besides which they can produce their goods at a cheaper rate, and unless a heavy protective duty is put on all merchandise arriving by sea Russia will not be able to compete with the Saxon races. It will be much more profitable if her merchants are established on the Amoor, to distribute European wares brought seaward; this too will materially benefit the people by making the various articles they require cheaper, while opening a market for their own products. They who now have to clothe themselves in fish skin, requiring a long time to prepare, will then be able to use articles from European looms at one-tenth part of their cost of production, by which means the resources of the country will be enabled to keep pace with its progress in civilisation.

The Manjourian merchants from Elan-Khala, or Etcha-Khoton, on the Soungaria, carry on a considerable trade with the inhabitants of the Amoor. They descend the Soungaria in large boats laden with Chinese produce, which they distribute here, charging an enormous price. The goods they supply are coarsely-printed calicoes, Chinese silk materials, rice, and millet; also bracelets, ear-rings, tobacco, and brandy; for which they receive in exchange valuable furs, isinglass, and the dried spinal bones of the sturgeon,—the latter are highly prized in Chinese cookery. The Mangoons from the Lower Amoor enter into this trade: they collect the furs from the hunters in every part of the region, and the other simple products from the people quite down to the Sea of Okhotsk. With these they ascend the river, bartering as they proceed, till they reach the Soungaria, and then ascend to Etcha-Khoton, exchange their commodities, and return with a Chinese cargo to their winter stations, where they remain till the following spring. So they pass their time; one voyage in the year realising enough for all their wants.

The Manjourians, who ought to be the best judges on the subject, claim for the Soungaria the honour of being parent to the Amoor, and say that that part of the river above its mouth is only an affluent. Although some discussion on this subject has taken place in the Imperial Geographical Society of St. Petersburg, I think it may be fairly inferred that Russia will not seriously dispute the point with the Chinamen, but leave them to establish the fact. This being done to their satisfaction, she may then have a few words to say about a treaty which has ceded to her the whole country north of the Amoor, and presently find herself possessed of the best and most densely peopled regions of Manjouria. The immediate establishment of her posts on the upper waters of the Soungaria will save her much trouble and expense, which is certain to be incurred a few years hence if they are formed on the spurious Amoor. Another advantage will also accrue to the Brother of the Sun — he will have a near neighbour to fly to in case his fanatical subjects of the north succeed in reaching his capital.

I shall say a few words on another point touching the Amoor. A good old proverb, "Give every one his due," induces me to put in a word in favour of an old acquaintance. It has been distinctly stated by a Russian authority that the Onon is the parent of the Amoor, as this river and the Ingoda form the Shilka, which runs to the head of the Amoor. Should the Chinese make the Amoor only an affluent, I cannot help entertaining a different opinion, and shall claim for it another origin. I apprehend that geographers will admit that the longest branch, measured from the point where the two rivers unite and form one, taking a new name, fairly claims the priority, and on this the Keroulun shall take its stand. The Onon and the Shilka have a course of 650 miles from the source to Oust-Strelka, whereas the Keroulun and the Argoun have a course of 850 miles to the same point where the Argoun and Shilka form the Amoor.

It is 209 years this summer since Khabaroff first saw the Soungaria. He descended the Amoor in 1651, on an expedition of discovery, and passed the mouth of the river without being stopped by the Chinese guard. He continued his voyage downward, and satisfied himself that the country would afford sufficient supply for all the wants of his people. As he had not taken a sufficient force to plunder, he returned with his party in the autumn to Albazin. In the following spring he again descended the river, accompanied by a strong party, succeeded in eluding the vigilance of the Chinese guards, and obtained a considerable quantity of grain and other provisions from the people, with which he passed down the Soungaria in the night, and carried his booty in safety to the forts. This became a constant practice, and Khabaroff, with his Cossacks, levied a "black mail" far into Manjouria. His daring deeds, and some cruelties, have caused his name to be handed down to the present race of Manjourians.

Stepanoff was the next leader who penetrated the proscribed region. In March 1654, he descended the Amoor, and sailed up the Soungaria. He was discovered by the Chinese in the evening of the third day, when a considerable number of boats gave chase, and compelled him to return. The following year Stepanoff made another descent on the Manjourians, accompanied by Poustchin and a strong party, when they succeeded in taking a large quantity of grain and other valuables, with which they returned to the fort, having provisioned themselves for a year.

Each spring a marauding expedition was led on by this indefatigable man, who determined that his neighbours should provide the supplies. These descents were made so suddenly, and sometimes with such ferocity, that the poor Manjourians fled like sheep, and left their homes to be sacked by the plunderers. At length the Chinese authorities were roused into action, and in the spring of 1658 a large body of Chinese troops were marched to the mouth of the Soungaria, and a strong fleet of their war boats concealed among the islands in readiness to kill or capture the band. On the night of the 30th of June 1658, Stepanoff dropped down with his little flotilla to the mouth of the Soungaria, and anchored to reconnoitre before sailing up the river. As soon as daylight appeared, he found himself in a trap; a division of war-boats rowed out into the water above him, and began to bear down upon them; another division formed across the river. Towards this he turned, hoping by the aid of the strong current to break through their line, but the Chinese were so numerous that the whole party were either killed or captured; and this stopped any further descent on the Manjourians.

Russian policy and commerce have already opened the Soungaria. The Manjourians have learned the value of silver roubles; these and scarlet cloth they willingly take in exchange for their sables, and the Russian steamers will, if needed, pass up the river in spite of any fleet of war-boats sent to oppose them. It is fortunate, however, that the valley of the Amoor has been added to the empire without a single contest with the people. The Cossack posts have been quietly placed at the different points, and Russian settlements are being established without opposition. Ten years hence the aspect of this region will be materially changed, flourishing towns will be seen on the banks of the Amoor, the vessels moored on the shore will show that the people are actively engaged in commerce and other industrial pursuits, while the white churches with their numerous turrets and green domes will prove that religion and civilisation have taken the place of idolatry and superstition. A country like this, where agriculture and cattle breeding can be carried to an unlimited extent by an industrious population, where all the necessaries of life can be easily produced, must prosper; and if a just and wise governor continues to rule in Oriental Siberia, this country is destined to have a great future.

Beside the Manjourian soldiers stationed on the Soungaria, the Toungouz have formed settlements in different parts near the mouth of the river, and their chief occupation is hunting and fishing. They are a quiet, inoffensive people, living in conical yourts covered with birch-bark, exactly like those I have seen on some of the lower affluents of the Yenissey. Like the Toungouz of that region, they

Touzemtz.

are tattooed; both the men and women adopting this decoration. There is also another race, the Touzemtz, dwelling here; they are of Toungouz origin, and have adopted the Manjourian manners and costume. Many are engaged in trading with the Goldi, and Mangoons; also with the other tribes on the Lower Amoor. They collect furs from the hunters, and exchange them with the Manjourian merchants for Chinese wares, which they distribute far over the country.

Others of this race are scattered about in villages on the Amoor, where they are employed as fishermen, and some of the fish they procure and dry, are sent to Pekin. In addition to this branch of their trade, they supply the Manjourian population on the Soungaria with the principal part of their food. The Touzemtz may be considered as the most industrious race on the Amoor.

CHAP. XVIII.

THE MIDDLE AMOOR.

Below the mouth of the Soungaria the Amoor stretches out, and several islands have been formed in its bed. Its course is to the north-east, which seems to be a direct continuation of the Soungaria, extending for about twenty-five miles. As the Amoor enters it in this place nearly at right angles, I think the Chinese have reason for their opinion as to its being the affluent. There are numerous large islands here that appear to have been formed by the waters of the Soungaria, which is now being swept away by the more rapid stream of the Amoor.

A little further down the river greatly expands, giving it the character of a large lake, which idea, however, is quickly dispelled as the rapid current floats the traveller past the islands. Flat shores extend for some distance on each side; they are covered with long grass, and the bank is fringed with willows. In many parts where the rocks protrude through the plains their summits are clothed with shrubs and flowers, while around their base there are rich pastures, which prove the fertility of this virgin soil. Vast tracts of country are spread out, where it is probable man has never broken the turf. Beyond rise well-wooded mountain slopes, where timber can be easily obtained for constructing dwellings and for fuel. Numerous rivulets cross these plains, well stored with fish, and game is abundant; but so long as its scanty populations are compelled to pay their tax in sable skins they will form no permanent settlements, nor turn their attention to the riches of the soil.

The river still runs on among clusters of islands, covered with luxuriant vegetation and fine clumps of trees, under which are seen nestled the small straw and bark dwellings of the inhabitants. A few miles further down, the aspect of the country changes, the Gai-djen is seen winding its course across the plain, and a chain of blue mountains, in which it has its source, is visible in the distance. It falls into the Amoor on the right bank, and opposite to its mouth there is a large island, on which a few Toungouz families have taken up their abodes. Some of the islands are inhabited by a single family, who seem to be cut off from all intercourse with their brethren. Although they are living on these isolated spots, like so many Crusoes, the hand of oppression grasps them, and the Chinaman obliges them to leave their quiet abodes and seek the sable in the wild region to the north.

Beyond the mouth of the Gai-djen the Amoor runs at the foot of rocky cliffs, where there is no vegetation. These extend for many miles through a branch of a small mountain chain, and in some parts they rise into rugged summits overhanging the water, by which deep ravines have been cut, giving them the appearance of huge forts placed to defend the river. At the eastern side of this chain a great plain stretches out to the south-east, and ends in a valley that seems to run far up into the mountains which forms the watershed between the Amoor and the Oussoure. Here is another vast space on which thousands might be settled, where, by a moderate share of industry, the soil could be made to supply not only the necessaries of life, but many of its luxuries. The plain is watered by numerous brooks that flow from the hills, and in many parts the ground is covered with a carpet of flowers, while in others the tall grass reaches above the head of a man when sitting on horseback.

The only inhabited spot visible on this great plain was the village of Khoun-garia; it extends along the shore for about a mile, and its background of luxuriant green foliage gives it a most refreshing aspect. The people are Toungouz, who live by hunting and fishing; they never think of cultivating the soil, and thereby place themselves beyond the reach of want that now often assails them. No doubt it is somewhat difficult to change the habits of the wild hunter and make him till the ground, nor will it be accomplished in my time. The example of the Russian colonist will do much to bring about this change; his labour too will become more valuable than killing sables, and then the rising generation will enter on a new mode of life without the prejudices of their parents.

At a distance of about twenty miles beyond Khoungaria another branch of the mountain chain approaches the river. In the course of ages the Amoor has changed its course, sweeping away the lower slopes and cutting the elevated ridges into high and picturesque headlands, that give singular variety and beauty to the scenery on the river. One of these is Derke, a fine bold mass of igneous rocks that rises to a great elevation, and terminates in pinnacles far above the ridge. Tigers are numerous in this chain, especially to the south, where the people, in consequence, find it impossible to keep horses. The panther is also found in the forests, and these animals deter the sable hunters from visiting the mountain region, as their rifles and bows are poor weapons to use against such dangerous beasts.

On the left side of the river the country contains some extensive plains, and wooded hills stretch across them. Many are covered with a thick forest of oaks, elms, and lime; the latter growing to a great size. Another flat shore extends beyond Derke, and a valley runs at the foot of the mountains far to the southward. Further down another mass of rocks is thrown up, named Etau; portions are exceedingly rugged, and crowned with huge pinnacles of bare rock, while in other places they are covered with larch trees that have taken root on every ledge. On the opposite side there are similar cliffs, also well wooded; and between them the great river rolls on its flood more than a mile in width. This may be considered a great cleft cut through the mountain, which the river is constantly making wider. At the lower end nature has been most prodigal; she has thrown together many stony masses, that are piled up in singular and picturesque forms, rising from the water that dashes against their base like waves in a gale. In some of the deep recesses magnificent oaks and the Manjourian lime-trees are growing most luxuriantly; the latter attaining the height of sixty feet, while birches are to be found in the upper clefts draping the rocks with their pendant foliage.

Beyond, the islands become numerous, the banks less elevated, and the current less rapid. On one part the shore was strewn with blocks of stone, extending over a great space, and appearing as if the cliffs had been uprooted and hurled into a heap; among these were gigantic ferns and various shrubs. This is a considerable fishing station, and the Manyargs come here in great numbers at certain seasons and procure vast quantities. A little further down the river Bou-ka-tcha falls into the Amoor: it descends from the elevated land on the right side, in a series of rapids, and makes a thundering noise.

Not far from this place the Manyargs have their summer dwellings; they are conical, and formed by a number of poles, like those of the Kalmucks in the Saian Mountain, with this difference, that the Manyargs cover theirs with reeds instead of birch bark. In winter the latter live in more substantial dwellings, which they build of wood. Like the

Kalmucks, they are fond of finery; they will exchange anything for rings, ear-rings, and calico, or silk of vivid colour, especially red or crimson. Tobacco and brandy are temptations they cannot resist, and the Manjourian merchants employ both to obtain the hard-earned furs at one-third their value. By these means the Manjourians keep the people constantly in their power, and always in a state of abject poverty.

I trust that General Mouravioff will exercise the same benevolence towards the tribes on the Amoor, that have now come under his charge, he previously displayed towards the Sayots. This race would soon have been extinct,—caused solely by the Russian traders stripping them of everything for wodky, and then keeping them in their grasp by supplying them with ammunition for the following year: fortunately for them, the General prohibited wodky being bartered for their furs, and only allowed the exchange of their skins for such goods as were necessary to them. After two days the yermak is closed, when both traders and hunters are obliged to depart for their homes.

Should the General adopt the same plan on the Amoor, a thriving population will arise in the place of those whom the Chinese have reduced to a condition as pitiable as slavery. This will shortly give the Russians a moral influence that will spread rapidly over Manjouria and destroy the power by which China holds the people in thraldom. The punishments and tortures the authorities inflict on the unfortunate men when unable to pay the tax are so atrocious that I will not distress my readers by relating them. I may, however, mention that it is no uncommon circumstance for the hunter to sell himself for life for a single sable skin to ransom himself from their cruelty. The sooner, therefore, General Korsakoff and his Cossacks sweep the Chinese out of Manjouria the better.

Not far from the Bou-ka-tcha there is a large island

where the cork trees grow, which, under proper management, may become a source of wealth to many in this region. The Amoor at this part is two miles in width; in some parts the whole breadth is visible, and its mighty current is seen rolling on. Below the island the right bank of the river again rises into cliffs that continue for a considerable distance, but at no great elevation till they reach Koun-olee, a high craggy mass about five miles in length; in some parts the water washes the rocks, in others they recede, forming a vast crescent, encircling a natural garden covered with plants, shrubs, and flowers. Again the rocks turn, and jut out into the stream, where the water is gradually undermining the lofty crags, and one after another they are being hurled into the flood.

After passing this the Amoor is divided into innumerable branches, forming islands of great magnitude, and on both sides of the river the country stretches out into immense plains, which are admirably adapted for colonisation; thousands of families might find homes here, and soon surround themselves with every comfort; and as the mountain chain to the south of the Oussoure is supposed to be rich in minerals, a wide field may be opened for the more adventurous spirits. Some of my friends, the mining engineers, have an idea that a second California exists in this region. I have no reason to doubt this, seeing that the country is on the same parallel with the gold deposits which are known to exist on the southern slopes of the Altai.

Since these opinions were expressed exploration has proved that the Manjourians are already working gold mines on the La-ou-djan, one of the southern affluents of the Soungaria. The investigation of other portions of this region will soon make known its mineral wealth.

Still further to the east is the village of Sel-gha-koo, which stands near the mouth of a small river coming from the great plain. The people are Manyargs, and on the opposite side of the river there is another village. The men have all adopted the Chinese mode, having their hair plaited into long tails. Fishing and hunting is their occupation; the river teems with the finny tribe, and many large sturgeons are caught. The plain and the hills beyond form a good hunting-ground; on the former wild boars are numerous, and these they usually kill with a spear, as their

Manyarg.

rifles have a very small bore. They meet Bruin in the same manner; the conflict is hand to paw, and is often dangerous. The elk, the maral, and wild goat, they shoot. Looking at the weapon they use, it appears surprising that they ever succeed; this is, however, owing to their thorough acquaintance with the habits of the animals they pursue, their untiring efforts in the chase, and their unflinching courage.

They eat the bear, believing that his flesh gives a zest

for the chase, and renders them proof against fear. They need such a stimulant occasionally, especially in their encounters with the wild boar, as he is one of the most dangerous animals the hunter has to grapple with, and a stroke from his tusk often proves fatal to man and horse. In their encounters with the bear they are careful not to injure his head; as they offer it to their god, and it must be without blemish, enclosed in birch bark, and suspended from a tree: this they believe to be a certain antidote against evil spirits.

About twenty miles below Sel-gha-koo the Amoor expands to more than three miles in width, with many islands scattered over its bed; it then narrows again, and runs past the foot of Ak-dar, beyond a broad arm makes a curve to the south, having more the appearance of a lake than a river: this is named Tar-gong. The country on the right is a plain covered with long grass—clumps of willows and trees are scattered over it. On the north side a series of small valleys and wooded hills extend to a great distance; beyond these are seen the summits of a mountain chain.

After a winding course of many miles the different branches are united, and the river flows on in one great stream, more than two miles in width. The banks are sand and clay, thickly covered with timber; in some places vistas are formed through the dense forest, leading to a fine open country beyond, where rich pastures stretch out to a great distance; but the grass is never cropped except by the wild animals. Both banks partake of the same character, and, notwithstanding their luxuriance, they wear a desolate aspect, neither man nor his works being visible, and nature pours forth her bounties only to wither and die unheeded.

Russia has obtained a territory more valuable than all the supposed cotton districts of Africa, watered by hundreds of streams flowing into the great artery that passes through its entire length. The climate is good, and well suited for

Europeans; its animals belong to both the cold and warm regions, while its luxuriant herbage and magnificent flora prove that the temperature is neither severe in winter nor excessively hot in summer. It is possible that some of these great plains may be suited for the culture of the cotton plant; if so, a supply of this valuable product will, ere long, be found at the Russian ports in the Sea of Japan and in the Gulf of Tartary.

Again the Amoor stretches out, with numerous islands dotted over its surface; most of these are low, and covered with willows. At the time of the spring floods they are inundated, and then it exhibits a mighty stream, near five miles in width, that extends for thirty or forty miles. The hills now close in and force the flood into a narrow channel till it reaches another great expanse, named Sen-dha-koo. The country becomes highly interesting; on the north several valleys run far up among wooded hills, which extend towards the Khingan Mountains, whose summits are so distant that they appear almost like clouds on the horizon. To the south the mountains of Khouk-tcher-khoorene are seen stretching far beyond the Oussoure, and into the supposed Manjourian "El-dorado." Fertile plains extend along the bank of the river, watered by numerous rivulets that descend from the distant hills. Clumps of maple, poplar, and lime-trees are dispersed over this tract, and willows fringe the borders of the streams. This scene would be improved by herds of cattle browsing on the plain, and waving crops of corn on the hill sides. Time, however, will bring about this change, and even the Manyargs and Mangoons may become an agricultural people.

As the river continues on its downward course the aspect of the country changes; cliffs begin to rise on both shores, in which many ravines have been cut by the torrents that come tumbling from the higher ground into the Amoor.

These continue for many miles without any material change till they reach Khor-roko, where the river expands into a deep bay on its southern shore, and this is named Noung-gia. There is a Toungouz settlement here, and although the chief occupations of the people are fishing and hunting, each dwelling is surrounded by its garden, in which both vegetables and flowers are cultivated. The women are exceedingly industrious, and, unlike the Toungouz and Kalmucks of Siberia, keep their dwellings neat and clean. Both men and women possess all the qualities required in an industrious population. They are an exceedingly imitative race, and example will go far towards changing their habits.

Beyond the bay a large tract of meadow land runs up into a great curve turned by the mountains, where they sweep round towards the Oussoure, ending in high cliffs on the bank of the Amoor, and these are the rocks of Kirma, which form a bold and picturesque headland. A small arm of the Amoor makes a turn to the south at this point, and runs on towards the mouth of the Oussoure, having a narrow tract of flat land along the bank.

On a rocky eminence which juts out into the river a little beyond Kirma are the remains of an ancient fort, and near it the ruins of Atchanska. The rocks run nearly perpendicular down to the water, and form a little sheltered cove that can only be approached in a boat, and a narrow neck connects this mass with the high bank. In the summer of 1651 Khabaroff visited the Oussoure, and after deciding to form a permanent settlement near its mouth, selected this place, as nature had done much towards rendering the position secure. Without loss of time he commenced operations, first securing his little fleet of boats in the cove that formed a good and safe harbour; a path was soon formed that enabled the men to scale the cliffs, and then he began building a fort in which to spend the winter.

His position was discovered by the Chinese in the autumn before he had completed his works, and a body of Manjourian troops was sent to dislodge him. They were numerous enough to sweep him and his followers into the Amoor, but his prowess had already made an impression on the minds of the Celestials, and they behaved like curs, barking at the lion at bay, but taking especial care to keep out of the reach of his teeth. When the winter set in he was left in peace, and his enemies retired to their cantonments to brood over their disappointment.

After their departure Khabaroff set about finishing his works, and did everything he could to render his position impregnable, as he was well aware that a large army would return in the spring. Another difficulty beset him, far more to be dreaded than Chinese soldiers, and that was the want of supplies. Fish was abundant in the Amoor, and game could be obtained in the mountains, but he required more than these to enable him to stand a siege, and corn for bread could only be procured from the foe. Khabaroff had overcome too many obstacles to permit this to daunt him, and his men were ready to go wherever he led.

Before the "braves" were established in their winter quarters, the commander of the fort, with a strong party, ascended the Oussoure and passed several of their towns. This was not his first voyage up the river, for he had previously ascended far beyond the Nora, and knew all their positions. Having reached a depôt, the boats were run in, and he made an attack on the place so sudden and desperate that the Manjourians were taken by surprise and driven out. With a few of his picked men, he kept in check a strong body of Chinese soldiers, while others helped themselves to what they wanted. When this was accomplished he retreated, sprung into the boats, and pushed out into the river without the slightest loss. It was not so with his opponents, for every shot that had been fired had been fatal, and the rifles of Khabaroff's Cossack hunters became the terror of the whole Chinese army.

As the party descended the river it was soon obvious that an alarm had been spread, and that they would have to run the gauntlet in passing the towns where Manjourian troops were stationed. On drawing near the first, the commander saw a line of boats filled with men pushing out into the river to cut him off. A strong current and a breeze was in his favour; they carried him rapidly down, and he ordered his men not to fire till they were near the enemy, then to sweep the two nearest boats, and the current would take them past in the confusion. His plan was successful, and his boats cut through the line—but this time his men did not escape unscathed, several being wounded; wind and current, however, soon carried them out of danger from Chinese missiles, while the Cossack rifles speedily checked any daring spirits that approached too near. The other towns were passed in the night, and in little more than a week, Khabaroff had provisioned his garrison at the cost of his enemies. Such was the daring of this man that his fame among the people was like that of Nelson among English sailors. The Cossacks of the Argoun have many traditions concerning him, and his name is ever associated with victory.

Khabaroff and his band were not idle during the winter, and as large game was abundant in the Khouk-tcher-Khoorene there was no lack of provisions. He had also secured some Toungouz in his service, who visited the Manjour towns and informed him of the preparations that were there being made for a siege. A vast armament was coming to assail them, under the command of two distinguished Manjourian officers, who had promised to kill or capture every man; nevertheless, no one appeared alarmed. All had confidence in their leader, and calmly waited the event, without even discontinuing their hunting excursions.

At length the winter passed and spring returned, when the spies announced the movement of the Chinese troops; and early in April a great body of men took up a position before the fort. Before hostilities commenced the generals summoned the garrison to surrender, and promised that all the men should be escorted to the frontier, but their commander they demanded as a prisoner. This was answered with a shout of defiance, and an invitation to come and take him.

The besiegers commenced throwing up batteries, but were not permitted to accomplish this in quiet. Khabaroff opened on them with his few small guns, while the Cossacks picked off the men with their rifles whenever they could get within range, and many fell, with little loss to the garrison. Although retarded in their operations, the loss of men was of little moment to the Chinese commanders, and by the aid of the numbers at their disposal the works advanced rapidly. It was not many days before they replied to the Russian guns with five times the number. Had they been as well served and pointed, the affair would soon have been ended. As it was, each day robbed Khabaroff of one or more of his men, while the loss to the enemy was considerable. Three weeks had passed, the bombardment still continued, and reinforcements were constantly arriving at the Chinese camp; but though the Cossacks made several sorties, inflicting great losses on their enemies, no great advantage was gained.

Khabaroff became aware that with his limited resources it was impossible to drive away his numerous assailants. Beside which, his ammunition was so reduced that he could no longer use his guns, and his enemies were only kept at bay by his rifles. After standing this unequal siege for a month, and learning from his spies that a fleet of boats was approaching, he decided to retreat. Before, however, abandoning his position, he determined to give them one more lesson, as a parting remembrance. He proposed to burn the Chinese camp, if half a dozen of his Cossacks would volunteer to accompany him. This call was instantly responded to by all, but the men coupled it with a condition that their commander should not be permitted to join in the expedition; and so eager were they to go on this dangerous errand, that the fort would have been deserted.

Khabaroff selected six men and one of his officers, and a boat's crew was ordered to row them to a ravine in the rocks about half a mile off, by which they could approach the rear of the enemy's camp. After giving them time to reach within a short distance of the tents, he ordered the guns to open on the Chinese forts, and personally led a sortie into the enemy's lines, which quickly threw the whole army into confusion. This secured the success of the expedition, and very soon the tents were seen in flames at several different points. The sudden attack and conflagration so bewildered the Chinese that the little party retreated to the boat unmolested, and reached the fort in safety, though some of the other men were wounded in the sortie.

The camp continued burning for some time before it could be extinguished, and in the morning Khabaroff had the satisfaction of seeing half of it destroyed. At an early hour the boats were loaded with the remaining stores, and only a few sentinels remained at their posts; when all was ready these were withdrawn, and the men sent down the cliffs to the boats. Their commander remained in the fort, and was the last to descend. Directly he stepped on board the oars were vigorously used, and they were soon out of reach of their enemies. The Chinese at last discovered that the fort was deserted, but Khabaroff and his companions had eluded their vengeance and escaped to Albazin. After his retreat the enemy demolished the fort, and the Chinese have remained in undisturbed possession for more than 200 years; but during this long period the daring acts of this Cossack leader have not been forgotten, for tradition has handed down his name to the present race.

The Oussoure is one of the great affluents of the Amoor; its source is in the lake Khin-kai, and its course more than 400 miles. The Noro and Mouren, which fall into the Oussoure on the west, are large rivers, and numerous affluents bring their waters from the mountains to the east to swell its flood. In some parts this runs through sandy plains; and here, in exactly the same parallel of latitude as on the Kirghis steppes, near 4,000 miles to the westward, the tortoise rears her young in the beds of warm sand.

The mouth is about a mile in width, and on its western bank there are numerous lakes, most probably the remains of spring inundations. This is a low and fenny district, extending far to the south; the high reeds and rank grass which it produces are suggestive of ague. On the opposite side of the river the country assumes a very different aspect; the Khouk-tcher-Khoorene Mountains are seen rising from the water, in some places abrupt, in others in long wooded slopes, terminating in craggy summits. Here the tiger and the leopard rule, but the time is approaching when Russian colonists will dispute their right, and either kill or drive them into other regions. In addition to the prospect of agricultural riches to be acquired here, mineral wealth is to be obtained; and I do not believe that anything could stop the adventurous spirits of this age in their search after gold.

A little below the Oussoure is the Toungouz settlement of Tourme, and not far off is a village containing a variety of these migratory races. There are to be found Manjour officers and soldiers, Touzemtz, Toungouz, and some of the Goldi race, congregated by mercantile interests, each having something to exchange. These people obtain great quantities of sable skins, as the animals are numerous in the district. They also procure the tortoise-shells from the banks of the Noro and other parts of the valley of the Oussoure. The villages and settlements are surrounded by gardens, where excellent vegetables are grown, and there can be no doubt as to the successful cultivation of European varieties. The maple, the lime, and the oak thrive, and wheat is also grown.

A Goldi.

Tourme and several other villages are dotted in small valleys at the foot of Khouk-tcher-Khoorene, near its slopes and abrupt faces, which run down to the Amoor. Most of these are covered with forest, and numerous deep ravines have been cut in the mountains by torrents that keep up a constant roar. In many of the gorges the vegetation has a most luxuriant character, and it is among these thick and tangled masses that the tiger makes his lair. Here, again, neither the Manjourian officers nor the people are able to keep horses; they speedily become food for these feline ravagers. Bears and foxes are also numerous, and their skins are articles of barter.

There are many villages on the right bank of the southern branch of the Amoor, the bed of the river being many miles to the north, and enclosing an enormous island, round which the branch makes a considerable curve to the northward, and meets the great stream at the rocks of Beree. These are cliffs which run down into the water; the whole body of the Great Amoor is poured at a right angle against them, and here the two streams unite. The result is a tremendous eddy that causes this part of the river to whirl and boil up like waves breaking on a rocky shore. The Toungouz have built a village, whence they have this vast mass of surging water constantly in view.

The rocky heights of Beree extend for a long distance; in some parts they recede from the river and become less abrupt, and these places are thickly covered with trees. Further down is Khol-Yakee, where the sandstone formation is heaved up in enormous masses that rise perpendicularly out of the flood; in other parts huge blocks have fallen from above and lie scattered on the shore. Beyond them the shore falls into a broad valley, in which runs the river Daou-sa-man, and here the country is inhabited by Goldi and Toungouz. Many of their villages are placed in lovely and romantic spots. These semi-civilised people show great taste and judgment in the selection of a site for their dwellings. Their positions are not the effect of accident, as I have seen numerous instances of their sacrificing convenience for picturesque effect.

Beyond these pretty villages the shore continues sloping

at a moderate elevation for a long distance, and the country beyond is covered with fine timber. In one of its open glades another village appeared, and some ten miles further are the sandstone cliffs of Kirmis-Khon-Konee. Afterwards the mountains recede on each side, and a broad valley opens out, through which the Amoor winds its course, having many islands sprinkled over a surface more than two miles in width.

Numerous settlements are dotted down on the banks of the Amoor in this region; some are nestling at the edge of a dark forest, and look gay with their gardens around them. Others are placed under clumps of trees on the verge of great tracts of pasture land that extend far into the interior. If industrious colonists are sent here they will find it better and much easier to raise their crops than in the far west in America, where it takes years to clear even a small space;—pastures are already formed to their hands, where thousands of cattle would find food.

Like the inhabitants of the western plains of Asia, these people are attracted by gay colours; their fondness for them carries them in extravagance beyond my friends the Kirghis, who love to clothe their persons in "bright array," whereas the inhabitants of the Amoor paint all their household goods and portions of their dwellings with the most vivid tints; and, like the Chinese, possess an excellent knowledge of the harmony of colours.

Sakha-tche is a bold mass of basaltic rocks that forms a fine promontory on one side of the Bay of Gas-si-en-ga. The Amoor spreads at this point to a great width. A slightly undulating country stretches out to the north, and the summits of a mountain chain are seen in the distance. Many small and some large islands have been formed in this part of the river; several are covered with trees, and inhabited by a few Toungouz, and others by Goldi. They seem quite cut off from the world, and live on fish, with which Providence has bountifully stored this mighty stream. By a ramble in the forest on either shore they can procure game, and their gardens grow sufficient vegetables for all their wants, while fur-bearing animals are so numerous as to render it easy to obtain valuable skins; and thus they have everything around them to render life comfortable. Unfortunately, a bane which is the ruin of thousands in civilised life, finds its way to these solitary spots, and brings misery into their abodes.

The Chinese trader penetrates to every inhabited spot, with tea and various articles of clothing, but the greatest portion of his cargo is brandy, and he here, as elsewhere, soon strips the people of their valuable skins for one-tenth part of their value, paid in this most disagreeable composition. His customers are then compelled to make over to him a portion of the next year's produce to procure the few necessaries they require, which are only to be obtained at an enormous price. These scoundrels become rich by the demoralisation and ruin they produce.

Opposite to one of the large islands are the high volcanic cliffs of Saen-doo; they jut far into the river, and stand out of the water like gigantic castles, quite in keeping with the vast flood at their feet. Several miles beyond this is another volcanic mass, Mo-dad-ze, a picturesque group of rocks rising to a great height, with deep recesses at intervals, which give the appearance of towers; the tops of some are split into turrets and pinnacles, that when viewed at a distance, assume the character of an enormous Gothic structure. In some of the recesses clumps of elm and pine trees are growing, while in other parts birch and ash have taken root on the terraces, and their graceful foliage is seen waving in the breeze.

This part of the Amoor, for a space of from forty to fifty miles, is not surpassed by any river scenery. Its great breadth, the numerous islands that seem floating on its surface, and the high cliffs that rise out of its bed, produce a series of grand and constantly changing scenes. Ouk-se-me is one of the last; it stands at the lower end of this vast line of crags, rising like a wall from the water to the height of 150 feet, and extends more than a mile in

Above Ouk-se-me.

length. Deep ravines have been cut in the mass by torrents which come tumbling down. They can only be heard, as groups of elm, ash, and birch screen their falling streams, while the pine, aspen, and other trees crown the summit.

After passing Ouk-se-me the islands disappear, and the Amoor rolls on in one great stream; a broad valley has taken the place of the rocky cliffs, which, after a few miles, extends into a great plain. The plain spreads till both water and land are lost in haze on the horizon; but before reaching the village of Tcher-e-me the Amoor is again divided into two great branches, of which one turns a little more to the north, and leaves a long and broad island between them. Near the junction of these two arms stands Tcher-e-me, surrounded with bushes and willows. It is a village of Toungouz: on an island nearly opposite is another village, and a Manjourian merchant from a town on the Soungaria has an establishment here. He carries on a considerable trade, being paid for his merchandise in skins.

About twenty miles below Tcher-e-me the Amoor expands to about six miles in width, and here are numerous islands, some inhabited by Goldi. Further down is the Doon-doon; it has its source in the mountains to the south-east, and after a course of near 400 miles falls into the Amoor on the right bank. Near this place are many Goldians and Touzemtz, and a considerable trade in skins is carried on with the Chinese, who arrive with their well-laden boats in the early part of summer, and then commence the barter of sable skins for brandy. These fairs are not of long duration, for when the men become intoxicated the barter goes on rapidly. The crafty traders in a few days transfer all their valuables to the boats, when they sail away to plunder other settlements in the same manner, and leave their deluded victims to misery.

It is to be hoped that Russia will introduce a better system by limiting the supply of wodky, and on no account permit her traders to make that the principal article of exchange. So long as the Chinese have possession of the Soungaria, no restriction on the Russian side will avail; a whole army of Cossacks would not be able to check the introduction of the demoralising liquid. That river is the great highway into the eastern provinces of the Chinese empire; by it every article travels to supply the wants of the whole region of the Amoor and the Oussoure. Both the Soungaria and the Oussoure have been explored—the first step towards occupation—and I hope, ere long, to hear that my friend General Korsakoff has established his Cossacks from Dalai-noor to the sources of the Soungaria. When this is accomplished, a new and a better era will commence for the Daourians and all the people on the Amoor.

About thirty miles below the river Doon-doon the cliffs of Doloe commence: they are rocks of igneous origin, and extend over a distance of more than thirty miles. At this part the Amoor opens out to a great width, and a large bay sweeps past the upper end of the cliffs, in which there are several islands. The rocks of Doloe are neither abrupt nor of great elevation, except in a few places, where they form headlands and project into the water; all the others are thickly covered with timber. Sometimes a flat shore is formed at the foot of the rocks, and on one of these stands the large Goldi village of Doloe. A short distance further is another, called Sou-zoo.

The Amoor is divided again by several large islands, bearing willows and a few trees; a flat shore stretches along, and extends up to the foot of the Giong Mountains. This chain has no great elevation, it is covered with timber to its summit, and continues down the left bank, enclosing the Amoor in a narrow valley, but without curtailing its width. Tigers and leopards are said to be numerous in the Giong chain, and as game and large animals abound in the district, they find plenty of food, as well as an almost impenetrable cover, from which it is impossible to dislodge them; they not unfrequently attack the people.

On a beautiful spot, where an open glade runs up towards the mountains, the Touzemtz have placed their village Daeso. It seems to have been erected in this situation solely to save their neighbours the tigers a long walk in search of prey, for by all accounts they never fail to make a feast on any unfortunate person who wanders even a short distance into their domain.

Further down the Tchol-yat-se Mountains close in on the Amoor, and stretch far to the northward along its course. The Nootch-Koutch is a rapid torrent that enters the Amoor through a great chasm in the mountains. High precipices of hornblende rise up on the shore, forming a magnificent portal through which the foaming water rushes, while luxuriant vegetation is growing at their base. A few miles beyond the mouth of this torrent the Amoor is divided into several streams, and between two is the island Kerella.

At this part some of the spurs of the Tchol-yat-se run quite down to the river and form several rocky headlands, and all the arms of the Amoor become united into one great stream that rolls on without interruption till it strikes against the bold rocky promontory of Sar-koo, from which it is thrown back in sheets of white foam. A little beyond the Sar-koo is the An-gooa, and then comes another series of cliffs that terminate in a small headland rising from the shore. A Manjourian merchant has formed an establishment here, and holds a fair in the spring, when the sable hunters come and exchange their furs. There are several islands on this part of the river, and immediately opposite, on the left rises the mountain Ou-ot-ze-arl, or "Moung-goo-Khong-ko" (silver mountain).

In all ages and countries, wherever the precious metals have been found, the position, it is said, has been guarded by spirits, whose only duty was to prevent mortals procuring even a small portion of the treasure. In Europe these superstitions have long lost their power. In South America they still exist, and on the banks of the Amoor they are implicitly believed.

Moung-goo-Khong-ko is represented by the natives as one

of those mysterious mountains where a host of spirits watch over its mineral riches, which they represent to be unbounded. They relate traditions of former races who perished in their attempts to elude the spectral guardians and snatch only a handful of the precious metal; and aver that whoever approaches the spot will be shrouded in a fearful storm, from which it is impossible to escape, when the culprits will be seized and hurled into an unfathomable abyss in the centre of the mountain. They also relate stories of a more recent period, handed down from their grandfathers, telling of bands of men who, being driven to desperation, rushed to the mountain determined to possess some of its wealth, but that thunderings were heard so terrible that several ran away in the greatest alarm; the rest, more daring, proceeded, but the thunder became more fearful, shaking the mountains and heaving up the water in the Amoor: after which, they say, it became calm, but not one of these reckless adventurers was ever again seen.

A few years ago, when the expedition descended the Amoor, two mining engineers and half-a-dozen Cossacks dared the anger of these dangerous spirits, though warned by more tales of horror than I have space or inclination to relate. No one could be induced to bear them company or guide them to the spot, and when they departed they were looked upon as men doomed to a terrible death. In a few days they returned, having destroyed two illusions of the people by proving — first, that no spirits were there; and, secondly, that there was no treasure to guard. The bright metallic veins seen in the rocks, that had given rise to this terrible tradition, were arsenic.

CHAP. XIX.

THE LOWER AMOOR.

The Bokee Mountains rise on the right of the Amoor, extending northward for more than ten miles, and then the slopes descend to a plain that stretches out to a great distance. The Amoor is more than six miles in width at this point, and when the whole stream is seen running onward during the spring floods, with thousands of trees floating on its surface, it shows what vast tracts of forest are uprooted every year. On the left shore the country rises gradually towards a mountain chain that is visible far in the distance. Islands become more frequent in this broad channel, on some of which the Goldi have their villages.

Further down a small mountain chain descends to the river on the left side, and then turns to the westward, extending far up toward the sources of the Gorina. The river Elbean-bera has its rise in this chain, and here it is expected that mineral treasures will be found. A little beyond this, on the right side of the Amoor, the Ong-mee-Khang-koo Cliffs commence, and continue for a great many miles. Sometimes these rocks rise from the water, in other places they recede, leaving broad spaces of flat shore covered with clumps of trees and a luxuriant vegetation. On one of these secluded spots is the village of Ong-mee: the dwellings are shaded by clumps of splendid trees, while picturesque rocks form a background to a beautiful rural scene.

At a considerable distance below the village the rocky

island of Omou-an rises out of the water, covered with trees and plants—in most parts the rocks are quite perpendicular. A little beyond is the Goldi village of Kho-da-le, standing on a slope above. Shortly after passing it the shore presents a long line of igneous cliffs, and on the opposite side of the river is the village of Sam-bae. The people on this part of the Amoor are mostly Goldis, and of the Shaman creed, and the priests possess great power over them.

The Amoor becomes much narrower where it flows between the high igneous shores, that extend a distance

A Group of Goldi Children.

of nearly one hundred miles. Islands are frequent even here, where the stream is more confined, and numbers of Goldi villages are found on both shores. The country is covered with forest as far as the eye can reach. Tigers and panthers are very numerous, and they often visit the villages searching for prey. One of the latter, Mil-ke, stands on a beautiful spot surrounded with fine cedar and other trees. The Amoor becomes still narrower till it reaches the village of Djong-me. Although there are many inhabitants along the shores in this district, and the settlements numerous, there is space for one hundred times the population, and the country is exceedingly rich in fur-bearing animals.

Shortly after passing Djong-me the land on the right bank of the Amoor becomes better adapted for agriculture; meadow stretches along the shore, and broad tracts of pasture are seen in the distance. The change is made immediately obvious by the number of villages that are scattered about, and almost invariably beautiful situations have been chosen. Nature has been exceedingly bountiful in this region, and has bestowed on the people some of her most valuable gifts. Magnificent forests contain timber suited for every purpose, oak for ship-building, with elm, birch, and pine for domestic purposes. She has stocked these vast forests with animals—many suited for the food of man, while others produce furs of great value, for which he can always find a market; and all multiply around him without giving him a moment's care.

She has provided rich pastures for domestic animals, and the luxuriant vegetation which springs up everywhere shows that man need only scatter the seed into the earth, to ensure an abundant harvest, while the Amoor and its affluents afford an inexhaustible supply of various kinds of fish.

Again the Amoor expands in width, and numerous islands appear as it approaches one of its great affluents, the Goreena, which enters on the left side by two mouths, that pour a great body of water into this vast drain of Asia. The Goreena, it is supposed, has its source far to the west in a part of the Khingan Mountains, but it has not been explored by the Cossacks further than about fifty miles from its mouth. The Goldi and Toungouz ascend this valley on hunting expeditions.

In several of the Goldi villages near the mouth of this river bears and eagles are domesticated; that is, the former are accommodated in separate apartments, formed like a penfold, with wooden palings secured at the top, and the latter are sometimes in cages, but are usually chained to a stump. The bear is held in great veneration by these people, who bestow much care upon him; his dwelling is kept clean, and he is well fed; in short, it may be said that he leads the life of a gentleman, living in luxury, and receiving every attention. Unfortunately for Bruin, he finds out to his cost that a selfish motive has produced all this attention, and procured for him the delicious fruits with which his palate has been pampered. Notwithstanding the endearing epithets of son and brother, he is at last removed from his room, paraded about with marked consideration, and then barbarously murdered in the presence of all his friends; and what is still worse, they finish by showing themselves cannibals, and feast on the body of him whom they constantly addressed as their nearest relative. This is a sacrifice made on their great festivals.

The natives here have also a custom which I found prevailing in other parts of Asia among the Kalmucks, some tribes of the Kalkas, and the Toungouz, of providing their deceased brother with all the tools and implements necessary to enable him to carry on his trade or occupation in the land of ghosts. If this duty be neglected, they believe that his spirit wanders for ever through dark and dismal forests, without finding a place of rest. The custom varies among different people, but all tend to the same end. For instance, the Kirghis chief has his favourite horses buried with him, that he may not be compelled to walk in his ghostly state, — a thing he abhors when living. The Kalmuck and Kalkas have their weapons, clothes, and implements placed in their graves, that they may appear suitably apparelled before their friends, and able to engage in their ordinary pursuits. But the Toungouz races have similar articles placed on their grave, to be ready for service the moment they awake from what they consider to be their temporary repose.

The Goldi and some other tribes have a slight knowledge

of astronomy, which I believe is common to the Asiatic races. The Kirghis and Kalkas are obliged to know the stars, for they are their only guides through many a dark and dreary night, when riding over the vast plains.

A Goldi Man and Woman.

Nearly opposite the mouth of the Goreena is the river Belgo-Kha-van-e-bera; Tchieng-ka, and some other large villages, were on its bank. Here the Goldi and Mangoon races begin to mix. Even in this region, so far removed from civilisation and refinement, a jeweller finds occupation, the men wearing rings of iron, copper, and silver on their thumbs and fingers, while a Goldi village belle hangs an ornament from her nose, to give greater effect to her charms.

Whatever may be the opinion of my fair readers as to

her personal appearance, I can assure them that the most favoured of them arrayed in all the splendour necessary for a Court presentation, does not regard herself with half the satisfaction the Goldian belle feels when beholding her nasal ornament and large ear-rings. To the portrait of her presented on the opposite page, is added that of a Goldi exquisite, bearing a pipe of a new pattern.

The Goreena and Se-du-bera are considered by Russian authorities to mark the division between the Middle and Lower Amoor. With this the local geological change from igneous rocks to sandstone has nothing to do; but the change that takes place in the flora and fauna is deemed sufficient to establish a line of demarcation between the two regions.

A short distance below the Goreena the mountains recede and form a deep crescent, with a flat shore covered with rich vegetation, where stands the settlement of Ka-our-me, also containing a mixed population of the two races. Six miles further down is the village of Goolda, occupied by the Mangoons. Looking across the Amoor to the mouth of the Goreena, a mountain chain is seen branching to the north and the west, while the Amoor is girded on both sides with hills, and is in most parts covered with wood. From this point several islands are visible, and the river extends to a great width till it reaches the Onee, which falls into it on the right bank; a little beyond is the Mangoon village of Tchoue-tcha. A flat shore stretches along for many miles, containing a numerous population, all of whom are engaged in hunting and fishing.

The Mangoons, like the Goldi, are descendants from the Toungouz race, retaining their language and religion. The Shaman is all-powerful with them, and nothing of importance is undertaken without consulting him. Besides being the spiritual adviser, he is the family physician, and by the influence which he acquires in the two characters, he moulds the people to his will, and directs many of their actions. No hunting expeditions are planned without him, and, like all other good priests, he has his tithes.

The Mangoons have now frequent intercourse with the Cossacks at their posts, and the Russians at their settlements. Many have adopted the costume of their new neighbours instead of their fish-skin coverings, and have already begun to speak the Russian language. The example of these industrious colonists will show them the advantage of agricultural pursuits. The Mangoons are a highly imitative race; even in their present rude state they cultivate the fine arts, and apply their genius in decorating their clothing. Some of their articles of dress are beautiful; while their caps and hats, of birch bark, are graceful in form and chastely ornamented. Many of the patterns they design and work would throw into the shade much of the stiff and unmeaning decoration invented in classic Greece. Nor do I think they will be slow in adopting a better mode of constructing their dwellings. Russian stoves and glass windows will take the place of their ineffective heating apparatus and of the fish-skin covering for their windows.

Such improvements will tend to establish and spread the power of Russia in these regions. If her officers govern the people with justice, few families will remain on the Manjourian side of the river to endure cruelty and oppression. Nor will it be long before the Mandarin and his satellites will be made to beat a retreat towards the great wall.

Descending the river towards Addee-Adze, several moderately high summits are seen on both banks. The right is not much elevated above the water; in some parts it is covered with fine timber, and in others extensive tracts of pasture seem to stretch up to the lower slopes of the Peueso Mountains. Many of the summits in this chain rise into rocky peaks, while the ridges beneath are covered with a thick forest. The left bank is formed by rocks rising perpendicular from the water. In some places they recede, and a narrow flat shore extends along, which is occupied by Mangoon dwellings.

Beyond Addee-Adze the country assumes another aspect. The mountains have become bare and bleak; narrow rocky valleys and ravines extend from the Amoor far up among the hills, and numerous torrents pour into the river. Clumps of birch and picta grow in the rocky glens, and scattered groups are visible on the distant slope; while cliffs of slate on each side bound the great stream, whose course at this part is uninterrupted. No islands are visible, and the vast flood runs smoothly along till it reaches the Mangoon settlements of Tasch-e-go and Poso. After this it increases in width; the mountains recede, leaving flat shores of considerable extent; and several small villages appear. Not far beyond is the settlement of Deren.

A few years ago the people in this neighbourhood committed a most atrocious act. Two Catholic missionaries, De la Bruniere and Venault, after a residence of some years in different parts of China, had found their way into Manjouria. They visited many of the towns in this portion of the Celestial Empire, and exercised their vocation whereever there was an opportunity of making converts. It is said that among the settlers on the upper part of the Oussoure they were successful, and remained with their proselytes some time. From the Manjourian merchants they acquired information about the different tribes inhabiting the banks of the Amoor, and learned that the whole population were Shaman.

Intent on attacking Shamanism in its stronghold, they made their way down the Oussoure, and exercised their calling at all the towns on their route, with what success I cannot say, as most of the people are followers of Confucius. They, however, arrived at one of the towns on the lower part of the river in the autumn of 1845; too late to proceed further, therefore here they spent the winter.

In the following spring, when the ice broke up, they prepared to continue their journey, and arranged with some Manjour merchants for a passage in their boats as far as the villages of the Goldi. After a voyage of several days they reached the tribe, who received them hospitably; and here their guides left them. Up to this period all is certainty, but with regard to their subsequent proceedings this is by no means the case.

The Goldi admit that the strangers visited them in 1846, and remained for a considerable period, travelling from one village to another, disputing with their Shamans, and assuring them that the god whom their priest called upon in his song could neither hear nor answer his prayer, and that he had no power to do them good or evil. The missionaries, it appeared, had also stated that their God created the world; that without him not only the sun would not shine, but that it would be constant winter and darkness. Also that Shaitan had been chained deep in the earth, whence he could never reappear, not even at the call of the Shaman. These were startling assurances; they astonished the people, but did not convince them—the Shaman and his sorcery had too strong a hold on their minds.

Having laboured hard, but in vain, the good fathers continued their journey, and at length reached the Mangoons, whom they also tried to convert. They travelled from village to village, using every argument at their disposal to shake the belief of the people in the power of the Shaman, which so enraged the priests that their position became critical. The Mangoons are a quiet, inoffensive race, and could not easily be roused to acts of violence. Notwithstanding the threats of the priests, and the fear they inspired, these brave men did not relax in what they deemed a duty; they were, however, forced to leave the Mangoons and resume their labours in another direction.

De la Bruniere and his companion entered the country of the Gelyaks, among whom Shamanism is more deeply rooted than in any other race in Asia. In short, they are fanatics of the deepest cast, and constantly practise sorcery. Here is the seat of the Arch-Shaman, whose priests delude the people by their pretended enchantments and jugglery, and over their minds exert unlimited sway.

Nevertheless the missionaries were not daunted; they commenced their labours with energy, and exposed the impious tricks of the high-priests of Satan, which so roused the malignant feelings of the latter that they never rested till they had induced their dupes to put the strangers to death. The Gelyaks admit that this diabolical murder was perpetrated among their tribes, at the instigation of the Shaman.

A little below Deren the Amoor is divided by an island, on which there is a Mangoon settlement. Further on the banks are formed by a series of rocky declivities consisting of aphanite, with stunted trees and shrubs growing in the clefts. In many parts deep ravines intersect these stony masses, and some are filled with trees. About eight or ten miles below, the rocks recede on each side, and the Amoor opens out into a broad expanse that extends as far as Kil-ban. From here the scenery changes, and the river narrows to about a mile in width, with high cliffs rising on each shore, in many parts thickly covered with pine and birch trees.

It retains the same character till it reaches the settlement of Polsia, when islands again appear, and not far from this is Dar-ach-ta. From this point it makes a turn to the east and approaches a mountain chain seen in that direction; a spur from which extends down to the river and forms a fine rocky headland, that projects out into the water. This is exposed to the full force of the current, causing the waves to recoil and form a dangerous whirlpool. As it cannot be approached without risk in a small boat, the natives take care to give it a wide berth. In a sheltered nook looking down upon this turmoil of water, the Mangoons have built a village; its picturesque position being apparently the only inducement for selecting the site.

From this place the valley of the Amoor expands, and mountain chains are visible on each side. Some of the summits are of considerable elevation, and terminate in rugged crags, while beneath the ridges are covered with forests. Flat shores extend for a long distance, across

A Group of Mangoon Children.

which the river Nu-re-me winds its course, and enters the Amoor on its right bank. Beyond is the village of Dzare, snugly placed in a sheltered nook overtopped by pine trees, each house having a garden.

After passing Dzare, the Amoor is divided into two great branches and several small channels. One of the large streams turns to the right, and passes the village of Gobnee; a few miles further is the entrance to the lake of Kezee. On the lower side, and at a short distance from the outlet, is Mariensk post, one of the most important stations that Russia has planted on the Amoor. A battery has been erected that commands both the river and the entrance to this inland port, and a town is rapidly rising.

The entrance from the Amoor is about one third of a mile in width, but several small islands interrupt the passage, rendering the navigation difficult; a steam-tug will, however, obviate this.

The lake is about twenty-seven miles long, and its greatest width is three miles, but it becomes considerably narrower as it extends to the eastward. A chain of mountains, which attain a considerable elevation, runs along its southern shore, and terminates on Castries Bay. The Aï has its source in this chain, and after a course of near 200 miles, pours a considerable body of water into the lake. A small chain of hills extends along the north side, and numerous minor streams flow into the lake on both shores. Only twenty miles of high land intervene between the eastern end of the Kezee lake and the Gulf of Tartary.

A channel through these hills would be invaluable to Russia, and save the great expense that must be incurred by constructing a railway from Mariensk to Castries Bay. The distance between the two points is about fifty-three miles, and over a difficult country. As neither labour nor materials for such an undertaking can be procured here, or even from Siberia, the cost of making a single line of iron-way will far exceed that of any line that has yet been constructed in Russia; nor is commerce sufficiently developed in this new acquisition to pay by its transit one-hundredth part of the expense of working it. The time, however, must come when the locomotive will be seen sending out its puffs of steam in this remote part of Asia.

A short distance below Mariensk the Amoor takes a course nearly due north, and contains many islands. Both shores are flat, but hills appear in the distance on each side. Further down they approach nearer, forming the valley of the Amoor, which is thickly covered with a forest of pines and birch. But little change takes place in the aspect of the country for a long distance, except that the hills become a little more abrupt, while many small valleys branch to the right and left, in which the Mangoons have formed settlements.

About 100 miles below Mariensk is the village of Pul, the Nijne-Novgorod of these regions, where the hunters and traders assemble from all quarters. Toungouz hunters from the Zeya and the Yablonoi bring the produce of their rifles. Gelyaks from the shore of the Sea of Okhotsk attend

Gelyaks.

with their furs, and the Mangoons, with their neighbours, the Goldi, bring skins from the Oussoure and Goreena. Manjour merchants from the Soungaria meet them with wares from China, and Japanese come to barter their goods with the hunters for the produce of their forests. Such an assemblage can only be collected on this spot, where curious and highly-characteristic scenes take place between the daring hunter and the crafty Manjour and Japanese.*

At one of these singular gatherings, in 1841, men of a different race appeared, carrying skins like other hunters, but their features and language showed the Asiatics that they were not descended from any of their tribes. They had, however, proved themselves good woodsmen, had gained the esteem of the Toungouz, among whom they had been living, and were introduced as belonging to the brotherhood.

In the summer of 1839 three Polish exiles disappeared from the neighbourhood of Nertchinsk; a strict search was made in every direction, but no clue was found by which they could be traced. A few of their comrades alone knew their plans and the direction they had taken, which was down the Amoor. Escapes were not uncommon in this district, notwithstanding the vigilance of the guards, and a reward offered to the Manjours for every prisoner they found beyond their frontier. Many fugitives were brought back and severely punished, as an example to their comrades.

The Poles were officers who had served in the wars, and knew that a flogging and hard labour in the mines would be their fate if caught; and their comrades were well assured that no force of the Manjourians would ever take them alive when once they had got across the frontiers. It has since been ascertained that these men provided themselves with rifles and descended the Amoor as far as the Onon, where they joined a party of Toungouz hunters, whom they accompanied on an expedition to the sources of the Selindja. By a display of courage and intelligence they succeeded in establishing a mutual friendship between these simple people and themselves, and spent two winters in their dwellings. In the autumn of 1841 they went with their friends to Pul; after the fair the exiles bade them adieu, and proceeded with the Japanese traders to the island of Saghalien, where one of them died. The others made their way to the eastern coast, and after a stay of some months had the satisfaction of seeing a ship anchor off the coast, bearing a flag with the stars and stripes. A boat's crew, with the captain, landed to obtain provisions, and were astonished at being addressed in English by one of the exiles, who explained his position, and requested a passage to any place where he and his comrade might find a ship for Europe.

The kind-hearted seaman instantly consented to take them on board and land them in America if no better opportunity offered of sending them to Europe; but he informed them that he was an American whaler, and as his ship had not her full cargo, that they would probably be delayed some months on the voyage. He kept his word; and when he put them on shore made known their history to his countrymen, which excited both their sympathy and generosity.

Ten years afterwards one of them reached Paris, and succeeded in making known his escape to his unfortunate comrades in Siberia, from one of whom I obtained the particulars.

From Pul to Michaeloffsk the country retains much of the same character, but the river becomes narrower, and attains a depth of 115 feet. Several streams fall into it both on the right and left shores. About twenty miles lower down the Omogun falls into the river on the left side, and this is the great affluent of the Lower Amoor. It has its source in the Khingan chain, and its course is about 450 miles. Beyond this the river becomes wider, and makes a great curve to the north-west; after passing Tebak, when within a short distance of Lake Orel, it turns suddenly to the south-east, and extends to more than two miles in width, with many islands dotted over its bed. Here there are numerous Gelyak villages, inhabited by people said to be the least civilised on the Amoor.

From Tebak high mountains rise on both sides the river, the banks are frequently formed by rugged cliffs, and the country is thickly covered with timber. After passing the settlement of Vait, all the branches of the Amoor are united in one stream near two miles in width, and varying from 150 feet to 200 feet in depth. This broad tide rolls on to Nicholaiofsk, the great defence of the Amoor. These works have been designed and constructed under the superintendence of eminent engineers, and their armament would speedily stop any ships that attempted to enter, while the fleet would remain safely moored higher up the stream.

The long winter here is a great detriment, and the place can never become a first-rate commercial port, as the ships will always be obliged to leave early. Frost approaches at the end of October or the first few days in November, and seals up the river, which for six long months is one vast sheet of ice, and during a greater part of the seventh it is impossible for vessels to move from their moorings on account of the floating masses. So that five months is the only period during the year when this part of the Amoor can be used for commercial purposes. Bad as it is for ships to be frozen in at Cronstadt, it would be much worse at Nicholaiofsk; and this will ever remain a serious disadvantage, and check the development of the various resources of the country.

Martello towers are built on Cape Tebak and Cape Pronge, to defend the mouth of the river; they would not be easy to pass; and similar towers have been raised on the coast between Cape Pronge and Castries Bay, at every point best suited for defence.

The latter will ultimately be the port of the Amoor. It is only for three months in the winter that vessels would be sealed up here, even if caught in the ice; a circumstance that would rarely happen, as sailing a degree or two south would take the ship into a more genial clime.

I have many friends among the numerous Russian settlers who have left their homes and service in Europe to pitch their tents in the country between Pronge and Castries Bay: I sincerely wish them success, and feel assured that they will establish a hardy and industrious race here, that must ultimately play a great part in these regions.

Both sides of this Strait will before long be peopled by Russians, and the Island of Saghalien be added to their empire. The latter contains valuable beds of coal, whence Russia can draw supplies for either a steam navy or for industrial purposes; it will also give her splendid harbours in the Pacific, and leave her fleets free for operations throughout every part of the year.

APPENDIX.

MAMMALIA

IN

THE VALLEY OF THE AMOOR.

A Group of Hunting Dogs.

UPPER AMOOR.

ARVICOLA	rutila	
CERVUS	Alces	Elk.
	Capreolus	Roebuck.
	Elephus	Stag.
CANIS	Lupus	Wolf.
	Vulpes	Fox.
EQUUS	Hemionus	
ERINACEUS	auritus	Hedgehog.

FELIS	Caracal	Lynx.
GULO	borealis	Glutton.
LAGOMYS	alpinus	Alpine hare.
LEPUS	Tolai	Hare.
	variabilis	
LUTRA	vulgaris	Otter.
MELES	Taxus	Badger.
MOSCHUS	moschiferus	
MUS	decumanus	Rat.
MUSTELA	erminea	Ermine.
	sibirica	Polecat.
	zibellina	Sable.
MYOSPALAX	talpinus	Bear.
NYCTIREUTES	procyonoïdes	Racoon dog.
SCIURUS	vulgaris	Squirrel.
SOREX	vulgaris	
SUS	scrofa	Wild boar.
TAMIAS	striatus	Striped squirrel
VESPERTILIO	Daubentonii	Bat.
	borealis	

MIDDLE AMOOR.

CANIS	alpinus	Red wolf.
	Lupus	Wolf.
	Vulpes	Fox.
CERVUS	Capreolus	Roebuck.
	Elephus	Stag.
FELIS	Caracal	Lynx.
	Irbis	Panther.
	Tigris	Tiger.
LEPUS	variabilis	
MELES	Taxus	Badger.
MOSCHUS	moschiferus.	
MUS	decumanus	Rat.
MUSTELA	erminea	Ermine.
	sibirica	Polecat.
	zibellina	Sable.
NYCTIREUTES	procyonoïdes	Racoon dog

SOREX	pygmæus	
	vulgaris	
SUS	scrofa	Wild boar.
URSUS	Arctos	Brown bear.
VESPERTILIO	Daubentonii	Bat.

LOWER AMOOR.

CANIS	alpinus	Red wolf.
	Lupus	Wolf.
	Vulpes	Fox.
CERVUS	Alces	Elk.
	Capreolus	Roebuck.
	Tarandus	Reindeer.
ERINACEUS	auritus	Hedgehog.
FELIS	Caracal	Lynx.
LEPUS	variabilis	
MUS	decumanus	Rat.
MUSTELA	erminea	Ermine.
	sibirica	Polecat.
	zibellina	Sable.
SOREX	pygmæus	
	vulgaris.	
TAMIAS	striatus	Striped squirrel.
URSUS	Arctos	Brown bear.
VESPERTILIO	Daubentonii	Bat.

BIRDS

IN

THE VALLEY OF THE AMOOR.

UPPER AMOOR.

Accentor		Sparrow
Alauda	alpestris	Lark.
	pratensis	
Alcedo	ispida	Kingfisher.
Anas	acuta	Pintail duck.
	Boschas	Duck.
	Clangula	Golden eye.
	Crecca	Teal.
	falcata	Duck.
	Fuligula	Tufted duck.
	glocitans	Duck.
	nigra	Black scoter.
	Querquedula	Teal.
Bombycilla	garrula	Bohemian chatterer.
Caprimulgus	Jotaka	Night-jar.
Charadrius	(Ægialites) curonicus	Plover.
	pluvialis	
Ciconia	nigra	Black stork.
Circus	cyaneus	Marsh harrier.
Columba	gelastes	Dove.
Colymbus	glacialis	
Corvus	cyaneus	Blue jay.
	Corax	Raven.
	Corone	Crow.
	dauricus	Daw.
Cuculus	canorus	Cuckoo.
Cypselus	Apus	Swift.
	Ciris.	

EMBERIZA	aureola	
	pithyornus	
	rutila	
	spodocephala	
FALCO	atra	
	candicans	Hawk.
	Tinnunculus	Kestrel.
FRINGILLA	Montifringilla	
GARRULUS	glandarius	
GRUS	leucogeranus	White crane.
HIRUNDO	domestica	Swallow.
	riparia	
	urbica	
LAGOPUS	albus	Ptarmigan
LANIUS	phœnicurus	
LARUS	minutus	Gull.
MOTACILLA	alba	Wagtail.
	flava	Yellow wagtail.
NUMENIUS	arquata	Common curlew.
ORIOLUS	sinensis	Chinese oriole.
PANDION	Haliaëtos	Osprey.
PARUS	caudatus	Long tailed tit.
	cyaneus	Blue tit.
	palustris	Marsh tit.
PLECTROPHANES	nivalis	Snow bunting.
PICA	cyanea	Blue jay.
PICUS	martius	Woodpecker.
	major	
	minor	Little woodpecker.
PODICEPS	cornutus	
SALICARIA	Aëdon	
SCOLOPAX	major	Double snipe.
SITTA	europæa	Nuthatch.
	uralensis	
STERNA	leucoptera	White-winged tern.
	longipennis	Tern.
STRIX	brachyotus	Short-eared owl.
	Bubo	Horned owl.
	funerea	
	Nyctea	Snowy owl.
	Otus	Owl.
STURNUS	dauricus	Starling.
SYLVIA	aurorea	
	Calliope	

Sylvia	cyanura	
	kamschatkensis	Red-necked nightingale.
	Locustella	
	Proregulus	
	sibirica	
Tetrao	bonasia	Wood hen.
	Tetrix	Black grouse.
Totanus	Glareola	
	glottis	
Tringa	minuta	
	Temminckii	
Turdus	fuscatus	Blackbird
Upupa	Epops	Hoopoe.
Vanellus	cristatus	Lapwing

MIDDLE AMOOR.

Actitis	hypoleucos	
Alcedo	Ispida	King-fisher.
Anas	acuta	Pintail duck.
	Boschas	Duck.
	Crecca	Teal.
	clypeata	
	falcata	Duck.
	galericulata	
	histrionica	Harlequin duck.
	nigra	Black scoter.
	Querquedula	Teal.
Anser	Bernicla	Goose.
	cygnoïdes	
	grandis	
Aquila	albicilla	Eagle.
	pelagica	
Ardea	cinerea	Heron.
	virescens	
Buteo	vulgaris	Buzzard.
Caprimulgus	Jotaka	Night-jar.
Charadrius	mongolicus	
Ciconia	nigra	Black stork.
Columba	gelastes	Dove.
Colymbus	glacialis	

CORVUS	Corone	Crow.
	dauricus	Daw.
CUCULUS	sp.	
CYGNUS	musicus	Swan.
CYPSELUS	Ciris	
EMBERIZA	aureola	
	spodocephala	
FALCO	candicans	Hawk.
	Tinnunculus	Kestrel.
FRINGILLA	Montifringilla	
GARRULUS	glandarius	
GRUS	leucogeranus	White crane
HÆMATOPUS	ostralegus	Oyster-catcher.
HIRUNDO	riparia	Swallow.
LANIUS	phœnicurus	
LARUS	canus	Gull.
	minutus	
MOTACILLA	alba	Wagtail.
	flava	Yellow wagtail.
	lugubris	
MUSCICAPA	cinereo-alba	
	narcissina	
	sp.	
NUCIFRAGA	caryo-catactes	
ORIOLUS	sinensis	Chinese oriole.
PANDION	Haliaëtos	Osprey.
PARUS	ater	
	cyaneus	Blue tit.
PASTOR	sturninus	
PHASIANUS	sp.	Pheasant.
PICA	caudata	Magpie.
	cyanea	Blue jay.
PICUS	minor	Woodpecker.
SALICARIA	Aëdon	
SITTA	europæa	Nuthatch.
STERNA	Hirundo	Common tern.
	leucoptera	White-winged tern.
	longipennis	Tern.
STRIX	brachyotus	Short-eared owl.
	Bubo	Horned owl.
	Otus	Owl.
SYLVIA	cyanura	
	kamschatkensis	Red-necked nightingale.
	Proregulus	

SYLVIA	sibirica	
	(Zosterops) chloronotus	
	sp.	
TETRAO	bonasia	Wood hen.
	canadensis	
	Tetrix	Black grouse.
TOTANUS	Glareola	
TRINGA	minuta	
	Temminckii	
TURDUS	fuscatus	Blackbird.

LOWER AMOOR.

ACTITIS	hypoleucos	
ALCEDO	Ispida	Kingfisher
ANAS	acuta	Pintail duck.
	Boschas	Duck.
	clypeata	
	Crecca	Teal.
	falcata	Duck.
	galericulata	
	nigra	Black scoter.
	Querquedula	Teal.
AQUILA	albicilla	Eagle
	pelagica	
ARDEA	cinerea	Heron.
BUTEO	Lagopus	Buzzard.
COLYMBUS	glacialis	
CORVUS	Corax	Raven.
CYPSELUS	Ciris	
EMBERIZA	aureola	
	spodocephala	
FALCO	candicans	Hawk.
	Tinnunculus	Kestrel
FRINGILLA	Montifringilla	
GRUS	leucogeranus	White crane.
HÆMATOPUS	ostralegus	Oyster-catcher.
HIRUNDO	riparia	Swallow.
LARUS	minutus	Gull.
MOTACILLA	alba	Wagtail.
	lugubris	

PANDION	Haliaëtos	Osprey.
PICA	cyanea	Blue jay.
PICUS	martius	Woodpecker.
	minor	Little woodpecker.
SALICARIA	Aëdon	
SITTA	europæa	Nuthatch.
STERNA	leucoptera	White-winged tern.
	longipennis	Tern.
STRIX	brachyotus	Short-eared owl.
	Otus	Owl.
SYLVIA	cyanura	
	kamschatkensis	Red-necked nightingale.
	Proregulus	
	sibirica	
TETRAO	bonasia	Wood hen.
	canadensis	
TOTANUS	Glareola	
TRINGA	crassirostris	
	minuta	
	Temminckii	
TURDUS	fuscatus	Blackbird.

TREES, SHRUBS, AND FLOWERS,

IN

THE VALLEY OF THE AMOOR.

UPPER AMOOR.

ABIES	obovata	Fir.
ACER	Ginnala	Maple.
ACHILLEA	setacea	Milfoil.
ACHYROPHORUS	grandiflorus	
ADENOPHORA	verticillata	
ADONIS	apennina	Adonis.
	daurica	
AJUGA	genevensis	Bugle.
ALLIUM	angulosum	Garlic.
	majus	
ALNOBETULA	fruticosa	
ALNUS	hirsuta	Alder.
ALSINE	laricina	Chickweed.
ALYSSUM	lenense	Madwort.
ANDROSACE	villosa	Androsace.
ANTHRISCUS	nemorosa	Rough chervil.
AQUILEGIA	atropurpurea	Columbine.
	leptoceras	
	oxysepala	
	parviflora	
	vulgaris	
ARTEMISIA		Wormwood.
ASPARAGUS	oligoclonos	Asparagus.
	Sieboldi	
ASTERANTHEMUM	dauricum	Starwort.
ATRAGENE	sibirica	
	platysepala	

AURICULA	minima	Auricula.
BETULA	alba	Birch.
	daurica	
	palustris	
	palustris Gmelini	
CALLISACE	daurica	
CALTHA	palustris	Marsh-marigold.
CALYPSO	borealis	Calypso.
CALYSTEGIA	dauricum	Bearbind.
CAMPANULA	punctata	Bell-flower.
CAREX	cæspitosa	Carex.
	Maackii	
	Meyeriana	
	pediformis	
	pedunculata	
	stricta	
CENOMYCE	rangiferina	Cenomyce.
CERASTIUM	arvense	Ceratium.
CHAMÆDAPHNE	calyculata	
CHELIDONIUM	majus	Celandine.
CHRYSOSPLENIUM	alternifolium	Golden saxifrage.
CLEMATIS	angustifolia	Virgin's bower.
	fusca	
	Manjouria	
CONVALLARIA	majalis	Lily of the valley.
CORNUS	alba	Dogwood.
	sibirica	
CORYDALIS	remota	Corydalis.
CORYLUS	heterophylla	Nut-tree.
	manjouria	
COTYLEDON		Navelwort.
CRATÆGUS	pinnatifida	Hawthorn.
	sanguinea	
CYNOCTEMUM	(Rhodostegia) roseum	
CYPRIPEDIUM	Calceolus	Lady's slipper.
	guttatum	
	macranthum	
	ventricosum	
DENTARIA	tenuifolia	Dentaria.
DIANTHUS	dentosus	Pink.
DICTAMNUS	albus	Fraxinella.
DOLICHOS		Dolichos.
DRABA	lutea	Whitlow-grass.
ERITRICHIUM	Maackii	

ERITRICHIUM	obovatum	
ERYSIMUM	altaicum	Hedge-mustard.
EUONYMUS	Maackii	Spindle-tree.
EUPHORBIA	Esula	Spurge.
FRAGARIA	vesca	Strawberry.
FRITILLARIA	Dagana	Fritillary.
GALIUM	verum	Bedstraw.
GENTIANA	humilis	Gentian.
GERANIUM	eriostemon	Crane's-bill.
	sibiricum	
GULDENSTADTIA	pauciflora	
HEMEROCALLIS	flava	Day-lily.
	graminea	
HYPERICUM	Ascyron	St. John's-wort.
IMPATIENS	nolitangere	Balsam.
	parviflora	
IRIS	Bloudowii	Iris.
	dichotoma	
	Güldenstadtii	
	lævigata	
	pauciflora	
	sibirica	
	uniflora	
	ventricosa	
IXERIS	versicolor	
JUGLANS	manjourica	Walnut.
JUNIPERUS	daurica	Juniper.
LAMPYRIS	sibirica	
LARIX	daurica	Larch.
LATHYRUS	humilis	Lathyrus.
LEDUM	palustre	Labrador.
LEONTOPODIUM	sibiricum	Lion's-foot.
LESPEDEZA	bicolor	Lespedeza.
LILIUM	Martagon	Lily.
	pulchellum	
	spectabile	
	tenuifolium	
LYCHNIS	sibirica	Lychnis.
LYSIMACHIA	brachystachys	Loose-strife.
	daurica	
MAACKIA	amurensis, nov. gen. Rupr.	
MAJANTHEMUM	bifolium	
MAXIMOVICZIA	amurensis, nov. gen. Rupr.	

MELICA	Gmelini	Melic-grass.
MENISPERMUM	dauricum	Moon-seed.
MŒHRINGIA	lateriflora	Mœhringia.
MYOSOTIS	cæspitosa	Scorpion-grass.
	sylvaticus	
	sylvestris	
PÆONIA	daurica	Pæony.
	tenuifolia	
PANAX	sessiliflorum	Panax.
PAPAVER	alpinum	Poppy.
	nudicaule	
PARIS	obovata	Paris.
	quadrifolia	
PATRINIA	scabiosæfolia	Patrinia.
PERULARIA	fuscescens	
PHELODENDRON	amurense, nov. gen. Rupr.	
PICEA	Pichta	Pitch-pine.
PINUS	Cembra	Pine.
	manjourica	
	pumila	
	sylvestris	
PLATANTHERA	chlorantha	Platanthera.
PLATYCODON	grandiflorum	
PLECOSTIGMA	pauciflorum	
POLEMONIUM	cæruleum	Greek valerian.
POLYGONATUM	officinale	Solomon's seal.
	stenophyllum	
	vulgare	
POLYSTICHUM	fragrans	
POPULUS	tremula	Poplar.
	suaveolens	
POTENTILLA	fragarioïdes	Cinquefoil.
	subacaulis	
PRIMULA	cortusoïdes	Primrose.
PRUNUS	Padus	Plum.
PULSATILLA	vulgaris	
PYROLA	rotundifolia	Winter-green.
QUERCUS	mongolica	Oak.
RANUNCULUS	auricomus	Crowfoot.
	propinquus	
RHAMNUS	daurica	Buckthorn.
RHAPONTICUM	uniflorum	
RHODODENDRON	dauricum	Rhododendron.
RIBES	Dikuscha	Currant.

RIBES	glabellum	Currant.
	nigrum	
	procumbens	
	rubrum	
ROSA	acicularis	Rose.
	cinnamomea	
	daurica	
RUBIA	cordifolia	Madder.
RUBUS	idæus	Bramble.
SALIX	cinerascens	Willow.
	depressa	
	pentandra	
	rosmarinifolia	
	viminalis	
SAMBUCUS	racemosa	Elder.
SAXIFRAGA	septentrionalis	Saxifrage.
SCORZONERA	austriaca	Viper's grass.
SEDUM	aizoon	Stonecrop.
SELAGINELLA	sanguinolenta	
SENECIO	campestris	
SILENE	repens	Catchfly.
SOLANUM	persicum	Nightshade.
SOPHORA	flavescens	Sophora.
SORBUS	aucuparia	
SPIRÆA	angustifolia	Spiræa.
	chamædrifolia	
	digitata	
	lobata	
	salicifolia	
	sericea	
	tomentosa	
STACHYS	baicalensis	Hedge-nettle.
STELLARIA	radians	Stitchwort.
STELLERA	Chamæjasme	Stellera.
SYRINGA	amurensis	Lilac.
TARAXACUM	collinum	
THALICTRUM	amurense	Meadow-rue.
	angustifolium	
	aquilegifolium	
THLASPI	cochleariforme	Shepherd's purse.
THYMUS	Serpyllum	Thyme
TILIA	cordata	Lime-tree.
TRIENTALIS	europæa	Winter-green.
TRIFOLIUM	Lupinaster	Trefoil.
TROLLIUS	asiaticus	Globe-flower.

ULMUS	glabra	Elm-tree.
	pumila	
URTICA		Nettle.
VACCINIUM	Vitis idæa	Whortle-berry.
	uliginosum	
VALERIANA	officinalis	Valerian.
VERATRUM	nigrum	Veratrum.
VERONICA	tubiflora	Speedwell.
VIBURNUM	Opulus	Viburnum.
VICIA	multicaulis	Vetch.
VINCETOXICUM	atratum	
VIOLA	acuminata	Violet.
	dactyloïdes	
	discuta	
	Gmeliniana	
	Ircutiana	
	macrantha	
	mirabilis	
	multicaulis	
	Patrini	
	subglabra	
	variegata	
VITIS	amurensis	Vine.
	cordifolia	
	indivisa	
	riparia	
XYLOSTEUM	cæruleum	

MIDDLE AMOOR.

ABIES	obovata	Fir.
	ajanensis	
ACARNA	chinensis	Acarna.
ACER	Dedyle	Maple.
	Ginnala	
	Mono	
	tegmentosum	
ACONITUM	arcuatum	Wolf's-bane
	volubile	
ACTÆA	erythrocarpa	Actæa.
	spicata	

ADENOPHORA	latifolia	
ADIANTUM	pedatum	Maiden-hair.
AGRIMONIA	pilosa	Agrimony.
ALLIUM	anisopodium	Garlic.
	lineare	
ALNOBETULA	fruticosa	
ALNUS	hirsuta	Alder.
AMARANTUS		Amaranth.
AMETHYSTEA	cærulea	Amethystea.
ARABIS	pendula	Wall-cress.
ARALIA	manjourica	Aralia.
ARISTOLOCHIA	contorta	Aristolochia.
ARTEMISIA	latiloba	Wormwood.
	sacrorum	
	samamisica	
	scoparia	
	selengensis	
	sylvatica	
ASPIDIUM	Filix fœmina	Shield-fern.
ASTERANTHEMUM	dauricum	
ASTRAGALUS	uliginosus	Milk-vetch.
BECKMANNIA	erucæformis	Beckmannia.
BERBERIS	amurensis	Berberry.
BETULA	alba	Birch.
	Maackii	
	Maximowiczii	
	ovalifolia	
	reticulata	
BIDENS	tripartita	Bidens.
	pinnatifida	
BUPLEURUM	longiradiatum	Hare's-ear.
CACALIA	auriculata	Cacalia.
CALAMAGROSTIS	epigejos	
CALAMINTHA	chinensis	Calamint.
CALLISACE	daurica	
CALYSTEGIA	daurica	Bearbind.
CAMPANULA	punctata	Bell-flower.
CARAGANA	Altagana	Siberian Pea-tree.
CARDUUS	crispus	Thistle.
CAULOPHYLLUM	robustum	Caulophyllum.
CELASTRUS	flagellaris	Staff-tree.
CHAMÆDAPHNE	calyculata	
CHAMÆMELUM	limosum	
CHENOPODIUM	ficifolium	Goosefoot.

CHLORANTHUS	manjouricus	Chloranthus.
CHYLOCALYX	perfoliatus	
CIRCÆA	alpina	Enchanter's night-shade.
	lutetiana	
CIRSIUM	Maackii	
	pendulum	
CLEMATIS	angustifolia	Virgin's bower.
	fusca	
	manjourica	
CLINTONIA	udensis	
COMMELINA	communis	Commelina.
CORISPERMUM	elongatum	Tick-seed.
	latifolium	
CORNUS	canadensis	Dogwood.
	sibirica	
CORYDALIS	Maackii	Corydalis
	speciosa	
CORYLUS	heterophylla	Nut-tree.
	manjourica	
	rostrata	
COTYLEDON		Navel-wort.
CRATÆGUS	pinnatifida	Hawthorn.
CUSCUTA	systyla	Dodder.
DIANTHUS	dentosus	Pink.
DICTAMNUS	albus	Fraxinella.
DIOSCOREA	quinqueloba	Yam.
ECHINOSPERMUM	deflexum	Echinospermum.
ELÆOCHARIS	acicularis	
	ovata	
	palustris	
ELEUTHERO-COCCUS	senticosus, nov. gen. Maxim.	
ERIGERON	acre	Erigeron
EUONYMUS	gibbiflorus	
	Maackii	
	verrucosus	
EUPHORBIA	lucorum	Spurge.
FIMBRISTYLIS	leiocarpa	Fimbristylis.
FRAXINUS	manjourica	Ash-tree.
GALIUM	boreale	Bedstraw.
	latifolium	
GEBLERA	sungariensis	

GEBLERA	suffruticosa	
GERANIUM	vlassovianum	Crane's-bill.
GLYCERIA	fluitans	Glyceria.
	leptorhiza	
GLYCYRRHIZA	pallidiflora	Glycyrrhiza.
GYPSOPHILA	latifolia	Gypsophila.
	perfoliata	
HABENARIA	linearifolia	Habenaria.
HETEROPAPPUS	decipiens	
HOTEIA	chinensis	
HYPERICUM	Ascyron	St. John's-wort.
	attenuatum	
INULA	britannica	Inula.
	linariæfolia	
	salicina	
ISOLEPIS	Micheliana	Isolepis.
JUGLANS	manjourica	Walnut.
LACTUCA	amurensis	Lettuce.
LARIX	daurica	Larch.
LATHYRUS	palustris	Lathyrus.
	pilosus	
LESPEDEZA	bicolor	Lespedeza.
LIBANOTIS	seseloïdes	
LIGULARIA	sibirica	
LILIUM	callosum	Lily.
LIMNANTHEMUM	nymphoïdes	
LINARIA	vulgaris	Toad-flax.
LUZULA	campestris	Luzula.
	minor	
LYCHNIS	fulgens	Lychnis
LYCOPODIUM	complanatum	Club-moss.
	clavatum	
LYCOPUS	lucidus	Water-horehound.
LYSIMACHIA	barystachys	Loose-strife.
LYTHRUM	Salicaria	Lythrum.
MAACKIA	amurensis, nov. gen. Rupr.	
MAJANTHEMUM	bifolium	
MAXIMOVICZIA	amurensis, nov. gen. Rupr.	
MELAMPYRUM	roseum	Cow-wheat.
MENISPERMUM	dauricum	Moon-seed.
MENTHA	origanoïdes	Mint.
METAPLEXIS	Stauntonii	

MITROSICYOS	lobatus, nov. gen. Maxim.	
MULGEDIUM	sibiricum	Mulgedium.
NYMPHÆA	Wenzellii	Water-lily.
ONOCLEA	interrupta	Onoclea.
	sensibilis	
OROBUS	lathyroïdes	
PÆONIA	albiflora	Pæony.
	obovata	
PANAX	sessiliflorum	Panax.
PARIS	obovata	Paris.
	quadrifolia	
PATRINIA	rupestris	Patrinia.
	scabiosæfolia	
PEDICULARIS	resupinata	Lousewort.
	sceptrum	
PHELLODENDRON	amurense, nov. gen. Rupr.	
PHILADELPHUS	tenuifolius	Syringa.
PHRYMA	leptostachya	Phryma.
PICEA	Pichta	Pitch-pine.
PICRIS	japonica	Ox-tongue.
PINUS	manjourica	Pine.
	Pichta	
PLATANTHERA	hologlottis	Platanthera
PLATYCODON	grandiflorum	
POA	coarctata	Meadow-grass.
	nemoralis	
POLYGONUM	nodosum	Persicaria.
	Convolvulus	
	minus	
POLYPODIUM	Phegopteris	Polypody.
	vulgare	
POLYSTICHUM	spinulosum	
POPULUS	tremula	Poplar.
	suaveolens	
POTENTILLA	bifurca	Cinquefoil.
PRUNUS (PADUS)	Maackii	Plum.
PTARMICA	mongolica	
PYROLA	renifolia	Winter-green.
PYRUS	baccata	Pyrus.
	ussuriensis	
QUERCUS	mongolica	Oak.
RANUNCULUS	amurensis	Crowfoot.

RANUNCULUS	amuricus	Crow foot.
	chinensis	
RHAMNUS	daurica	Buckthorn.
RHODODENDRON	dauricum	Rhododendron.
RIBES	rubrum	Currant.
ROSA	cinnamomea	Rose.
RUBUS	cratægifolius	Bramble.
	idæus	
RUMEX	maritimus	Dock.
SALVINIA	natans	
SAMBUCUS	racemosa	Elder.
SANGUISORBA	officinalis	Great burnet.
	tenuifolia	
SAUSSUREA	pulchella	Saussurea.
SAXIFRAGE	bronchialis	Saxifrage.
	congesta	
SCHIZOPEPON	bryoniæfolius, nov. gen. Maxim.	
SCORZONERA	macrosperma	Viper's grass.
SCUTELLARIA	dependens	Skull-cap.
	galericulata	
	japonica	
SEDUM	Aïzoon	Stonecrop.
	Middendorffii	
SELAGINELLA	pulvinata	
SETARIA	glauca	Setaria.
SILENE	foliosa	Catchfly.
SIUM	cicutæfolium	Water-parsnip.
SOLIDAGO	Virgaurea	Golden-rod.
SOPHORA	flavescens	Sophora.
SORBUS	aucuparia	
SPIRÆA	flexuosa	Spiræa.
	salicifolia.	
	sericea.	
SPIRANTHES	australis	Spiranthes.
STACHYS	baikalensis	Hedge-nettle.
STYLOCALYX	perfoliatus	
SYNEILEISIS	aconitifolia, nov. gen. Maxim.	
SYRINGA	amurensis	Lilac.
	vulgaris	
TANACETUM	boreale	Tansy.
	vulgare	
TAXUS	baccata	Yew-tree.

THALICTRUM		Meadow-rue.
THYMUS	latifolia	Thyme.
	Serpyllum	
TILIA	cordata	Lime-tree.
	manjourica.	
	parviflora	
TRAPA	natans	Water-caltrops.
TRIFOLIUM	Lupinaster	Trefoil.
TRISETUM	flavescens	Trisetum.
TROCHOSTIGMA	Kolomikta	
ULMUS	glabra	Elm-tree.
	montana	
	suberosa	
VACCINIUM	Vitis idæa	Whortle-berry.
	uliginosum	
VERONICA	grandis	Speedwell.
	longifolia	
VIBURNUM	Opulus	Viburnum.
VICIA	pallida	Vetch.
VINCETOXICUM	volubile	
VITIS	amurensis	Vine.
WOODSIA	major	Woodsia.
	subcordata	
XYLOSTEUM	gibbiflorum	
	Maackii	
	Maximoviczii	

LOWER AMOOR.

ABIES	ajensis	Fir.
ACER	Dedyle	Maple.
	Mono	
ACTÆA	spicata	Actæa.
ALNOBETULA	fruticosa	
ALNUS	hirsuta	Alder.
AQUILEGIA	volubilis	Columbine.
ARTEMISIA	integrifolia	Wormwood,
BETULA	reticulata	Birch.
	Maximoviczii	
CHAMÆDAPHNE	calyculata	

Cimicifuga	simplex	Bugwort.
Clematis	fusca	Virgin's bower.
Clintonia	udensis.	
Cornus	sibirica	Dogwood.
	alba	
Corydalis	Maackii	Corydalis.
Corylus	manjourica	Nut-tree.
Cratægus	pinnatifida	Hawthorn.
Cyperus	bufonicus	Cyperus.
	limosus.	
Eleuthero-coccus	senticosus, nov. gen. Maxim.	
Euonymus	macropterus	Spindle-tree.
Gentiana	triflora	Gentian.
Juglans	manjourica	Walnut.
Juniperus	daurica	Juniper.
Ledum	(palustre) dilatum	Labrador.
Maackia	amurensis, nov. gen. Rupr.	
Picea	Pichta	Pitch-pine.
Polygonum		Persicaria.
Populus	tremula	Poplar.
Pyrola		Winter-green.
Quercus	mongolica	Oak.
Rhaponticum		
Rhododendron	dauricum	Rhododendron.
Rubus	idæus	Bramble.
Sambucus	racemosa	Elder.
Sorbus	aucuparia	
Spiræa	salicifolia	Spiræa.
Thymus	Serpyllum	Thyme.
Tilia	cordata	Lime-tree.
Vaccinium	uliginosum	Whortle-berry.
	Vitis idæa	
Xylosteum	cæruleum	
	gibbiflorum	
	Maximoviczii	

MAMMALIA

OF THE

KIRGHIS STEPPE, ALA-TAU, KARA-TAU, AND TARBAGATAI.

ARCTOMYS	Bobac	Marmot.
	fulvus	
	leptodactylis	
	mugosaricus	
BOS	Bubalus	Buffalo.
CANIS	aureus	Jackal.
	Caragan	
	Corsac	Corsac fox.
	Lupus	Wolf.
	sylvestris	
	Vulpes	Fox.
CAPRA	Ammon	Argali, or Wild sheep.
	Ibex	Ibex.
CASTOR	Fiber	Beaver.
CERVUS	Alces	Elk.
	Capreolus	Roebuck.
	Elephus	Stag.
	Pygargus	Wild goat.
EQUUS	Caballus sylvestris	Wild horse.
ERINACEUS	auritus	Hedgehog.
FELIS	Catus	Wild cat.
	Lynx	Lynx.
	Tigris	Tiger.
LEPUS	Tolai	Hare.
LUTRA		Otter.
MARAL		Stag.
MELES	Taxus	Badger.
MUS		Mouse.
	citillus	

Mus	jaculus	
	Rattus	Rat.
	typhlus	
Mustela	erminea	Ermine.
	putorius	Polecat.
	Martes	Marten.
Phoca		Seal.
Sorex	fodiens	
Sus	scrofa	Wild boar.
Talpa		Mole.
Ursus		Bear.
Vespertilio		Bat.
	discolor	
	pipistrellus	

BIRDS

OF THE

KIRGHIS STEPPE, ALA-TAU, KARA-TAU, AND TARBAGATAI.

ALAUDA	alpestris	Lark.
ANAS	Olor	Swan.
	rutila	Red duck.
	Tadorna	
ARDEA	comata	Heron.
CHARADRIUS	asiaticus	Plover.
	tartaricus	Plover.
CICONIA		Stork.
	nigra	Black stork.
COLUMBA		Wood pigeon.
CORACIAS	garrula	
CORVUS	Monedula	Jackdaw.
	Corax	Raven.
	frugilegus	Rook.
	glandarius	Jay.
COTURNIX	dactylisonans	
EMBERIZA	aureola	
	hortulana	Wheatear.
FRINGILLA	Spinus	Siskin.
	Spinus asiaticus	
FALCO	apivorus	Honey buzzard.
	Chrysaëtos	Eagle.
	Chrysaëtos ragouja	
	nobilis	Bearcoot.
	gentilis	
	Pygargus	
GRUS	cinerea	Crane.

Grus	leucogeranus	White crane.
Hæmatopus	ostralegus	Oyster-catcher.
Hirundo	alpestris	Swallow.
Larus	canus	Seagull.
Loxia	persica	
Mergus	Merganser	
Motacilla	flava	Yellow wagtail.
	Luscinia	Nightingale.
Otis	tarda	Bustard.
	Tetrax	Bustard.
Perdrix	cinerea	Grey partridge.
Phasianus	colchicus	Pheasant.
Phalacrocorax	carbo	Cormorant.
Pelecanus	Onocrotalus	Pelican.
Pica	caudata	Magpie.
Platalea	leucorodia	Spoonbill.
Pyrrhula		Bullfinch.
Saxicola	Œnanthe	Wheatear.
	stapazina	Russet wheatear.
Scolopax	gallinago	Small snipe.
Sterna	Hirundo	Common tern.
Strix	Nyctea	Snowy owl.
	Otus	Owl.
	Scops	Scops-eared owl.
Sturnus		Starling.
Tantalus	falcinellus	
Tetrao	longicaudata	Quail.
	paradoxus	
Tringa	Vanellus	Lapwing.
Upupa	Epops	Hoopoe.

TREES, SHRUBS, AND FLOWERS,

FOUND ON THE

KIRGHIS STEPPE, ALA-TAU, KARA-TAU, AND TARBAGATAI.

ACHILLEA	Millefolium	Milfoil.
ACORUS	Calamus	Acorus.
ADONIS	apennina	Adonis.
	autumnalis	
	vernalis	
AIRA	aquatica	Hair-grass.
	truncata	
ALCHEMILLA	vulgaris	Lady's mantle.
ALISMA	Plantago	Water-plantain.
ALLIUM	bisulcum	Garlic.
	Cepa	
	sativum	
	tartaricum	
ALOPECURUS	pratensis	Foxtail-grass.
ALYSSUM	micropetalum	Madwort.
AMARYLLIS	tartarica	Amaryllis.
AMYGDALUS	nana	Almond.
ANABASIS	aphylla	Anabasis.
ANCHUSA	rupestris	Bugloss.
ANCYPERUS	esculentus	
ANEMONE	alba	Anemone.
	cærulea	
	narcissiflora	
	patens	
	sylvaticus	
ANTHEMIS	nobilis	Chamomile.
ANTIRRHINUM	genistifolium	Snapdragon.

Antirrhinum	Linaria	Snapdragon.
Arabis	pendula	Wall-cress.
Artemisia	Abrotanum	Wormwood.
	Absinthium	
	Dracunculus	
	nivea	
	nutans	
	Santonica	
	tartarica	
Asclepias	sibirica	Swallow-wort.
Asphodelus		Asphodel.
Aster	altaicus	
	chinensis	
	elegans	
	sibiricus	
Astragalus	contortuplicatus	Milk-vetch.
	falcatus	
	fruticosus	
	longiflorus	
	melilotoïdes	
	physodes	
	sulcatus	
	tenuifolius	
	uliginosus	
	verticillaris	
	virgatus	
	vulpinus	
Atraphaxis	frutescens	Atraphaxis.
Atriplex	hortensis	Orache.
	sibirica	
	tartarica	
Avena	sylvestris	Oat-grass.
Belladonna		Amaryllis.
Berberis	emarginata	Barberry.
	sibirica	
Betonica	grandiflora	Betony.
	officinalis	
Betula	alba	Birch.
	daurica	
	fruticosa	
Bubon	Galbanum	Bubon.
Butomus	umbellatus	Flowering rush.
Cachrys	odontalgica	Cachrys
Campanula	coronata	Bell-flower.

CAMPANULA	grandiflora	Bell-flower.
	lilifolia	
	macrantha	
	punctata	
	sarmatica	
	verticillata	
CAMPHOROSMA	monspeliensis	Camphorosma.
CAPPARIS	spinosa	Caper-tree.
CARDUUS	Arundo	Thistle.
	cyanoïdes	
CAREX	arenaria	Carex.
	curta	
CARUM	Carui	Caraway.
	simplex	
CARYOPHYLLUS	aromaticus	Clove-tree.
CENTAUREA	alata	Centaury.
	glastifolia	
	maculosa	
	orientalis	
	radiata	
	tartarica	
	trichocephala	
CERCIS	Siliquastrum	Judas-tree.
CHEIRANTHUS		Wallflower.
CHENOPODIUM	salsum	Goosefoot.
CHONDRILLA	graminea	Gum-succory.
CIMICIFUGA	(Ledum) palustre	Bugwort.
CLEMATIS	daurica	Virgin's bower.
	glauca	
	graveolens	
CNICUS	carthamoïdes	
	ciliatus	
	desertorum	
	helenioïdes	
	serratuloïdes	
COCHLEARIA	officinalis	Scurvy-grass.
COTONEASTER		Cotoneaster.
COTYLEDON	malacophyllum	Navelwort.
	serrata	
	spinosa	
CRATÆGUS	monogyna	Hawthorn.
	Oxyacantha	
CUCUBALUS	baccifer	Campion.
CYPERUS	longus	Cyperus.

CYPRIPEDIUM	guttatum	Lady's slipper.
	humile	
	macranthum	
	ventricosum	
CYTISUS	dentatus	Cytisus.
DODARTIA	orientalis	Dodartia.
DRABA	verna	Whitlow-grass.
ECHINOPS		Globe-thistle.
ECHIUM	vulgare	Vipers' bugloss.
ELÆAGNUS	angustifolius	Oleaster.
ELYMUS	arenarius	Lyme-grass.
	junceus	
	sabulosus	
	sibiricus	
	tener	
EPHEDRA	monostachya	Ephedra.
EQUISETUM		Horse-tail.
ERIOPHORUM		Cotton-grass.
ERUCA		Rocket.
EUPHORBIA	helioscopia	Spurge.
	palustris	
FALKIA		Falkia.
FERULA	persica	Giant fennel.
	sibirica	
FESTUCA		Fescue-grass.
FRAGARIA	vesca	Strawberry.
FRANKENIA	hirsuta	Sea-heath.
GENTIANA	adscendens	Gentian.
	algida	
	aquatica	
	macrophylla	
	triflora	
GLYCYRRHIZA	asperrima	Glycyrrhiza
HESPERIS	aprica	Rocket.
	arabidiflora	
	tartarica	
HIERACIUM	Gmelini	Hawkweed.
	murorum	
HYOSCYAMUS	niger	Henbane.
	physaloïdes	
INULA	Helenium	Inula.
IRIS	flavissima	Iris
	longispatha	
	setosa	

Isatis	tinctoria	Woad.
Juncus	Typha	Rush.
Juniperus	communis	Juniper.
	excelsa	
	nana	
	sylvia	
Kochia	hyssopifolia	Kochia.
Leontice	incerta	Leontice.
Lepidium	coronopifolium	Pepperwort.
	latifolium	
Lithospermum		Gromwell.
Lonicera	pulchra	Lonicera.
	punicea	
	tartarica	
Lotus	ornithopodioïdes	Bird's-foot trefoil.
Lychnis	fulgens	Lychnis.
Lycium	tartaricum	Box-thorn.
	ruthenicum	
Lysimachia	vulgaris	Loose-strife.
Lythrum	Salicaria	Lythrum.
Malva	Althæa	Mallow.
Medicago		Medick.
Mentha	crispa	Mint.
	crispata	
	sativa	
	undulata	
Myosotis		
Nymphæa	nitida	Water-lily.
	salsa	
Onobrychis		Saintfoin.
Onosma	simplicissimum	Onosma.
Ornithogalum	uniflorum	Star of Bethlehem.
Orobanche	cæruleum	Broom-rape.
Phalaris		Canary-grass.
Phlomis	alpina	Phlomis.
	tuberosa	
Pinus	Cembra	Pine.
	orientalis	
	Pallasiana	
	Pichta	
	sibirica	
Plantago	asiatica	Plantain.
	maxima	

PLANTAGO	minuta	Plantain.
	salsa	
PODALYRIA		Podalyria.
POLYGONUM	acidulum	Persicaria.
	crispulum	
	divaricatum	
	frutescens	
	ocreatum	
	salignum	
	tartaricum	
	undulatum	
POPULUS	balsamifera	Poplar.
	nigra	
	suaveolens	
PORTULACA	oleracea	Purslane.
POTENTILLA	astracanica	Cinquefoil.
	bifurca	
	fragarioïdes	
	grandiflora	
	hispida	
	multifida	
	nivea	
	prostrata	
	ruthenica	
	Salesovii	
	sericea	
	stipularis	
	supina	
PRUNUS	dasycarpa	Plum.
	sibirica	
RANUNCULUS	aquaticus	Crowfoot.
	aquatilis	
	cassubicus	
	falcatus	
	fluvialis	
	salsuginosus	
RAPHANUS	tenellus	Radish.
RHEUM	capsicum	Rhubarb.
	compactum	
	hybridum	
	palmatum	
	tartaricum	
	undulatum	
RIBES	aciculare	Currant.

RIBES	Diacantha	Currant.
	Grossularia	
	procumbens	
	saxatile	
	triste	
ROBINIA	sibirica	Robinia.
	frutescens	
	Halodendron	
ROSA	acicularis	Rose.
	berberifolia	
	daurica	
	flore semipleno	
	grandiflora	
	lutescens	
	Pallasii	
	pauciflora	
	pimpinellifolia	
	reversa	
	sanguisorbifolia	
RUMEX		Dock.
	Patientia	
SALICORNIA	herbacea	Glasswort.
SALIX	pentandra	Willow.
SALSOLA	arbuscula	Saltwort.
	laniflora	
	oppositifolia	
	vermiculata	
SALVIA	Hablitziana	Sage.
	mollis	
	officinalis	
SCABIOSA	arvensis	Scabious.
	isetensis	
	stellata	
SCIRPUS	acicularis	Club-rush.
	(Arundo) Phragmites	
	lacustris	
	palustris	
SCORZONERA	caricifolia	Viper's grass.
	eriosperma	
	purpurea	
SEDUM	acre	Stone-crop.
	Aïzoon	
	hybridum	
	quadrifidum	

SEDUM	populifolium	Stone-crop.
	spinosum	
SEMPERVIVUM	tectorum	House-leek.
SENECIO		Groundsel.
SERRATULA	amara	Saw-wort.
	angustifolia	
	centaurioïdes	
	coronata	
	salicifolia	
	tinctoria	
SINAPIS		Mustard.
SISYMBRIUM	altissimum	Sisymbrium.
	integrifolium	
STATICE	ferulacea	Sea-lavender.
	flexuosa	
	Gmelini	
	graminifolia	
	latifolia	
	Limonium	
	scoparia	
	suffruticosa	
STIPA	sibirica	Feather-grass.
TAMARIX	germanica	Tamarisk.
THLASPI	bursa pastoris	Shepherd's purse.
	ceratocarpon	
TRAGOPOGON	mutabilis	Goat's-beard.
	pratense	
TRIFOLIUM	repens	Trefoil.
TRITICUM	repens	Wheat.
TULIPA	sylvestris	Tulip.
TYPHA	palustris	Cat's-tail.
ULEX	europæa	Furze.
ULMUS	campestris	Elm-tree.
	humilis	
	pumila	
VALERIANA	officinalis	Valerian.
VELLA	tenuissima	Cress-rocket.
VERBASCUM		Mullein.
VERONICA	angustifolia	Veronica.
	grandis	
	incisa	
	laciniata	
	multifida	
	neglecta	

VERONICA	pinnata	Veronica.
	sibirica	
	spuria	
VIBURNUM	dauricum	Viburnum.
	Opulus	
VIOLA	altaica	Violet.
	canina	
	uniflora	
ZYGOPHYLLUM		Bean caper.

MAMMALIA

OF

THE TRANS-BAIKAL AND SIBERIA.

ÆGOCEROS	Ammon	Argali, or Wild sheep.
	sibiricus	
ARCTOMYS	Bobac	Marmot.
ARVICOLA	amphibius	Water-rat.
	obscurus	
	rufocanus	
CANIS	aureus	Jackal.
	Corsac	Corsac fox
	Lagopus	Arctic fox.
	Lupus	Wolf.
	Vulpes	Fox.
CASTOR	Fiber	Beaver.
CERVUS	Alces	Elk.
	Capreolus	Roebuck.
	Elephus	Stag.
	Tarandus	Rein-deer.
DIPUS	sagitta	
ERINACEUS	auritus	Hedgehog.
FELIS	Lynx	Lynx.
	Tigris	Tiger.
GULO	borealis	Glutton.
LAGOMYS	alpinus	Alpine hare.
	hyperboreus	
	Ogotona	
LEPUS	Tolai	
	variabilis	
LUTRA	vulgaris	Otter.
MELES	Taxus	Badger.
MOSCHUS	moschiferus	

MUS	decumanus	Rat.
	minutus	
	musculus	Mouse.
MUSTELA	erminea	Ermine.
	sibirica	Polecat.
	vulgaris	
	zibellina	Sable
MYODES	gregarius	
PLECOTUS	auritus	
PTEROMYS	volans	Flying squirrel.
SCIURUS	vulgaris	Squirrel.
SOREX	vulgaris	
SPERMOPHILUS	Eversmanni	Siberian marmot.
SUS	scrofa	Wild boar.
TALPA	europæa	Mole.
TAMIAS	nigra	
	striatus	Striped squirrel.
URSUS	Arctos	Brown bear.
VESPERTILIO	borealis	Bat.
	dasycnemus	
	Daubentonii	

BIRDS

OF

THE TRANS-BAIKAL AND SIBERIA.

ACCENTOR	montanellus	Hedge-sparrow.
AËTITIS	hypoleucos	
ALAUDA	alpestris.	Lark.
	arvensis.	
ALCEDO	Ispida	King-fisher.
ANAS	acuta	Pintail duck.
	Boschas	Duck.
	Clangula	Golden eye.
	clypeata.	
	Crecca	Teal.
	Fuligula	Tufted duck.
	glacialis.	
	histrionica	Harlequin duck.
	nigra	Black scoter.
	Penelope	Whistler.
	Querquedula	Teal.
	rutila	Red duck.
ANSER	albifrons	Goose.
	Bernicla	
	cinereus	
	grandis	
	segetum	
ANTHUS	arboreus.	
	japonicus.	
	pratensis.	
AQUILA	albicilla	Eagle.
	nævia	
	nobilis	Bearcoot.

ASTUR	Nisus	
	palumbarius	
BOMBYCILLA	garrula	Bohemian chatterer.
BUTEO	Lagopus	Buzzard.
CAPRIMULGUS	europæus	Night-jar.
CHARADRIUS	(Ægialites) curonicus	Plover.
	(Ægialites) Hiaticula	Ringed plover.
	morinellus	Dottrel.
	pluvialis	
CICONIA	nigra	Black stork.
CINCLUS	Pallasii	
CIRCUS	cyaneus	Marsh harrier.
	rufus.	
COLUMBA	gelastes	Dove.
	Œnas.	
COLYMBUS	arcticus.	
	glacialis.	
	septentrionalis	Diver.
CORVUS	Corax	Raven.
	Cornix.	
	Corone	Crow.
	dauricus	Daw.
CREX	pratensis	Land-rail.
CUCULUS	canorus	Cuckoo.
CYPSELUS	Apus.	Swift.
	Ciris	
CYGNUS	Bewickii.	
	musicus	Swan.
EMBERIZA	aureola.	
	cioïdes.	
	pithyornus.	
	pusilla.	
	rustica.	
	rutila.	
	Schœniclus.	
	spodocephala	
FALCO	Æsalon	
	candicans	Hawk.
	peregrinus	
	subbuteo	
	Tinnunculus	Kestrel.
	vespertinus	
FRINGILLA	brunneonucha	
	linaria	
	Montifringilla	

FULICA	atra	Coot.
GARRULUS	infaustus	
GRUS	leucogeranus	White crane.
	cinerea	
HIRUNDO	riparia	Swallow.
	rustica	
	urbica	
JYNX	Torquilla	Wryneck.
LAGOPUS	albus	Ptarmigan.
LANIUS	major	Shrike.
	phœnicurus	
LARUS	cachinnans	
	canus	Gull.
	minutus	Gull.
	ridibundus	
LIMOSA	cinerea	
	rufa	
LOXIA	curvirostra	
	leucoptera	
MERGUS	albellus	White nun, or Smew.
	Merganser	
	serrator	
MILVUS	niger	Kite.
MOTACILLA	alba	Wagtail
	campestris	
	citreola	
	flava	Yellow wagtail.
	sulphurea	
NUCIFRAGA	caryo-catactes	
NUMENIUS	arquata	Common curlew.
ORIOLUS	Galbula	Oriole.
OTIS	tarda	Bustard.
PANDION	Haliaëtos	Osprey.
PARUS	caudatus	Long-tailed tit.
	major	
	palustris	Marsh tit.
	sibiricus	
PASSER	domesticus	
	montanus	
PASTOR	sturninus	
PERDIX	cinerea	Grey partridge.
PHALACROCORAX	carbo	Cormorant.
PHALAROPUS	cinereus	Phalarope.
	rufescens	

PHŒNICOPTERUS	roseus	Flamingo.
PICA	cyanea	Blue jay.
	caudata	Magpie.
PICUS	leuconotus	
	major	
	martius	Woodpecker.
	tridactylus	
PLECTROPHANES	lapponica	
	nivalis	Snow-bunting.
PODICEPS	cornutus	
	subcristatus	
PYRRHULA	erythrina	
	rosea	
	sibirica	
	vulgaris	Bullfinch.
SAXICOLA	Œnanthe	Wheatear.
	rubicola	
	saltatrix	
SCOLOPAX	gallinago	Snipe.
	gallinula	
	major	Large snipe.
	rusticola	Woodcock.
SITTA	europæa	Nuthatch.
STERNA	longipennis	Tern.
	minuta	
STREPSILAS	interpres	
STRIX	Bubo	Horned owl.
	brachyotus	Short-eared owl.
	funerea	
	nyctea	Snowy owl.
	Otus	Owl.
	Tengmalmi	
	uralensis	Oural owl.
STURNUS	vulgaris	Starling.
SYLVIA	aurorea	
	Certhiola	
	Eversmanni	
	kamschatkensis	Red-necked Nightingale.
	Locustella	
	Proregulus	
	sibirica	
	suecica	Blue-throated warbler.
TETRAO	bonasia	Wood hen.
	Tetrix	Black grouse.

TETRAO	urogalloïdes	
	Urogallus	
TOTANUS	Glareola	
	glottis	
	ochropus	
	pulverulentus	
TRINGA	Canutus	Knot.
	Cinclus	
	pugnax	Ruff.
	subarquata	
TURDUS	fuscatus	Blackbird.
	iliacus	Redwing.
	musicus	Thrush.
	pilaris	Fieldfare.
	ruficollis	
UPUPA	Epops	Hoopoe.
VANELLUS	cristatus	Lapwing.

TREES, SHRUBS, AND FLOWERS,

FOUND IN

SIBERIA AND MONGOLIA.

Genus	Species	Common name
ACER	palmatum	Maple.
	tartaricum	
ACHILLEA	alpina	Milfoil.
	Gerberi	
	impatiens	
ACONITUM	barbatum	Wolf's-bane.
	biflorum	
	versicolor	
	volubile	
ADENOPHORA	coronopifolia	
	tricuspidata	
ALLIUM	azureum	Garlic.
	baicalense	
	bisulcum	
	fistulosum	
	lineare	
	nutans	
	obliquum	
	pusillum	
	sibiricum	
	tartaricum	
ALTHÆA	leucantha	Marsh-mallow.
ALYSSUM	micropetalum	Madwort.
AMARYLLIS	tartarica	Amaryllis.
AMMODENDRON	Sieversii	
AMYGDALUS	dasycarpa	Almond.
	sibirica	
ANCHUSA	rupestris	Bugloss.

ANDROSACE	lactiflora	Androsace.
	macrocarpa	
ANEMONE	alba	Anemone.
	cærulea	
	Fischeriana	
	narcissiflora	
	patens	
	sibirica	
	ouralensis	
AQUILEGIA	anemonoïdes	Columbine.
	atropurpurea	
	bicolor	
	daurica	
	glandulosa	
	grandiflora	
	jucunda	
	leptoceras	
	pendula	
	sibirica	
	viridiflora	
ARABIS	pendula	Wall-cress.
ARENARIA	graminifolia	Sandwort.
	juniperina	
	longifolia	
	rigida	
	verticillata	
ARTEMISIA	annua	Wormwood.
	glauca	
	inodora	
	integrifolia	
	laciniata	
	neglecta	
	nivea	
	nutans	
	palustris	
	pauciflora	
	pectinata	
	repens	
	rupestris	
	Santonica	
	sericea	
	Sieversiana	
	tanacetifolia	
ASPARAGUS	dauricus	Asparagus.

ASTER	altaicus	
	elegans	
	sibiricus	
ASTRAGALUS	contortuplicatus	Milk-vetch.
	falcatus	
	fruticosus	
	galegiformis	
	Laxmanni	
	longiflorus	
	melilotoïdes	
	microphyllus	
	physodes	
	semibilocularis	
	sulcatus	
	tenuifolius	
	uliginosus	
	verticillaris	
	virescens	
	virgatus	
	vulpinus	
ATHAMANTA	condensata	Spignell.
	incana	
	sibirica	
ATRIPLEX	hortensis	Orache.
	rubra	
	sibirica	
	tartarica	
AXYRIS	amaranthoïdes	Axyris.
	hybrida	
	prostrata	
BALLOTA	lanata	Stinking horehound.
BARTSIA	pallida	Bartsia.
BERBERIS	emarginata	Berberry.
	sibirica	
BETONICA	grandiflora	Betony.
BETULA	daurica	Birch.
	fruticosa	
BIDENS	parviflora	Bidens.
BIEBERSTEINIA	odora	
BIOTA	pendula	Biota.
	tartarica	
BUPLEURUM	aureum	Hare's-ear.
CACALIA	hastata	Cacalia.
	rhombifolia	

CAMPANULA	coronata	Bell-flower.
	grandiflora	
	lactiflora	
	lilifolia	
	macrantha	
	punctata	
	sarmatica	
	sibirica	
	speciosa	
	stylosa	
	verticillata	
CARAGANA	Altagana	Siberian Pea-tree.
	arenaria	
	frutescens	
	Halodendron	
	jubata	
	pygmæa	
	Redovskii	
	sibirica	
	spinosa	
	tragacanthoïdes	
CARDAMINE	prorepens	Lady's smock.
CARDUUS	cyanoïdes	Thistle.
CARUM	simplex	Caraway.
CENTAUREA	Adami	Centaury.
	alata	
	Fischeri	
	glastifolia	
	maculosa	
	orientalis	
	radiata	
	sibirica	
	sordida	
	tartarica	
	trichocephala	
CEPHALARIA	albescens	Cephalaria.
	isetensis	
	ouralensis	
	Scabiosa	
CERATOCARPUS	arenarius	Ceratocarpus.
CHORISPORA	arcuata	Chorispora.
	sibirica	
	tenella	
CHRYSOCOMA	biflora	Goldylocks.

Chrysocoma	dracunculoïdes.	
Cimicifuga	fœtida	Bugwort.
Cineraria	glauca	Cineraria.
	macrophylla	
	sibirica	
	speciosa	
Claytonia	sibirica	Claytonia.
Clematis	daurica	Virgin's bower.
	glauca	
	graveolens	
	sibirica	
Cnicus	carthamoïdes	Horse-thistle.
	ciliatus	
	desertorum	
	elatior	
	helenioïdes	
	tartaricus	
	uniflorus	
Coluria	potentilloïdes	Coluria.
Cornus	alba	Dogwood.
	rossica	
Corydalis	longiflora	Corydalis.
	nobilis	
	ouralensis	
Cotyledon	serrata	Navel-wort.
Crambe	pinnatifida	Sea-kale.
	tartarica	
Cratægus	monogyna	Hawthorn.
Cunila	capitata	Cunila.
Cymbaria	daurica	Cymbaria.
Cypripedium	guttatum	Lady's slipper.
	macranthum	
	ventricosum	
Cytisus	wolgaricus	Cytisus.
Daphne	altaica	Daphne.
Datura	Metel	Thorn-apple.
Delphinium	amœnum	Larkspur.
	cheilanthum	
	cuneatum	
	dictyocarpum	
	elatum	
	flore pleno	
	glabellum	
	grandiflorum	

Delphinium	hybridum	Delphinium.
	laxiflorum	
	mesoleucum	
	palmatifidum	
	puniceum	
	revolutum	
	triste	
Diotis	ceratoïdes	Diotis.
Doronicum	altaicum	Leopard's-bane.
Dracocephalum	altaicum	Dragon's-head
	argunense	
	botryoïdes	
	grandiflorum	
	nutans	
	palmatum	
	peregrinum	
	sibiricum	
	speciosum	
	thymiflorum	
Echinospermum	squarrosum	
Elsholtzia	cristata	Elsholtzia.
Elymus	distichon	Lyme-grass.
	Hordeum	
	junceus	
	sabulosus	
	sibiricus	
	tener	
Ephedra	monostachya	Ephedra.
Epilobium	dauricum	Willow-herb.
Eremurus	spectabilis	Eremurus.
Erodium	serotinum	Heron's-bill.
Erysimum	ibericum	Hedge-mustard.
	sessiliflorum	
Euphorbia	pilosa	Spurge.
	ouralensis	
Ferula	sibirica	Giant fennel.
Filago	Lagopus	Cotton rose.
Frankenia	hirsuta	Sea heath.
Gagea	circinata	Gagea.
Genista	sibirica	Genista.
Gentiana	adscendens	Gentian.
	algida	
	gelida	
	laniflora	

GENTIANA	macrophylla	Gentian.
GERANIUM	collinum	Crane's-bill.
	dauricum	
	eriostemon	
	sibiricum	
GLYCYRRHIZA	asperrima	Glycyrrhiza
GROSSULARIA	aciculare	
GYPSOPHILA	acutifolia	Gypsophila
	altissima	
	paniculata	
	prostrata	
	repens	
	suffruticosa	
HEDYSARUM	alpinum	Hedysarum.
	argenteum	
	fruticosum	
	sennoïdes	
HEMEROCALLIS	flava	Day-lily.
	graminea	
HERACLEUM	giganteum	Cow-parsnip.
	Panaces	
	sibiricum	
HESPERIS	aprica	Rocket.
	arabidiflora	
HIERACIUM	Gmelini	Hawkweed
	lyratum	
	sibiricum	
HYOSCYAMUS	physaloïdes	Henbane
HYPECOUM	erectum	
HYPERICUM	attenuatum	St. John's-wort.
	Ascyron	
	elegans	
HYSSOPUS	Lophanthus	Hyssop.
IMPATIENS	parviflora	Balsam.
IPOMŒA	sibirica	Ipomœa.
IRIS	brachycuspis	Iris.
	dichostoma.	
	flavissima.	
	Güldenstadtii.	
	halophila.	
	Pallasii.	
	ruthenica.	
	setosa.	
	sibirica.	

Iris	spuria.	Iris
	tenuifolia.	
	ventricosa.	
Isopyrum	fumarioïdes	Isopyrum.
Ixiolirion	tartarica	Ixiolirion.
Juniperus	daurica	Juniper.
	excelsa.	
	nana.	
Kochia	hyssopifolia	Kochia.
Lagoseris	versicolor	Lagoseris.
Lathyrus	mutabilis	Lathyrus.
	pisiformis.	
Leonurus	crispus	Mother-wort.
	sibiricus.	
	supinus.	
Lepidium	coronopifolium	Pepper-wort.
Leptandra	Meyeri.	
Leuzea	altaica	Leuzea.
Ligusticum	longifolium.	Lovage.
Lilium	dauricum	Lily.
	pomponium	
	pumilum	
Lonicera	tartarica	Lonicera.
Lupinaster	pentaphyllus	Bastard lupine.
Lycium	ruthenicum	Box-thorn.
Macropodium	nivale	Macropodium.
Malcomia	laxa	Malcomia.
	taraxacifolia	
Marrubium	affine	Horehound.
	hirsutum	
Mentha	crispa	Mint.
	crispata	
	undulata	
Moluccella	tuberosa	Molucca balm.
Morus	tartarica	Mulberry.
Nasturtium	sagittatum	Nasturtium.
Nepeta	botryoïdes	Cat-mint.
	lamifolia	
	multifida	
	Mussini	
	teucriifolia	
Nitraria	Schoberi	Nitraria.
Nymphæa	nitida	Water-lily.
Onopordum	deltoïdeum	Cotton thistle.

Onosma	simplicissimum	Onosma.
Ornithogalum	uniflorum	Star of Bethlehem
Orobus	angustifolius	Bitter vetch.
	Fischeri	
	lathyroïdes	
	luteus	
Oxytropis	altaica	Oxytropis.
	deflexa	
	dichoptera	
	pilosa	
	uralensis	
Pæonia	albiflora	Pæony.
	anomala	
	daurica	
	hybrida	
	rubescens	
	sibirica	
	tartarica	
	tenuifolia	
	uniflora	
Papaver	armeniacum	Poppy.
	bracteatum	
	luteum	
	nudicaule	
	rubro-aurantiacum	
Patrinia	ruthenica	
	sibirica	
Pedicularis	compacta	Lousewort.
	euphrasioïdes	
	myriophylla	
	resupinata	
	uncinata	
Peganum	dauricum	Peganum.
Perdicium	Anandria	Perdicium.
Peucedanum	sibiricum	Sulphur-wort.
Phaca	arenaria	Bastard vetch.
Phlomis	agraria	Phlomis.
	alpina	
	pungens	
	tuberosa	
Physochlaina	physaloïdes	
Pinus	Cembra	Pine.
	Pallasiana	
	Pichta	

PLANTAGO	asiatica	Plantain.
	maxima	
	salsa	
PLATYCODON	grandiflorum	
PLATYSTEMON	leiocarpus	
POLEMONIUM	villosum	Greek valerian.
POLYGONUM.	acidulum	Persicaria.
	crispulum	
	divaricatum	
	frutescens	
	ocreatum	
	salignum	
	tartaricum	
	undulatum	
POPULUS	laurifolia	Poplar.
	suaveolens	
POTENTILLA		Cinquefoil.
PRIMULA	altaica	Primrose.
	cortusoïdes	
	daurica	
	dentiflora	
	integerrima	
	nivalis	
	Pallasii	
	sibirica	
PRUNUS	dasycarpa	Plum.
	sibirica	
PULMONARIA	daurica	Lungwort.
PUSCHKINIA	scilloïdes	Puschkinia.
PYRETHRUM	bipinnatum	Feverfew.
	millefoliatum	
PYRUS	baccata	Pyrus.
	prunifolia	
RANUNCULUS	cassubicus	Crowfoot.
	fumariæfolius	
	salsuginosus	
RHAMNUS	erythroxylon	Buckthorn.
RHODODENDRON	atrovirens	Rhododendron.
	chrysanthum	
	dauricum	
RIBES	Cynanchum	Currant.
	Diacantha	
	sibiricum	
ROSA	acicularis	Rose.

ROSA	astracanica	Rose.
	bifurca	
	daurica	
	flore semipleno	
	fragarioides	
	grandiflora	
	hispida	
	lutescens	
	multifida	
	nivea	
	Pallasii	
	pauciflora	
	pruinosa	
	reversa	
	ruthenica	
	sanguisorbifolia	
	sericea	
	stipularis	
	supina	
RUBIA	cordifolia	Madder.
SALSOLA	laniflora	Saltwort.
	vermiculata	
SALVIA	Hablitziana	Sage.
	mollis	
SAUSSUREA	pulchella	Saussurea.
SAXIFRAGA	cordifolia	Saxifrage.
	crassifolia	
	punctata	
	sibirica	
SCILLA	sibirica	Squill.
SCORZONERA	caricifolia	Viper's grass.
	eriosperma	
SCROPHULARIA	altaica	Figwort.
SCUTELLARIA	grandiflora	Skull-cap.
	lupulina	
	macrantha	
SEDUM	Aïzoon	Stone-crop.
	altaicum	
	dauricum	
	Ewersii	
	fulgens	
	hybridum	
	Lychnis	
	maximum	

SEDUM	nigrum	Stone-crop.
	populifolium	
	purpureum	
	spinosum	
SEMPERVIVUM	flagelliforme	Houseleek.
SERRATULA	angustifolia	Saw-wort.
	centaurioïdes	
	coronata	
	salicifolia	
SIBBALDIA	erecta	Sibbaldia.
SILENE	amœna	Catchfly.
	charæfolia	
	effusa	
	jeniseensis	
	procumbens	
	repens	
	saxatilis	
	sibirica	
	spergulifolia	
	tenuis	
	viscaginoïdes	
	volgensis	
SILYBUM	cernuum	Silybum.
SISON	salsum	Honey-wort.
SISYMBRIUM	altissimum	Sisybrium.
	integrifolium	
SONCHUS	sibiricus	Sow-thistle.
	tartaricus	
SPIRÆA	alpina	Spiræa.
	Aruncus	
	chamædrifolia	
	crenata	
	digitata	
	lævigata	
	lobata	
	sorbifolia	
	thalictroïdes	
	triloba	
STACHYS	lanata	Hedge-nettle.
	sibirica	
STATICE	ferulacea	Sea-lavender.
	flexuosa	
	Gmelini	
	graminifolia	

STATICE	latifolia	Sea-lavender.
	scoparia	
	suffruticosa	
STELLARIA	daurica	Stellera.
	Laxmanni	
STIPA	altissima	Feather-grass.
	melica	
	sibirica	
THALICTRUM	contortum	Meadow-rue.
	petaloïdeum	
	sibiricum	
	squarrosum	
THERMOPSIS	lanceolata	Thermopsis.
THLASPI	ceratocarpon	Shepherd's purse.
TRAGOPOGON	mutabilis	Goat's-beard.
TRIGONELLA	platycarpos	Fenugreek.
	ruthenica	
TROLLIUS	asiaticus	Globe-flower.
	hybridus	
	intermedius	
TOURNEFORTIA	Arguzia	Tournefortia.
TULIPA	tricolor	Tulip.
TURNERA	racemosa	Turnera.
ULMUS	humilis	Elm-tree.
	pumila	
URTICA	cannabina	Nettle.
VALANTIA	aspera	Valantia.
VERATRUM	nigrum	Veratrum.
VERONICA	angustifolia	Speedwell.
	grandis	
	incisa	
	laciniata	
	multifida	
	neglecta	
	pinnata	
	sibirica	
	spuria	
VICIA	biennis	Vetch.
VIOLA	altaïca	Violet.
	uniflora	
ZIZIPHORA	acinoïdes	Ziziphora.
	dasyantha	

INDEX.

B.

C.

D.

H.

I.

L.

M.

N.

U.

V.

W.

Y.

Z.

APPENDIX.

THE END.

MESSRS. HURST AND BLACKETT'S

NEW PUBLICATIONS.

DOMESTIC MEMOIRS of the ROYAL FAMILY, and of the COURT of ENGLAND, chiefly at SHENE and RICHMOND. By Folkestone Williams, F.G.S., F.R.G.S., &c. 3 vols. with Fine Portraits and other Illustrations, 31s. 6d. bound.

"In the prosecution of his labours, the author has consulted antiquaries and archæologists, and examined contemporary authorities. The result is, a work, pleasant and instructive, abundant in anecdote, and agreeably gossiping. It, moreover, evinces considerable research, and a generally sound historical judgment. Mr. Williams sketches the architectural arrangements of the King's Manor House at Shene in the time of Edward the Third, and adds an account of some of the sports and pastimes, the armour, costume, entertainments, tournaments, furniture, wardrobe, and court literature of the fourteenth century; the organization of the royal household, and the family of the King. We must pass over the doings of Richard II., and 'Good Queen Anne,' at the resplendent Manor House, over its restoration by Henry V, and his religious foundations, with the visit from the Emperor Sigismund, and William of Bavaria; over Henry the Sixth's residence there; over the romantic incidents that occurred there in Edward the Fourth's time. We must pass too, over the Court usages in Henry the Seventh's time. In the following reign we make acquaintance with the Princess Mary, welcoming and entertaining the gentlemen of France, with 'most goodly countenance,' and with 'pleasant pastime in playing on the virginals.' A more tender interest hallows the spot that witnessed the affection of Dudley Earl of Leicester and Amy Robsart, of Guilford and Lady Jane Grey, of Sir Philip Sydney and Elizabeth Walsingham, of Stella and Dean Swift. On the accession of Elizabeth to the throne, the splendour of the Court at Richmond revived with its gaiety. We then pass to Prince Henry, the next royal resident. The author describes the establishment and education of 'England's Darling,' as this accomplished Prince was designated; introduces us to Bishop Hall, Ben Jonson, and other notabilities, and to his gallery of paintings; Richmond under Charles I., the Protectorate and the Restoration, with Dr. Duppa and the Eikon Basilike, John Evelyn and William Lily; Richmond when the family of James II. resided there, when William of Orange 'lay there last night, and hunted this day,' when Anne 'sometimes counsel took, and sometimes tea,' when George I. and Sir Robert Walpole followed the hounds in the new park, when Queen Caroline walked in the gardens with that politic minister. Richmond under all these aspects is described and illustrated. Later, we come to Horace Walpole, the Princess Emily, Addington, and the Duke of Queensbury. Later still, we find the Sailor King, to whom we owe the terrace walk, delighting in the amenities of Richmond, and in our own day, we have seen the White Lodge selected for the educational residence of the Prince of Wales."—Spectator.

MEMOIRS of the COURT of GEORGE IV. From Original Family Documents. By the Duke of Buckingham and Chandos, K.G. 2 vols. 8vo. with Portraits, 30s. bound.

Among the many interesting subjects elucidated in this work will be found: The Trial of Queen Caroline—The King's Visits to Ireland, Scotland, and Hanover—Female Influence at Court—The Death of Lord Castlereagh—Junction of the Grenville Party with the Government—The Political and Literary Career of George Canning—O'Connell and the Catholic Claims—The Marquess Wellesley in Ireland—The Duke of Wellington's Administration—George the Fourth as a Patron of Art and Literature, &c.

"The country is very much indebted to the Duke of Buckingham for the publication of these volumes—to our thinking the most valuable of the contributions to recent history which he has yet compiled from his family papers. Besides the King, the Duke of Buckingham's canvas is full of the leading men of the day—Castlereagh, Liverpool, Canning, Wellington, Peel, and their compeers. We are sure that no reader, whether he seeks for gossip, or for more sterling information, will be disappointed by the book. There are several most characteristic letters of the Duke of Wellington."
John Bull.

The LIFE and TIMES of GEORGE VILLIERS, DUKE of BUCKINGHAM. From original and authentic sources. By Mrs. Thomson, Author of "The Life of the Duchess of Marlborough," &c. 3 vols. with Portrait, 31s. 6d. bound.

"These volumes will increase the well-earned reputation of their clever and popular author. The story of the royal favourite's career is told by Mrs. Thomson very honestly, and is enriched abundantly with curious and entertaining details drawn from the familiar letters of the time and the memorials of the State Paper Office, of which a full publication is now made for the first time. Labour and pains have, indeed, been well spent upon volumes that produce their evidence so fairly and are written so agreeably as these."—Examiner.

"Mrs. Thomson is entitled to great praise. She has written the most complete biography of Buckingham that has appeared in the language. Those who commence the work by being amused will end in being instructed."—Literary Gazette.

MESSRS. HURST AND BLACKETT'S

NEW PUBLICATIONS—CONTINUED.

LODGE'S PEERAGE and BARONETAGE for 1860, UNDER THE ESPECIAL PATRONAGE OF HER MAJESTY and H.R.H. THE PRINCE CONSORT, and corrected throughout by the Nobility. 29th Edition, 1 vol. royal 8vo. with the arms beautifully engraved, handsomely bound, with gilt edges, 31s. 6d.

LODGE'S PEERAGE AND BARONETAGE is acknowledged to be the most complete, as well as the most elegant, work of the kind. As an established and authentic authority on all questions respecting the family histories, honours, and connections of the titled aristocracy, no work has ever stood so high. It is published under the especial patronage of Her Majesty and His Royal Highness the Prince Consort, and is annually corrected throughout, from the personal communications of the Nobility. It is the only work of its class, in which, *the type being kept constantly standing*, every correction is made in its proper place to the date of publication, an advantage which gives it supremacy over all its competitors. Independently of its full and authentic information respecting the existing Peers and Baronets of the realm, the most sedulous attention is given in its pages to the collateral branches of the various noble families, and the names of many thousand individuals are introduced, which do not appear in other records of the titled classes. For its authority, correctness, and facility of arrangement, and the beauty of its typography and binding, the work is justly entitled to the high place it occupies on the tables of Her Majesty and the Nobility.

"Lodge's Peerage must supersede all other works of the kind, for two reasons; first, it is on a better plan; and, secondly, it is better executed. We can safely pronounce it to be the readiest, the most useful, and exactest of modern works on the subject."—SPECTATOR.

HISTORY of the REIGN of HENRY IV., KING of FRANCE and NAVARRE. From numerous Original Sources. By Miss FREER, Author of "The Lives of Marguerite D'Angoulême, Elizabeth de Valois, Henry III." &c. 2 vols. with Portraits, 21s.

"We know no works of this kind, with the exception, perhaps, of Macaulay's History, which are more pleasant reading than the histories of Miss Freer. The charm of the style and manner and the accuracy of the details combine to render her works a valuable addition to our literary treasures."
JOHN BULL.

"To become the chronicler of such a reign as that of Henry IV. was no mean task, and Miss Freer has accomplished it with singular taste, good sense, and vigour. The story never flags. Our authoress is always faithful, accurate, and intelligent. Her style is good, and her subject abounds with interest for every student of history."—HERALD.

NARRATIVE of a RESIDENCE at the COURT of MEER ALI MOORAD; with Wild Sports in the Valley of the Indus. By Capt. LANGLEY, late Madras Cavalry. 2 vols. with Illustrations.

The ENGLISHWOMAN in ITALY: Impressions of Life in the Roman States and Sardinia, during a Ten Years' Residence. By Mrs. G. GRETTON. 2 vols. 21s.

"Mrs. Gretton's book is timely, life-like, and for every reason to be recommended. It is impossible to close the book without liking the writer as well as the subject. The volumes are engaging, because real."—ATHENÆUM.

"A book fresh in manner and original in matter. It is as amusing as a novel, and has the solid value belonging to a faithful and lively delineation of real life."—SPECTATOR.

LORD WILLIAM LENNOX'S PICTURES of SPORTING LIFE and CHARACTER. 2 vols. 21s.

"This book should be in the library of every country gentleman, and of every one who delights in the sports of the field. It forms a complete treatise on sporting in every part of the World, and is full of pleasant gossip and anecdote. Racing, steeple chasing, hunting, driving, coursing, yachting, and fishing, cricket and pedestrianism, boating and curling, pigeon shooting, and the pursuit of game with the fowling-piece, all find an able exponent in Lord William Lennox."—HERALD.

REALITIES of PARIS LIFE. By the Author of "Flemish INTERIORS," &c. 3 vols. with Illustrations, 31s. 6d.

"'Realities of Paris Life' is a good addition to Paris books, and important as affording true and sober pictures of the Paris poor."—ATHENÆUM.

INTERESTING BOOKS OF TRAVELS

PUBLISHED BY

MESSRS. HURST AND BLACKETT.

TRAVELS in EASTERN AFRICA: with the Narrative of a Residence in Mozambique. By LYONS M'LEOD, Esq., F.R.G.S., late British Consul in Mozambique. 2 vols. with Map and Illustrations, 21s.

"Mr. M'Leod's volumes contain chapters for all readers—racy narrative, abundance of incident, compendious history, important matter-of-fact statistics, and many a page which will be perused with pleasure by the naturalist."—ATHENÆUM.

"Mr. M'Leod's work furnishes information concerning the commercial capabilities, not only of the Portuguese settlements, but also of the Cape and Natal, together with particulars concerning Mauritius, Madagascar, and the Seychelles. It likewise gives a peculiar insight into the combinations and influences which operate upon the Portuguese authorities in relation to the slave trade."—TIMES.

A SUMMER RAMBLE in the HIMALAYAS; with Sporting Adventures in the Vale of Cashmere. Edited by MOUNTAINEER. 8vo. with Illustrations, 15s.

"A book which we cannot commend too highly. It is a most interesting, pleasant, and well-written narrative. The sporting exploits which it describes are comparatively novel, and the account of the scenery among which they were performed is graphic and charming. A more satisfactory book could not be desired."—LITERARY GAZETTE.

SIX MONTHS in REUNION: a Clergyman's Holiday, and How he Passed it. By the Rev. P. BEATON, M.A. 2 vols. 21s.

"Mr. Beaton has done good service in the publication of these interesting volumes. He is an intelligent observer, enjoys himself heartily, and compels his readers to enjoy themselves also. Sagacity, practical good sense, a healthy animal nature, a well cultivated mind, are Mr. Beaton's qualifications as a traveller and a writer of travels. He possesses the advantages, too, of having selected ground that is comparatively untrodden. His work is written with taste and skill, and abounds with anecdote and information."—LITERARY GAZETTE.

LAKE NGAMI; or Explorations and Discoveries during Four Years' Wanderings in the Wilds of South-Western Africa. By CHARLES JOHN ANDERSSON. 1 vol. royal 8vo., with a Map and upwards of 50 Illustrations, representing Sporting Adventures, Subjects of Natural History, &c. Second Edition, 30s.

"This narrative of African explorations and discoveries is one of the most important geographical works that have lately appeared. It contains the account of two journeys; in the first of which the countries of the Damaras and the Ovambo, previously scarcely known in Europe, were explored; and in the second the newly-discovered Lake Ngami was reached by a route that had been deemed impracticable, but which proves to be the shortest and the best. The work contains much scientific and accurate information as to the geology, the scenery, products, and resources of the regions explored, with notices of the religion, manners, and customs of the native tribes. The continual sporting adventures, and other remarkable occurrences, intermingled with the narrative of travel, make the book as interesting to read as a romance, as, indeed, a good book of travels ought always to be. The illustrations by Wolf are admirably designed, and most of them represent scenes as striking as any witnessed by Jules Gerard or Gordon Cumming."—LITERARY GAZETTE.

SIXTEEN YEARS of an ARTIST'S LIFE in MOROCCO, SPAIN, and the CANARY ISLANDS. By Mrs. ELIZABETH MURRAY. 2 vols. 8vo. with Coloured Illustrations.

"Mrs. Murray, wife, we believe, of the English Consul at Teneriffe, is one of the first of female English Water Colour Artists. She draws well, and her colour is bright, pure, transparent and sparkling. Her book is like her painting, luminous, rich, and fresh. We welcome it (as the public, will also do) with sincere pleasure. It is a hearty book, written by a clever, quick-sighted, and thoughtful woman, who, slipping a steel pen on the end of her brush, thus doubly armed, uses one end as well as the other, being with both a bright colourer, and accurate describer of colours, outlines, sensations, landscapes and things. In a word, Mrs. Murray is a clever artist, who writes forcibly and agreeably."—ATHENÆUM.

A JOURNEY on a PLANK from KIEV to EAUX-BONNES. By LADY CHARLOTTE PEPYS. 2 vols. with Illustrations, 21s.

"A very beautiful and touching work. What must strike any reader is the extreme gracefulness of style and the utter forgetfulness of self in the writer. These qualities are so apparent that had the narrative been dull, which it is not, the volume could not have failed to charm."—CHRONICLE.